CAPTAIN AMERICA
★PATRIOT★

P9-EDL-100

Writer: Karl Kesel
Artist: Mitch Breitweiser
Color Artist: Bettie Breitweiser
Letterer: Jared K. Fletcher
Associate Editor: Lauren Sankovitch
Editor: Tom Brevoort
And for service to continuity above and beyond the call of duty, the thanks of a grateful nation go to Jeff Gelb, Michael Tiefenbacher, Mark Waid & Kurt Busiek

"Old Soldiers Never Die..."
Writer: Karl Kesel
Artist: Steve Uy
Letterer: Jared K. Fletcher
Associate Editor: Jeanine Schaefer
Editor: Tom Brevoort

"What If the Invaders Had Stayed Together after World War II?"
Writer: Roy Thomas
Penciler: Frank Robbins
Inker: Frank Springer
Colorist: George Bell
Letterers: Joe Rosen & John Costanza

Captain America created by Joe Simon & Jack Kirby

Collection Editor: Cory Levine
Editorial Assistants: James Emmett & Joe Hochstein
Assistant Editors: Matt Masdeu, Alex Starbuck & Nelson Ribeiro
Editors, Special Projects: Jennifer Grünwald & Mark D. Beazley
Senior Editor, Special Projects: Jeff Youngquist
Senior Vice President of Sales: David Gabriel

Editor in Chief: Joe Quesada
Publisher: Dan Buckley
Executive Producer: Alan Fine

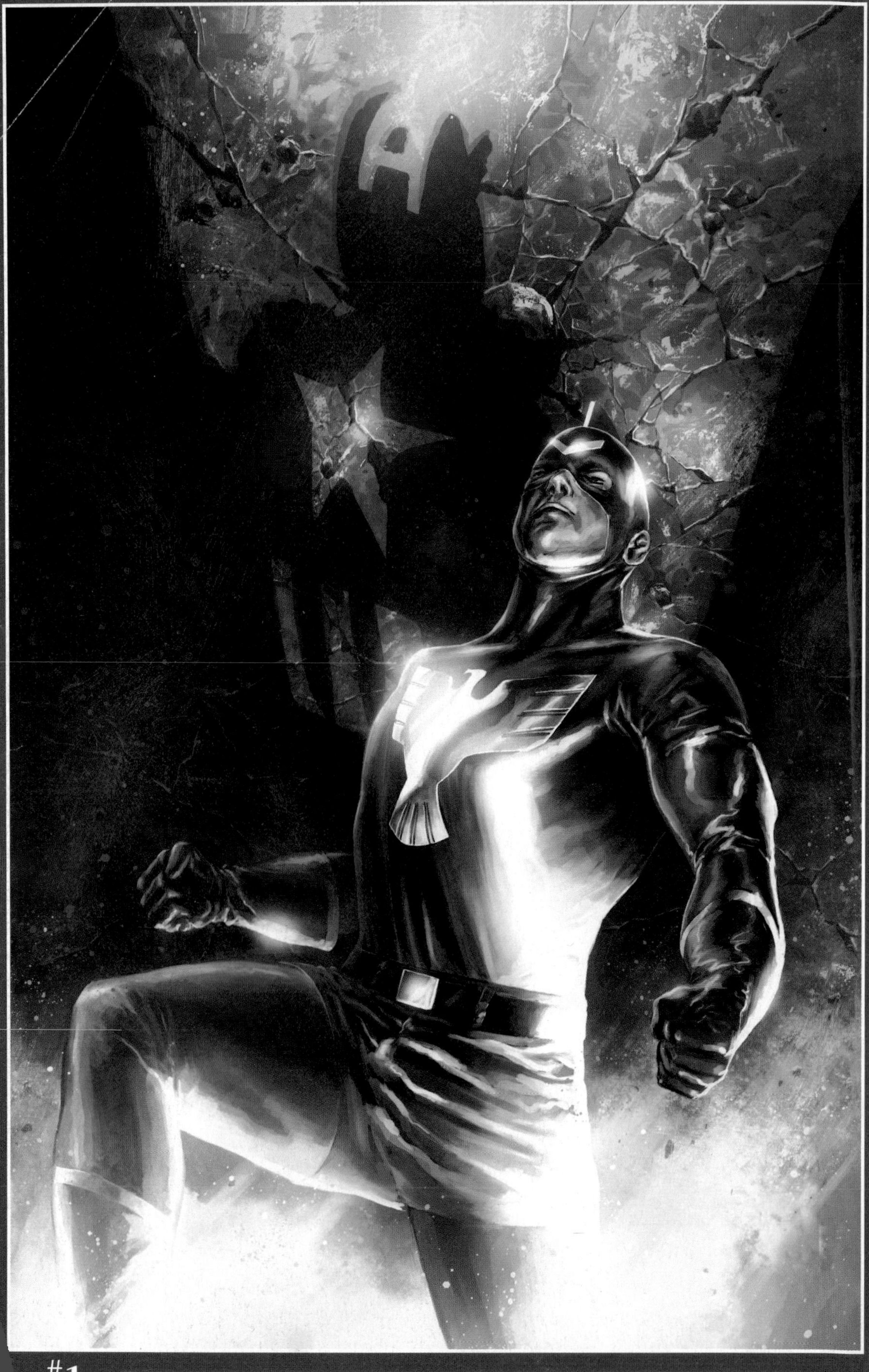

#1

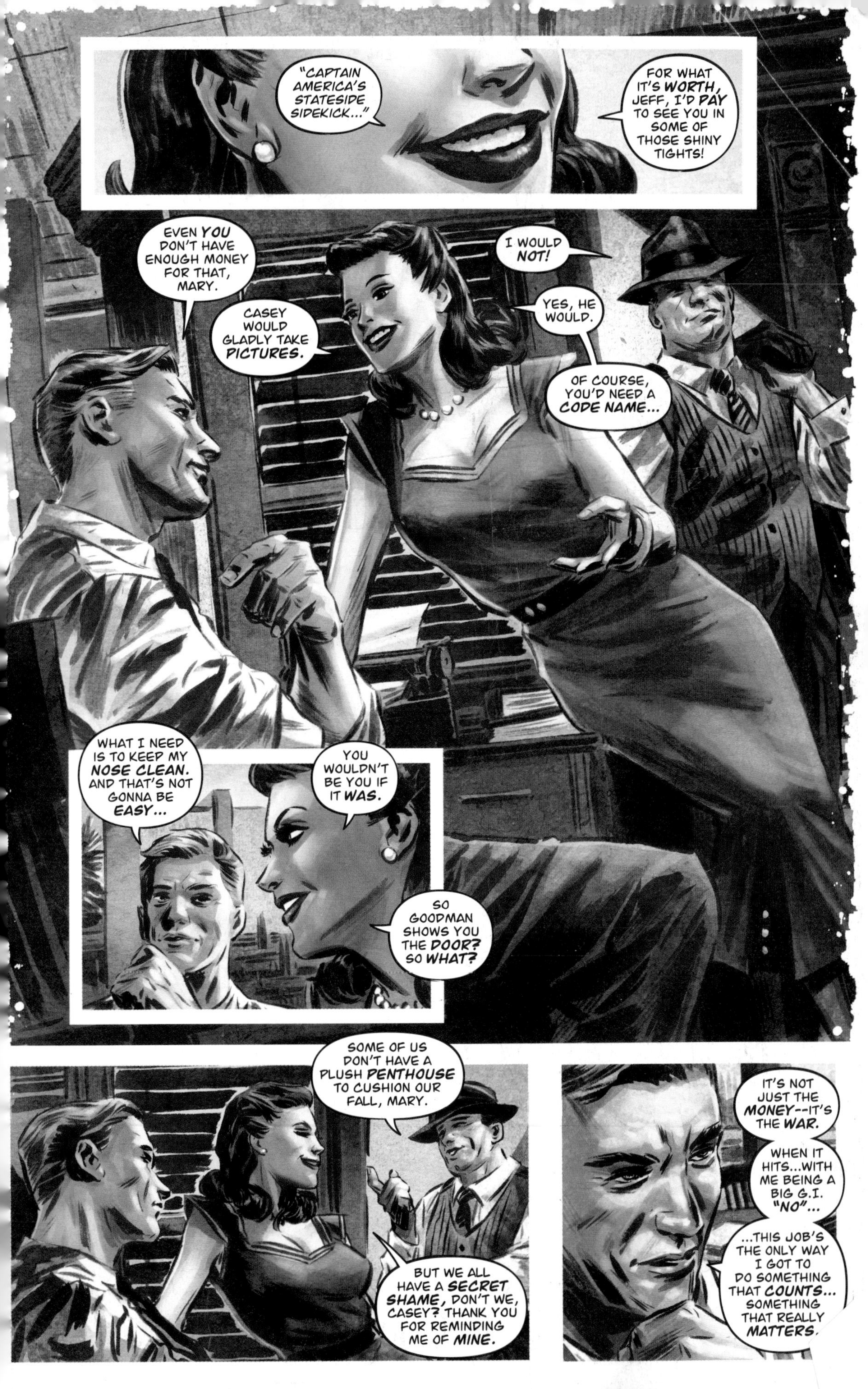
"CAPTAIN AMERICA'S STATESIDE SIDEKICK..."
FOR WHAT IT'S WORTH, JEFF, I'D PAY TO SEE YOU IN SOME OF THOSE SHINY TIGHTS!
EVEN YOU DON'T HAVE ENOUGH MONEY FOR THAT, MARY.
I WOULD NOT!
CASEY WOULD GLADLY TAKE PICTURES.
YES, HE WOULD.
OF COURSE, YOU'D NEED A CODE NAME...
WHAT I NEED IS TO KEEP MY NOSE CLEAN. AND THAT'S NOT GONNA BE EASY...
YOU WOULDN'T BE YOU IF IT WAS.
SO GOODMAN SHOWS YOU THE DOOR? SO WHAT?
SOME OF US DON'T HAVE A PLUSH PENTHOUSE TO CUSHION OUR FALL, MARY.
BUT WE ALL HAVE A SECRET SHAME, DON'T WE, CASEY? THANK YOU FOR REMINDING ME OF MINE.
IT'S NOT JUST THE MONEY--IT'S THE WAR.
WHEN IT HITS...WITH ME BEING A BIG G.I. "NO"...
...THIS JOB'S THE ONLY WAY I GOT TO DO SOMETHING THAT COUNTS... SOMETHING THAT REALLY MATTERS.

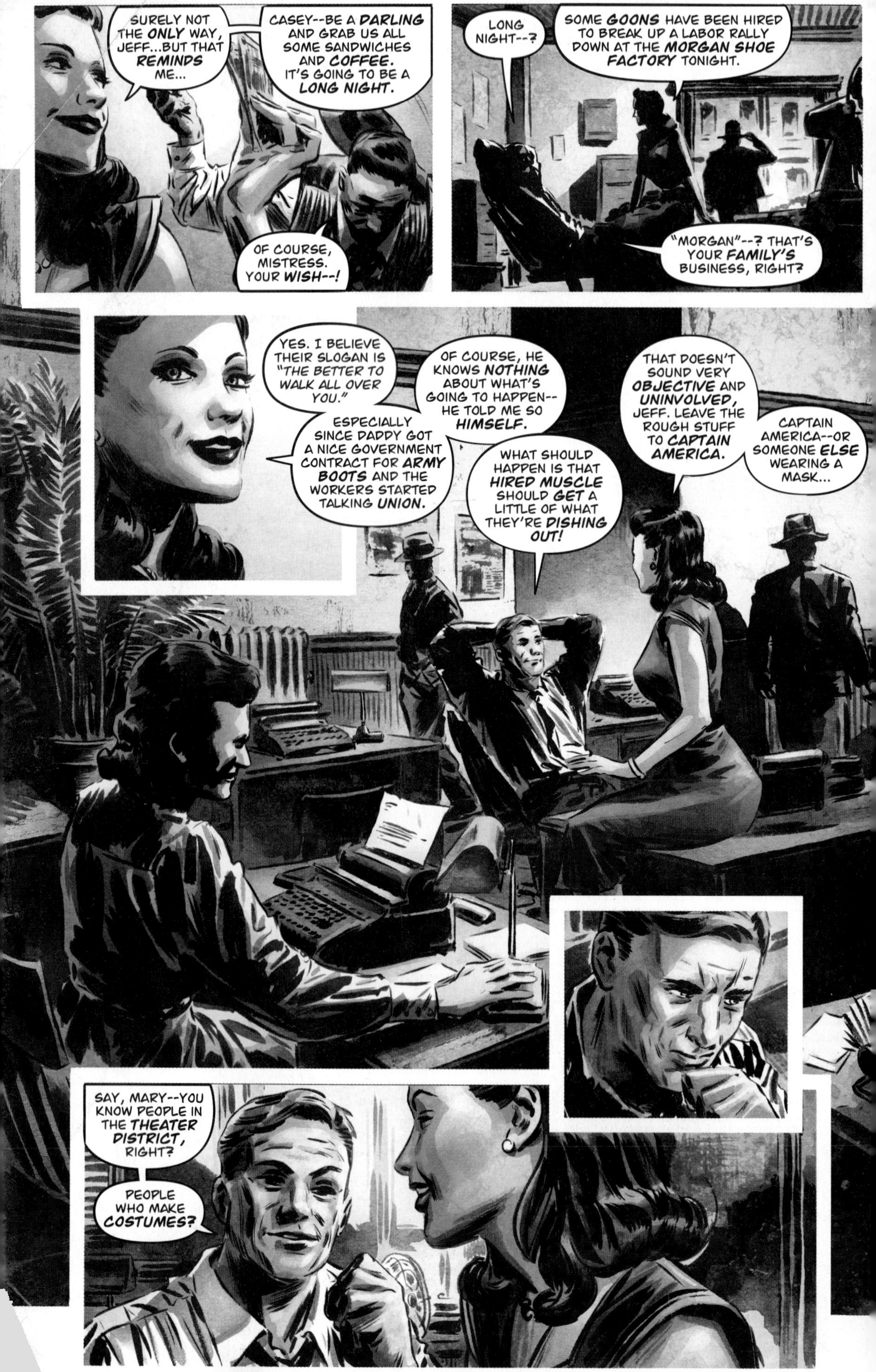
SURELY NOT THE ONLY WAY, JEFF...BUT THAT REMINDS ME...
CASEY--BE A DARLING AND GRAB US ALL SOME SANDWICHES AND COFFEE. IT'S GOING TO BE A LONG NIGHT.
OF COURSE, MISTRESS. YOUR WISH--!
LONG NIGHT--?
SOME GOONS HAVE BEEN HIRED TO BREAK UP A LABOR RALLY DOWN AT THE MORGAN SHOE FACTORY TONIGHT.
"MORGAN"--? THAT'S YOUR FAMILY'S BUSINESS, RIGHT?
YES. I BELIEVE THEIR SLOGAN IS "THE BETTER TO WALK ALL OVER YOU."
ESPECIALLY SINCE DADDY GOT A NICE GOVERNMENT CONTRACT FOR ARMY BOOTS AND THE WORKERS STARTED TALKING UNION.
OF COURSE, HE KNOWS NOTHING ABOUT WHAT'S GOING TO HAPPEN--HE TOLD ME SO HIMSELF.
WHAT SHOULD HAPPEN IS THAT HIRED MUSCLE SHOULD GET A LITTLE OF WHAT THEY'RE DISHING OUT!
THAT DOESN'T SOUND VERY OBJECTIVE AND UNINVOLVED, JEFF. LEAVE THE ROUGH STUFF TO CAPTAIN AMERICA.
CAPTAIN AMERICA--OR SOMEONE ELSE WEARING A MASK...
SAY, MARY--YOU KNOW PEOPLE IN THE THEATER DISTRICT, RIGHT?
PEOPLE WHO MAKE COSTUMES?

MASKED PATRIOT GIVES THUGS THE BOOT!

by JEFF MACE

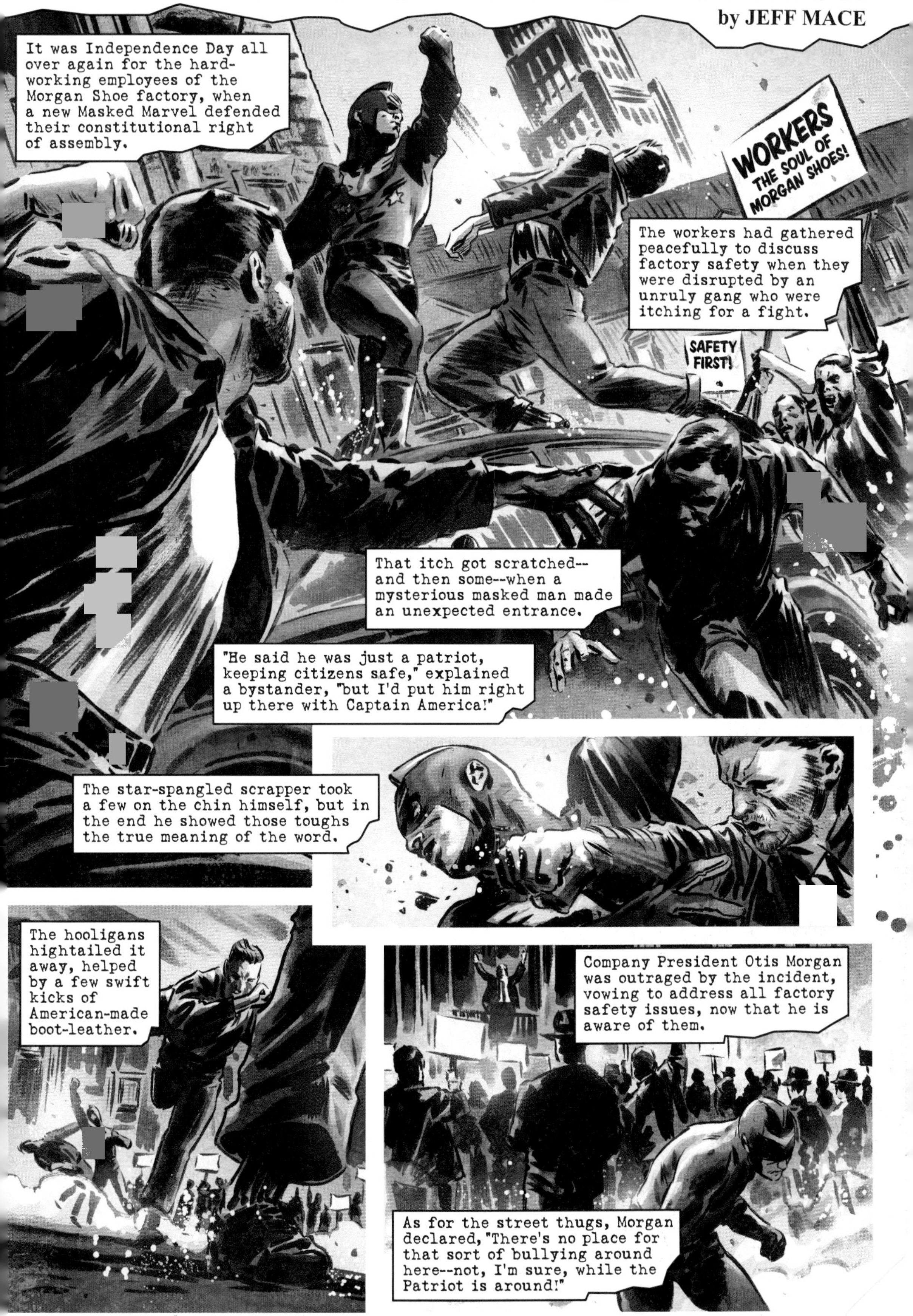
It was Independence Day all over again for the hard-working employees of the Morgan Shoe factory, when a new Masked Marvel defended their constitutional right of assembly.
WORKERS THE SOUL OF MORGAN SHOES!
The workers had gathered peacefully to discuss factory safety when they were disrupted by an unruly gang who were itching for a fight.
SAFETY FIRST!
That itch got scratched--and then some--when a mysterious masked man made an unexpected entrance.
"He said he was just a patriot, keeping citizens safe," explained a bystander, "but I'd put him right up there with Captain America!"
The star-spangled scrapper took a few on the chin himself, but in the end he showed those toughs the true meaning of the word.
The hooligans hightailed it away, helped by a few swift kicks of American-made boot-leather.
Company President Otis Morgan was outraged by the incident, vowing to address all factory safety issues, now that he is aware of them.
As for the street thugs, Morgan declared, "There's no place for that sort of bullying around here--not, I'm sure, while the Patriot is around!"

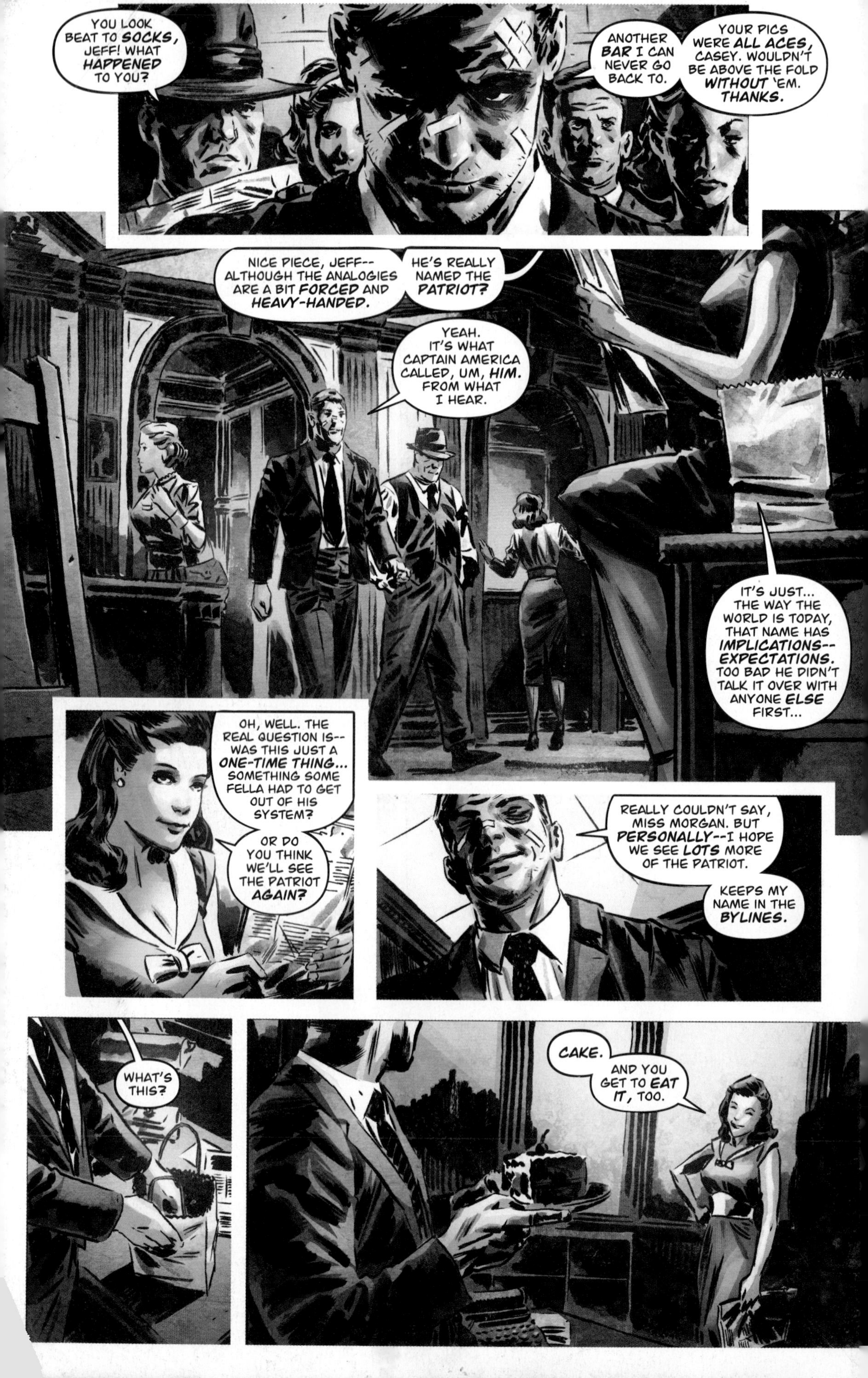
YOU LOOK BEAT TO SOCKS, JEFF! WHAT HAPPENED TO YOU?
ANOTHER BAR I CAN NEVER GO BACK TO.
YOUR PICS WERE ALL ACES, CASEY. WOULDN'T BE ABOVE THE FOLD WITHOUT 'EM. THANKS.
NICE PIECE, JEFF-- ALTHOUGH THE ANALOGIES ARE A BIT FORCED AND HEAVY-HANDED.
HE'S REALLY NAMED THE PATRIOT?
YEAH. IT'S WHAT CAPTAIN AMERICA CALLED, UM, HIM. FROM WHAT I HEAR.
IT'S JUST... THE WAY THE WORLD IS TODAY, THAT NAME HAS IMPLICATIONS-- EXPECTATIONS. TOO BAD HE DIDN'T TALK IT OVER WITH ANYONE ELSE FIRST...
OH, WELL. THE REAL QUESTION IS-- WAS THIS JUST A ONE-TIME THING... SOMETHING SOME FELLA HAD TO GET OUT OF HIS SYSTEM?
OR DO YOU THINK WE'LL SEE THE PATRIOT AGAIN?
REALLY COULDN'T SAY, MISS MORGAN. BUT PERSONALLY--I HOPE WE SEE LOTS MORE OF THE PATRIOT.
KEEPS MY NAME IN THE BYLINES.
WHAT'S THIS?
CAKE.
AND YOU GET TO EAT IT, TOO.

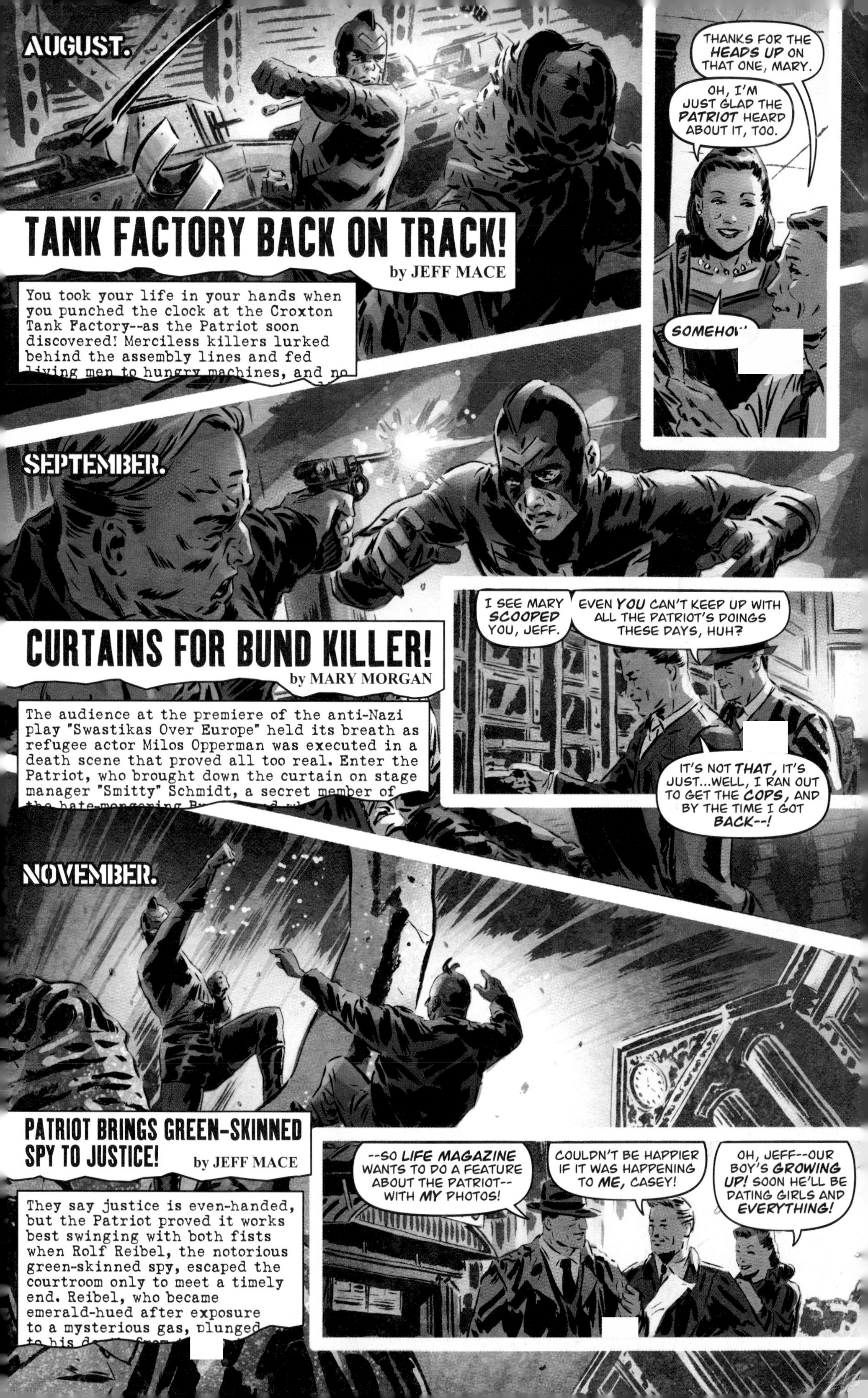

AUGUST.
THANKS FOR THE HEADS UP ON THAT ONE, MARY.
OH, I'M JUST GLAD THE PATRIOT HEARD ABOUT IT, TOO.
TANK FACTORY BACK ON TRACK!
by JEFF MACE
You took your life in your hands when you punched the clock at the Croxton Tank Factory--as the Patriot soon discovered! Merciless killers lurked behind the assembly lines and fed
SOMEHOW
SEPTEMBER.
CURTAINS FOR BUND KILLER!
by MARY MORGAN
The audience at the premiere of the anti-Nazi play "Swastikas Over Europe" held its breath as refugee actor Milos Opperman was executed in a death scene that proved all too real. Enter the Patriot, who brought down the curtain on stage manager "Smitty" Schmidt, a secret member of
I SEE MARY SCOOPED YOU, JEFF.
EVEN YOU CAN'T KEEP UP WITH ALL THE PATRIOT'S DOINGS THESE DAYS, HUH?
IT'S NOT THAT, IT'S JUST...WELL, I RAN OUT TO GET THE COPS, AND BY THE TIME I GOT BACK--!
NOVEMBER.
PATRIOT BRINGS GREEN-SKINNED SPY TO JUSTICE!
by JEFF MACE
They say justice is even-handed, but the Patriot proved it works best swinging with both fists when Rolf Reibel, the notorious green-skinned spy, escaped the courtroom only to meet a timely end. Reibel, who became emerald-hued after exposure to a mysterious gas, plunged
--SO LIFE MAGAZINE WANTS TO DO A FEATURE ABOUT THE PATRIOT--WITH MY PHOTOS!
COULDN'T BE HAPPIER IF IT WAS HAPPENING TO ME, CASEY!
OH, JEFF--OUR BOY'S GROWING UP! SOON HE'LL BE DATING GIRLS AND EVERYTHING!

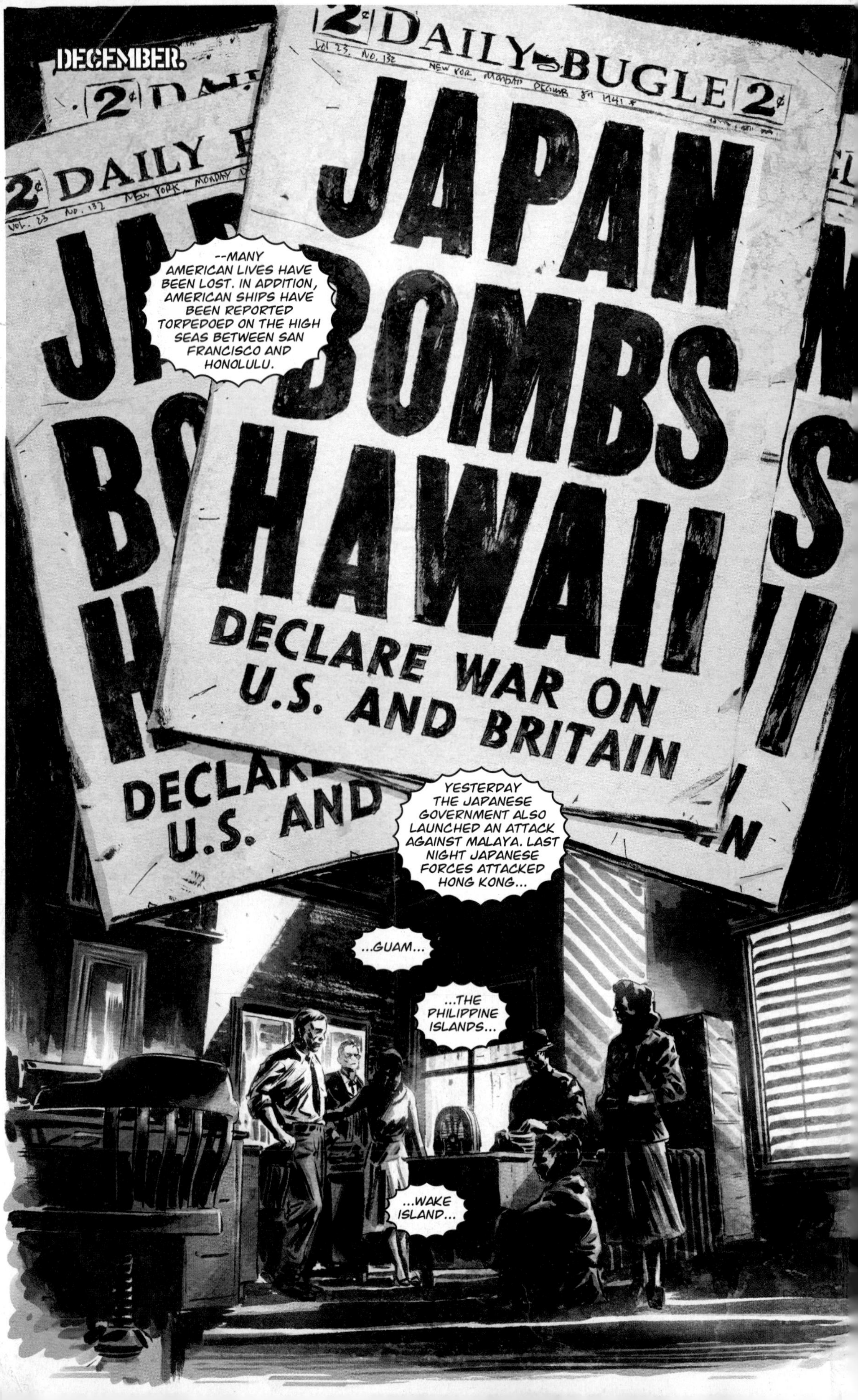
DECEMBER.
2¢ DAILY BUGLE 2¢
JAPAN BOMBS HAWAII
DECLARE WAR ON U.S. AND BRITAIN
--MANY AMERICAN LIVES HAVE BEEN LOST. IN ADDITION, AMERICAN SHIPS HAVE BEEN REPORTED TORPEDOED ON THE HIGH SEAS BETWEEN SAN FRANCISCO AND HONOLULU.
YESTERDAY THE JAPANESE GOVERNMENT ALSO LAUNCHED AN ATTACK AGAINST MALAYA. LAST NIGHT JAPANESE FORCES ATTACKED HONG KONG...
...GUAM...
...THE PHILIPPINE ISLANDS...
...WAKE ISLAND...

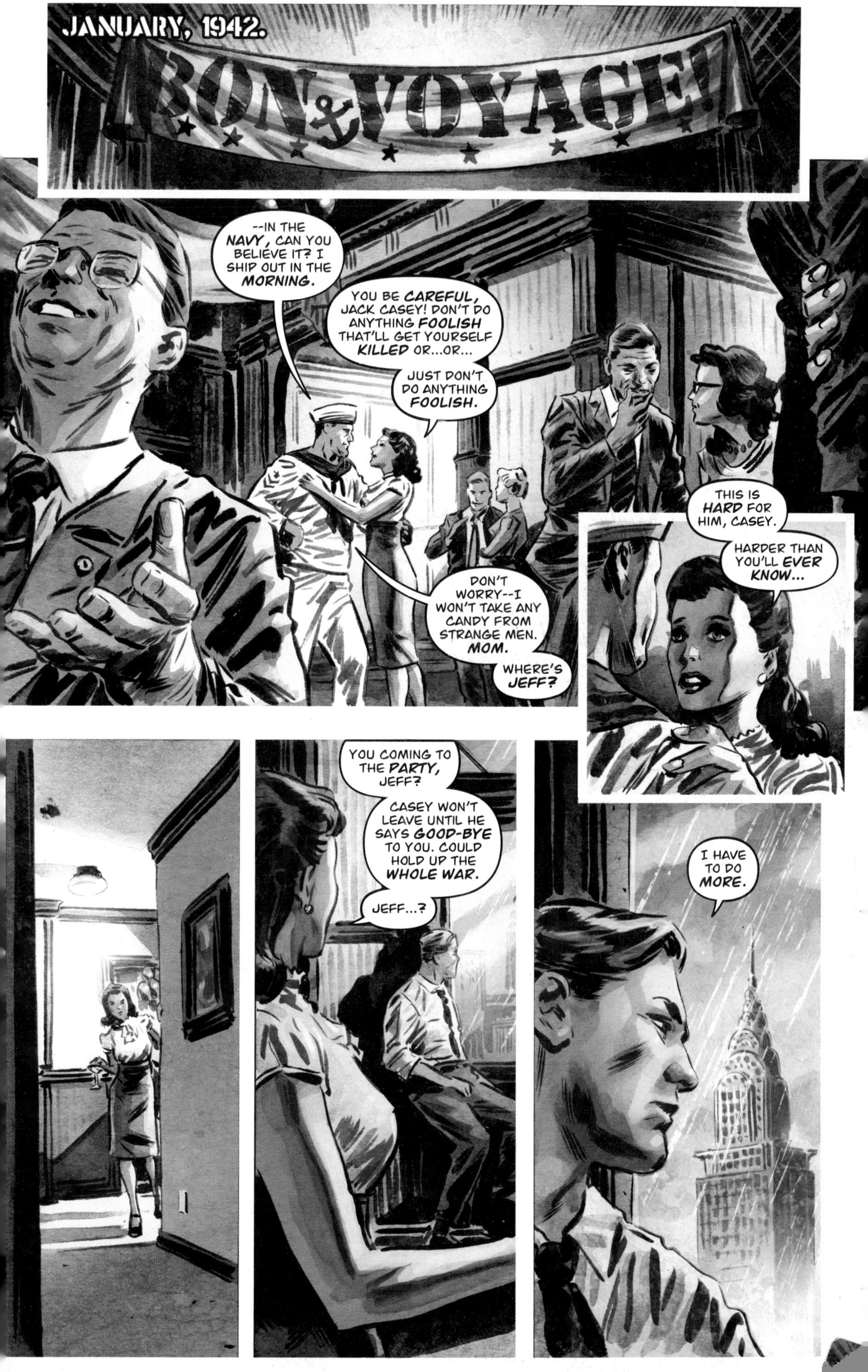
JANUARY, 1942.
BON VOYAGE!
--IN THE NAVY, CAN YOU BELIEVE IT? I SHIP OUT IN THE MORNING.
YOU BE CAREFUL, JACK CASEY! DON'T DO ANYTHING FOOLISH THAT'LL GET YOURSELF KILLED OR...OR...
JUST DON'T DO ANYTHING FOOLISH.
DON'T WORRY--I WON'T TAKE ANY CANDY FROM STRANGE MEN. MOM.
WHERE'S JEFF?
THIS IS HARD FOR HIM, CASEY.
HARDER THAN YOU'LL EVER KNOW...
YOU COMING TO THE PARTY, JEFF?
CASEY WON'T LEAVE UNTIL HE SAYS GOOD-BYE TO YOU. COULD HOLD UP THE WHOLE WAR.
JEFF...?
I HAVE TO DO MORE.

FEBRUARY. ...TOO CAN BE A

PATRIOT ...AR BOND

APRIL.

HELLO, AMERICA--THIS IS THE *PATRIOT*, WITH THIS WEEK'S... PATRIOT OF THE WEEK!

JEFF MACE

NOW, I KNOW IT'S BEEN PRETTY *GRIM* IN THE EAST COAST SHIPPING LANES--BUT LT. COMMANDER HAMILTON HOWE OF THE U.S.S. ROPER STARTED TO *CHANGE* THAT TWO NIGHTS AGO...

MAY.

...BOMBER PLANS RETRIEVED BY THE *PATRIOT*!

THE *DOUBLE-FISTED* DEFENDER OF DEMOCRACY EVEN HAD ENOUGH TIME TO ATTEND A CIVIL DEFENSE LUNCHEON AT THE *WHITE HOUSE*!

CAREFUL, LADIES! HIS FISTS BREAK JAWS--BUT HIS *BLUE EYES* BREAK HEARTS!

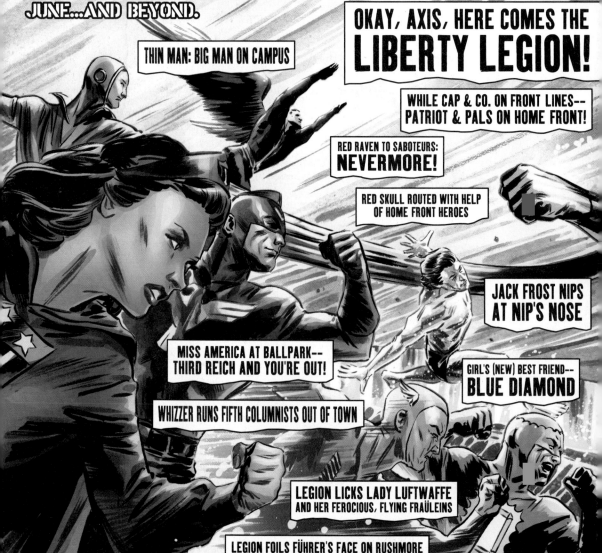

JUNE...AND BEYOND.

THIN MAN: BIG MAN ON CAMPUS

OKAY, AXIS, HERE COMES THE **LIBERTY LEGION!**

WHILE CAP & CO. ON FRONT LINES-- PATRIOT & PALS ON HOME FRONT!

RED RAVEN TO SABOTEURS: **NEVERMORE!**

RED SKULL ROUTED WITH HELP OF HOME FRONT HEROES

JACK FROST NIPS AT NIP'S NOSE

MISS AMERICA AT BALLPARK-- THIRD REICH AND YOU'RE OUT!

GIRL'S (NEW) BEST FRIEND-- **BLUE DIAMOND**

WHIZZER RUNS FIFTH COLUMNISTS OUT OF TOWN

LEGION LICKS LADY LUFTWAFFE AND HER FEROCIOUS, FLYING FRAÜLEINS

LEGION FOILS FÜHRER'S FACE ON RUSHMORE

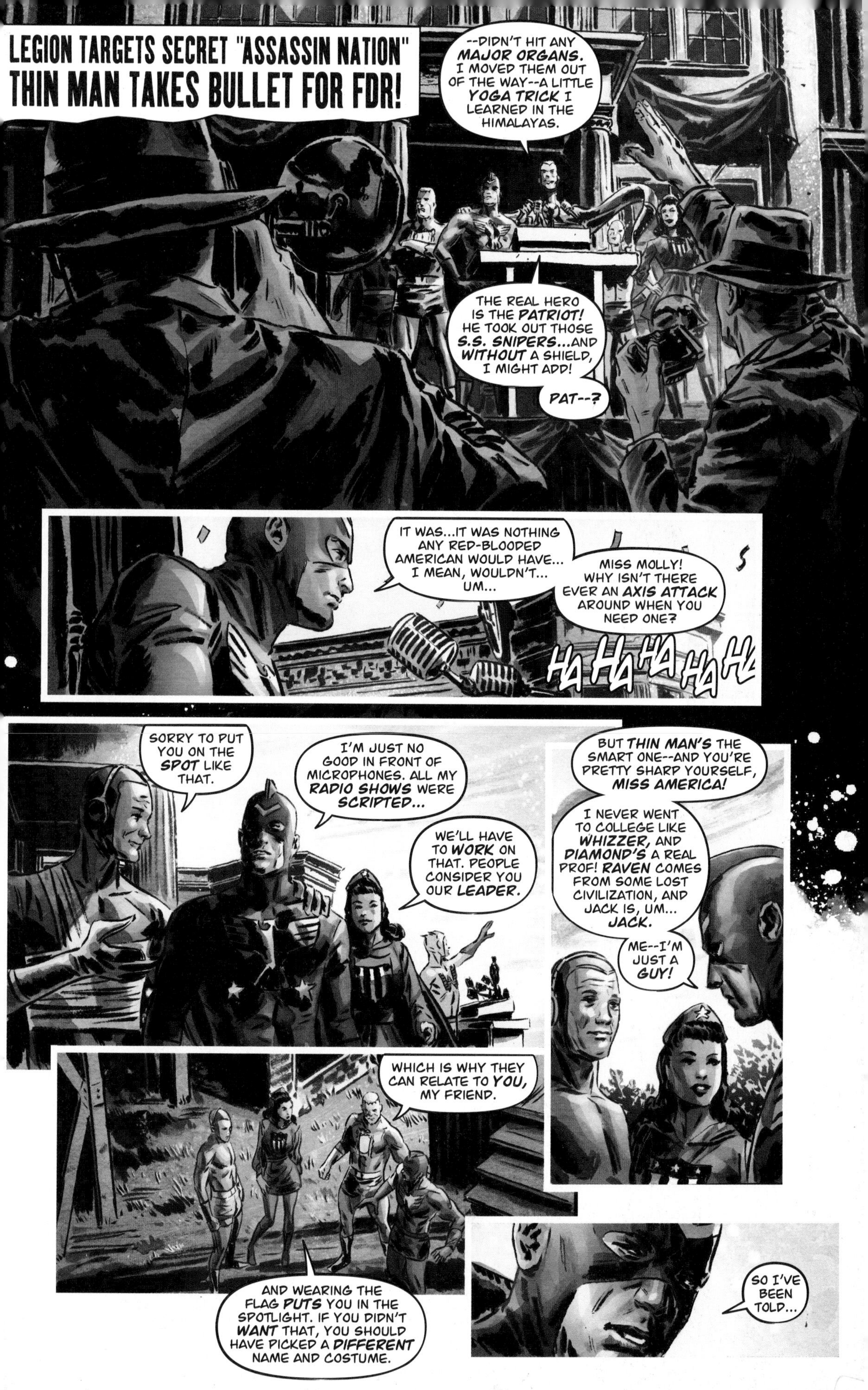
LEGION TARGETS SECRET "ASSASSIN NATION"
THIN MAN TAKES BULLET FOR FDR!
--DIDN'T HIT ANY MAJOR ORGANS. I MOVED THEM OUT OF THE WAY--A LITTLE YOGA TRICK I LEARNED IN THE HIMALAYAS.
THE REAL HERO IS THE PATRIOT! HE TOOK OUT THOSE S.S. SNIPERS...AND WITHOUT A SHIELD, I MIGHT ADD!
PAT--?
IT WAS...IT WAS NOTHING ANY RED-BLOODED AMERICAN WOULD HAVE... I MEAN, WOULDN'T... UM...
MISS MOLLY! WHY ISN'T THERE EVER AN AXIS ATTACK AROUND WHEN YOU NEED ONE?
HA HA HA HA HA
SORRY TO PUT YOU ON THE SPOT LIKE THAT.
I'M JUST NO GOOD IN FRONT OF MICROPHONES. ALL MY RADIO SHOWS WERE SCRIPTED...
WE'LL HAVE TO WORK ON THAT. PEOPLE CONSIDER YOU OUR LEADER.
BUT THIN MAN'S THE SMART ONE--AND YOU'RE PRETTY SHARP YOURSELF, MISS AMERICA!
I NEVER WENT TO COLLEGE LIKE WHIZZER, AND DIAMOND'S A REAL PROF! RAVEN COMES FROM SOME LOST CIVILIZATION, AND JACK IS, UM... JACK.
ME--I'M JUST A GUY!
WHICH IS WHY THEY CAN RELATE TO YOU, MY FRIEND.
AND WEARING THE FLAG PUTS YOU IN THE SPOTLIGHT. IF YOU DIDN'T WANT THAT, YOU SHOULD HAVE PICKED A DIFFERENT NAME AND COSTUME.
SO I'VE BEEN TOLD...

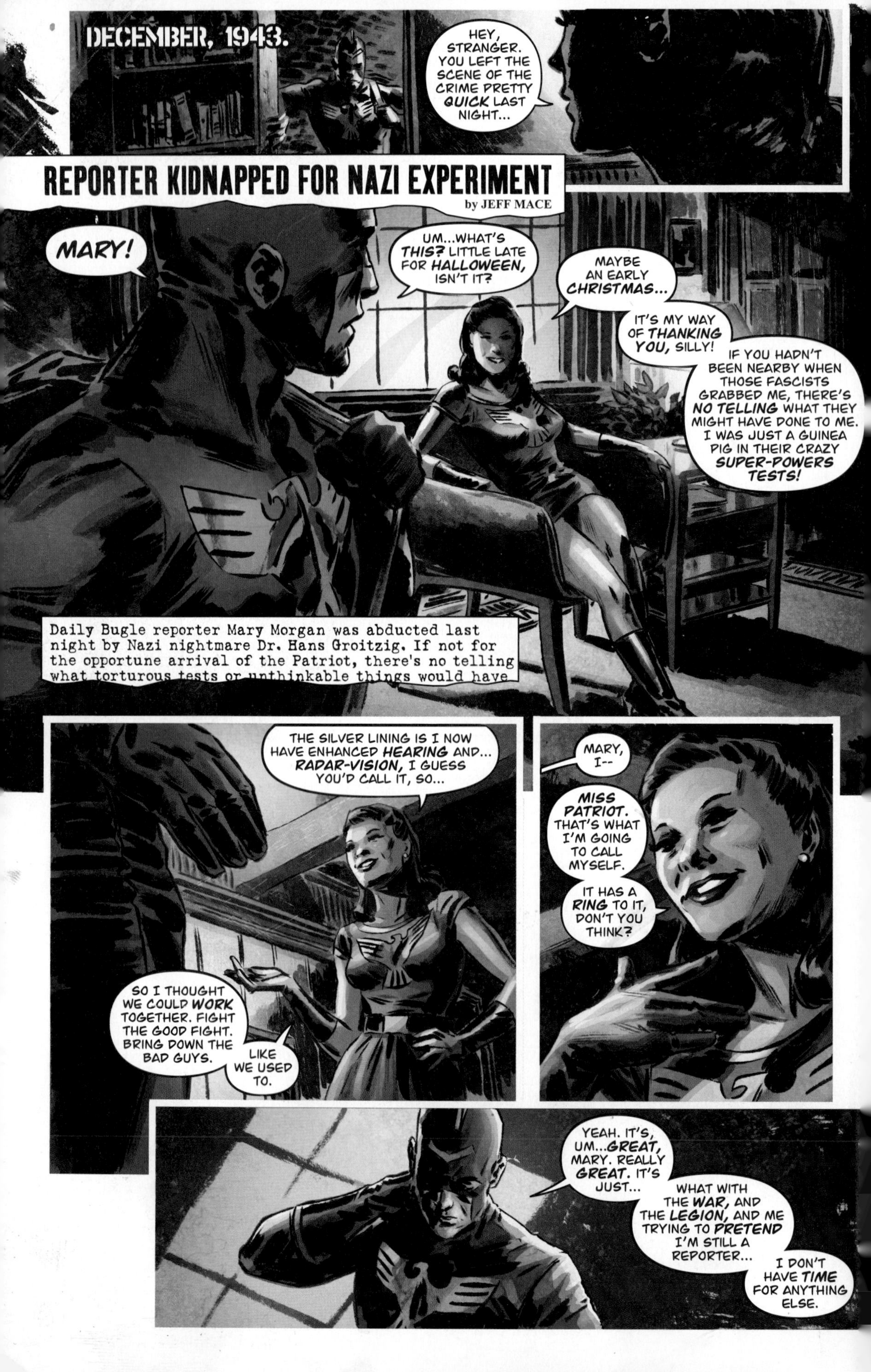
DECEMBER, 1943.
HEY, STRANGER. YOU LEFT THE SCENE OF THE CRIME PRETTY QUICK LAST NIGHT...
REPORTER KIDNAPPED FOR NAZI EXPERIMENT
by JEFF MACE
MARY!
UM...WHAT'S THIS? LITTLE LATE FOR HALLOWEEN, ISN'T IT?
MAYBE AN EARLY CHRISTMAS...
IT'S MY WAY OF THANKING YOU, SILLY!
IF YOU HADN'T BEEN NEARBY WHEN THOSE FASCISTS GRABBED ME, THERE'S NO TELLING WHAT THEY MIGHT HAVE DONE TO ME. I WAS JUST A GUINEA PIG IN THEIR CRAZY SUPER-POWERS TESTS!
Daily Bugle reporter Mary Morgan was abducted last night by Nazi nightmare Dr. Hans Groitzig. If not for the opportune arrival of the Patriot, there's no telling what torturous tests or unthinkable things would have
THE SILVER LINING IS I NOW HAVE ENHANCED HEARING AND... RADAR-VISION, I GUESS YOU'D CALL IT, SO...
SO I THOUGHT WE COULD WORK TOGETHER. FIGHT THE GOOD FIGHT. BRING DOWN THE BAD GUYS.
LIKE WE USED TO.
MARY, I--
MISS PATRIOT. THAT'S WHAT I'M GOING TO CALL MYSELF.
IT HAS A RING TO IT, DON'T YOU THINK?
YEAH. IT'S, UM...GREAT, MARY. REALLY GREAT. IT'S JUST...
WHAT WITH THE WAR, AND THE LEGION, AND ME TRYING TO PRETEND I'M STILL A REPORTER...
I DON'T HAVE TIME FOR ANYTHING ELSE.

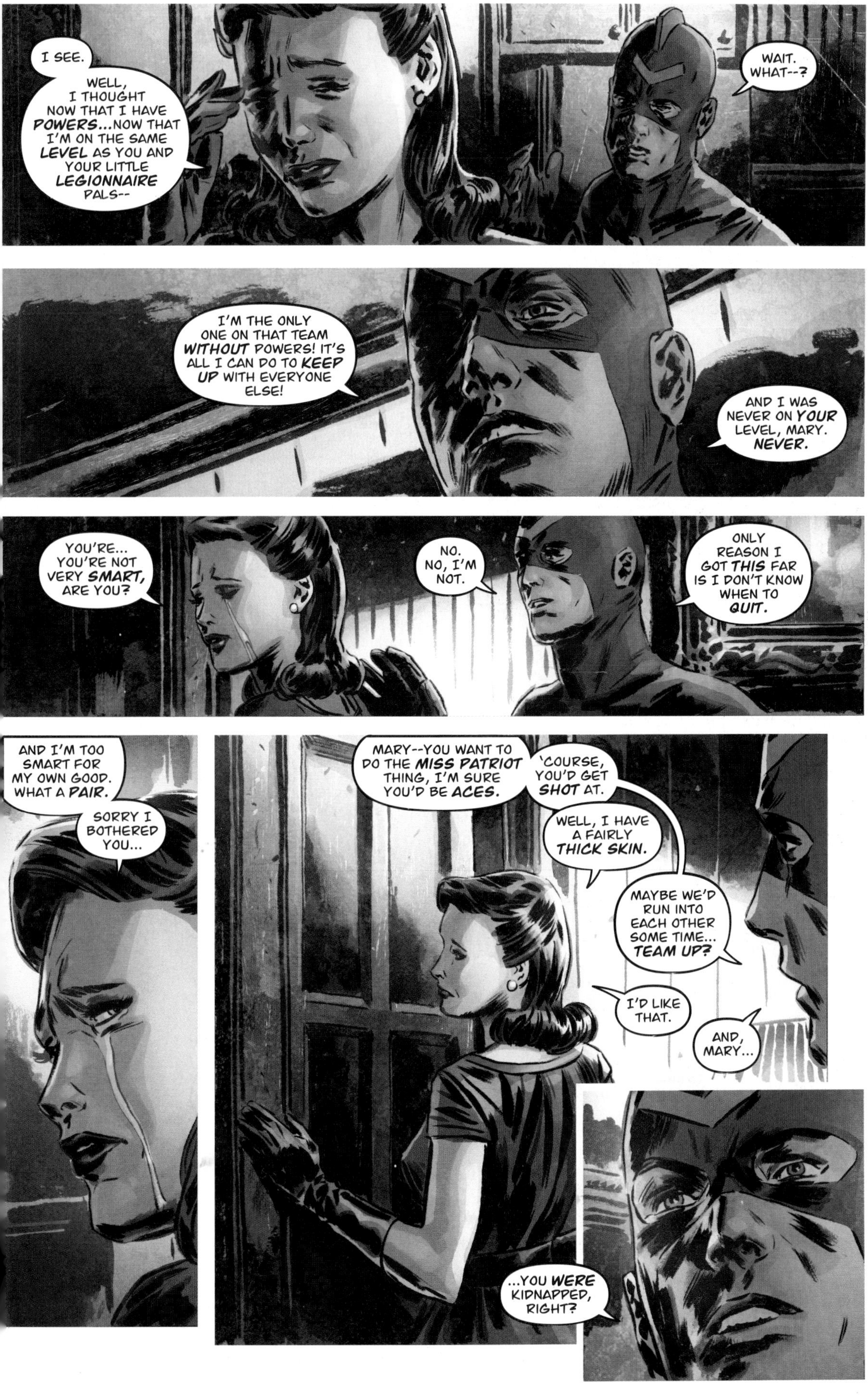
I SEE.
WELL, I THOUGHT NOW THAT I HAVE POWERS...NOW THAT I'M ON THE SAME LEVEL AS YOU AND YOUR LITTLE LEGIONNAIRE PALS--
WAIT. WHAT--?
I'M THE ONLY ONE ON THAT TEAM WITHOUT POWERS! IT'S ALL I CAN DO TO KEEP UP WITH EVERYONE ELSE!
AND I WAS NEVER ON YOUR LEVEL, MARY. NEVER.
YOU'RE... YOU'RE NOT VERY SMART, ARE YOU?
NO. NO, I'M NOT.
ONLY REASON I GOT THIS FAR IS I DON'T KNOW WHEN TO QUIT.
AND I'M TOO SMART FOR MY OWN GOOD. WHAT A PAIR.
SORRY I BOTHERED YOU...
MARY--YOU WANT TO DO THE MISS PATRIOT THING, I'M SURE YOU'D BE ACES.
'COURSE, YOU'D GET SHOT AT.
WELL, I HAVE A FAIRLY THICK SKIN.
MAYBE WE'D RUN INTO EACH OTHER SOME TIME... TEAM UP?
I'D LIKE THAT.
AND, MARY...
...YOU WERE KIDNAPPED, RIGHT?

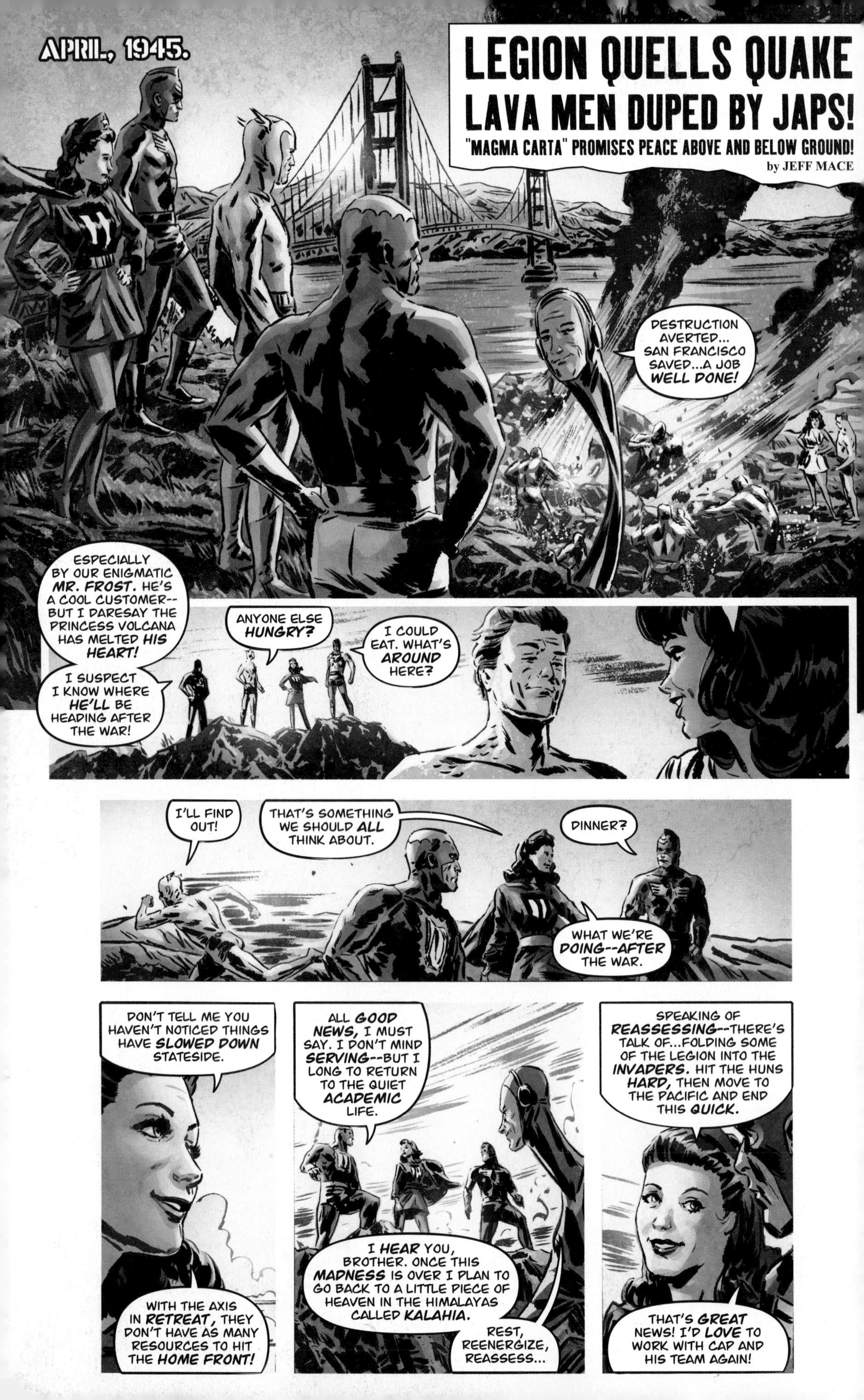

APRIL, 1945.
LEGION QUELLS QUAKE
LAVA MEN DUPED BY JAPS!
"MAGMA CARTA" PROMISES PEACE ABOVE AND BELOW GROUND!
by JEFF MACE
DESTRUCTION AVERTED... SAN FRANCISCO SAVED...A JOB WELL DONE!
ESPECIALLY BY OUR ENIGMATIC MR. FROST. HE'S A COOL CUSTOMER-- BUT I DARESAY THE PRINCESS VOLCANA HAS MELTED HIS HEART!
I SUSPECT I KNOW WHERE HE'LL BE HEADING AFTER THE WAR!
ANYONE ELSE HUNGRY?
I COULD EAT. WHAT'S AROUND HERE?
I'LL FIND OUT!
THAT'S SOMETHING WE SHOULD ALL THINK ABOUT.
DINNER?
WHAT WE'RE DOING--AFTER THE WAR.
DON'T TELL ME YOU HAVEN'T NOTICED THINGS HAVE SLOWED DOWN STATESIDE.
WITH THE AXIS IN RETREAT, THEY DON'T HAVE AS MANY RESOURCES TO HIT THE HOME FRONT!
ALL GOOD NEWS, I MUST SAY. I DON'T MIND SERVING--BUT I LONG TO RETURN TO THE QUIET ACADEMIC LIFE.
I HEAR YOU, BROTHER. ONCE THIS MADNESS IS OVER I PLAN TO GO BACK TO A LITTLE PIECE OF HEAVEN IN THE HIMALAYAS CALLED KALAHIA.
REST, REENERGIZE, REASSESS...
SPEAKING OF REASSESSING--THERE'S TALK OF...FOLDING SOME OF THE LEGION INTO THE INVADERS. HIT THE HUNS HARD, THEN MOVE TO THE PACIFIC AND END THIS QUICK.
THAT'S GREAT NEWS! I'D LOVE TO WORK WITH CAP AND HIS TEAM AGAIN!

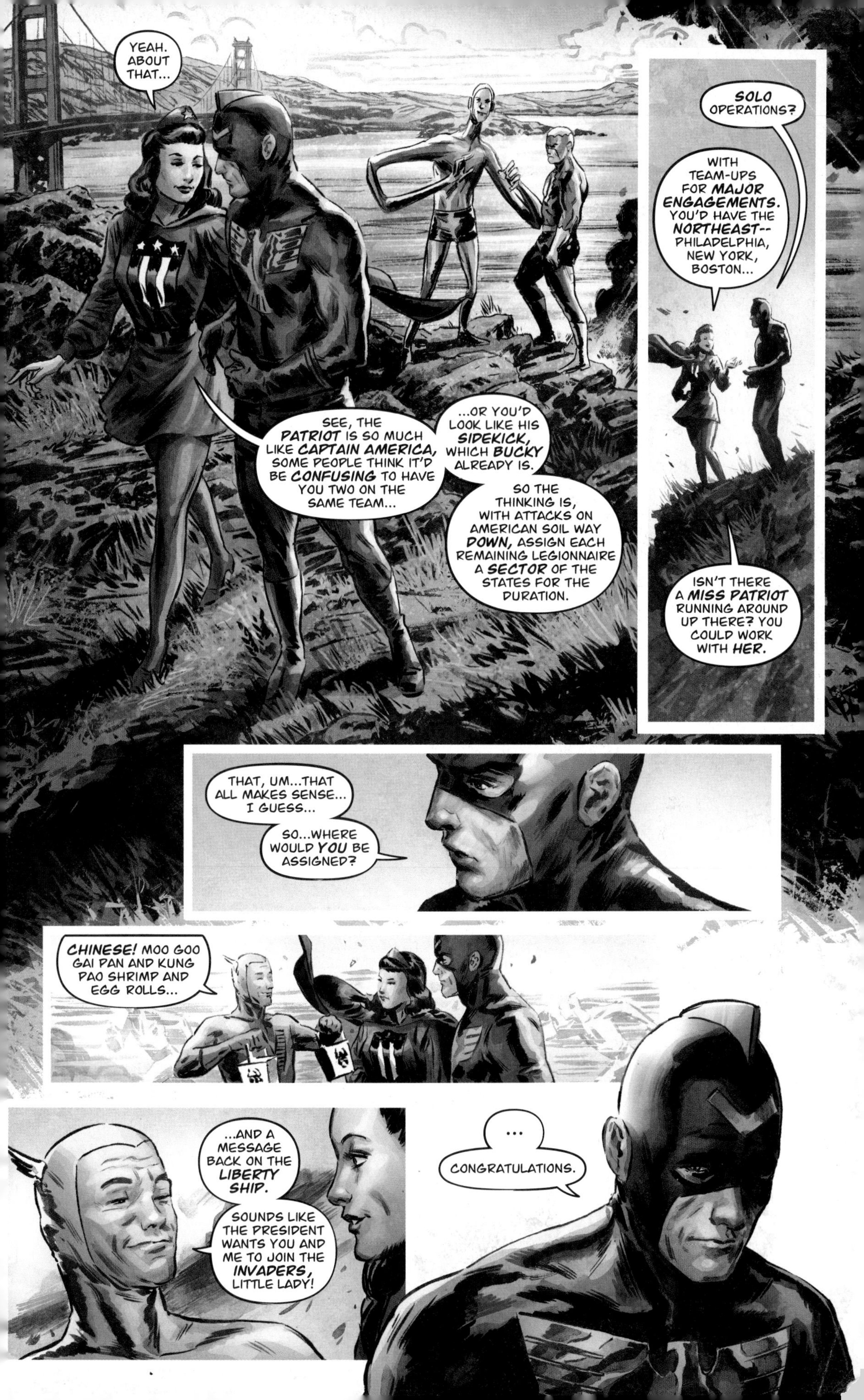
YEAH. ABOUT THAT...
SEE, THE PATRIOT IS SO MUCH LIKE CAPTAIN AMERICA, SOME PEOPLE THINK IT'D BE CONFUSING TO HAVE YOU TWO ON THE SAME TEAM...
...OR YOU'D LOOK LIKE HIS SIDEKICK, WHICH BUCKY ALREADY IS.
SO THE THINKING IS, WITH ATTACKS ON AMERICAN SOIL WAY DOWN, ASSIGN EACH REMAINING LEGIONNAIRE A SECTOR OF THE STATES FOR THE DURATION.
SOLO OPERATIONS?
WITH TEAM-UPS FOR MAJOR ENGAGEMENTS. YOU'D HAVE THE NORTHEAST--PHILADELPHIA, NEW YORK, BOSTON...
ISN'T THERE A MISS PATRIOT RUNNING AROUND UP THERE? YOU COULD WORK WITH HER.
THAT, UM...THAT ALL MAKES SENSE... I GUESS...
SO...WHERE WOULD YOU BE ASSIGNED?
CHINESE! MOO GOO GAI PAN AND KUNG PAO SHRIMP AND EGG ROLLS...
...AND A MESSAGE BACK ON THE LIBERTY SHIP.
SOUNDS LIKE THE PRESIDENT WANTS YOU AND ME TO JOIN THE INVADERS, LITTLE LADY!
...
CONGRATULATIONS.

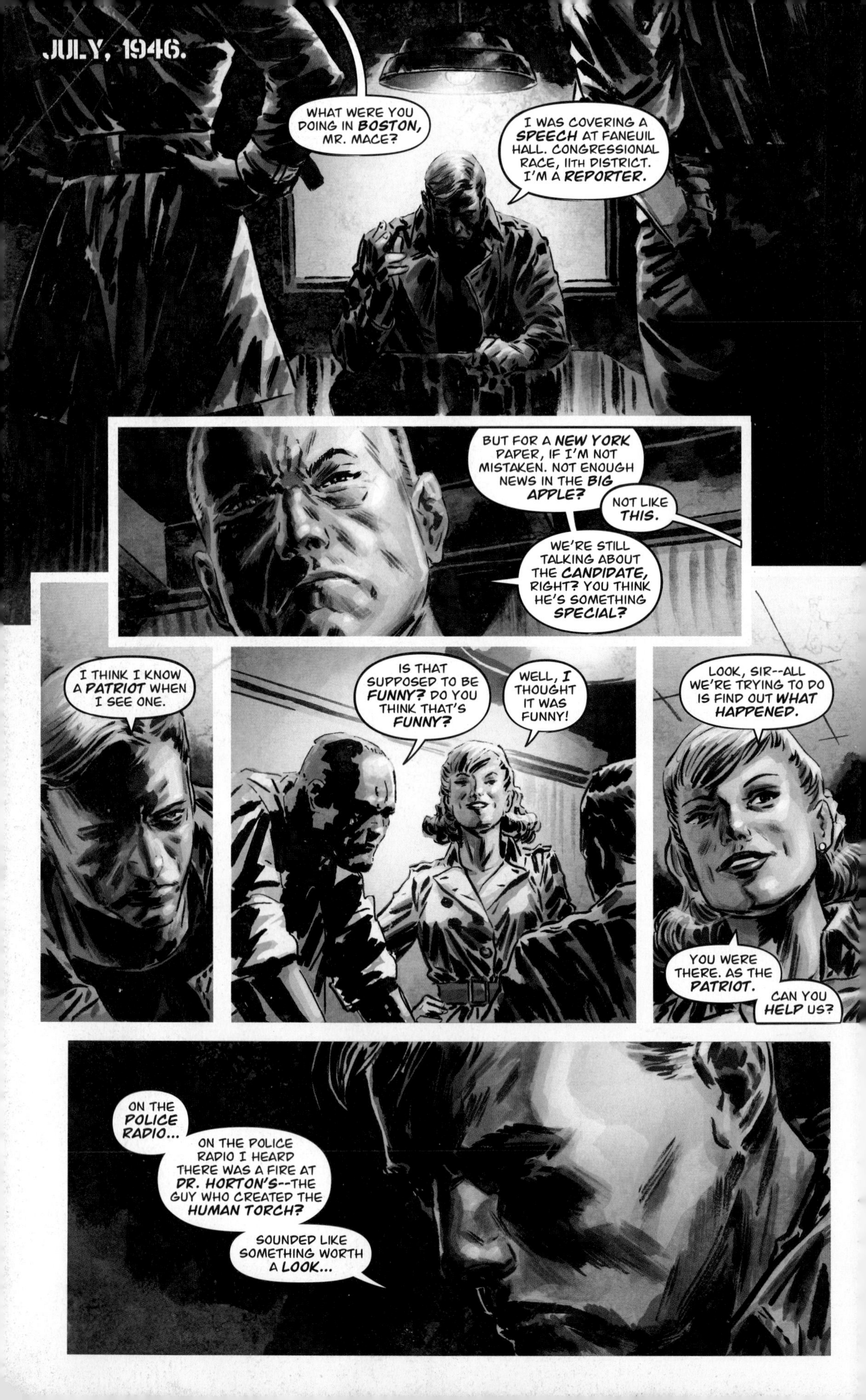
JULY, 1946.
WHAT WERE YOU DOING IN BOSTON, MR. MACE?
I WAS COVERING A SPEECH AT FANEUIL HALL. CONGRESSIONAL RACE, 11TH DISTRICT. I'M A REPORTER.
BUT FOR A NEW YORK PAPER, IF I'M NOT MISTAKEN. NOT ENOUGH NEWS IN THE BIG APPLE?
NOT LIKE THIS.
WE'RE STILL TALKING ABOUT THE CANDIDATE, RIGHT? YOU THINK HE'S SOMETHING SPECIAL?
I THINK I KNOW A PATRIOT WHEN I SEE ONE.
IS THAT SUPPOSED TO BE FUNNY? DO YOU THINK THAT'S FUNNY?
WELL, I THOUGHT IT WAS FUNNY!
LOOK, SIR--ALL WE'RE TRYING TO DO IS FIND OUT WHAT HAPPENED.
YOU WERE THERE. AS THE PATRIOT.
CAN YOU HELP US?
ON THE POLICE RADIO...
ON THE POLICE RADIO I HEARD THERE WAS A FIRE AT DR. HORTON'S--THE GUY WHO CREATED THE HUMAN TORCH?
SOUNDED LIKE SOMETHING WORTH A LOOK...

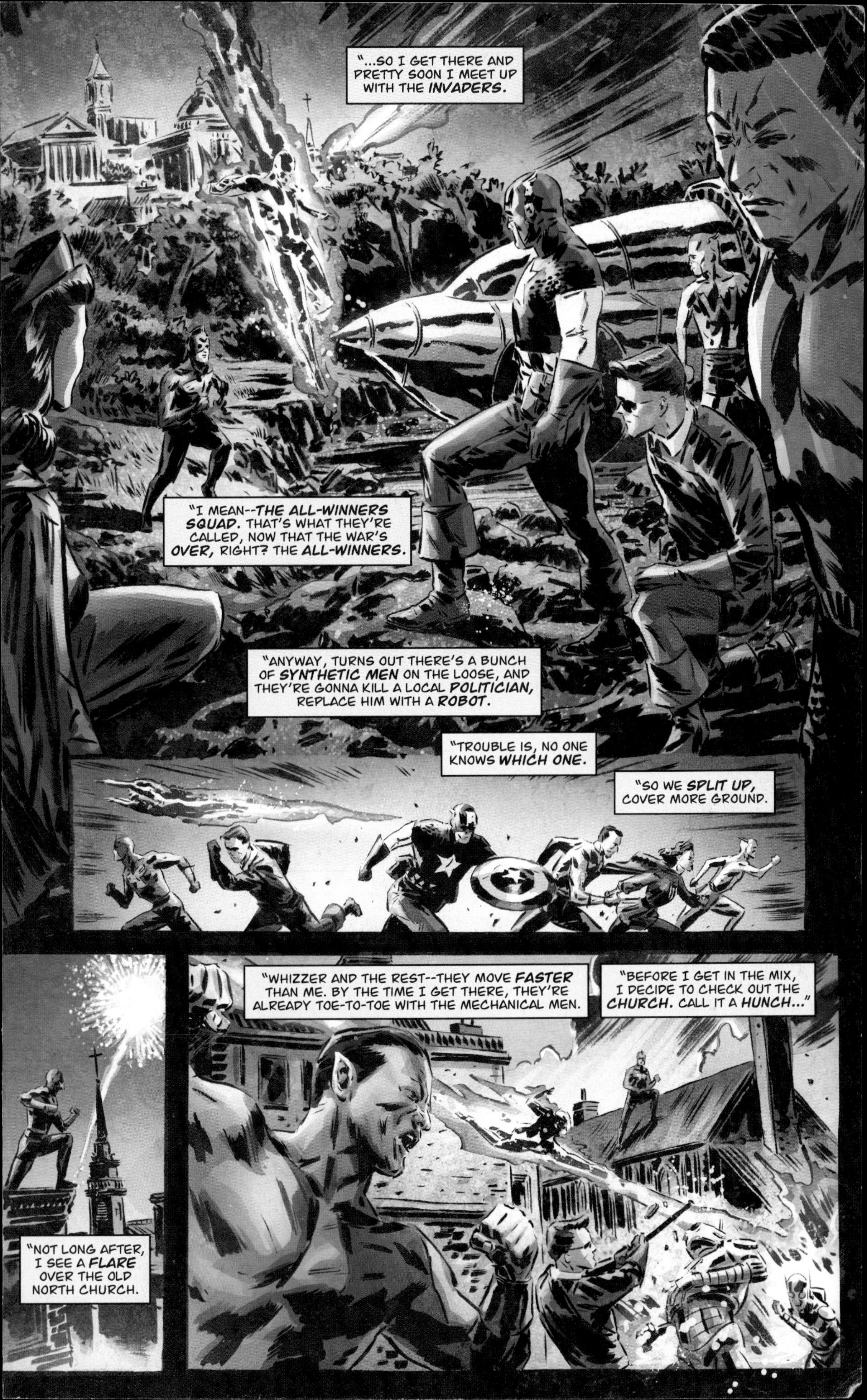
"...SO I GET THERE AND PRETTY SOON I MEET UP WITH THE INVADERS.
"I MEAN--THE ALL-WINNERS SQUAD. THAT'S WHAT THEY'RE CALLED, NOW THAT THE WAR'S OVER, RIGHT? THE ALL-WINNERS.
"ANYWAY, TURNS OUT THERE'S A BUNCH OF SYNTHETIC MEN ON THE LOOSE, AND THEY'RE GONNA KILL A LOCAL POLITICIAN, REPLACE HIM WITH A ROBOT.
"TROUBLE IS, NO ONE KNOWS WHICH ONE.
"SO WE SPLIT UP, COVER MORE GROUND.
"NOT LONG AFTER, I SEE A FLARE OVER THE OLD NORTH CHURCH.
"WHIZZER AND THE REST--THEY MOVE FASTER THAN ME. BY THE TIME I GET THERE, THEY'RE ALREADY TOE-TO-TOE WITH THE MECHANICAL MEN.
"BEFORE I GET IN THE MIX, I DECIDE TO CHECK OUT THE CHURCH. CALL IT A HUNCH..."

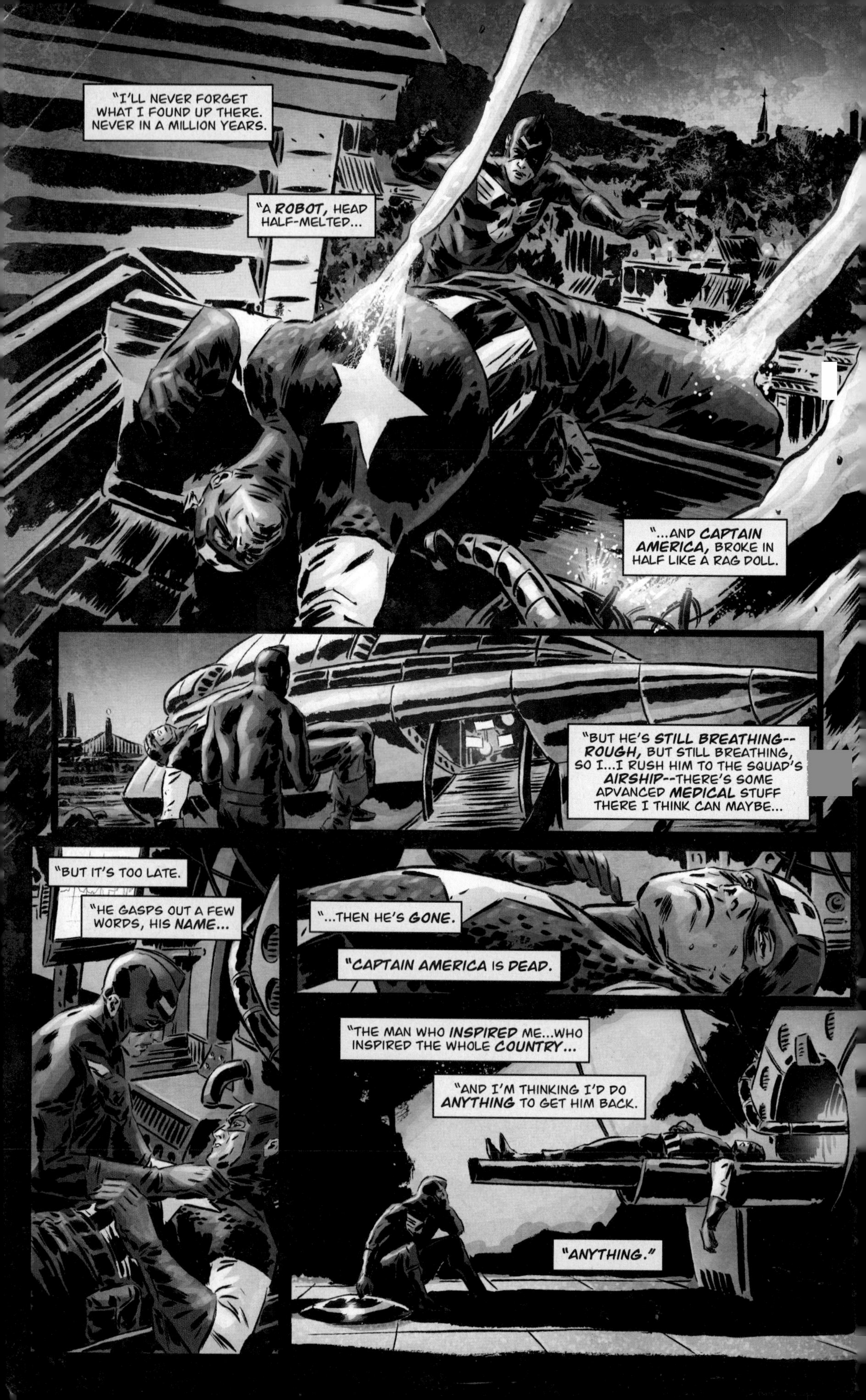
"I'LL NEVER FORGET WHAT I FOUND UP THERE. NEVER IN A MILLION YEARS.
"A ROBOT, HEAD HALF-MELTED...
"...AND CAPTAIN AMERICA, BROKE IN HALF LIKE A RAG DOLL.
"BUT HE'S STILL BREATHING-- ROUGH, BUT STILL BREATHING, SO I...I RUSH HIM TO THE SQUAD'S AIRSHIP--THERE'S SOME ADVANCED MEDICAL STUFF THERE I THINK CAN MAYBE...
"BUT IT'S TOO LATE.
"HE GASPS OUT A FEW WORDS, HIS NAME...
"...THEN HE'S GONE.
"CAPTAIN AMERICA IS DEAD.
"THE MAN WHO INSPIRED ME...WHO INSPIRED THE WHOLE COUNTRY...
"AND I'M THINKING I'D DO ANYTHING TO GET HIM BACK.
"ANYTHING."

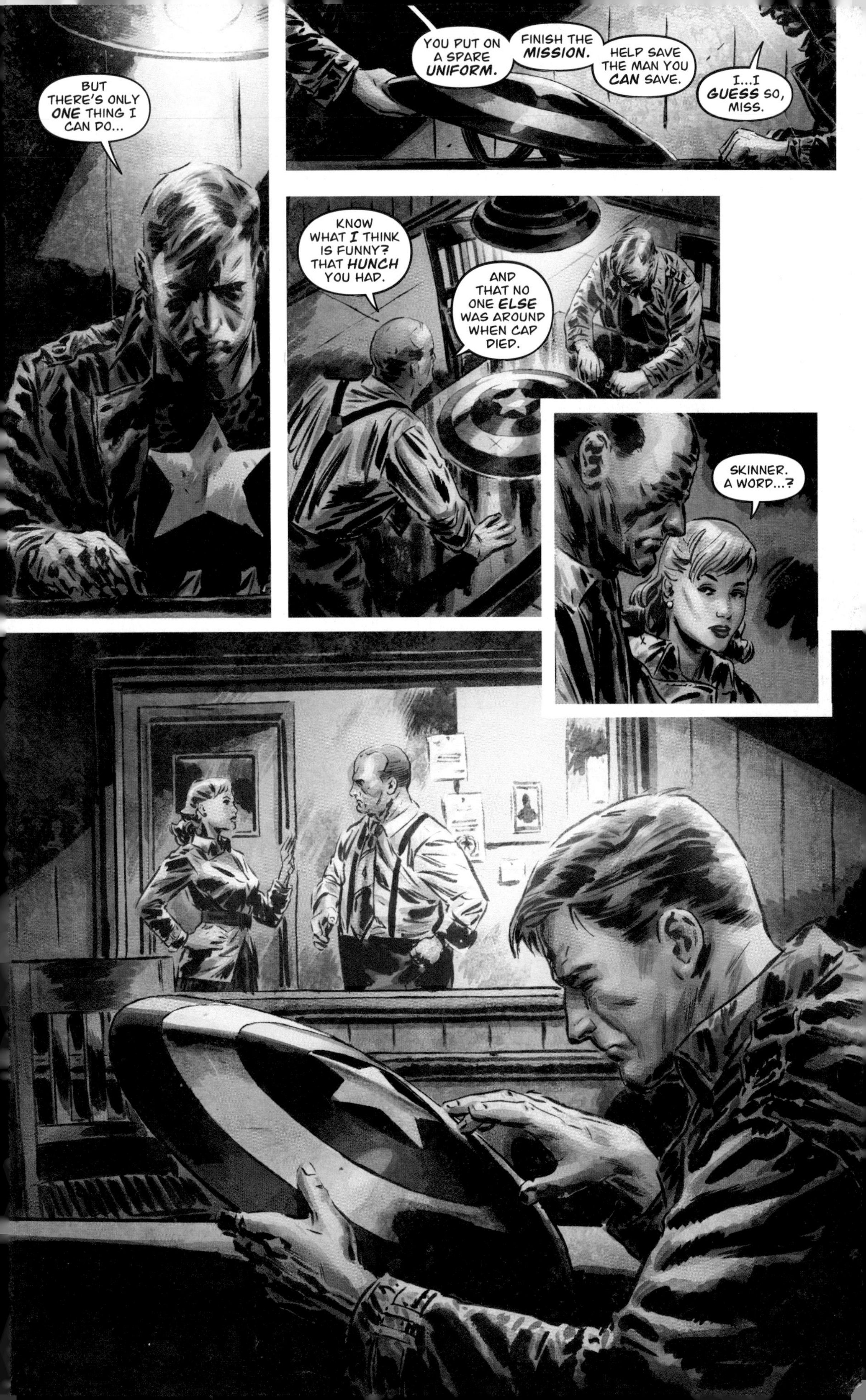
BUT THERE'S ONLY ONE THING I CAN DO...
YOU PUT ON A SPARE UNIFORM.
FINISH THE MISSION.
HELP SAVE THE MAN YOU CAN SAVE.
I...I GUESS SO, MISS.
KNOW WHAT I THINK IS FUNNY? THAT HUNCH YOU HAD.
AND THAT NO ONE ELSE WAS AROUND WHEN CAP DIED.
SKINNER. A WORD...?

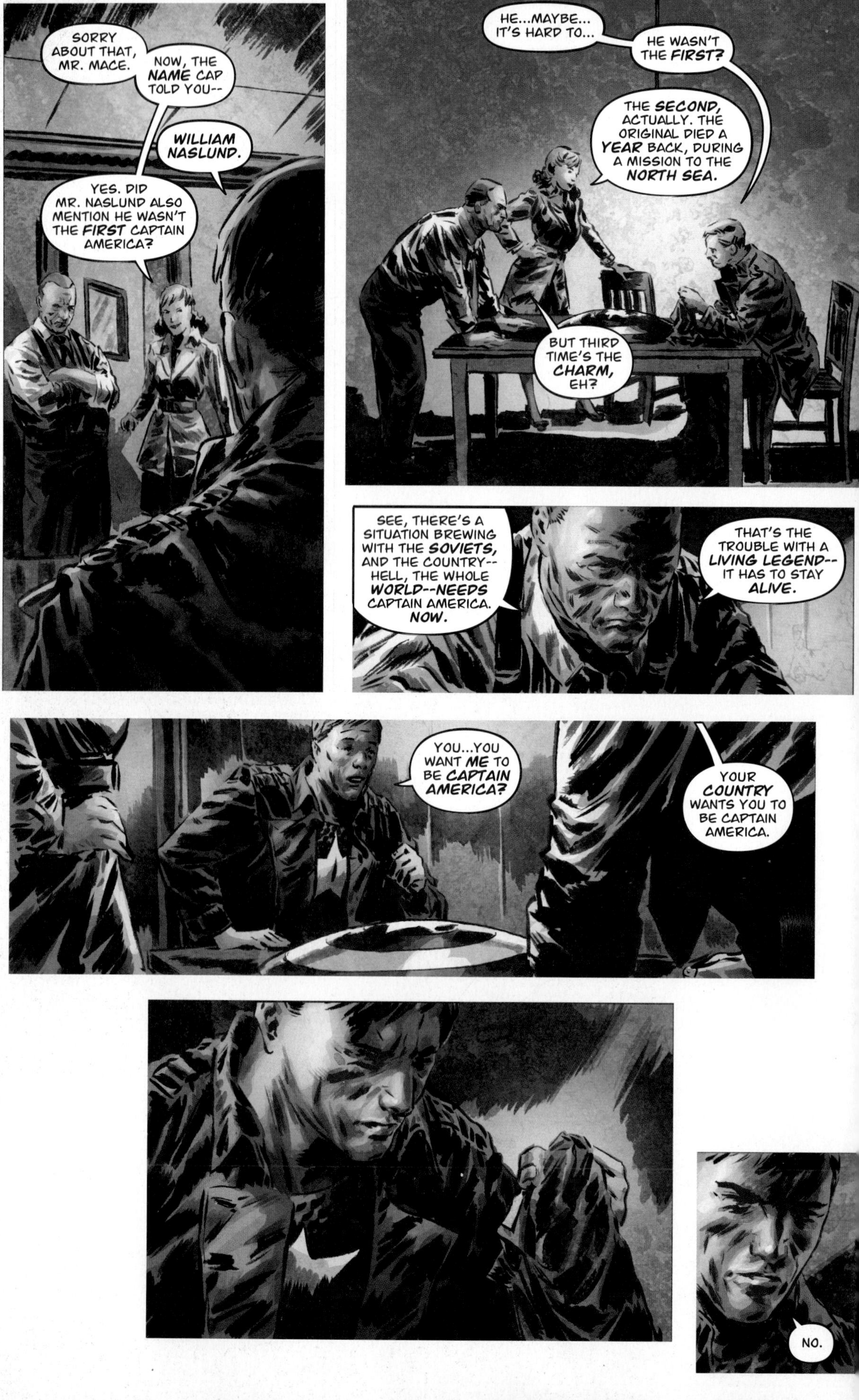
SORRY ABOUT THAT, MR. MACE.
NOW, THE NAME CAP TOLD YOU--
WILLIAM NASLUND.
YES. DID MR. NASLUND ALSO MENTION HE WASN'T THE FIRST CAPTAIN AMERICA?
HE...MAYBE... IT'S HARD TO...
HE WASN'T THE FIRST?
THE SECOND, ACTUALLY. THE ORIGINAL DIED A YEAR BACK, DURING A MISSION TO THE NORTH SEA.
BUT THIRD TIME'S THE CHARM, EH?
SEE, THERE'S A SITUATION BREWING WITH THE SOVIETS, AND THE COUNTRY-- HELL, THE WHOLE WORLD--NEEDS CAPTAIN AMERICA. NOW.
THAT'S THE TROUBLE WITH A LIVING LEGEND-- IT HAS TO STAY ALIVE.
YOU...YOU WANT ME TO BE CAPTAIN AMERICA?
YOUR COUNTRY WANTS YOU TO BE CAPTAIN AMERICA.
NO.

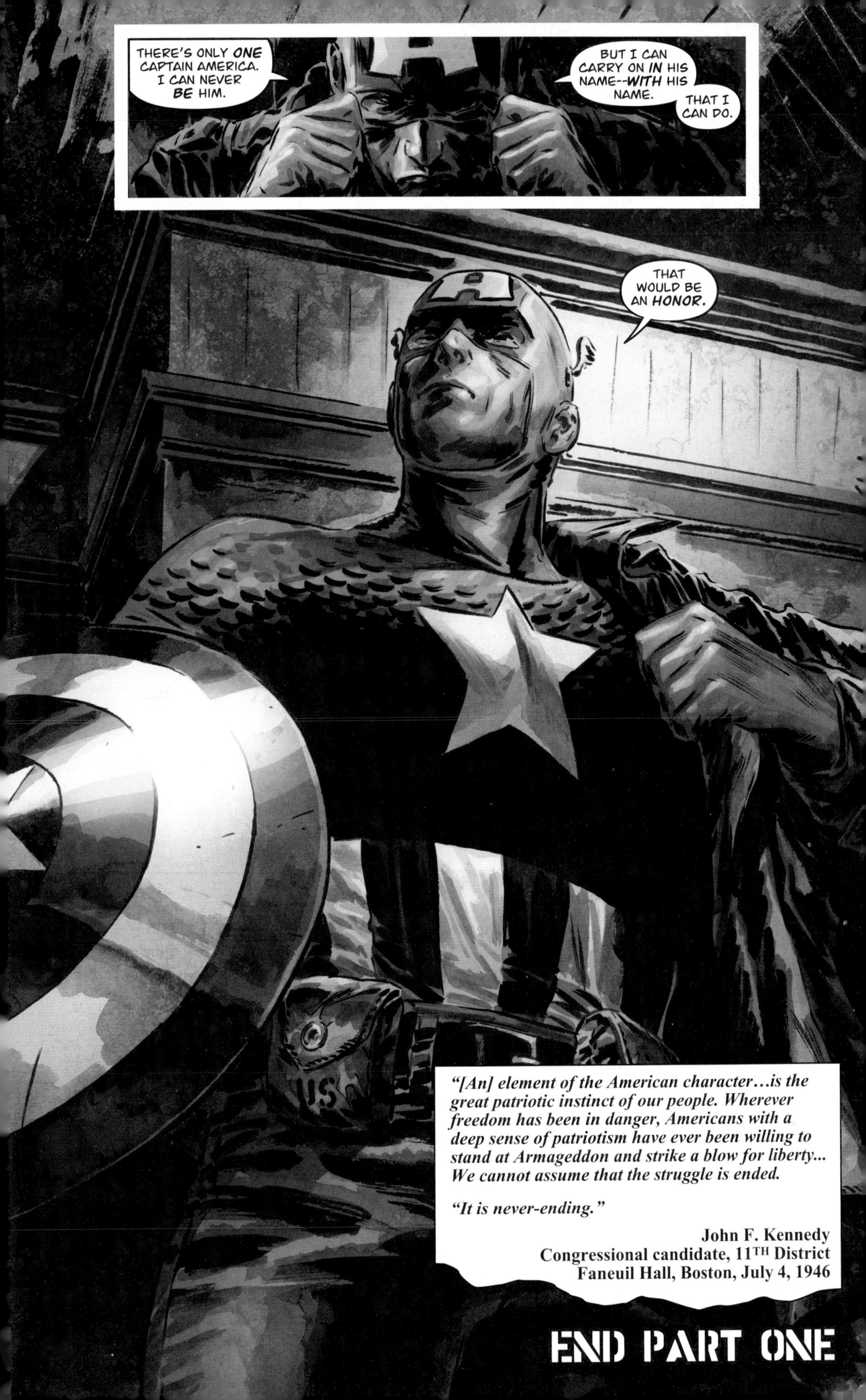
THERE'S ONLY ONE CAPTAIN AMERICA. I CAN NEVER BE HIM.
BUT I CAN CARRY ON IN HIS NAME--WITH HIS NAME.
THAT I CAN DO.
THAT WOULD BE AN HONOR.
"[An] element of the American character…is the great patriotic instinct of our people. Wherever freedom has been in danger, Americans with a deep sense of patriotism have ever been willing to stand at Armageddon and strike a blow for liberty... We cannot assume that the struggle is ended.
"It is never-ending."
John F. Kennedy
Congressional candidate, 11TH District
Faneuil Hall, Boston, July 4, 1946
END PART ONE

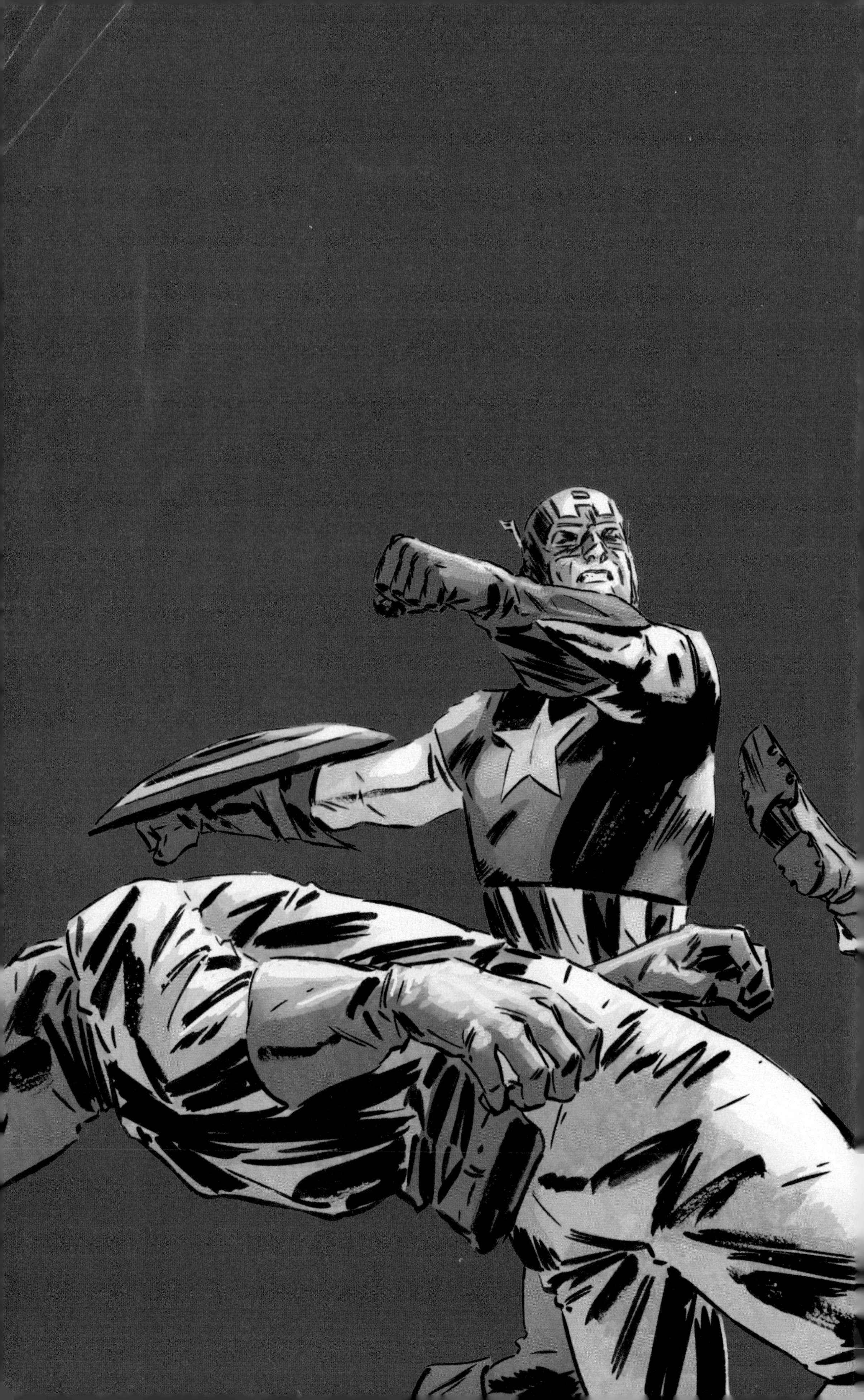

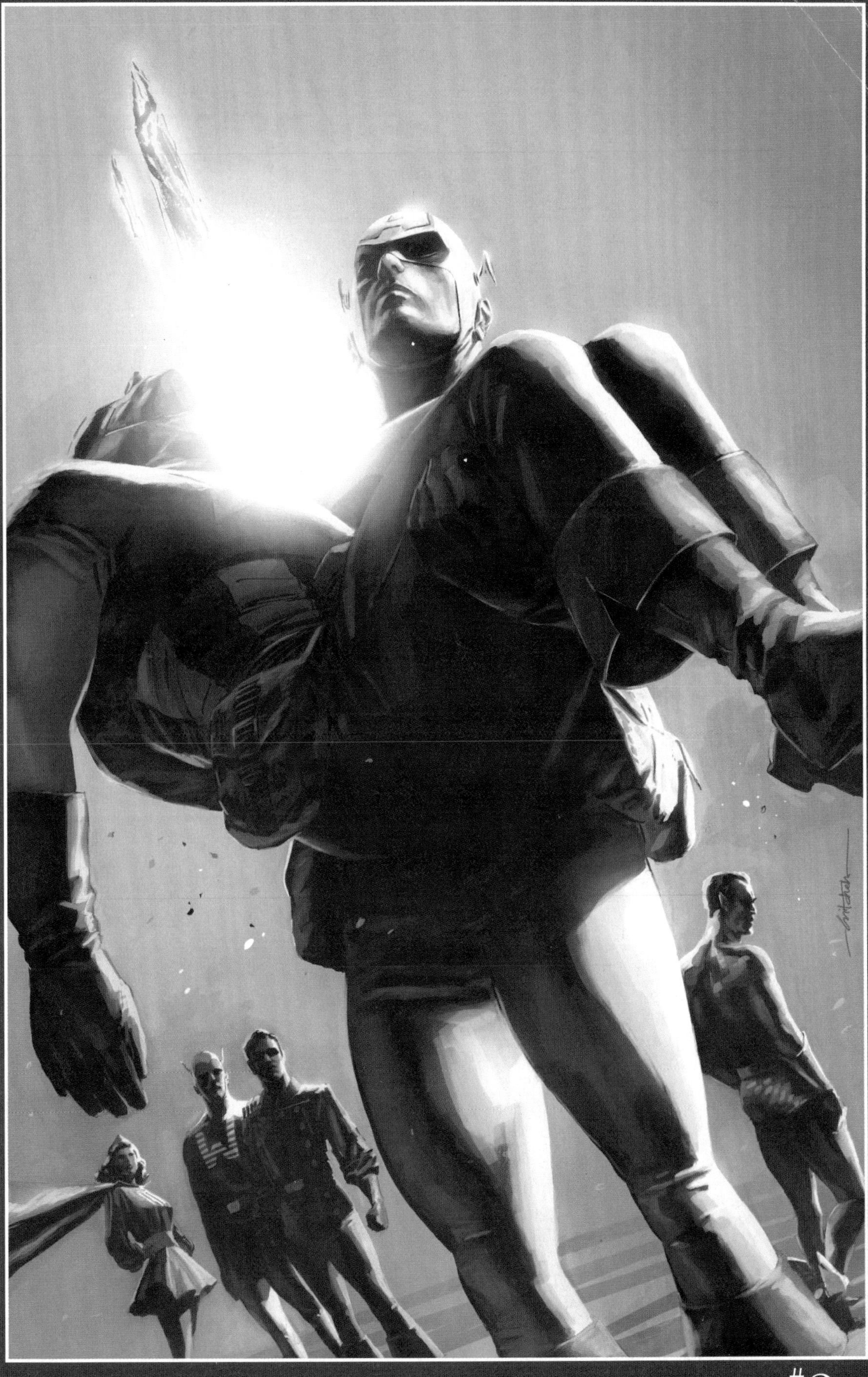

#2

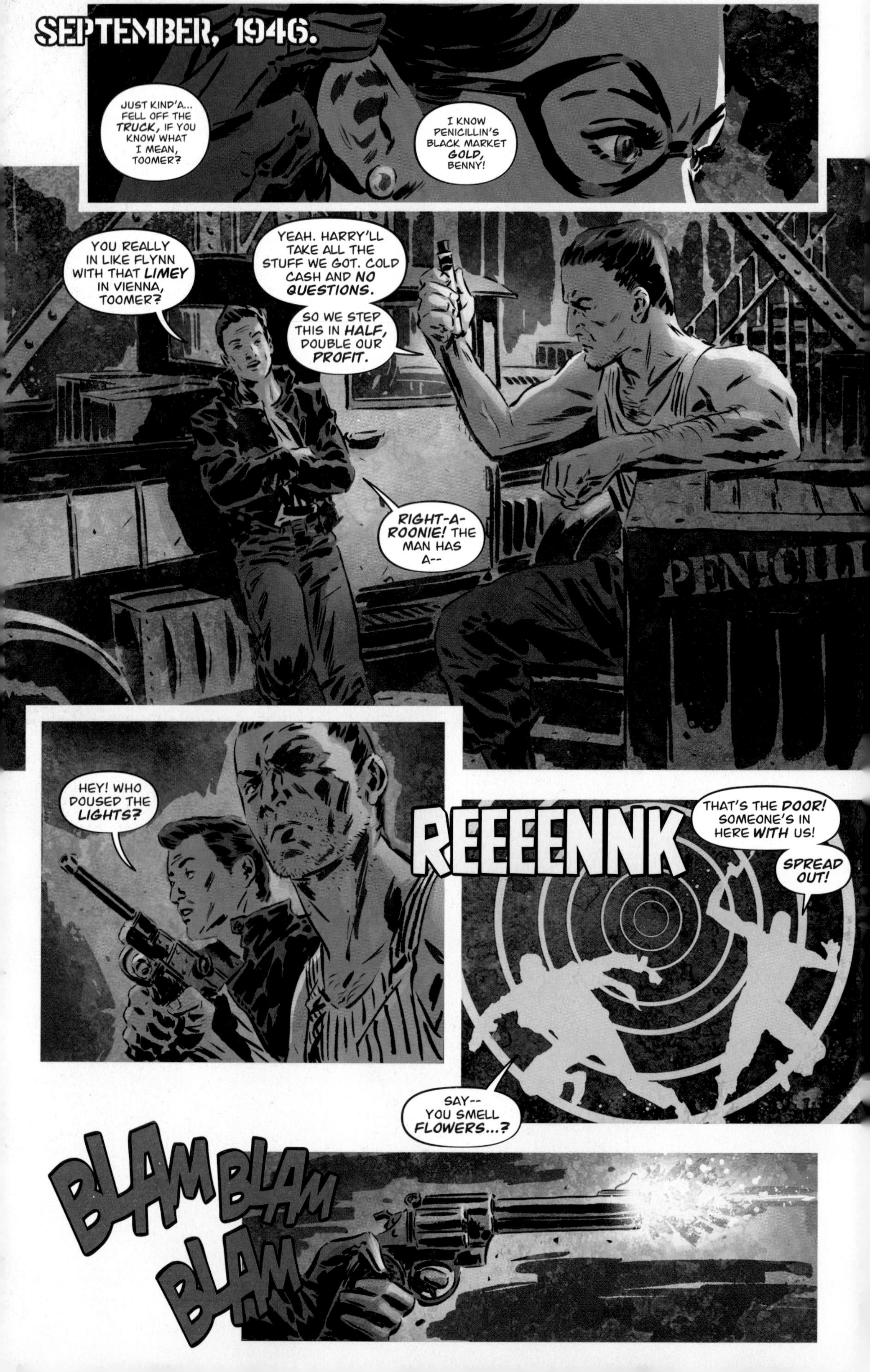
SEPTEMBER, 1946.
JUST KIND'A... FELL OFF THE TRUCK, IF YOU KNOW WHAT I MEAN, TOOMER?
I KNOW PENICILLIN'S BLACK MARKET GOLD, BENNY!
YOU REALLY IN LIKE FLYNN WITH THAT LIMEY IN VIENNA, TOOMER?
YEAH. HARRY'LL TAKE ALL THE STUFF WE GOT. COLD CASH AND NO QUESTIONS.
SO WE STEP THIS IN HALF, DOUBLE OUR PROFIT.
RIGHT-A-ROONIE! THE MAN HAS A--
PENICILL
HEY! WHO DOUSED THE LIGHTS?
REEEENNK
THAT'S THE DOOR! SOMEONE'S IN HERE WITH US!
SPREAD OUT!
SAY-- YOU SMELL FLOWERS...?
BLAM BLAM BLAM

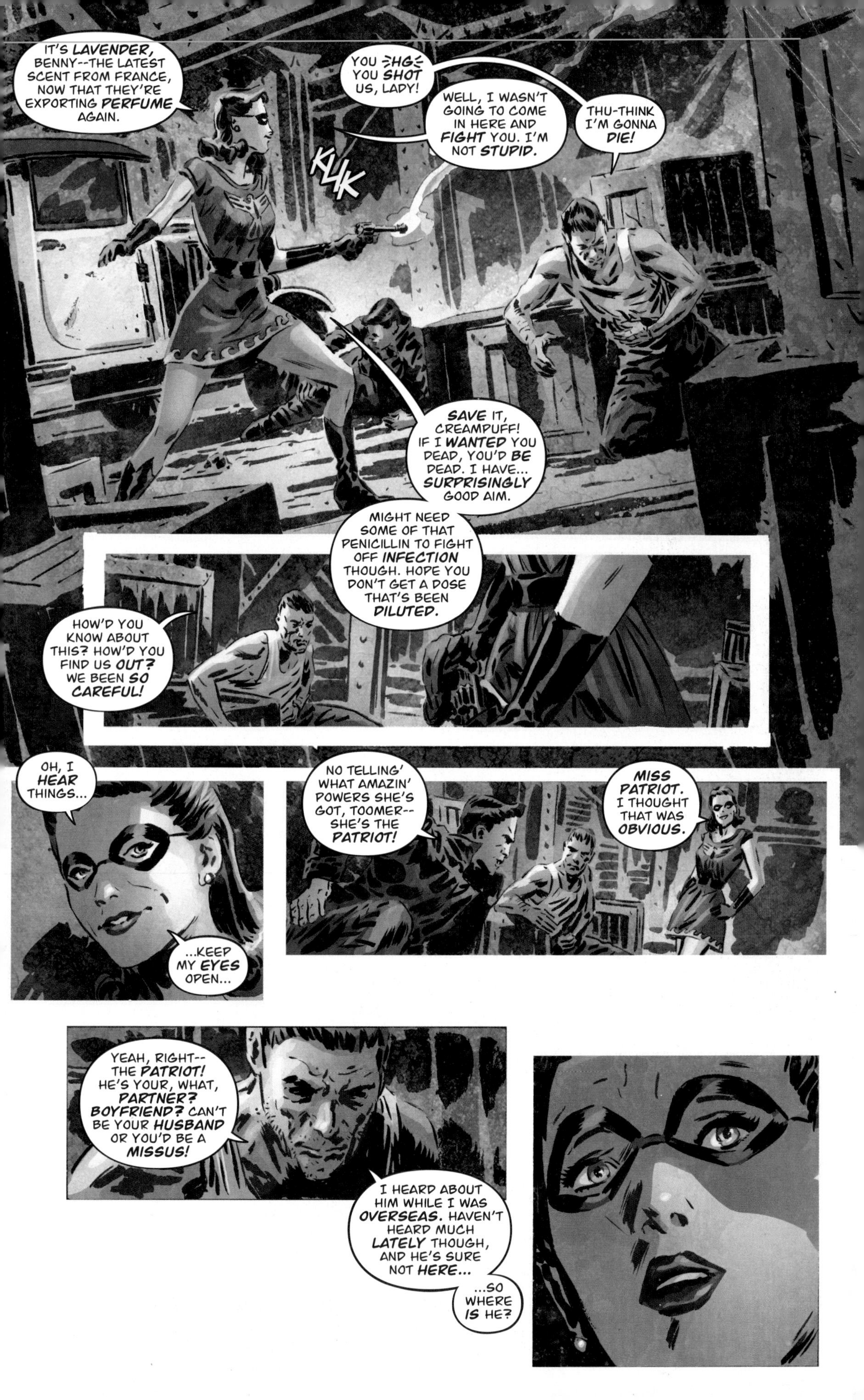
IT'S LAVENDER, BENNY--THE LATEST SCENT FROM FRANCE, NOW THAT THEY'RE EXPORTING PERFUME AGAIN.
YOU HG YOU SHOT US, LADY!
WELL, I WASN'T GOING TO COME IN HERE AND FIGHT YOU. I'M NOT STUPID.
THU-THINK I'M GONNA DIE!
KLIK
SAVE IT, CREAMPUFF! IF I WANTED YOU DEAD, YOU'D BE DEAD. I HAVE... SURPRISINGLY GOOD AIM.
MIGHT NEED SOME OF THAT PENICILLIN TO FIGHT OFF INFECTION THOUGH. HOPE YOU DON'T GET A DOSE THAT'S BEEN DILUTED.
HOW'D YOU KNOW ABOUT THIS? HOW'D YOU FIND US OUT? WE BEEN SO CAREFUL!
OH, I HEAR THINGS...
...KEEP MY EYES OPEN...
NO TELLING' WHAT AMAZIN' POWERS SHE'S GOT, TOOMER-- SHE'S THE PATRIOT!
MISS PATRIOT. I THOUGHT THAT WAS OBVIOUS.
YEAH, RIGHT-- THE PATRIOT! HE'S YOUR, WHAT, PARTNER? BOYFRIEND? CAN'T BE YOUR HUSBAND OR YOU'D BE A MISSUS!
I HEARD ABOUT HIM WHILE I WAS OVERSEAS. HAVEN'T HEARD MUCH LATELY THOUGH, AND HE'S SURE NOT HERE...
...SO WHERE IS HE?

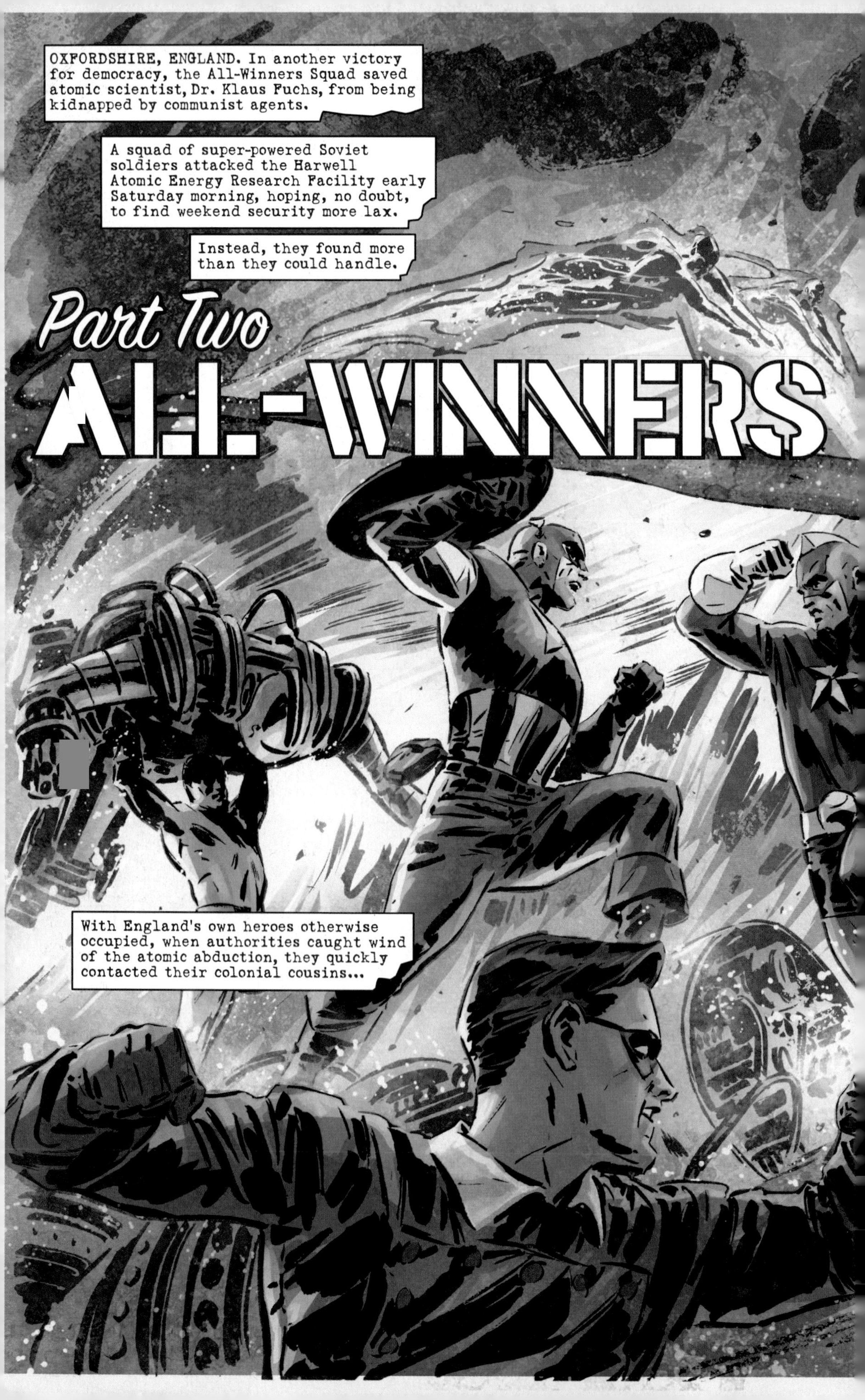
OXFORDSHIRE, ENGLAND. In another victory for democracy, the All-Winners Squad saved atomic scientist, Dr. Klaus Fuchs, from being kidnapped by communist agents.
A squad of super-powered Soviet soldiers attacked the Harwell Atomic Energy Research Facility early Saturday morning, hoping, no doubt, to find weekend security more lax.
Instead, they found more than they could handle.
Part Two
ALL-WINNERS
With England's own heroes otherwise occupied, when authorities caught wind of the atomic abduction, they quickly contacted their colonial cousins...

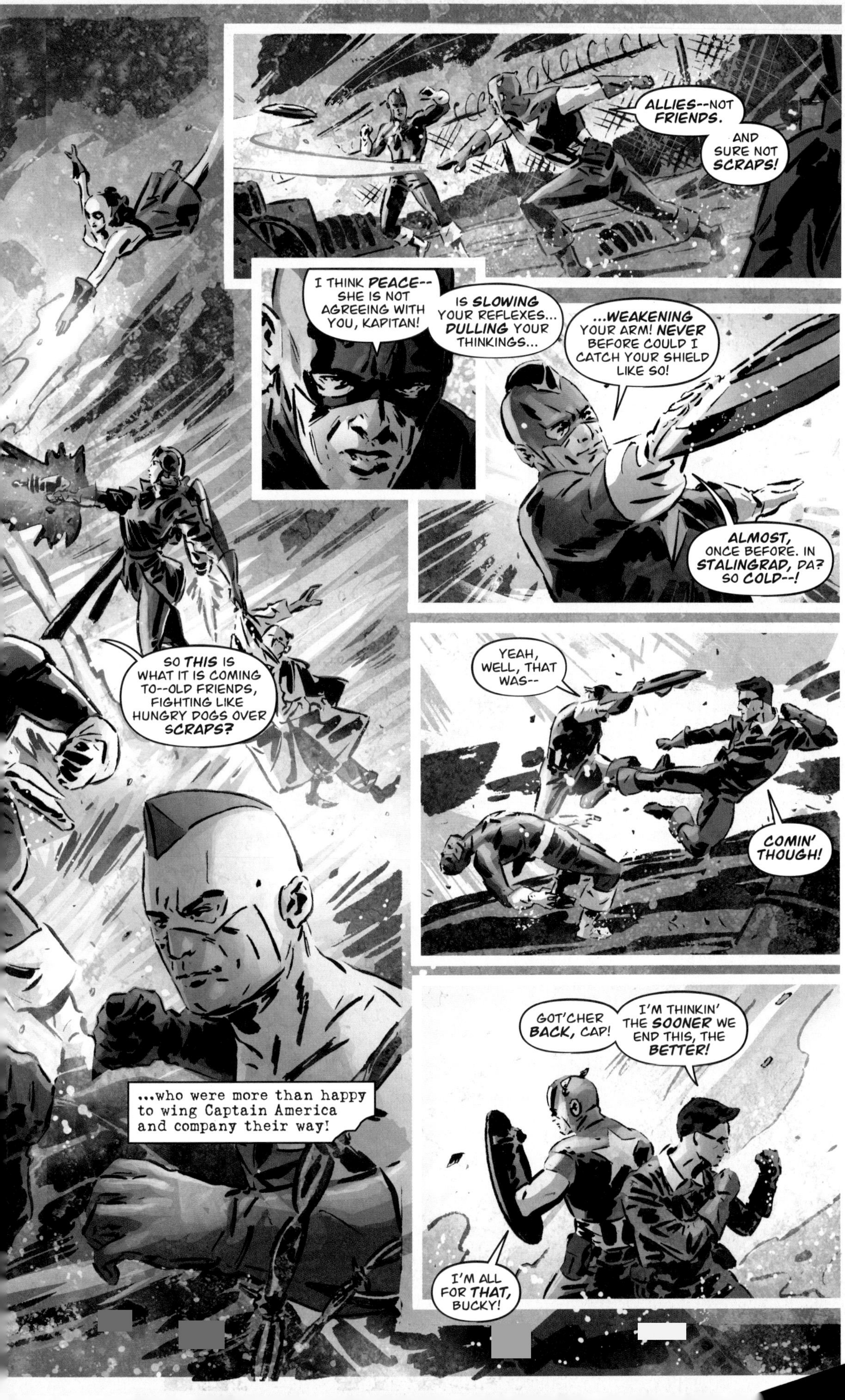
...who were more than happy to wing Captain America and company their way!
SO THIS IS WHAT IT IS COMING TO--OLD FRIENDS, FIGHTING LIKE HUNGRY DOGS OVER SCRAPS?
ALLIES--NOT FRIENDS.
AND SURE NOT SCRAPS!
I THINK PEACE--SHE IS NOT AGREEING WITH YOU, KAPITAN!
IS SLOWING YOUR REFLEXES... DULLING YOUR THINKINGS...
...WEAKENING YOUR ARM! NEVER BEFORE COULD I CATCH YOUR SHIELD LIKE SO!
ALMOST, ONCE BEFORE. IN STALINGRAD, DA? SO COLD--!
YEAH, WELL, THAT WAS--
COMIN' THOUGH!
GOT'CHER BACK, CAP!
I'M THINKIN' THE SOONER WE END THIS, THE BETTER!
I'M ALL FOR THAT, BUCKY!

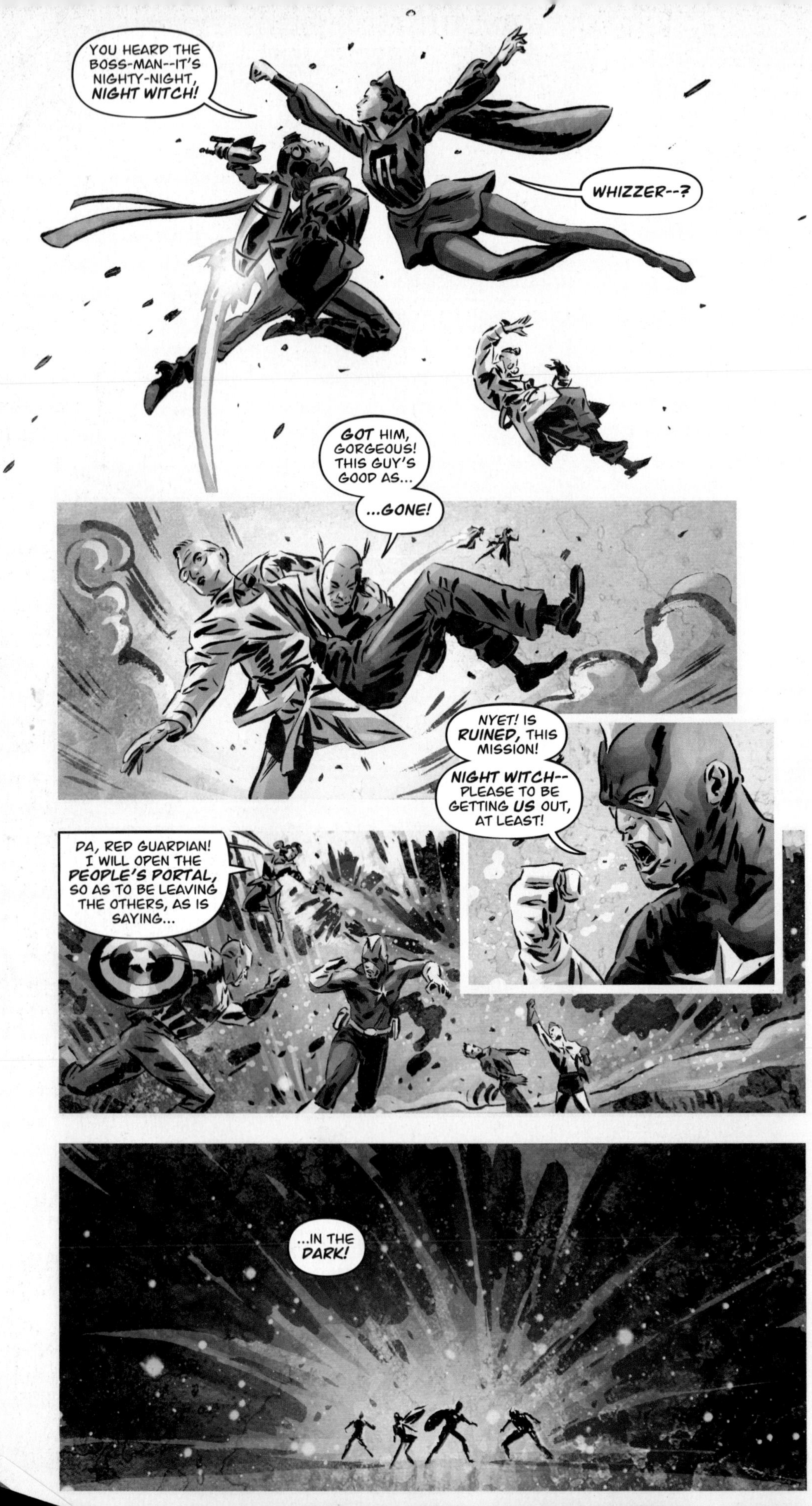
YOU HEARD THE BOSS-MAN--IT'S NIGHTY-NIGHT, NIGHT WITCH!
WHIZZER--?
GOT HIM, GORGEOUS! THIS GUY'S GOOD AS...
...GONE!
NYET! IS RUINED, THIS MISSION!
NIGHT WITCH-- PLEASE TO BE GETTING US OUT, AT LEAST!
DA, RED GUARDIAN! I WILL OPEN THE PEOPLE'S PORTAL, SO AS TO BE LEAVING THE OTHERS, AS IS SAYING...
...IN THE DARK!

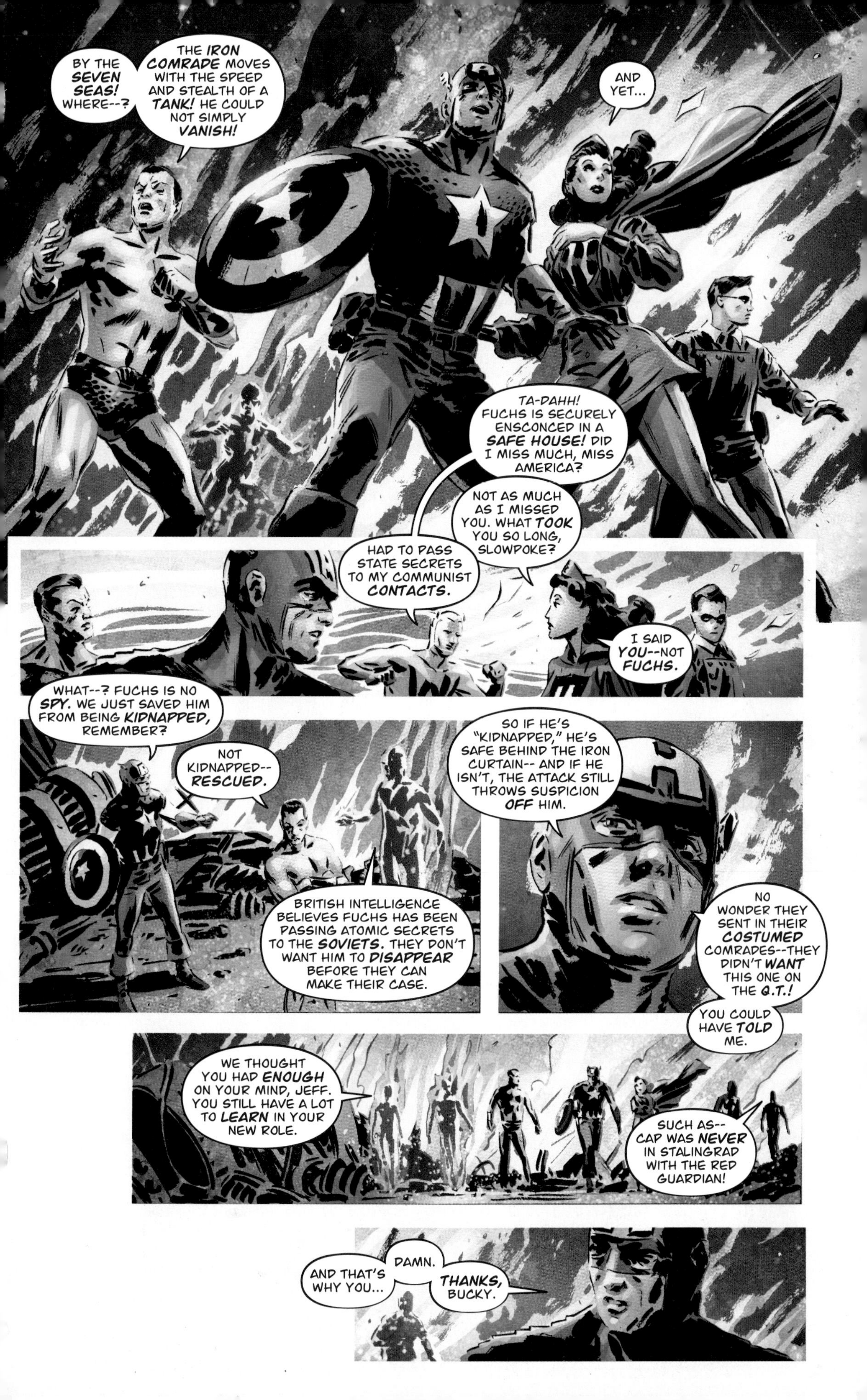
BY THE SEVEN SEAS! WHERE--?
THE IRON COMRADE MOVES WITH THE SPEED AND STEALTH OF A TANK! HE COULD NOT SIMPLY VANISH!
AND YET...
TA-DAHH! FUCHS IS SECURELY ENSCONCED IN A SAFE HOUSE! DID I MISS MUCH, MISS AMERICA?
NOT AS MUCH AS I MISSED YOU. WHAT TOOK YOU SO LONG, SLOWPOKE?
HAD TO PASS STATE SECRETS TO MY COMMUNIST CONTACTS.
I SAID YOU--NOT FUCHS.
WHAT--? FUCHS IS NO SPY. WE JUST SAVED HIM FROM BEING KIDNAPPED, REMEMBER?
NOT KIDNAPPED--RESCUED.
BRITISH INTELLIGENCE BELIEVES FUCHS HAS BEEN PASSING ATOMIC SECRETS TO THE SOVIETS. THEY DON'T WANT HIM TO DISAPPEAR BEFORE THEY CAN MAKE THEIR CASE.
SO IF HE'S "KIDNAPPED," HE'S SAFE BEHIND THE IRON CURTAIN-- AND IF HE ISN'T, THE ATTACK STILL THROWS SUSPICION OFF HIM.
NO WONDER THEY SENT IN THEIR COSTUMED COMRADES--THEY DIDN'T WANT THIS ONE ON THE Q.T.!
YOU COULD HAVE TOLD ME.
WE THOUGHT YOU HAD ENOUGH ON YOUR MIND, JEFF. YOU STILL HAVE A LOT TO LEARN IN YOUR NEW ROLE.
SUCH AS-- CAP WAS NEVER IN STALINGRAD WITH THE RED GUARDIAN!
AND THAT'S WHY YOU...
DAMN.
THANKS, BUCKY.

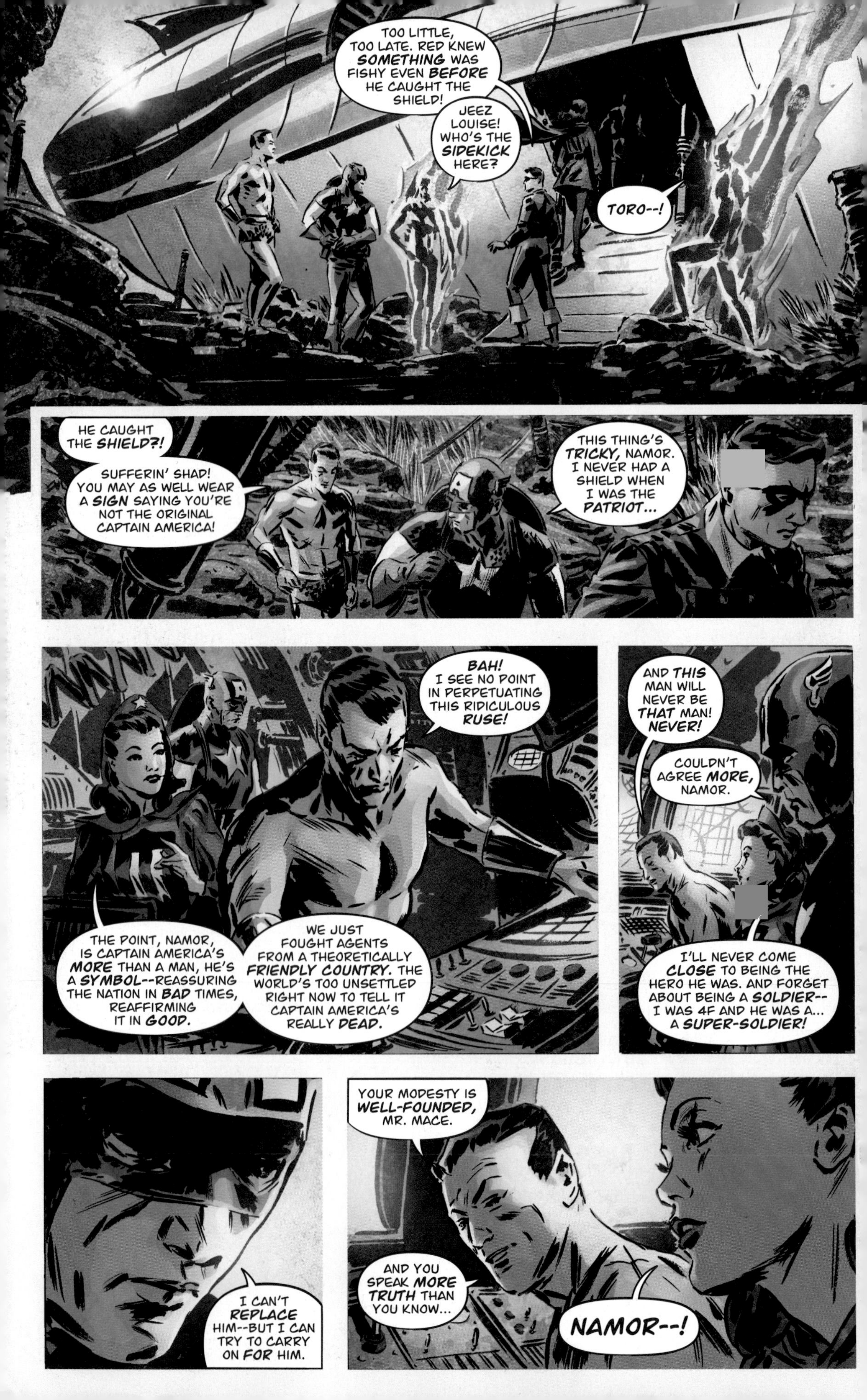
TOO LITTLE, TOO LATE. RED KNEW SOMETHING WAS FISHY EVEN BEFORE HE CAUGHT THE SHIELD!
JEEZ LOUISE! WHO'S THE SIDEKICK HERE?
TORO--!
HE CAUGHT THE SHIELD?!
SUFFERIN' SHAD! YOU MAY AS WELL WEAR A SIGN SAYING YOU'RE NOT THE ORIGINAL CAPTAIN AMERICA!
THIS THING'S TRICKY, NAMOR. I NEVER HAD A SHIELD WHEN I WAS THE PATRIOT...
BAH! I SEE NO POINT IN PERPETUATING THIS RIDICULOUS RUSE!
THE POINT, NAMOR, IS CAPTAIN AMERICA'S MORE THAN A MAN, HE'S A SYMBOL--REASSURING THE NATION IN BAD TIMES, REAFFIRMING IT IN GOOD.
WE JUST FOUGHT AGENTS FROM A THEORETICALLY FRIENDLY COUNTRY. THE WORLD'S TOO UNSETTLED RIGHT NOW TO TELL IT CAPTAIN AMERICA'S REALLY DEAD.
AND THIS MAN WILL NEVER BE THAT MAN! NEVER!
COULDN'T AGREE MORE, NAMOR.
I'LL NEVER COME CLOSE TO BEING THE HERO HE WAS. AND FORGET ABOUT BEING A SOLDIER-- I WAS 4F AND HE WAS A... A SUPER-SOLDIER!
I CAN'T REPLACE HIM--BUT I CAN TRY TO CARRY ON FOR HIM.
YOUR MODESTY IS WELL-FOUNDED, MR. MACE.
AND YOU SPEAK MORE TRUTH THAN YOU KNOW...
NAMOR--!

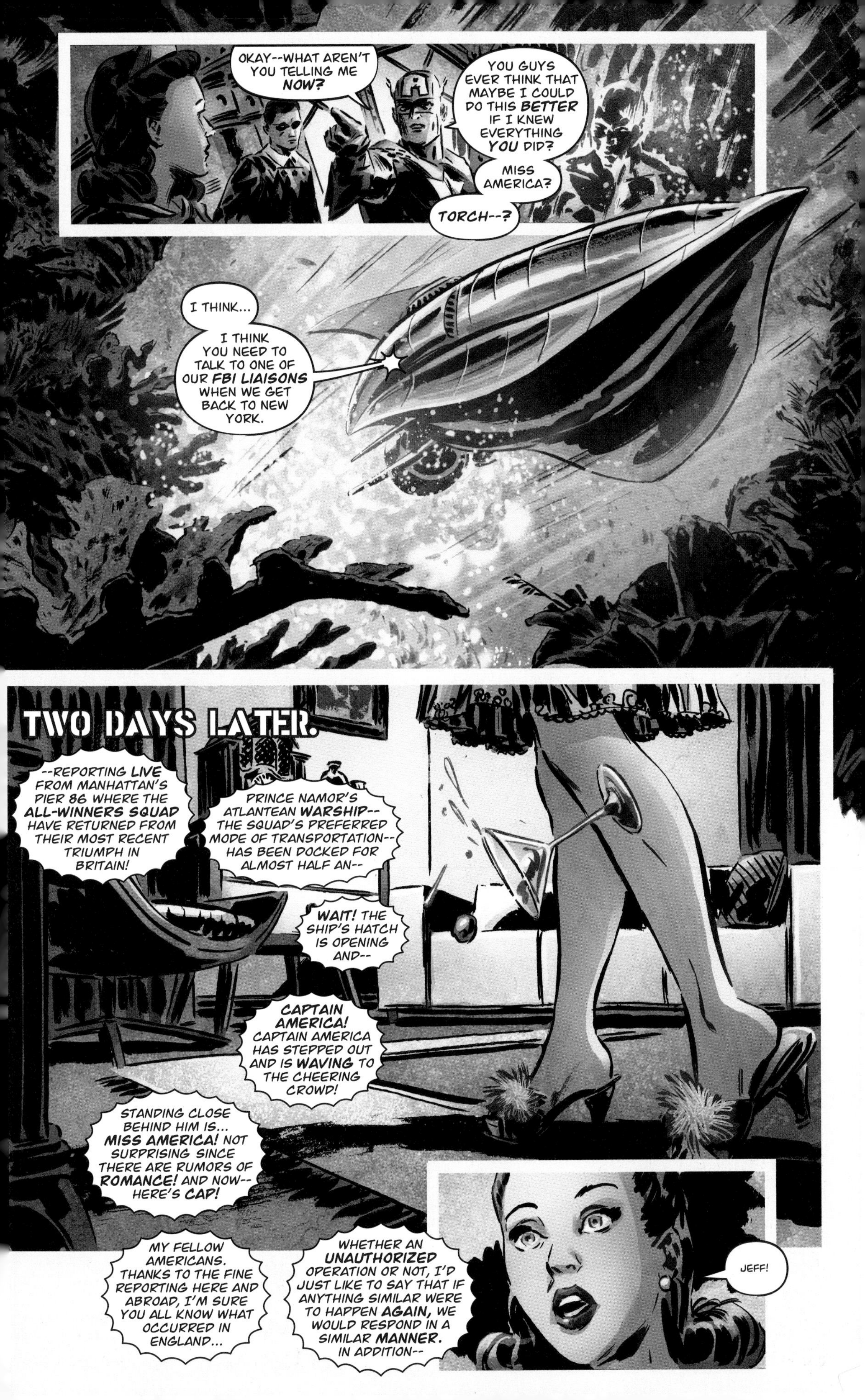
OKAY--WHAT AREN'T YOU TELLING ME NOW?
YOU GUYS EVER THINK THAT MAYBE I COULD DO THIS BETTER IF I KNEW EVERYTHING YOU DID?
MISS AMERICA?
TORCH--?
I THINK...
I THINK YOU NEED TO TALK TO ONE OF OUR FBI LIAISONS WHEN WE GET BACK TO NEW YORK.
TWO DAYS LATER.
--REPORTING LIVE FROM MANHATTAN'S PIER 86 WHERE THE ALL-WINNERS SQUAD HAVE RETURNED FROM THEIR MOST RECENT TRIUMPH IN BRITAIN!
PRINCE NAMOR'S ATLANTEAN WARSHIP-- THE SQUAD'S PREFERRED MODE OF TRANSPORTATION-- HAS BEEN DOCKED FOR ALMOST HALF AN--
WAIT! THE SHIP'S HATCH IS OPENING AND--
CAPTAIN AMERICA! CAPTAIN AMERICA HAS STEPPED OUT AND IS WAVING TO THE CHEERING CROWD!
STANDING CLOSE BEHIND HIM IS... MISS AMERICA! NOT SURPRISING SINCE THERE ARE RUMORS OF ROMANCE! AND NOW-- HERE'S CAP!
MY FELLOW AMERICANS. THANKS TO THE FINE REPORTING HERE AND ABROAD, I'M SURE YOU ALL KNOW WHAT OCCURRED IN ENGLAND...
WHETHER AN UNAUTHORIZED OPERATION OR NOT, I'D JUST LIKE TO SAY THAT IF ANYTHING SIMILAR WERE TO HAPPEN AGAIN, WE WOULD RESPOND IN A SIMILAR MANNER. IN ADDITION--
JEFF!

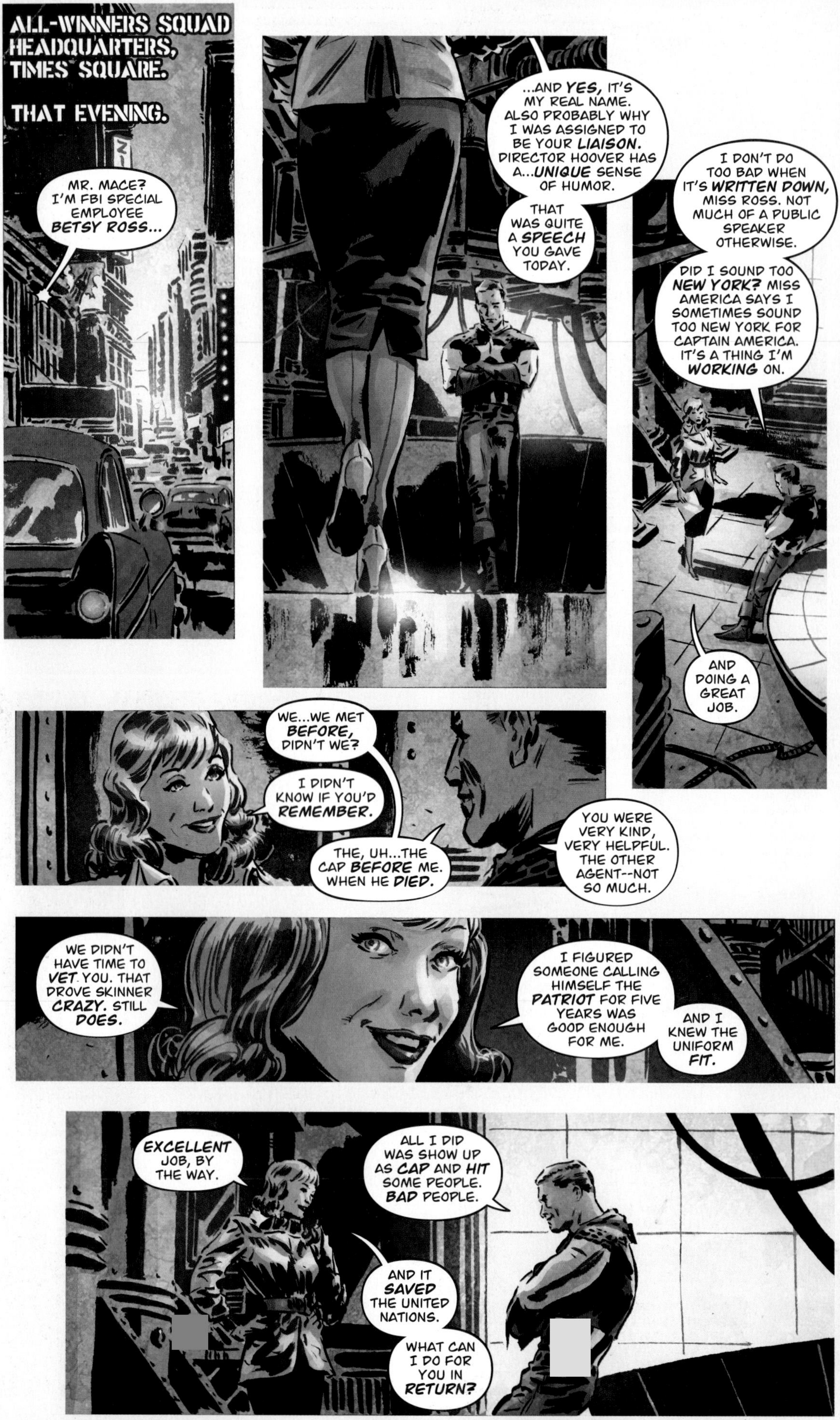
ALL-WINNERS SQUAD HEADQUARTERS, TIMES SQUARE.
THAT EVENING.
MR. MACE? I'M FBI SPECIAL EMPLOYEE BETSY ROSS...
...AND YES, IT'S MY REAL NAME. ALSO PROBABLY WHY I WAS ASSIGNED TO BE YOUR LIAISON. DIRECTOR HOOVER HAS A...UNIQUE SENSE OF HUMOR.
THAT WAS QUITE A SPEECH YOU GAVE TODAY.
I DON'T DO TOO BAD WHEN IT'S WRITTEN DOWN, MISS ROSS. NOT MUCH OF A PUBLIC SPEAKER OTHERWISE.
DID I SOUND TOO NEW YORK? MISS AMERICA SAYS I SOMETIMES SOUND TOO NEW YORK FOR CAPTAIN AMERICA. IT'S A THING I'M WORKING ON.
AND DOING A GREAT JOB.
WE...WE MET BEFORE, DIDN'T WE?
I DIDN'T KNOW IF YOU'D REMEMBER.
THE, UH...THE CAP BEFORE ME. WHEN HE DIED.
YOU WERE VERY KIND, VERY HELPFUL. THE OTHER AGENT--NOT SO MUCH.
WE DIDN'T HAVE TIME TO VET YOU. THAT DROVE SKINNER CRAZY. STILL DOES.
I FIGURED SOMEONE CALLING HIMSELF THE PATRIOT FOR FIVE YEARS WAS GOOD ENOUGH FOR ME.
AND I KNEW THE UNIFORM FIT.
EXCELLENT JOB, BY THE WAY.
ALL I DID WAS SHOW UP AS CAP AND HIT SOME PEOPLE. BAD PEOPLE.
AND IT SAVED THE UNITED NATIONS.
WHAT CAN I DO FOR YOU IN RETURN?

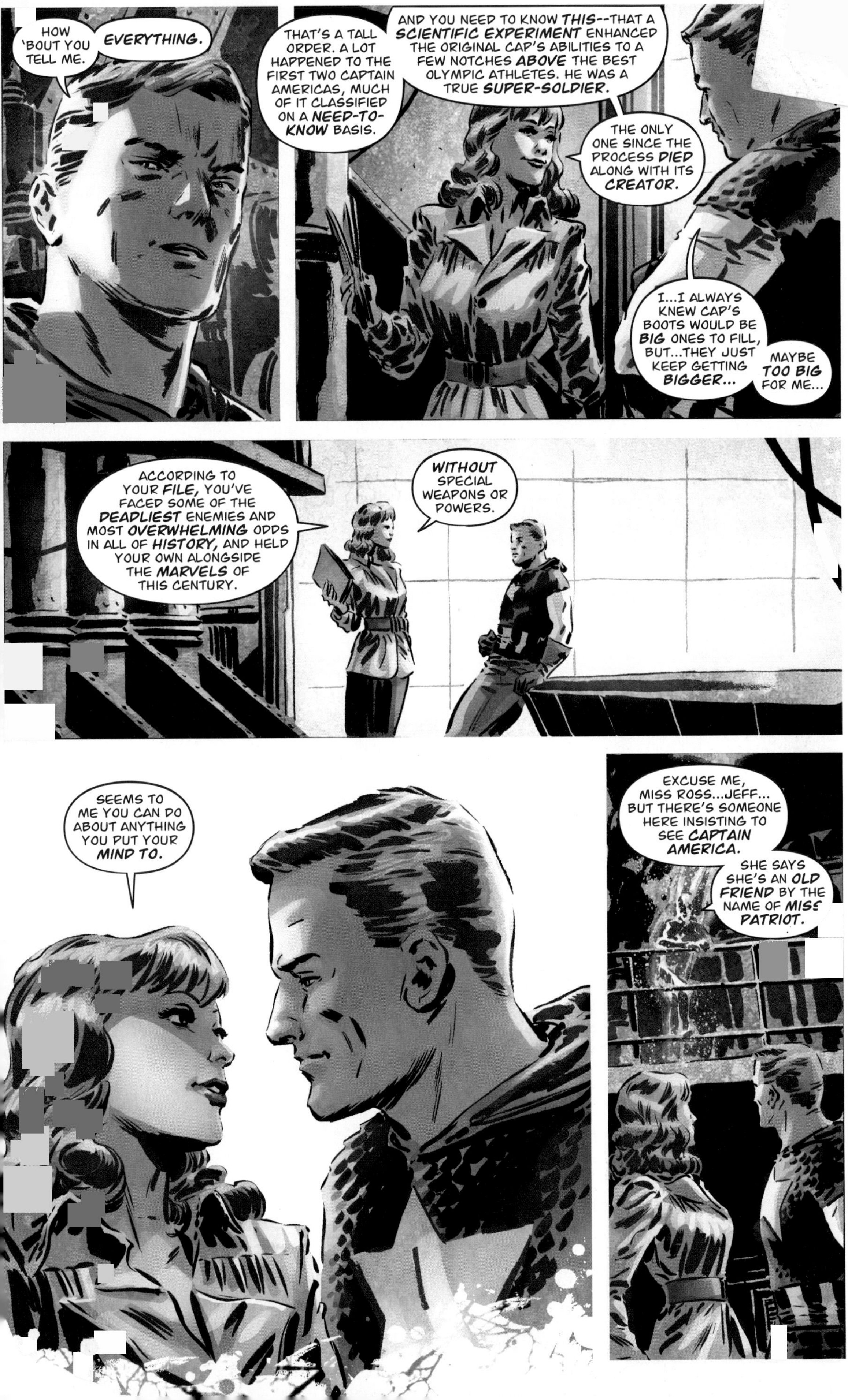

HOW 'BOUT YOU TELL ME.
EVERYTHING.
THAT'S A TALL ORDER. A LOT HAPPENED TO THE FIRST TWO CAPTAIN AMERICAS, MUCH OF IT CLASSIFIED ON A NEED-TO-KNOW BASIS.
AND YOU NEED TO KNOW THIS--THAT A SCIENTIFIC EXPERIMENT ENHANCED THE ORIGINAL CAP'S ABILITIES TO A FEW NOTCHES ABOVE THE BEST OLYMPIC ATHLETES. HE WAS A TRUE SUPER-SOLDIER.
THE ONLY ONE SINCE THE PROCESS DIED ALONG WITH ITS CREATOR.
I...I ALWAYS KNEW CAP'S BOOTS WOULD BE BIG ONES TO FILL, BUT...THEY JUST KEEP GETTING BIGGER...
MAYBE TOO BIG FOR ME...
ACCORDING TO YOUR FILE, YOU'VE FACED SOME OF THE DEADLIEST ENEMIES AND MOST OVERWHELMING ODDS IN ALL OF HISTORY, AND HELD YOUR OWN ALONGSIDE THE MARVELS OF THIS CENTURY.
WITHOUT SPECIAL WEAPONS OR POWERS.
SEEMS TO ME YOU CAN DO ABOUT ANYTHING YOU PUT YOUR MIND TO.
EXCUSE ME, MISS ROSS...JEFF... BUT THERE'S SOMEONE HERE INSISTING TO SEE CAPTAIN AMERICA.
SHE SAYS SHE'S AN OLD FRIEND BY THE NAME OF MISS PATRIOT.

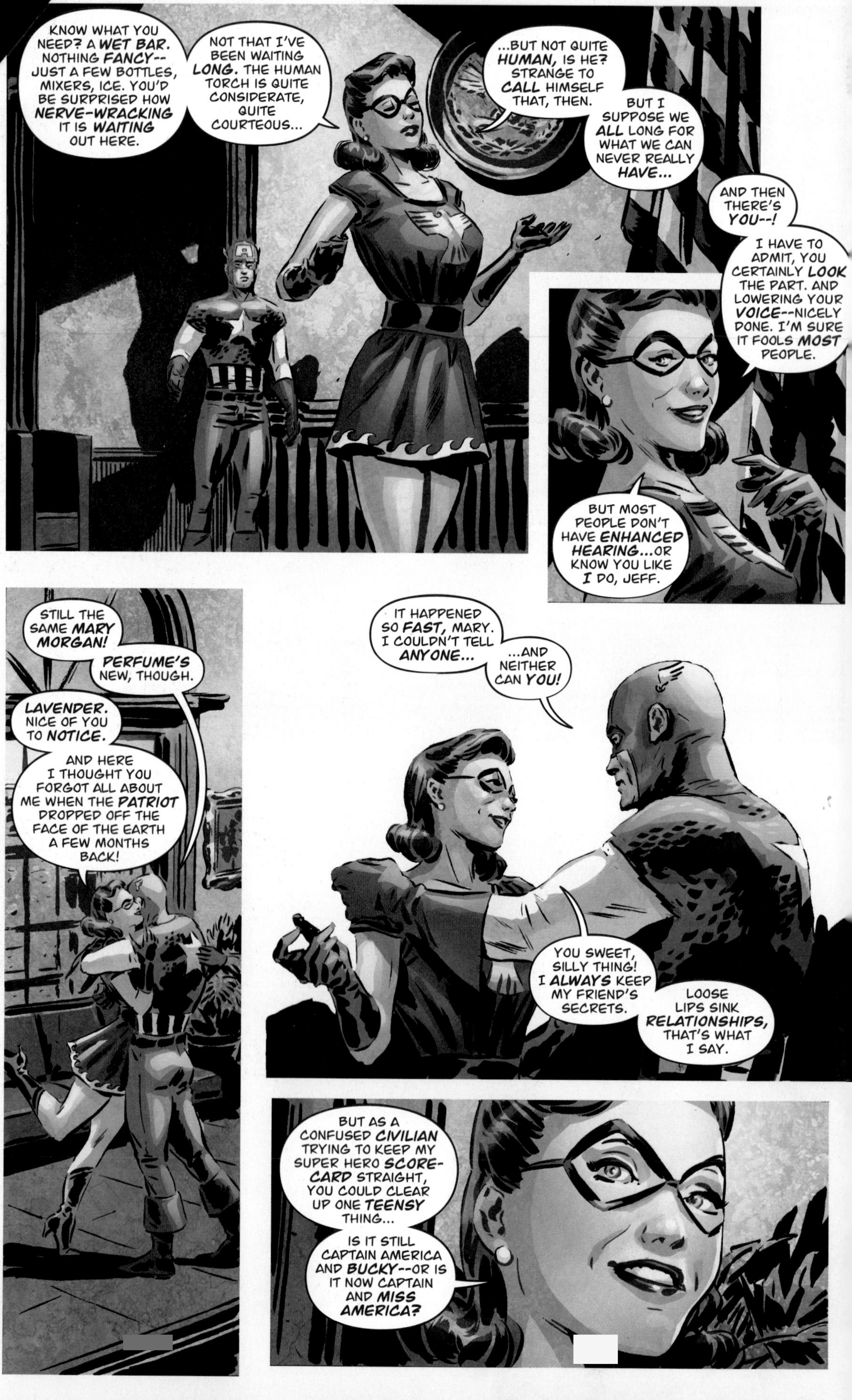
KNOW WHAT YOU NEED? A WET BAR. NOTHING FANCY-- JUST A FEW BOTTLES, MIXERS, ICE. YOU'D BE SURPRISED HOW NERVE-WRACKING IT IS WAITING OUT HERE.
NOT THAT I'VE BEEN WAITING LONG. THE HUMAN TORCH IS QUITE CONSIDERATE, QUITE COURTEOUS...
...BUT NOT QUITE HUMAN, IS HE? STRANGE TO CALL HIMSELF THAT, THEN.
BUT I SUPPOSE WE ALL LONG FOR WHAT WE CAN NEVER REALLY HAVE...
AND THEN THERE'S YOU--!
I HAVE TO ADMIT, YOU CERTAINLY LOOK THE PART. AND LOWERING YOUR VOICE--NICELY DONE. I'M SURE IT FOOLS MOST PEOPLE.
BUT MOST PEOPLE DON'T HAVE ENHANCED HEARING...OR KNOW YOU LIKE I DO, JEFF.
STILL THE SAME MARY MORGAN!
PERFUME'S NEW, THOUGH.
LAVENDER. NICE OF YOU TO NOTICE.
AND HERE I THOUGHT YOU FORGOT ALL ABOUT ME WHEN THE PATRIOT DROPPED OFF THE FACE OF THE EARTH A FEW MONTHS BACK!
IT HAPPENED SO FAST, MARY. I COULDN'T TELL ANYONE...
...AND NEITHER CAN YOU!
YOU SWEET, SILLY THING! I ALWAYS KEEP MY FRIEND'S SECRETS.
LOOSE LIPS SINK RELATIONSHIPS, THAT'S WHAT I SAY.
BUT AS A CONFUSED CIVILIAN TRYING TO KEEP MY SUPER HERO SCORE-CARD STRAIGHT, YOU COULD CLEAR UP ONE TEENSY THING...
IS IT STILL CAPTAIN AMERICA AND BUCKY--OR IS IT NOW CAPTAIN AND MISS AMERICA?

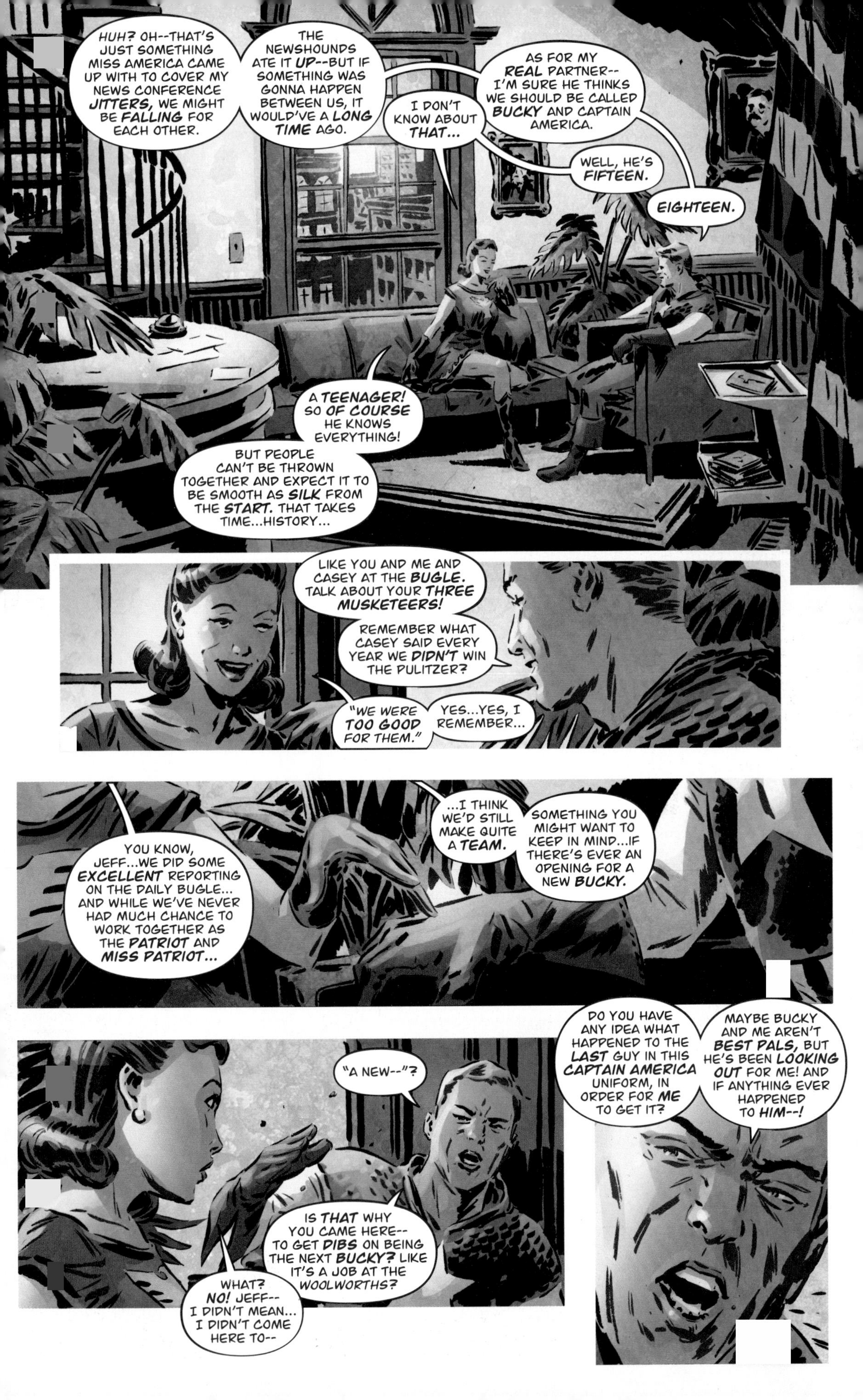
HUH? OH--THAT'S JUST SOMETHING MISS AMERICA CAME UP WITH TO COVER MY NEWS CONFERENCE JITTERS, WE MIGHT BE FALLING FOR EACH OTHER.
THE NEWSHOUNDS ATE IT UP--BUT IF SOMETHING WAS GONNA HAPPEN BETWEEN US, IT WOULD'VE A LONG TIME AGO.
I DON'T KNOW ABOUT THAT...
AS FOR MY REAL PARTNER-- I'M SURE HE THINKS WE SHOULD BE CALLED BUCKY AND CAPTAIN AMERICA.
WELL, HE'S FIFTEEN.
EIGHTEEN.
A TEENAGER! SO OF COURSE HE KNOWS EVERYTHING!
BUT PEOPLE CAN'T BE THROWN TOGETHER AND EXPECT IT TO BE SMOOTH AS SILK FROM THE START. THAT TAKES TIME...HISTORY...
LIKE YOU AND ME AND CASEY AT THE BUGLE. TALK ABOUT YOUR THREE MUSKETEERS!
REMEMBER WHAT CASEY SAID EVERY YEAR WE DIDN'T WIN THE PULITZER?
"WE WERE TOO GOOD FOR THEM."
YES...YES, I REMEMBER...
YOU KNOW, JEFF...WE DID SOME EXCELLENT REPORTING ON THE DAILY BUGLE... AND WHILE WE'VE NEVER HAD MUCH CHANCE TO WORK TOGETHER AS THE PATRIOT AND MISS PATRIOT...
...I THINK WE'D STILL MAKE QUITE A TEAM.
SOMETHING YOU MIGHT WANT TO KEEP IN MIND...IF THERE'S EVER AN OPENING FOR A NEW BUCKY.
"A NEW--"?
IS THAT WHY YOU CAME HERE-- TO GET DIBS ON BEING THE NEXT BUCKY? LIKE IT'S A JOB AT THE WOOLWORTHS?
WHAT? NO! JEFF-- I DIDN'T MEAN... I DIDN'T COME HERE TO--
DO YOU HAVE ANY IDEA WHAT HAPPENED TO THE LAST GUY IN THIS CAPTAIN AMERICA UNIFORM, IN ORDER FOR ME TO GET IT?
MAYBE BUCKY AND ME AREN'T BEST PALS, BUT HE'S BEEN LOOKING OUT FOR ME! AND IF ANYTHING EVER HAPPENED TO HIM--!

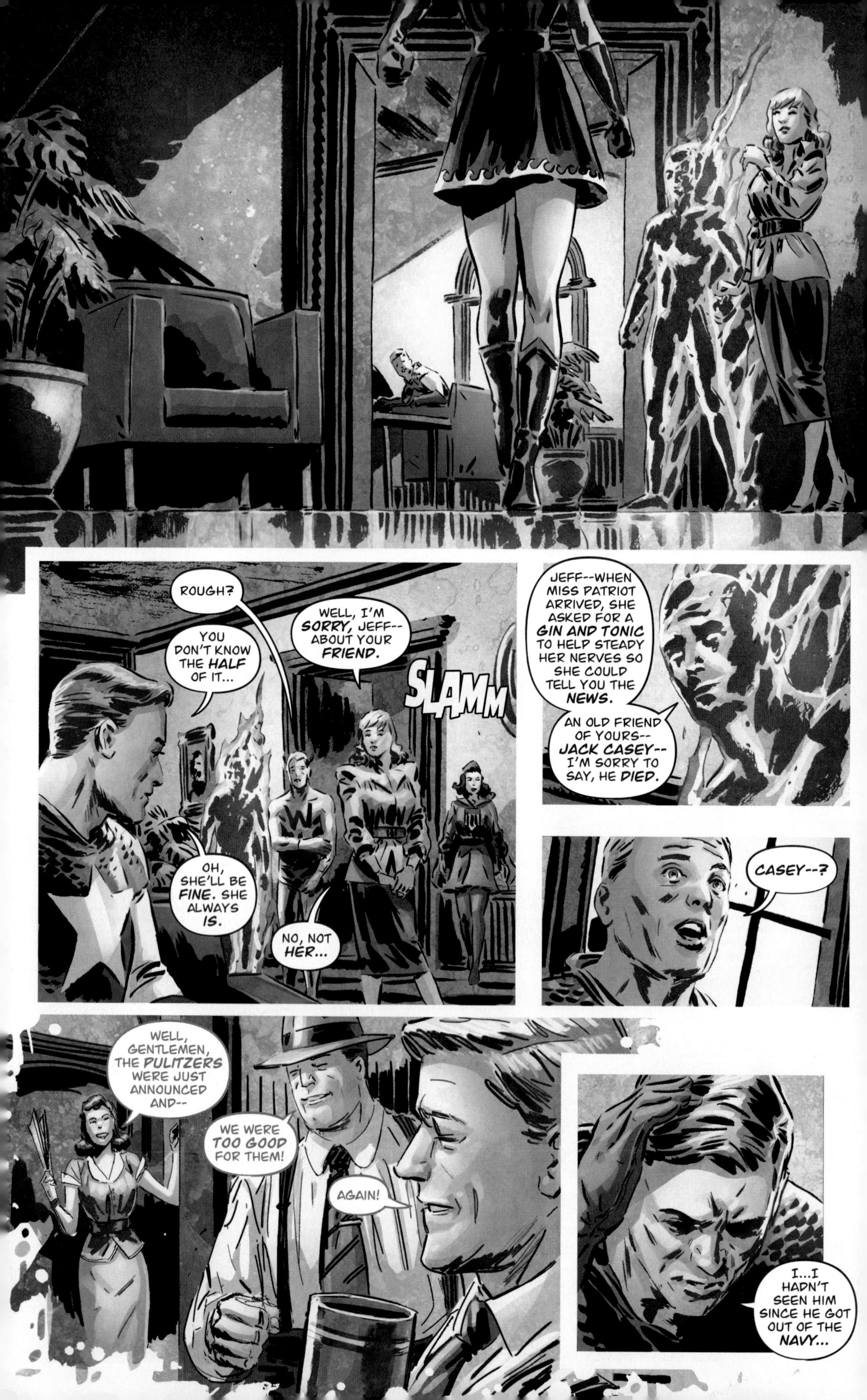

ROUGH?
YOU DON'T KNOW THE HALF OF IT...
WELL, I'M SORRY, JEFF-- ABOUT YOUR FRIEND.
SLAMM
OH, SHE'LL BE FINE. SHE ALWAYS IS.
NO, NOT HER...
JEFF--WHEN MISS PATRIOT ARRIVED, SHE ASKED FOR A GIN AND TONIC TO HELP STEADY HER NERVES SO SHE COULD TELL YOU THE NEWS.
AN OLD FRIEND OF YOURS-- JACK CASEY-- I'M SORRY TO SAY, HE DIED.
CASEY--?
WELL, GENTLEMEN, THE PULITZERS WERE JUST ANNOUNCED AND--
WE WERE TOO GOOD FOR THEM!
AGAIN!
I...I HADN'T SEEN HIM SINCE HE GOT OUT OF THE NAVY...

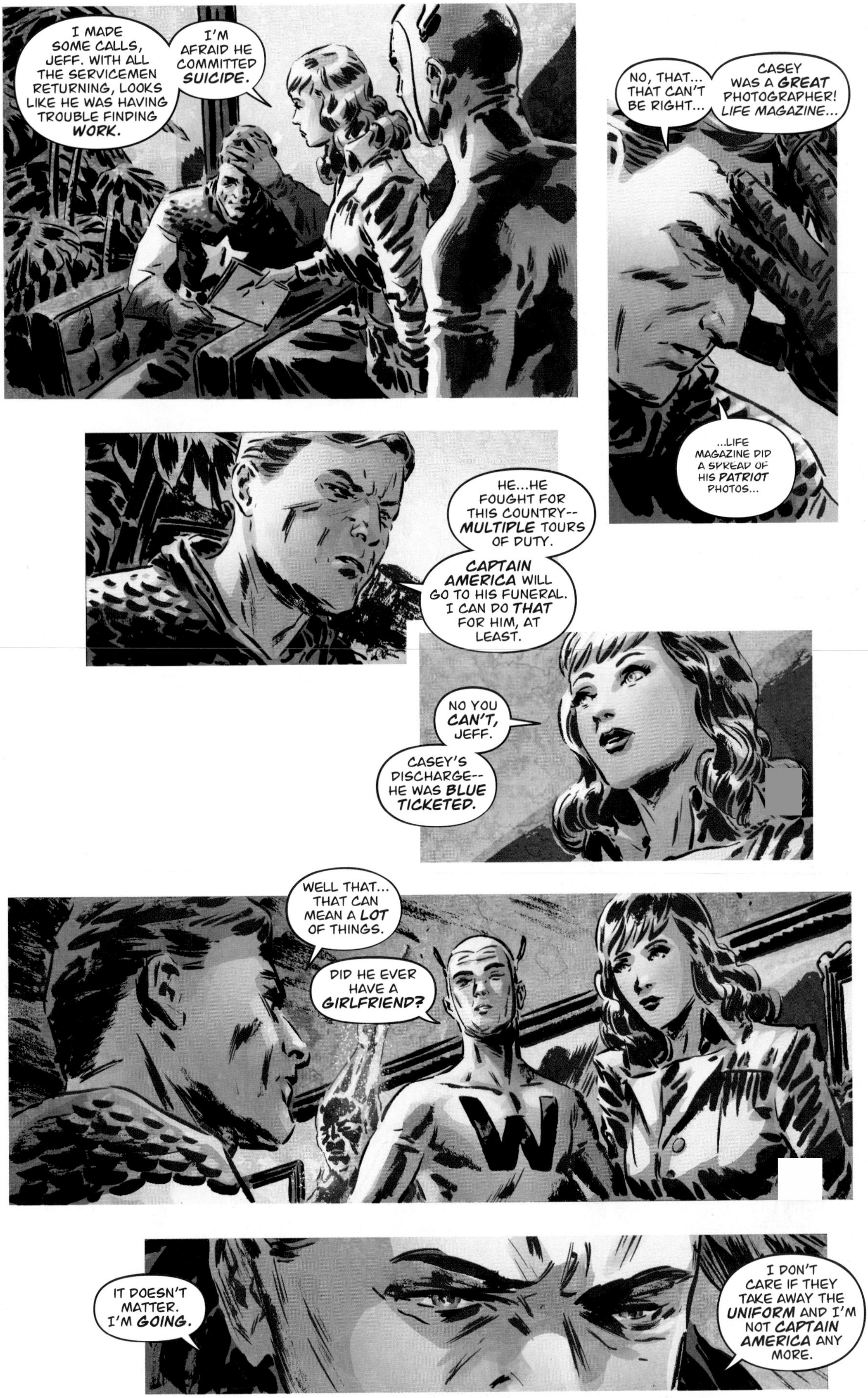

I MADE SOME CALLS, JEFF. WITH ALL THE SERVICEMEN RETURNING, LOOKS LIKE HE WAS HAVING TROUBLE FINDING WORK.
I'M AFRAID HE COMMITTED SUICIDE.
NO, THAT... THAT CAN'T BE RIGHT...
CASEY WAS A GREAT PHOTOGRAPHER! LIFE MAGAZINE...
...LIFE MAGAZINE DID A SPREAD OF HIS PATRIOT PHOTOS...
HE...HE FOUGHT FOR THIS COUNTRY-- MULTIPLE TOURS OF DUTY.
CAPTAIN AMERICA WILL GO TO HIS FUNERAL. I CAN DO THAT FOR HIM, AT LEAST.
NO YOU CAN'T, JEFF.
CASEY'S DISCHARGE-- HE WAS BLUE TICKETED.
WELL THAT... THAT CAN MEAN A LOT OF THINGS.
DID HE EVER HAVE A GIRLFRIEND?
IT DOESN'T MATTER. I'M GOING.
I DON'T CARE IF THEY TAKE AWAY THE UNIFORM AND I'M NOT CAPTAIN AMERICA ANY MORE.

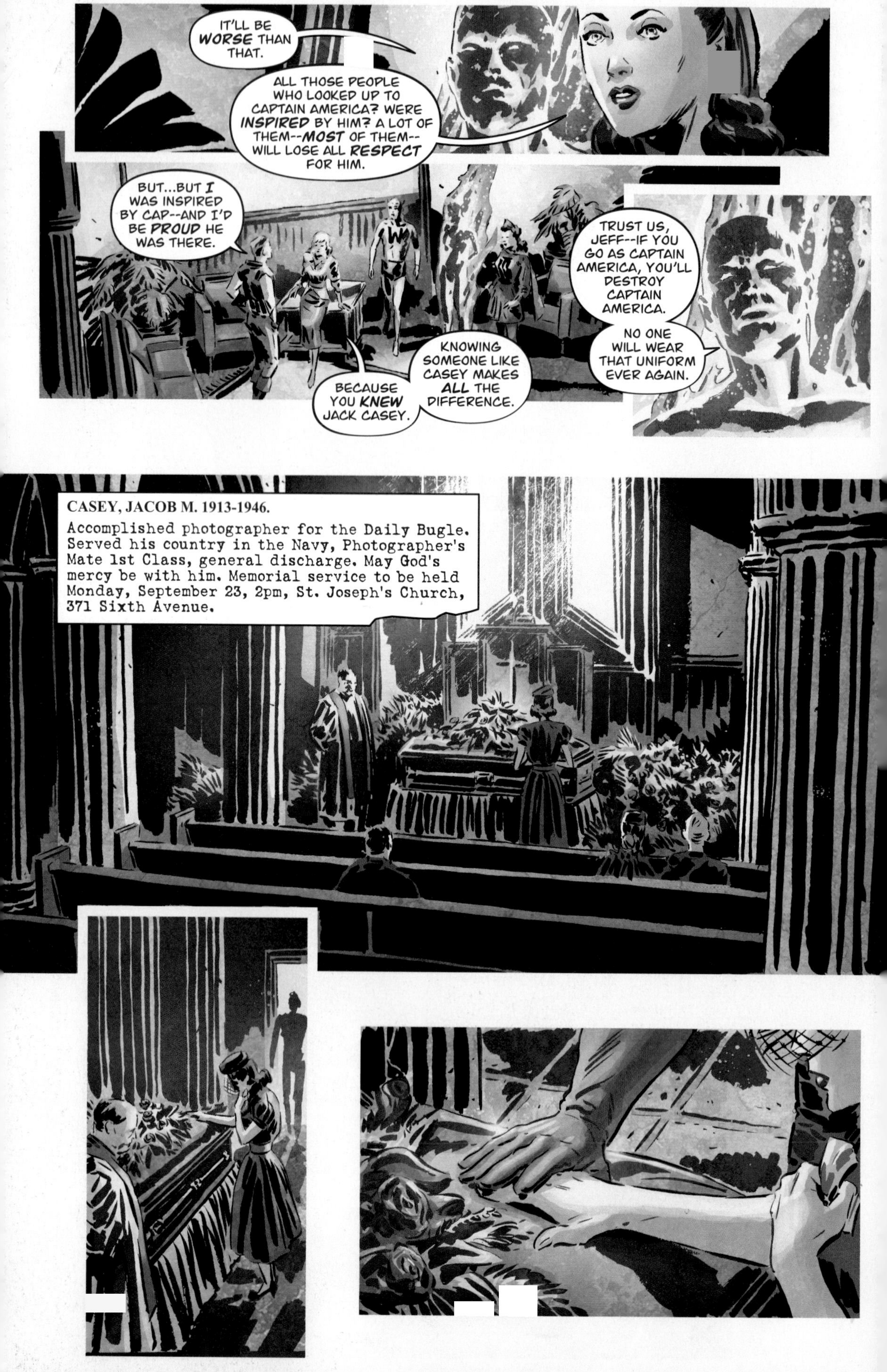
IT'LL BE WORSE THAN THAT.
ALL THOSE PEOPLE WHO LOOKED UP TO CAPTAIN AMERICA? WERE INSPIRED BY HIM? A LOT OF THEM--MOST OF THEM--WILL LOSE ALL RESPECT FOR HIM.
BUT...BUT I WAS INSPIRED BY CAP--AND I'D BE PROUD HE WAS THERE.
BECAUSE YOU KNEW JACK CASEY.
KNOWING SOMEONE LIKE CASEY MAKES ALL THE DIFFERENCE.
TRUST US, JEFF--IF YOU GO AS CAPTAIN AMERICA, YOU'LL DESTROY CAPTAIN AMERICA.
NO ONE WILL WEAR THAT UNIFORM EVER AGAIN.
CASEY, JACOB M. 1913-1946.
Accomplished photographer for the Daily Bugle. Served his country in the Navy, Photographer's Mate 1st Class, general discharge. May God's mercy be with him. Memorial service to be held Monday, September 23, 2pm, St. Joseph's Church, 371 Sixth Avenue.

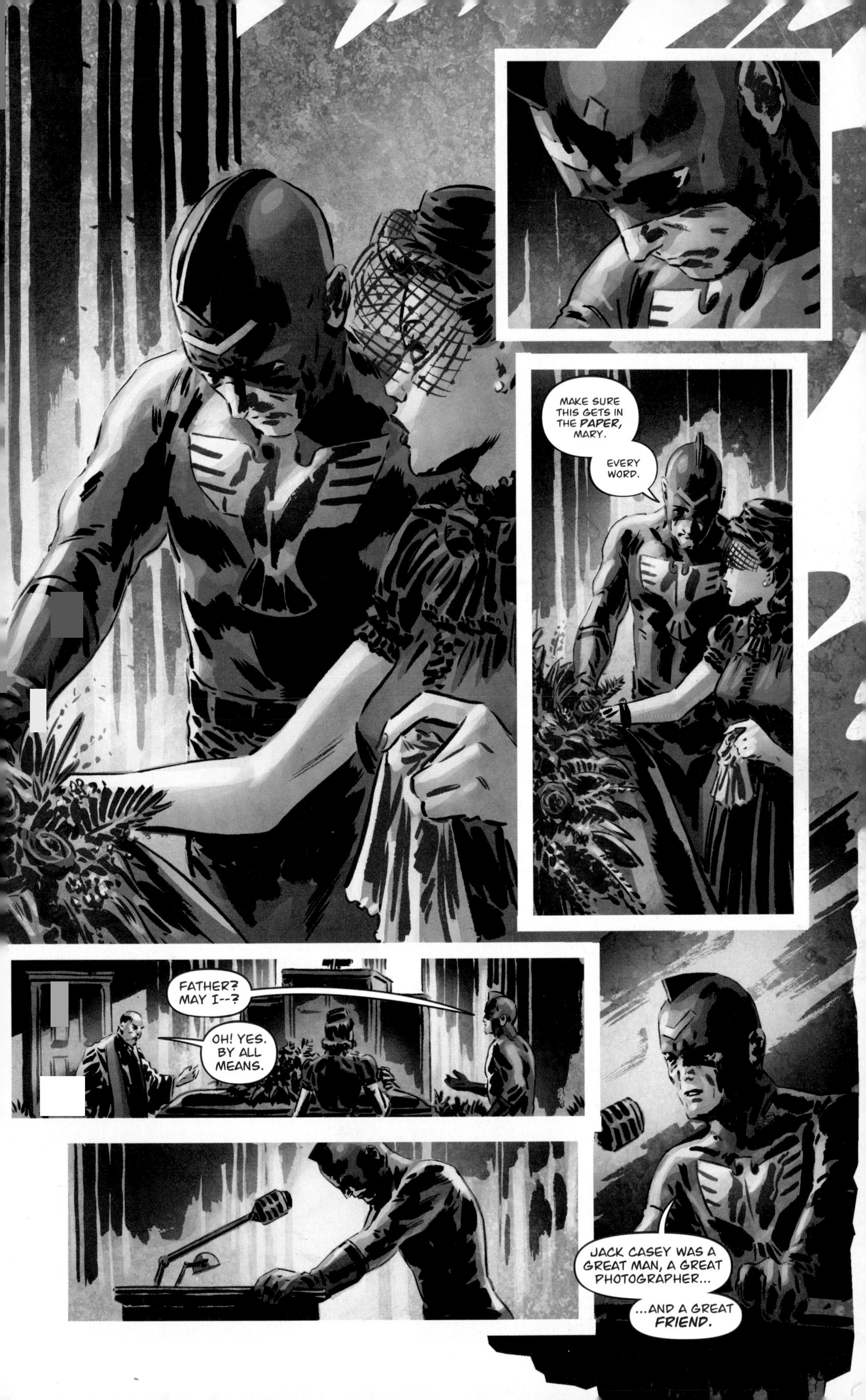

MAKE SURE THIS GETS IN THE PAPER, MARY.
EVERY WORD.
FATHER? MAY I--?
OH! YES. BY ALL MEANS.
JACK CASEY WAS A GREAT MAN, A GREAT PHOTOGRAPHER...
...AND A GREAT FRIEND.

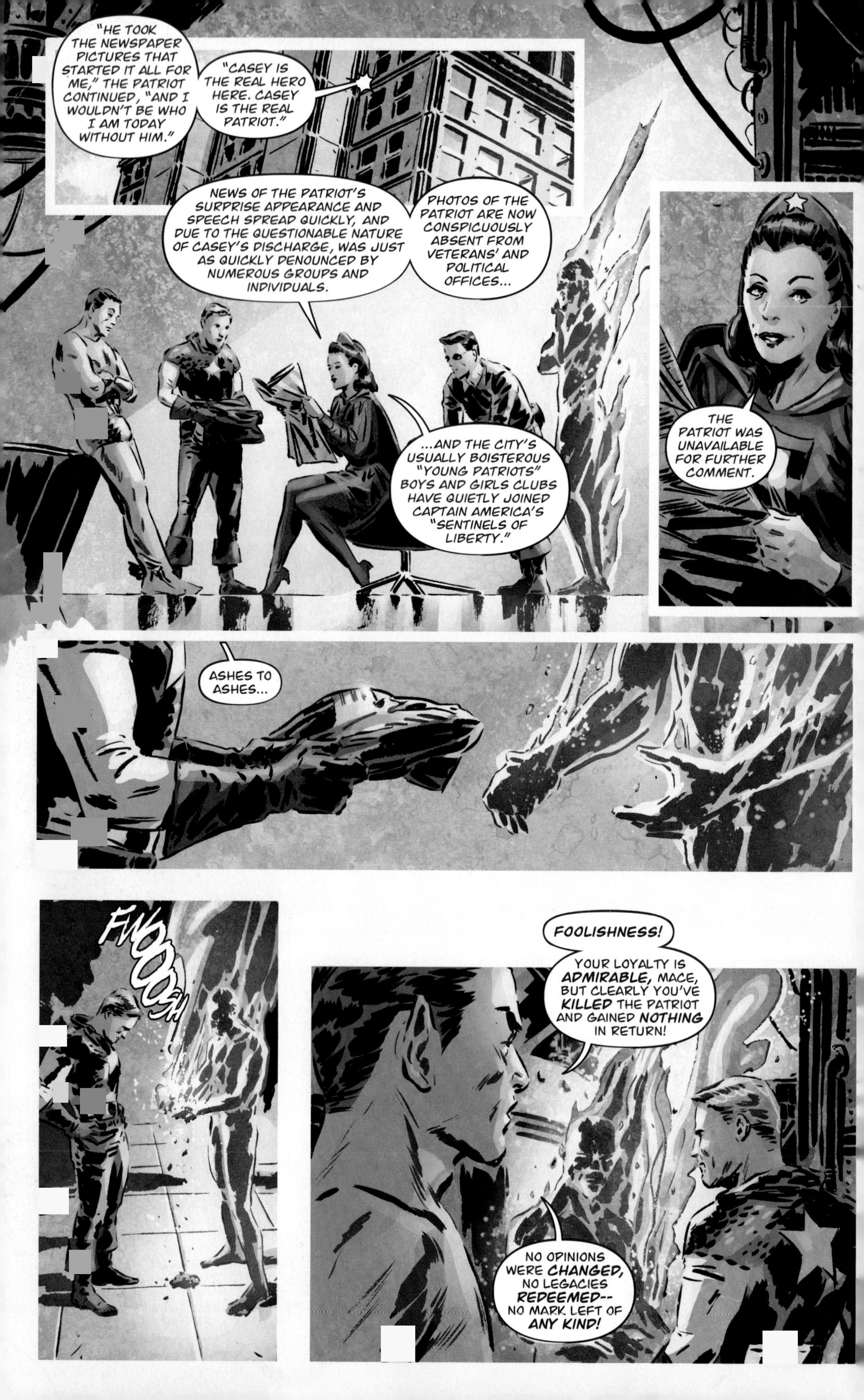
"HE TOOK THE NEWSPAPER PICTURES THAT STARTED IT ALL FOR ME," THE PATRIOT CONTINUED, "AND I WOULDN'T BE WHO I AM TODAY WITHOUT HIM."
"CASEY IS THE REAL HERO HERE. CASEY IS THE REAL PATRIOT."
NEWS OF THE PATRIOT'S SURPRISE APPEARANCE AND SPEECH SPREAD QUICKLY, AND DUE TO THE QUESTIONABLE NATURE OF CASEY'S DISCHARGE, WAS JUST AS QUICKLY DENOUNCED BY NUMEROUS GROUPS AND INDIVIDUALS.
PHOTOS OF THE PATRIOT ARE NOW CONSPICUOUSLY ABSENT FROM VETERANS' AND POLITICAL OFFICES...
...AND THE CITY'S USUALLY BOISTEROUS "YOUNG PATRIOTS" BOYS AND GIRLS CLUBS HAVE QUIETLY JOINED CAPTAIN AMERICA'S "SENTINELS OF LIBERTY."
THE PATRIOT WAS UNAVAILABLE FOR FURTHER COMMENT.
ASHES TO ASHES...
FWOOOOSH
FOOLISHNESS!
YOUR LOYALTY IS ADMIRABLE, MACE, BUT CLEARLY YOU'VE KILLED THE PATRIOT AND GAINED NOTHING IN RETURN!
NO OPINIONS WERE CHANGED, NO LEGACIES REDEEMED-- NO MARK LEFT OF ANY KIND!

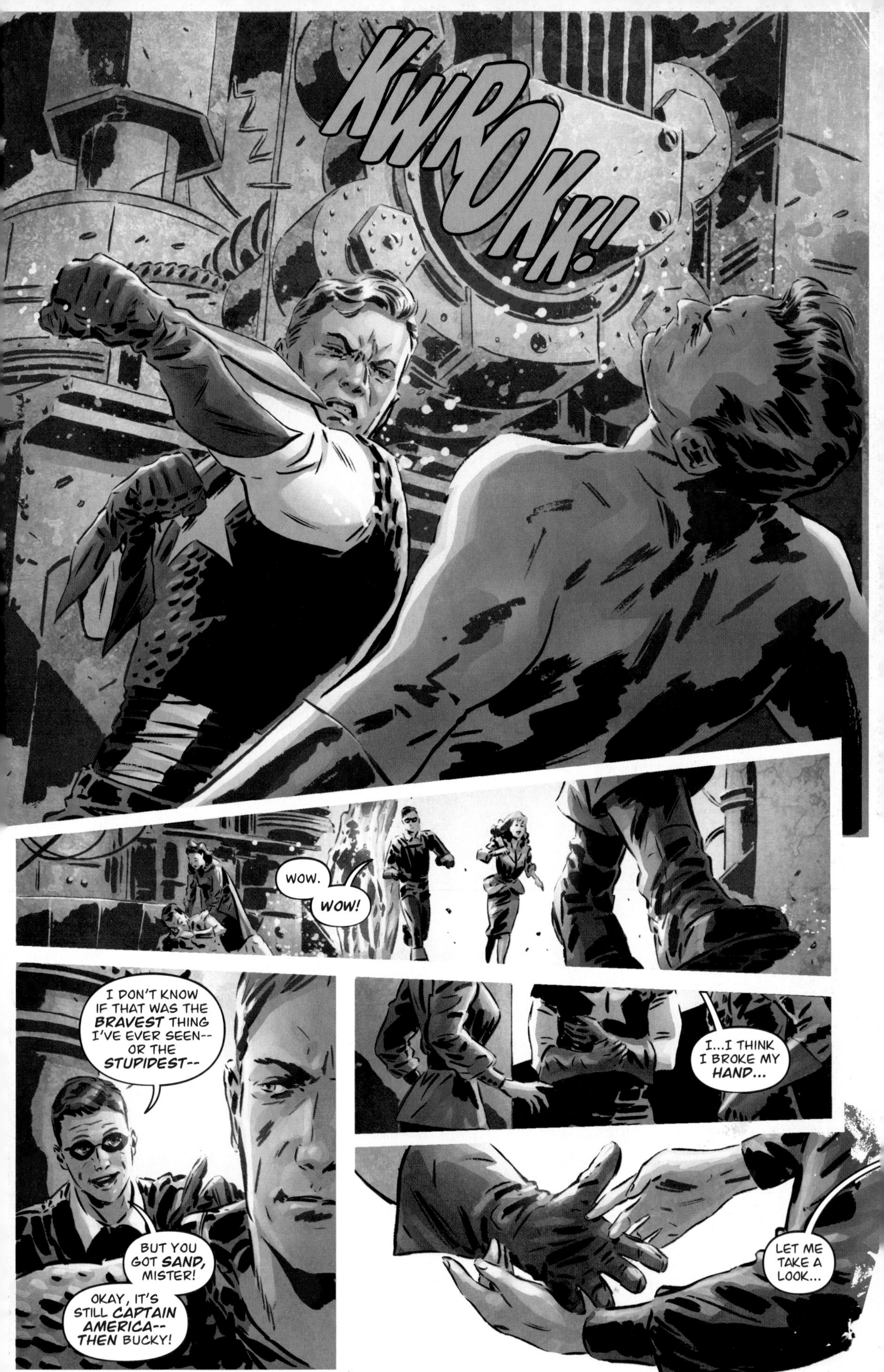
KWROKK!
WOW.
WOW!
I DON'T KNOW IF THAT WAS THE BRAVEST THING I'VE EVER SEEN-- OR THE STUPIDEST--
BUT YOU GOT SAND, MISTER!
OKAY, IT'S STILL CAPTAIN AMERICA-- THEN BUCKY!
I...I THINK I BROKE MY HAND...
LET ME TAKE A LOOK...

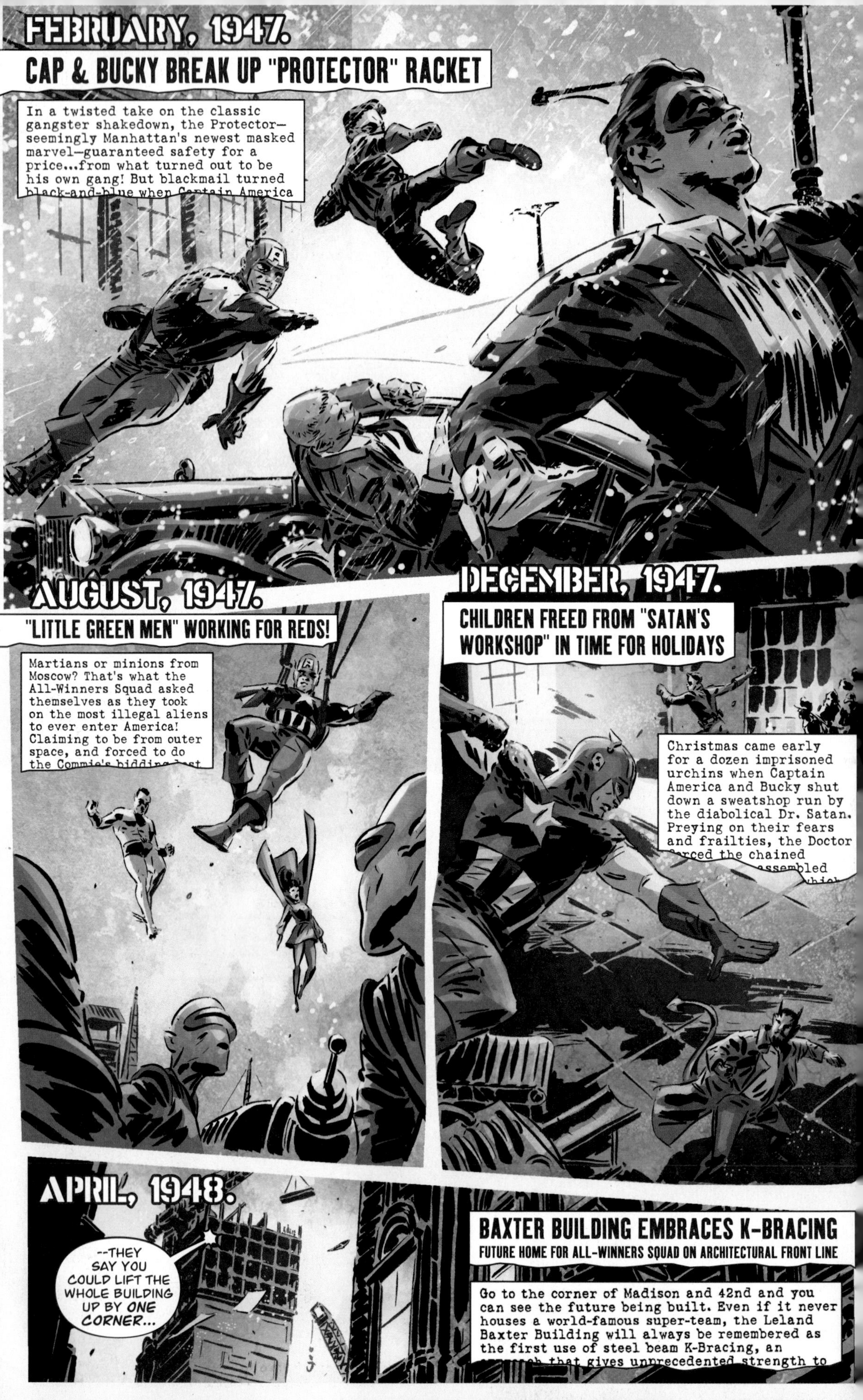
FEBRUARY, 1947.
CAP & BUCKY BREAK UP "PROTECTOR" RACKET
In a twisted take on the classic gangster shakedown, the Protector—seemingly Manhattan's newest masked marvel—guaranteed safety for a price...from what turned out to be his own gang! But blackmail turned black-and-blue when Captain America
AUGUST, 1947.
"LITTLE GREEN MEN" WORKING FOR REDS!
Martians or minions from Moscow? That's what the All-Winners Squad asked themselves as they took on the most illegal aliens to ever enter America! Claiming to be from outer space, and forced to do the Commie's bidding
DECEMBER, 1947.
CHILDREN FREED FROM "SATAN'S WORKSHOP" IN TIME FOR HOLIDAYS
Christmas came early for a dozen imprisoned urchins when Captain America and Bucky shut down a sweatshop run by the diabolical Dr. Satan. Preying on their fears and frailties, the Doctor forced the chained
APRIL, 1948.
--THEY SAY YOU COULD LIFT THE WHOLE BUILDING UP BY ONE CORNER...
BAXTER BUILDING EMBRACES K-BRACING
FUTURE HOME FOR ALL-WINNERS SQUAD ON ARCHITECTURAL FRONT LINE
Go to the corner of Madison and 42nd and you can see the future being built. Even if it never houses a world-famous super-team, the Leland Baxter Building will always be remembered as the first use of steel beam K-Bracing, an approach that gives unprecedented strength to

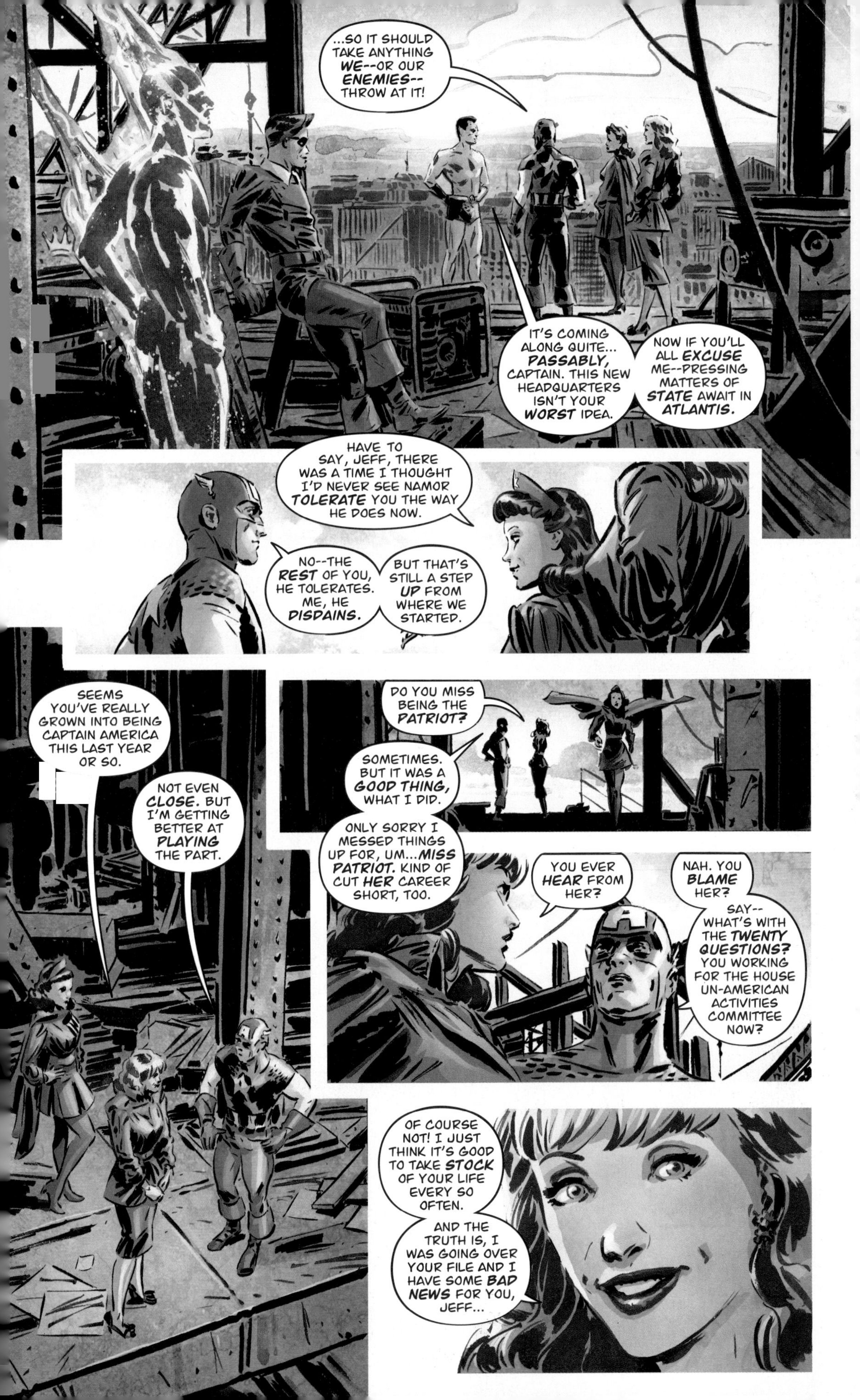

...SO IT SHOULD TAKE ANYTHING WE--OR OUR ENEMIES--THROW AT IT!
IT'S COMING ALONG QUITE... PASSABLY, CAPTAIN. THIS NEW HEADQUARTERS ISN'T YOUR WORST IDEA.
NOW IF YOU'LL ALL EXCUSE ME--PRESSING MATTERS OF STATE AWAIT IN ATLANTIS.
HAVE TO SAY, JEFF, THERE WAS A TIME I THOUGHT I'D NEVER SEE NAMOR TOLERATE YOU THE WAY HE DOES NOW.
NO--THE REST OF YOU, HE TOLERATES. ME, HE DISDAINS.
BUT THAT'S STILL A STEP UP FROM WHERE WE STARTED.
SEEMS YOU'VE REALLY GROWN INTO BEING CAPTAIN AMERICA THIS LAST YEAR OR SO.
NOT EVEN CLOSE. BUT I'M GETTING BETTER AT PLAYING THE PART.
DO YOU MISS BEING THE PATRIOT?
SOMETIMES. BUT IT WAS A GOOD THING, WHAT I DID.
ONLY SORRY I MESSED THINGS UP FOR, UM...MISS PATRIOT. KIND OF CUT HER CAREER SHORT, TOO.
YOU EVER HEAR FROM HER?
NAH. YOU BLAME HER?
SAY--WHAT'S WITH THE TWENTY QUESTIONS? YOU WORKING FOR THE HOUSE UN-AMERICAN ACTIVITIES COMMITTEE NOW?
OF COURSE NOT! I JUST THINK IT'S GOOD TO TAKE STOCK OF YOUR LIFE EVERY SO OFTEN.
AND THE TRUTH IS, I WAS GOING OVER YOUR FILE AND I HAVE SOME BAD NEWS FOR YOU, JEFF...

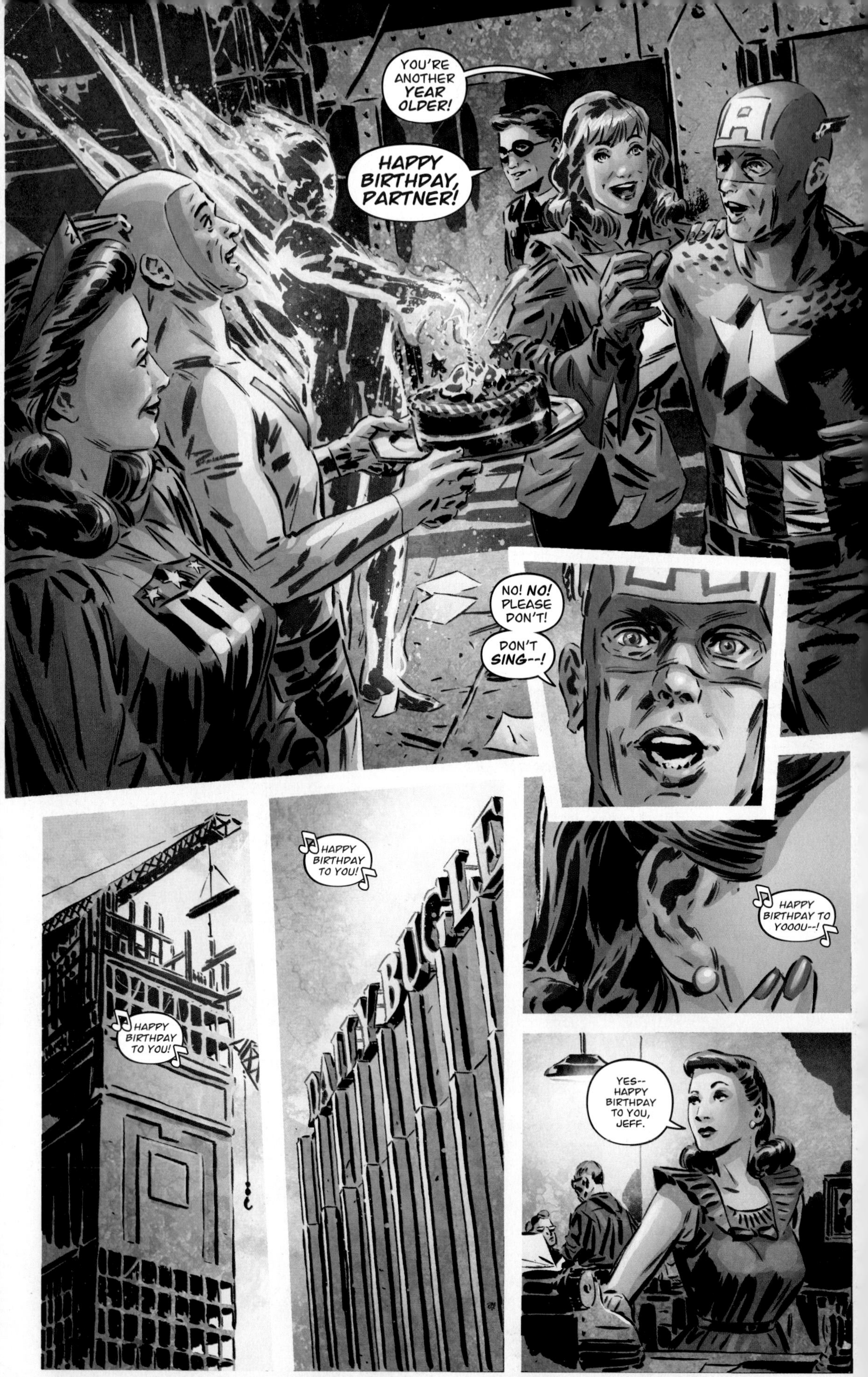
YOU'RE ANOTHER YEAR OLDER!
HAPPY BIRTHDAY, PARTNER!
NO! NO! PLEASE DON'T!
DON'T SING--!
HAPPY BIRTHDAY TO YOU!
HAPPY BIRTHDAY TO YOU!
HAPPY BIRTHDAY TO YOOOU--!
YES-- HAPPY BIRTHDAY TO YOU, JEFF.

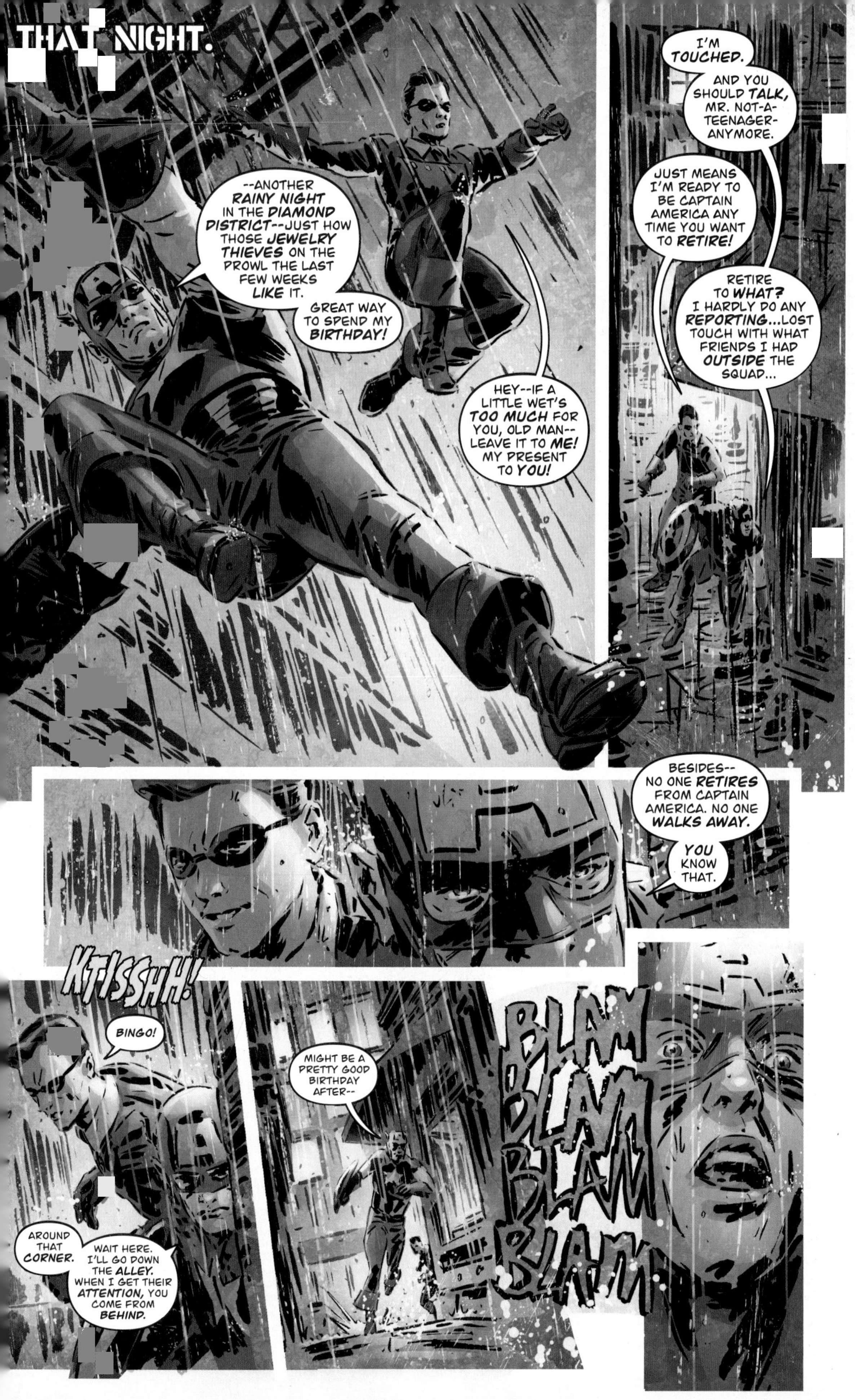
THAT NIGHT.
--ANOTHER RAINY NIGHT IN THE DIAMOND DISTRICT--JUST HOW THOSE JEWELRY THIEVES ON THE PROWL THE LAST FEW WEEKS LIKE IT.
GREAT WAY TO SPEND MY BIRTHDAY!
HEY--IF A LITTLE WET'S TOO MUCH FOR YOU, OLD MAN--LEAVE IT TO ME! MY PRESENT TO YOU!
I'M TOUCHED.
AND YOU SHOULD TALK, MR. NOT-A-TEENAGER-ANYMORE.
JUST MEANS I'M READY TO BE CAPTAIN AMERICA ANY TIME YOU WANT TO RETIRE!
RETIRE TO WHAT? I HARDLY DO ANY REPORTING...LOST TOUCH WITH WHAT FRIENDS I HAD OUTSIDE THE SQUAD...
BESIDES--NO ONE RETIRES FROM CAPTAIN AMERICA. NO ONE WALKS AWAY.
YOU KNOW THAT.
KTISSHH!
BINGO!
AROUND THAT CORNER.
WAIT HERE. I'LL GO DOWN THE ALLEY. WHEN I GET THEIR ATTENTION, YOU COME FROM BEHIND.
MIGHT BE A PRETTY GOOD BIRTHDAY AFTER--
BLAM BLAM BLAM BLAM BLAM

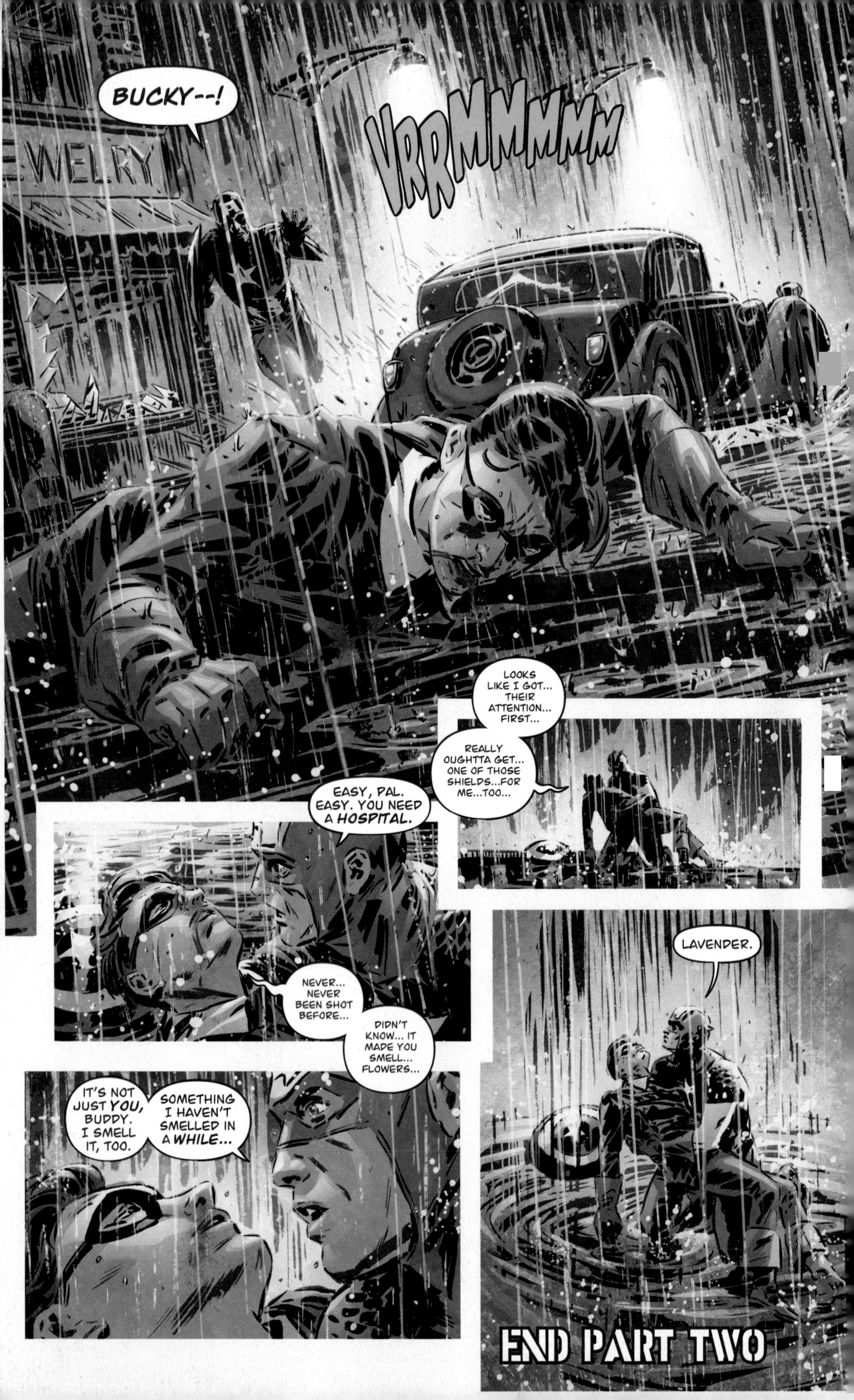
BUCKY--!
WELRY
VRRMMMMM
LOOKS LIKE I GOT... THEIR ATTENTION... FIRST...
REALLY OUGHTTA GET... ONE OF THOSE SHIELDS...FOR ME...TOO...
EASY, PAL. EASY. YOU NEED A HOSPITAL.
NEVER... NEVER BEEN SHOT BEFORE...
DIDN'T KNOW... IT MADE YOU SMELL... FLOWERS...
LAVENDER.
IT'S NOT JUST YOU, BUDDY. I SMELL IT, TOO.
SOMETHING I HAVEN'T SMELLED IN A WHILE...
END PART TWO

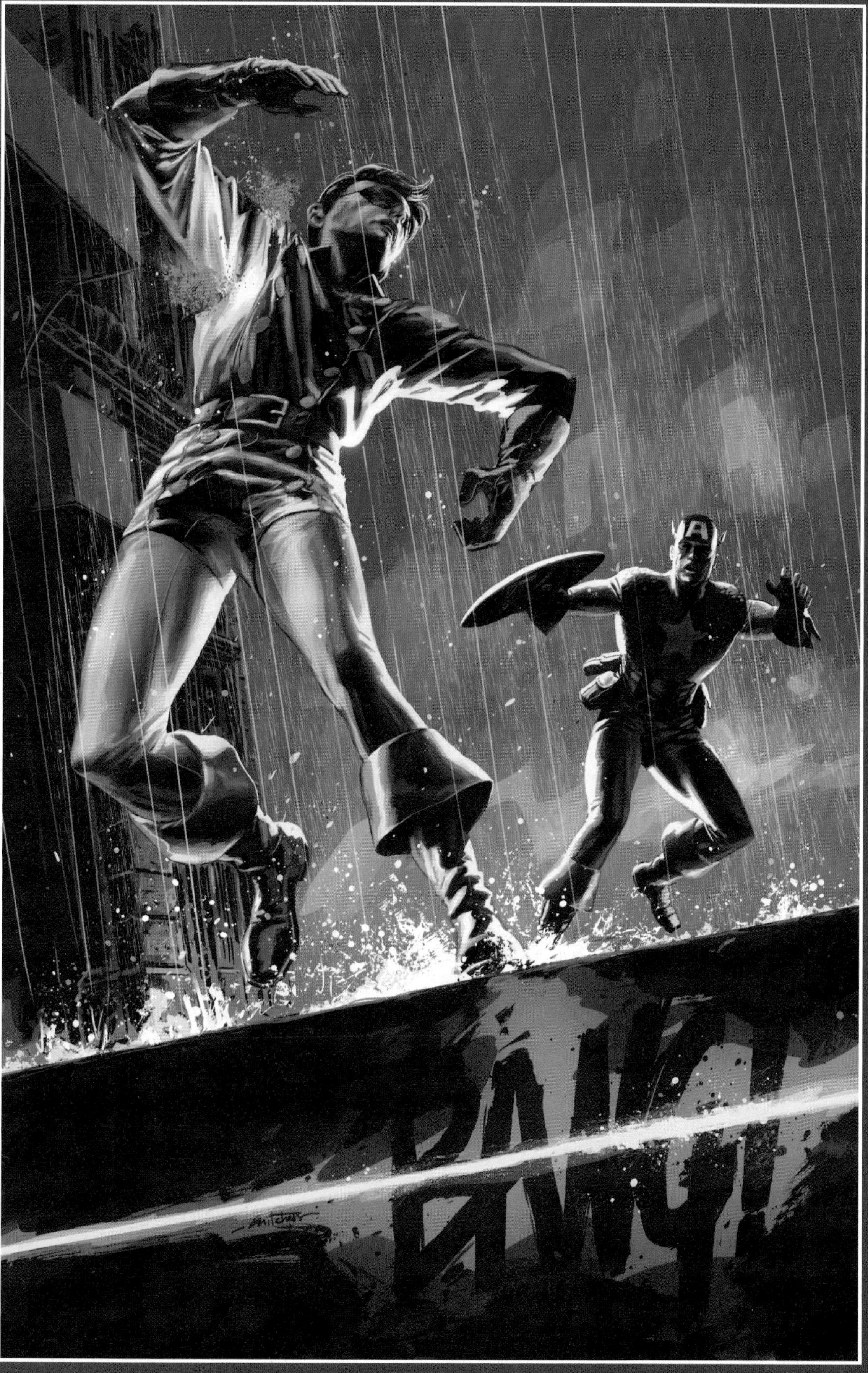

#3

CAPTAIN AMERICA:
PATRIOT PART 3: TRUTH & JUSTICE★

BUCKY SHOT!
LIFE HANGS BY THREAD

The rain-slicked streets of Manhattan's Diamond District ran red last night when Captain America's young partner, Bucky, was brutally gunned down while attempting to stop a robbery. An FBI source confirmed the star-spangled super-soldier rushed Bucky to an undisclosed hospital, where he is in critical condition. Doctors have been working tirelessly throughout the night and morning to save his life. The perpetrators remain unknown and at large.

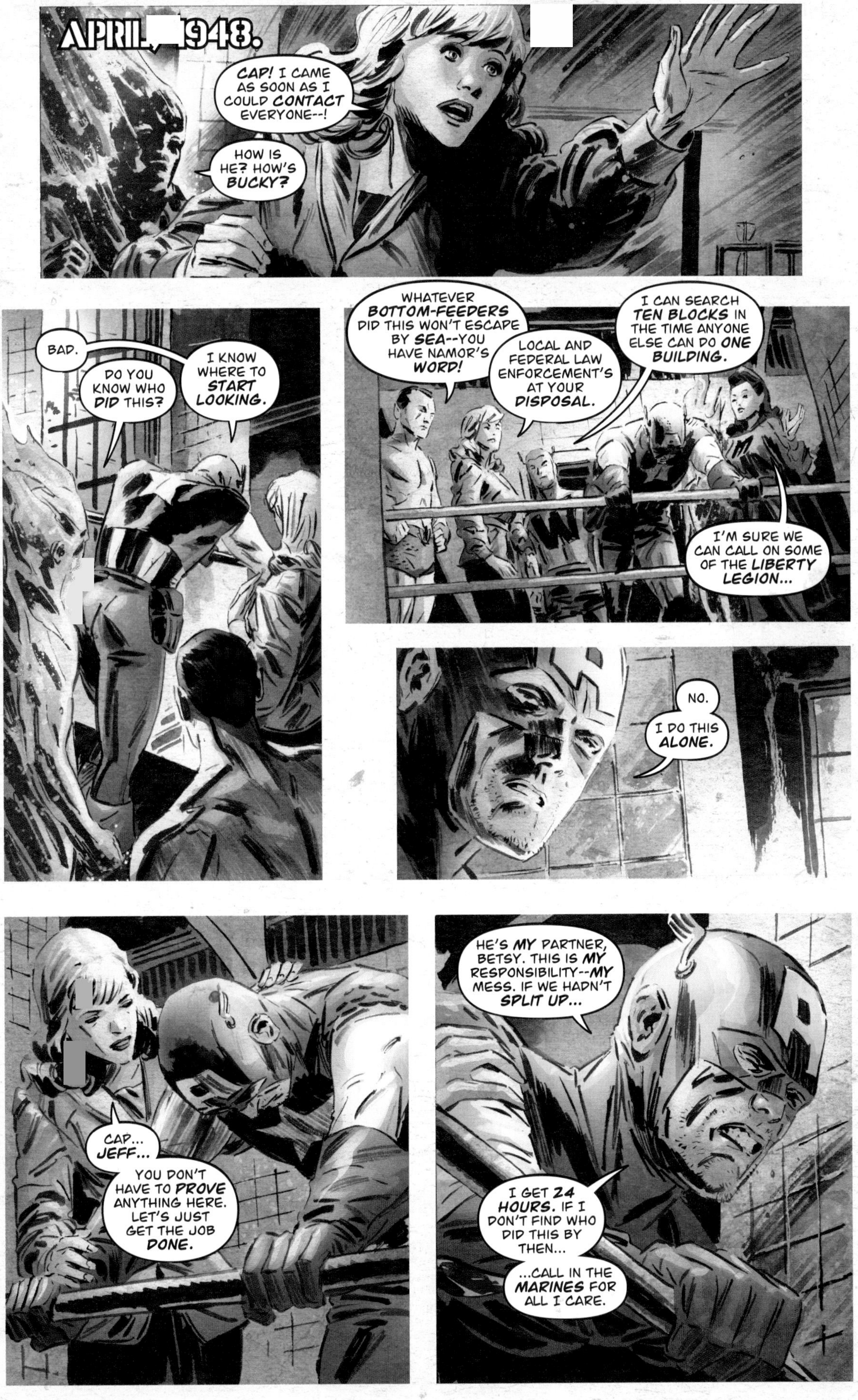
APRIL, 1948.
CAP! I CAME AS SOON AS I COULD CONTACT EVERYONE--!
HOW IS HE? HOW'S BUCKY?
BAD.
DO YOU KNOW WHO DID THIS?
I KNOW WHERE TO START LOOKING.
WHATEVER BOTTOM-FEEDERS DID THIS WON'T ESCAPE BY SEA--YOU HAVE NAMOR'S WORD!
LOCAL AND FEDERAL LAW ENFORCEMENT'S AT YOUR DISPOSAL.
I CAN SEARCH TEN BLOCKS IN THE TIME ANYONE ELSE CAN DO ONE BUILDING.
I'M SURE WE CAN CALL ON SOME OF THE LIBERTY LEGION...
NO.
I DO THIS ALONE.
CAP... JEFF...
YOU DON'T HAVE TO PROVE ANYTHING HERE. LET'S JUST GET THE JOB DONE.
HE'S MY PARTNER, BETSY. THIS IS MY RESPONSIBILITY--MY MESS. IF WE HADN'T SPLIT UP...
I GET 24 HOURS. IF I DON'T FIND WHO DID THIS BY THEN...
...CALL IN THE MARINES FOR ALL I CARE.

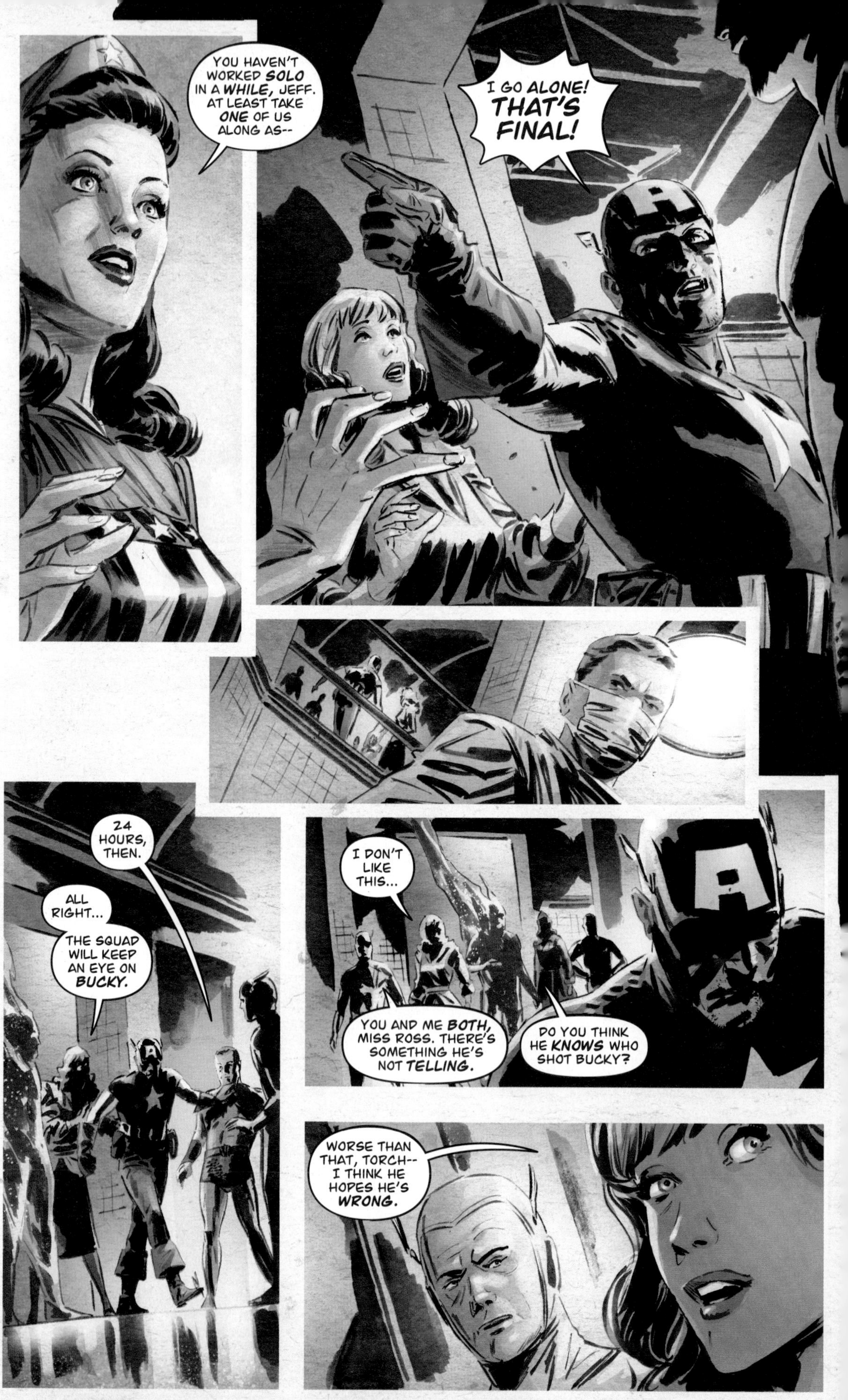
YOU HAVEN'T WORKED SOLO IN A WHILE, JEFF. AT LEAST TAKE ONE OF US ALONG AS--
I GO ALONE! THAT'S FINAL!
24 HOURS, THEN.
ALL RIGHT...
THE SQUAD WILL KEEP AN EYE ON BUCKY.
I DON'T LIKE THIS...
YOU AND ME BOTH, MISS ROSS. THERE'S SOMETHING HE'S NOT TELLING.
DO YOU THINK HE KNOWS WHO SHOT BUCKY?
WORSE THAN THAT, TORCH-- I THINK HE HOPES HE'S WRONG.

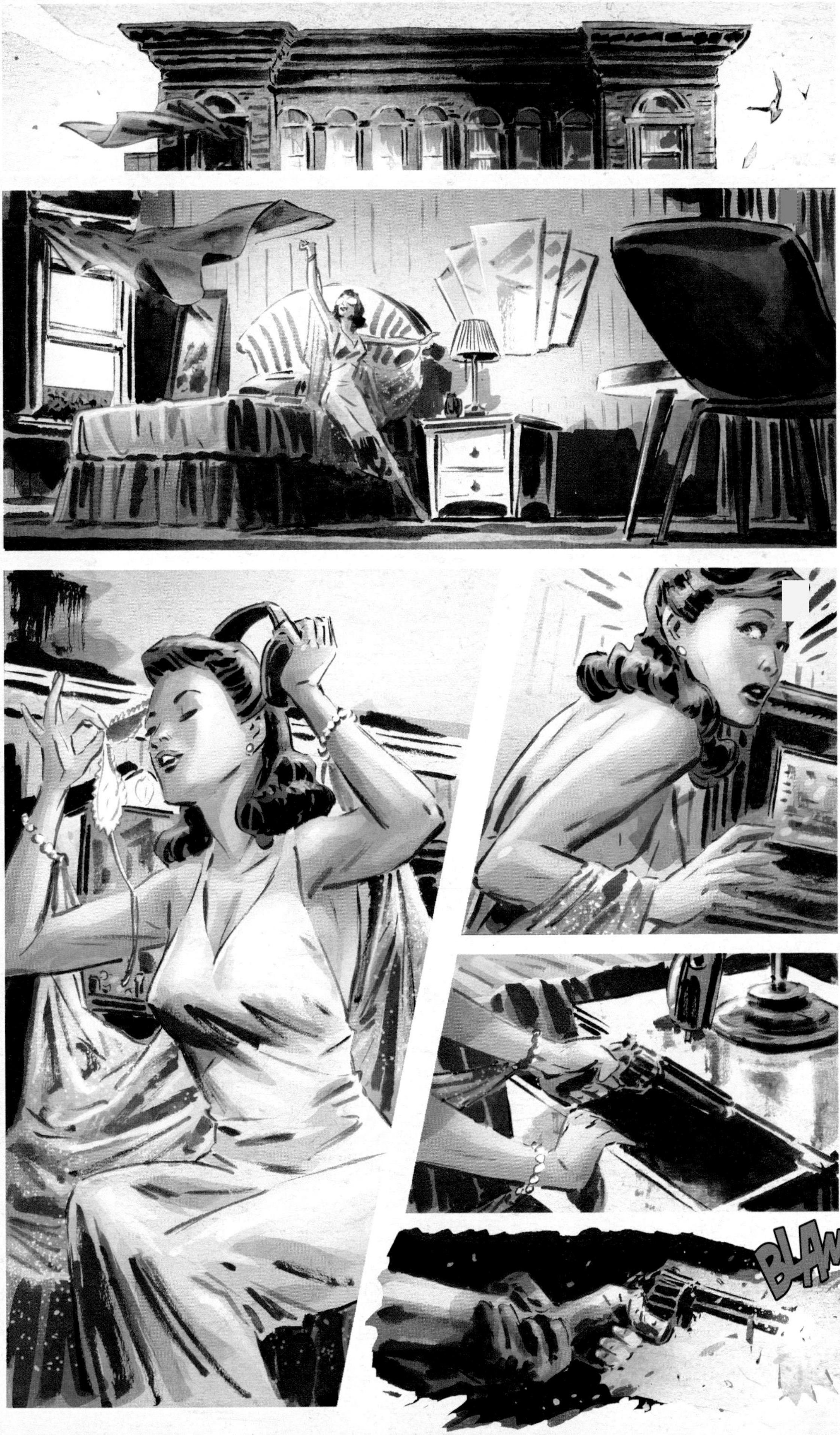
BLAM

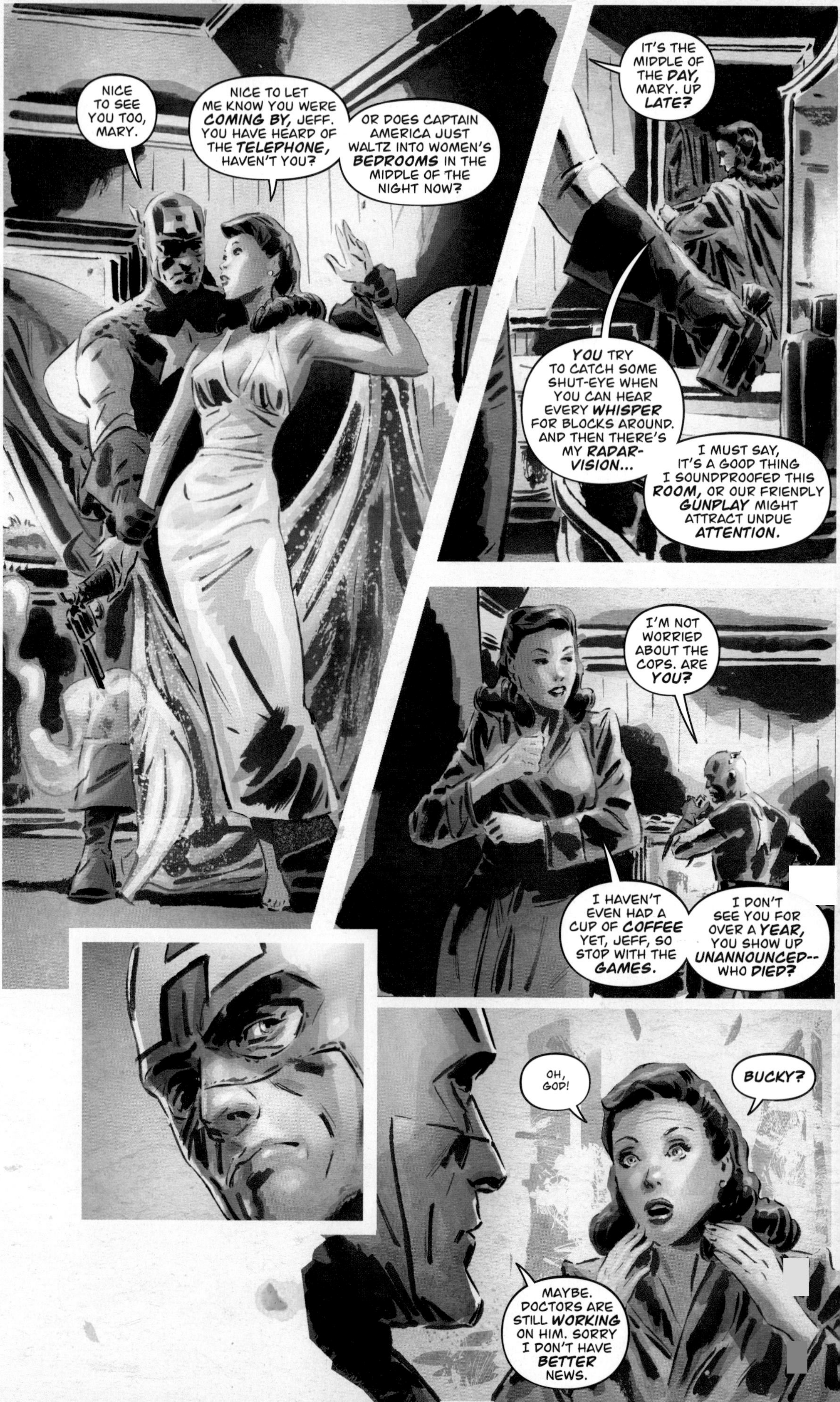

NICE TO SEE YOU TOO, MARY.
NICE TO LET ME KNOW YOU WERE COMING BY, JEFF. YOU HAVE HEARD OF THE TELEPHONE, HAVEN'T YOU?
OR DOES CAPTAIN AMERICA JUST WALTZ INTO WOMEN'S BEDROOMS IN THE MIDDLE OF THE NIGHT NOW?
IT'S THE MIDDLE OF THE DAY, MARY. UP LATE?
YOU TRY TO CATCH SOME SHUT-EYE WHEN YOU CAN HEAR EVERY WHISPER FOR BLOCKS AROUND. AND THEN THERE'S MY RADAR-VISION...
I MUST SAY, IT'S A GOOD THING I SOUNDPROOFED THIS ROOM, OR OUR FRIENDLY GUNPLAY MIGHT ATTRACT UNDUE ATTENTION.
I'M NOT WORRIED ABOUT THE COPS. ARE YOU?
I HAVEN'T EVEN HAD A CUP OF COFFEE YET, JEFF, SO STOP WITH THE GAMES.
I DON'T SEE YOU FOR OVER A YEAR, YOU SHOW UP UNANNOUNCED-- WHO DIED?
OH, GOD!
BUCKY?
MAYBE. DOCTORS ARE STILL WORKING ON HIM. SORRY I DON'T HAVE BETTER NEWS.

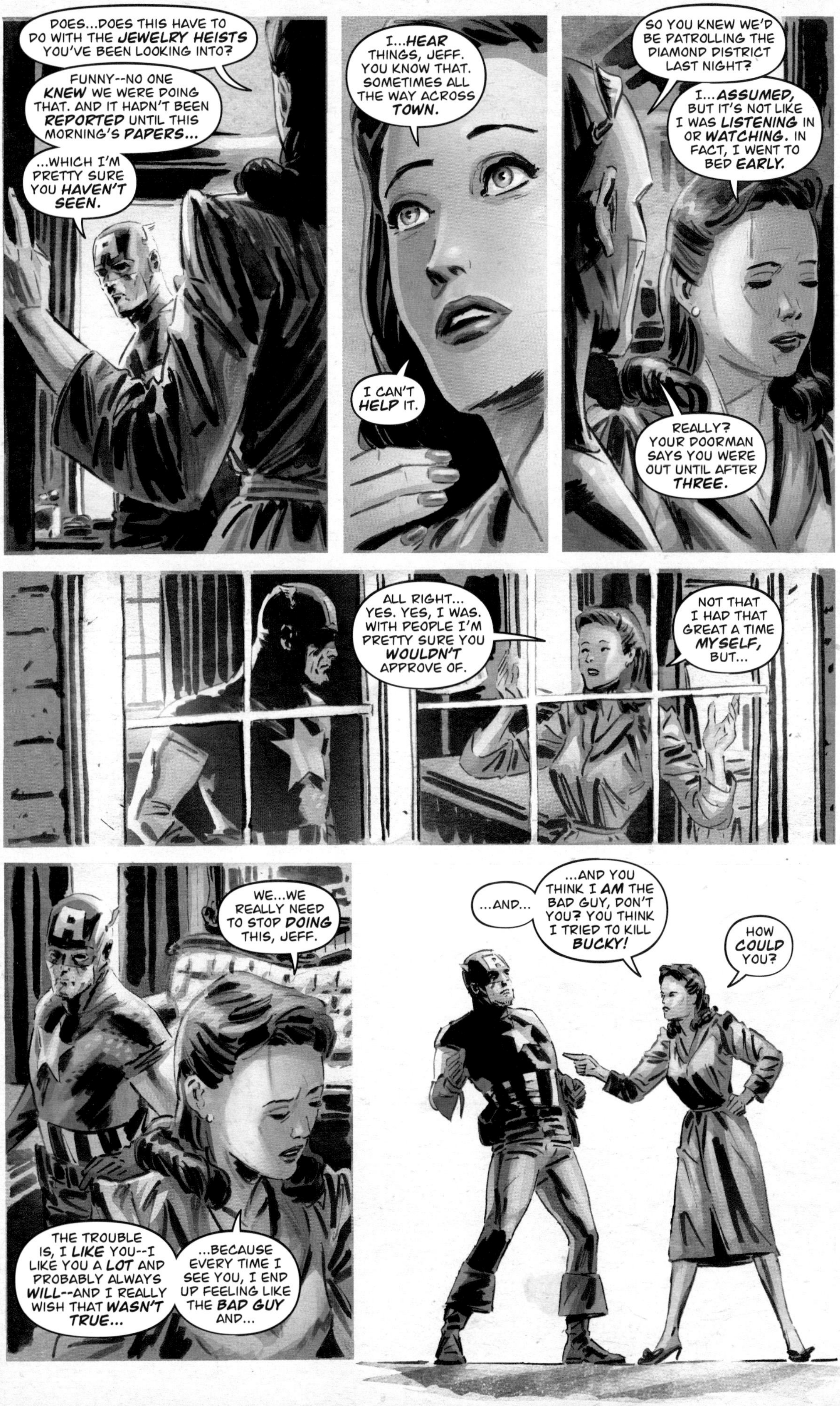
DOES...DOES THIS HAVE TO DO WITH THE JEWELRY HEISTS YOU'VE BEEN LOOKING INTO?
FUNNY--NO ONE KNEW WE WERE DOING THAT. AND IT HADN'T BEEN REPORTED UNTIL THIS MORNING'S PAPERS...
...WHICH I'M PRETTY SURE YOU HAVEN'T SEEN.
I...HEAR THINGS, JEFF. YOU KNOW THAT. SOMETIMES ALL THE WAY ACROSS TOWN.
I CAN'T HELP IT.
SO YOU KNEW WE'D BE PATROLLING THE DIAMOND DISTRICT LAST NIGHT?
I...ASSUMED, BUT IT'S NOT LIKE I WAS LISTENING IN OR WATCHING. IN FACT, I WENT TO BED EARLY.
REALLY? YOUR DOORMAN SAYS YOU WERE OUT UNTIL AFTER THREE.
ALL RIGHT... YES. YES, I WAS. WITH PEOPLE I'M PRETTY SURE YOU WOULDN'T APPROVE OF.
NOT THAT I HAD THAT GREAT A TIME MYSELF, BUT...
WE...WE REALLY NEED TO STOP DOING THIS, JEFF.
THE TROUBLE IS, I LIKE YOU--I LIKE YOU A LOT AND PROBABLY ALWAYS WILL--AND I REALLY WISH THAT WASN'T TRUE...
...BECAUSE EVERY TIME I SEE YOU, I END UP FEELING LIKE THE BAD GUY AND...
...AND...
...AND YOU THINK I AM THE BAD GUY, DON'T YOU? YOU THINK I TRIED TO KILL BUCKY!
HOW COULD YOU?

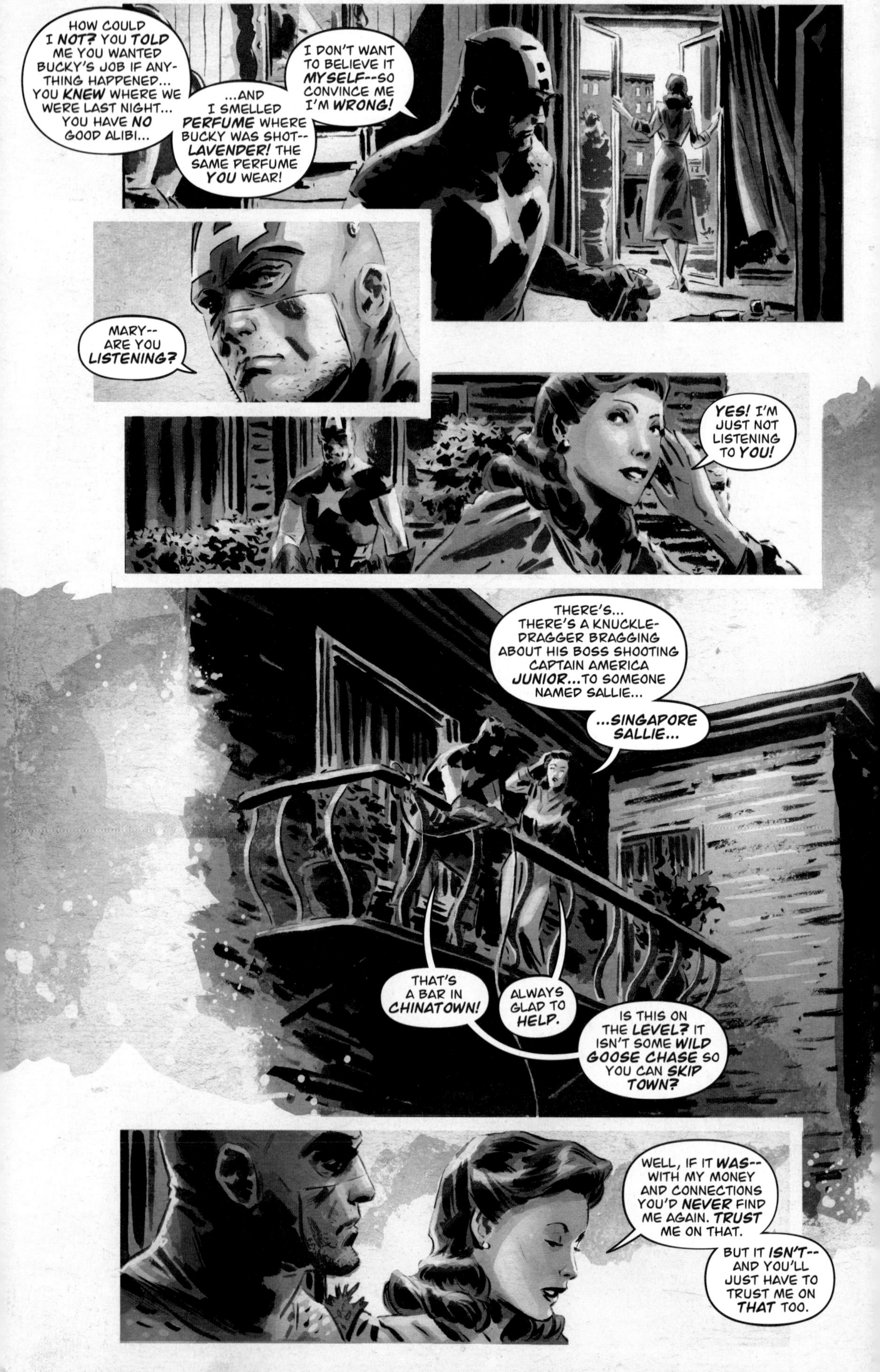
HOW COULD I NOT? YOU TOLD ME YOU WANTED BUCKY'S JOB IF ANY-THING HAPPENED... YOU KNEW WHERE WE WERE LAST NIGHT... YOU HAVE NO GOOD ALIBI...
...AND I SMELLED PERFUME WHERE BUCKY WAS SHOT--LAVENDER! THE SAME PERFUME YOU WEAR!
I DON'T WANT TO BELIEVE IT MYSELF--SO CONVINCE ME I'M WRONG!
MARY--ARE YOU LISTENING?
YES! I'M JUST NOT LISTENING TO YOU!
THERE'S... THERE'S A KNUCKLE-DRAGGER BRAGGING ABOUT HIS BOSS SHOOTING CAPTAIN AMERICA JUNIOR...TO SOMEONE NAMED SALLIE...
...SINGAPORE SALLIE...
THAT'S A BAR IN CHINATOWN!
ALWAYS GLAD TO HELP.
IS THIS ON THE LEVEL? IT ISN'T SOME WILD GOOSE CHASE SO YOU CAN SKIP TOWN?
WELL, IF IT WAS--WITH MY MONEY AND CONNECTIONS YOU'D NEVER FIND ME AGAIN. TRUST ME ON THAT.
BUT IT ISN'T--AND YOU'LL JUST HAVE TO TRUST ME ON THAT TOO.

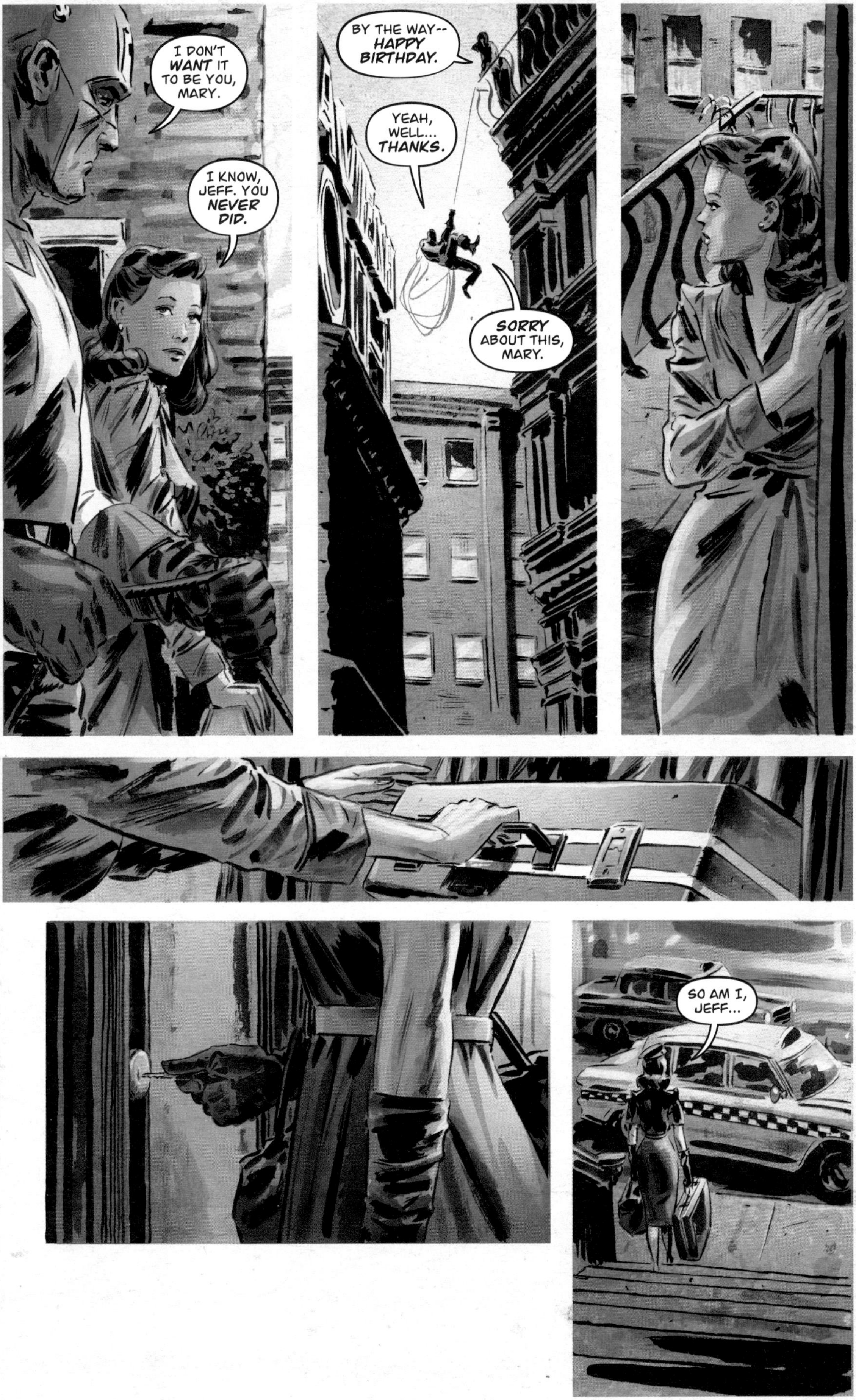
I DON'T WANT IT TO BE YOU, MARY.
I KNOW, JEFF. YOU NEVER DID.
BY THE WAY-- HAPPY BIRTHDAY.
YEAH, WELL... THANKS.
SORRY ABOUT THIS, MARY.
SO AM I, JEFF...

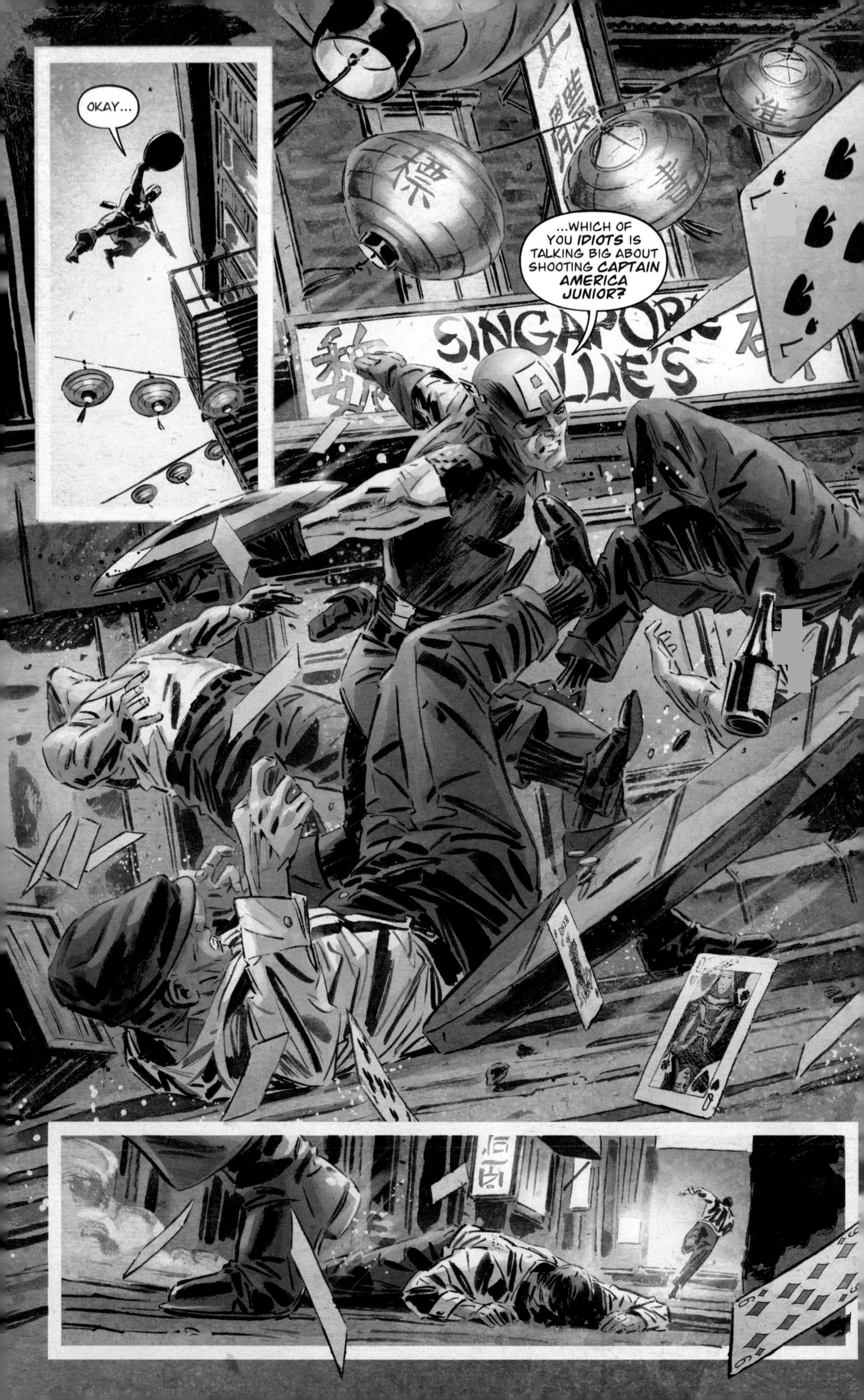
OKAY...
...WHICH OF YOU IDIOTS IS TALKING BIG ABOUT SHOOTING CAPTAIN AMERICA JUNIOR?
SINGAPORE LILLIE'S

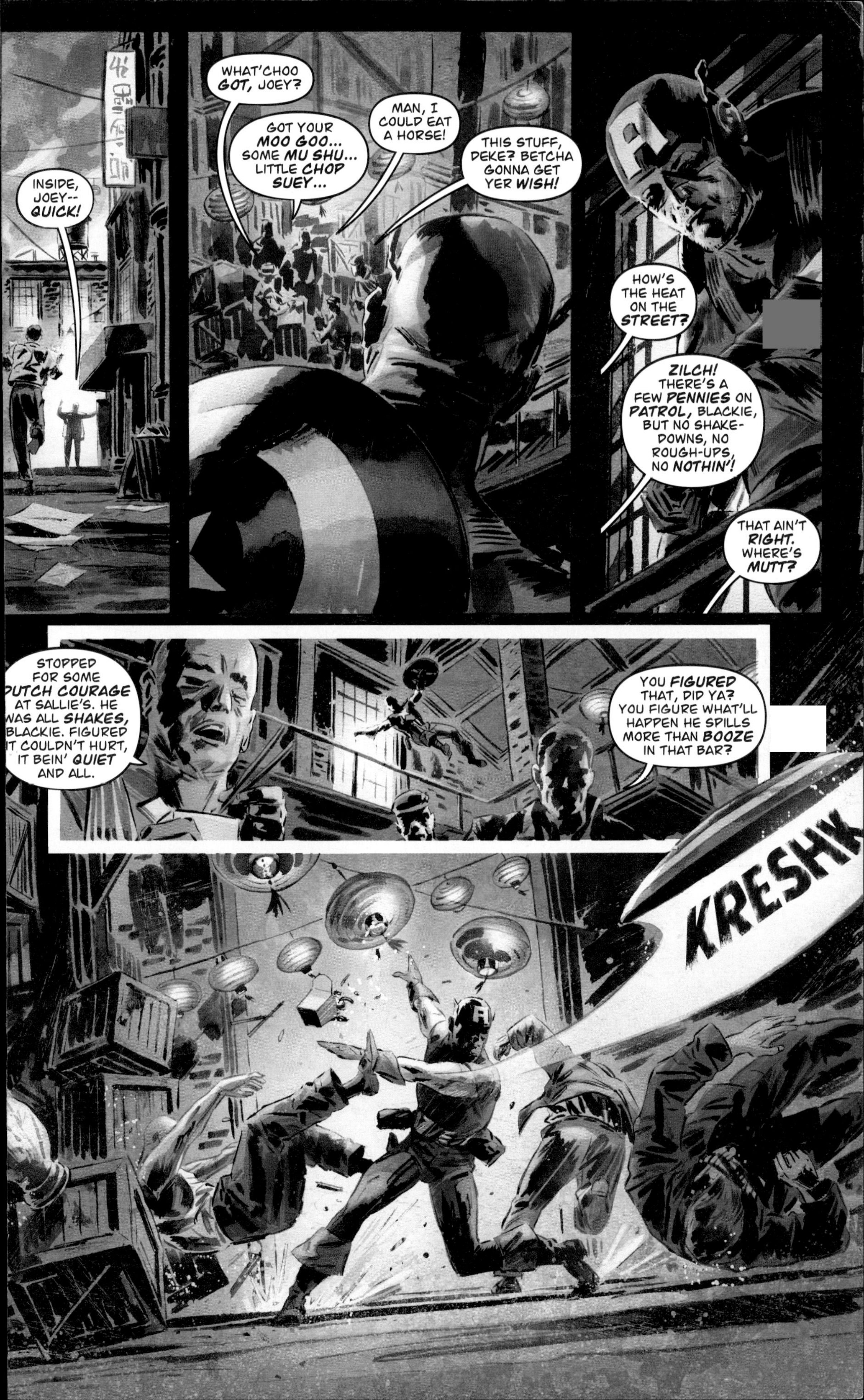
INSIDE, JOEY-- QUICK!
WHAT'CHOO GOT, JOEY?
GOT YOUR MOO GOO... SOME MU SHU... LITTLE CHOP SUEY...
MAN, I COULD EAT A HORSE!
THIS STUFF, DEKE? BETCHA GONNA GET YER WISH!
HOW'S THE HEAT ON THE STREET?
ZILCH! THERE'S A FEW PENNIES ON PATROL, BLACKIE, BUT NO SHAKE-DOWNS, NO ROUGH-UPS, NO NOTHIN'!
THAT AIN'T RIGHT. WHERE'S MUTT?
STOPPED FOR SOME DUTCH COURAGE AT SALLIE'S. HE WAS ALL SHAKES, BLACKIE. FIGURED IT COULDN'T HURT, IT BEIN' QUIET AND ALL.
YOU FIGURED THAT, DID YA? YOU FIGURE WHAT'LL HAPPEN HE SPILLS MORE THAN BOOZE IN THAT BAR?
KRESHK

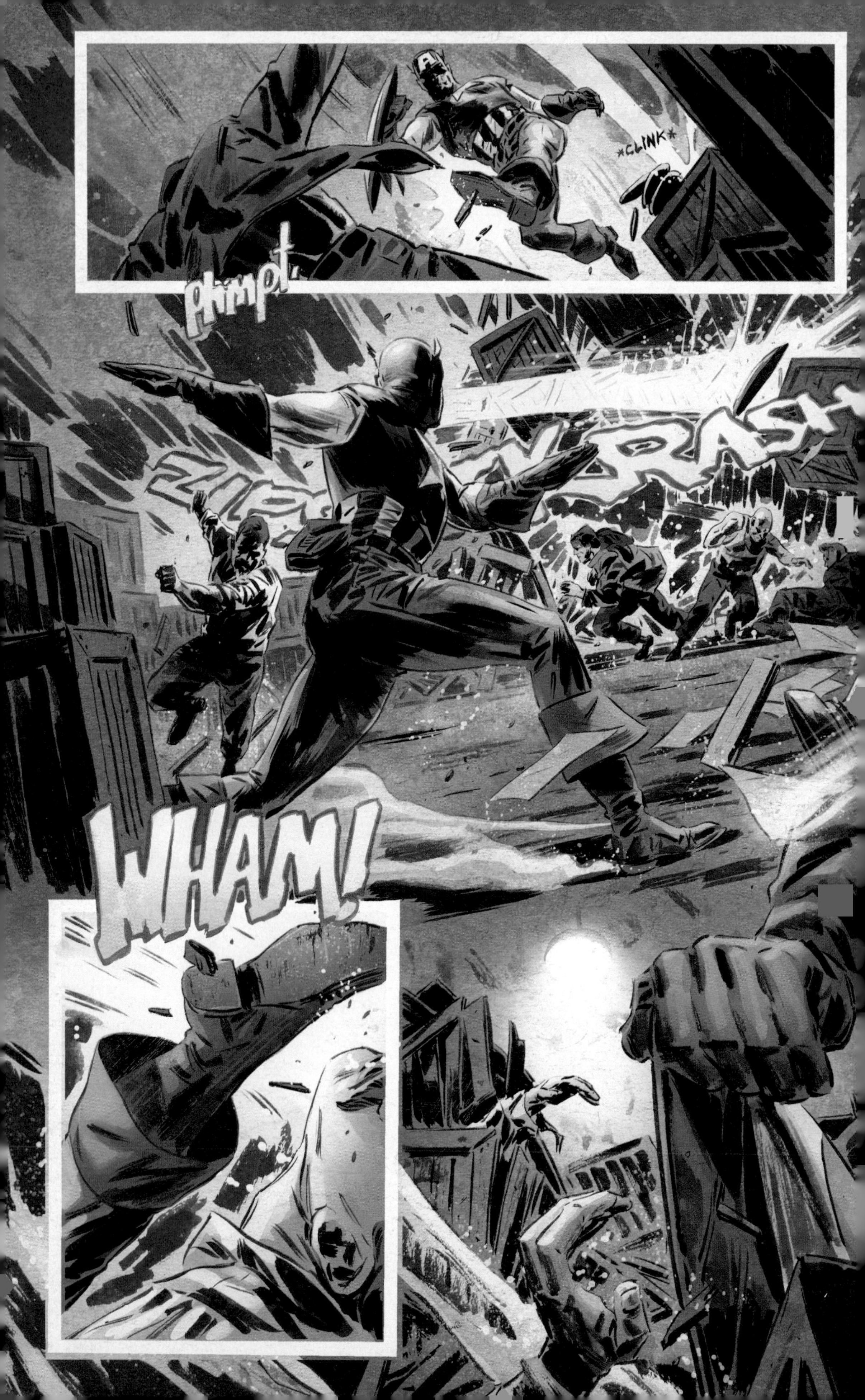
CLINK
phimpt.
WHAM!

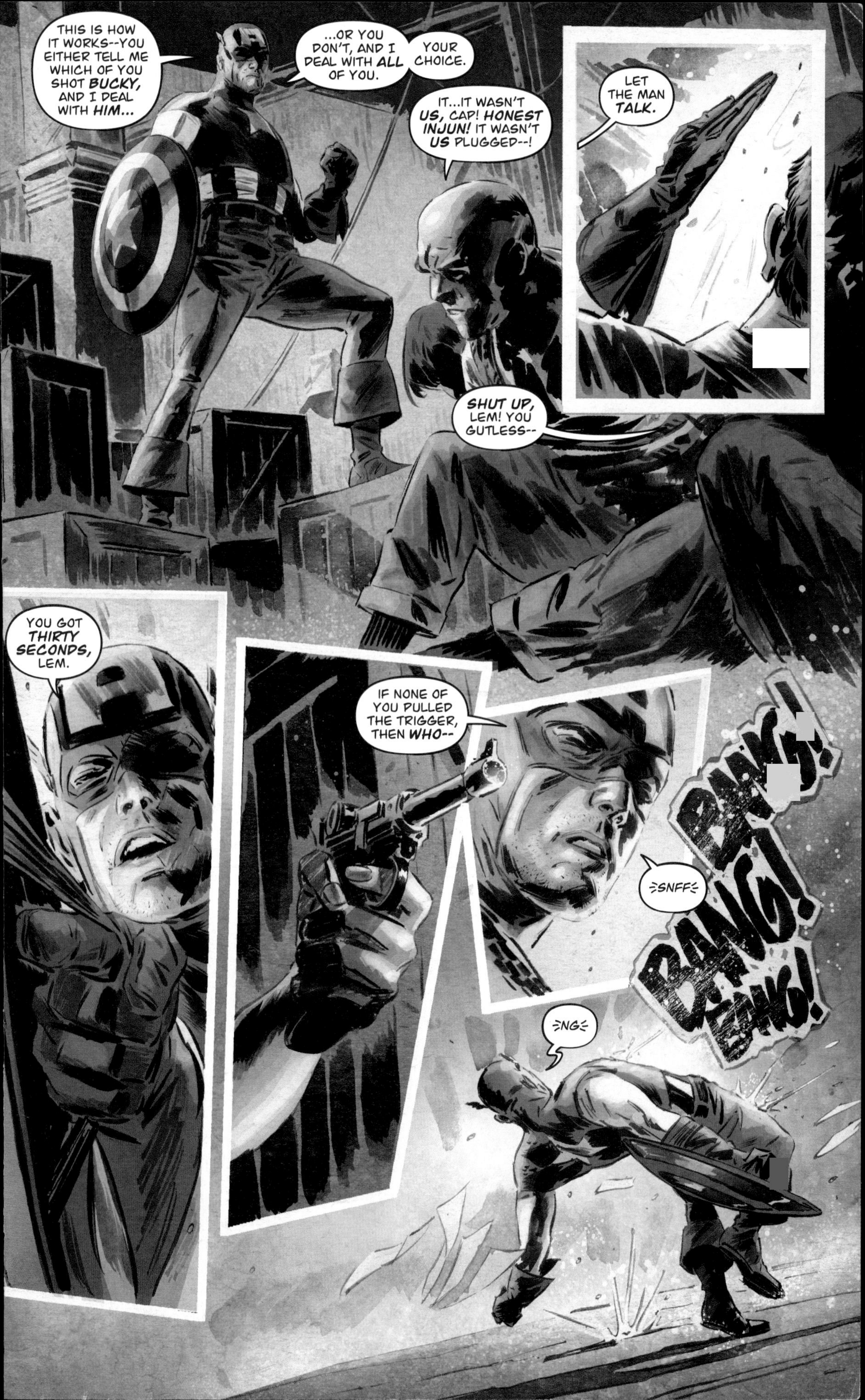
THIS IS HOW IT WORKS--YOU EITHER TELL ME WHICH OF YOU SHOT BUCKY, AND I DEAL WITH HIM...
...OR YOU DON'T, AND I DEAL WITH ALL OF YOU.
YOUR CHOICE.
IT...IT WASN'T US, CAP! HONEST INJUN! IT WASN'T US PLUGGED--!
LET THE MAN TALK.
SHUT UP, LEM! YOU GUTLESS--
YOU GOT THIRTY SECONDS, LEM.
IF NONE OF YOU PULLED THE TRIGGER, THEN WHO--
SNFF
BANG! BANG! BANG! BANG!
NG

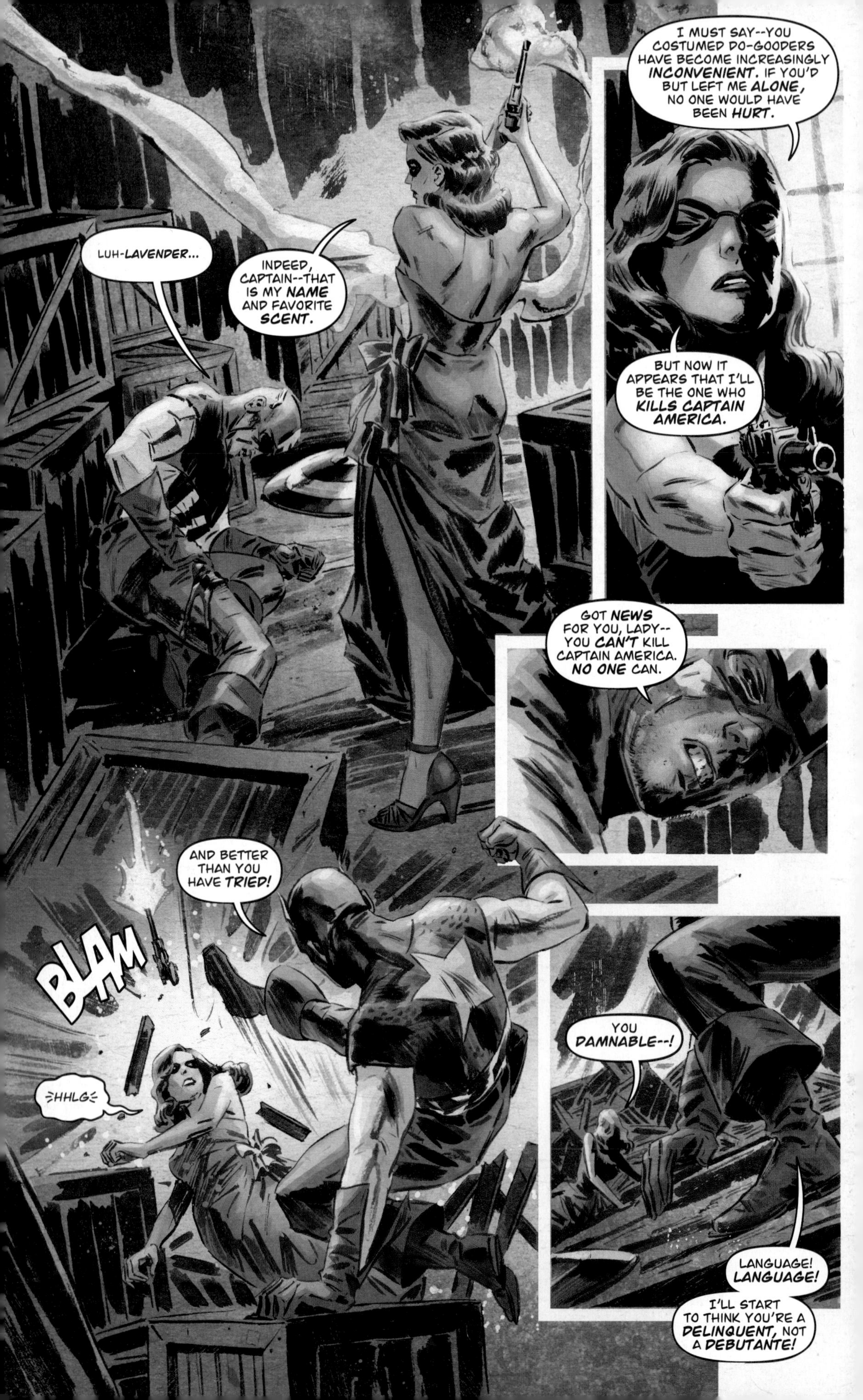
LUH-LAVENDER...
INDEED, CAPTAIN--THAT IS MY NAME AND FAVORITE SCENT.
I MUST SAY--YOU COSTUMED DO-GOODERS HAVE BECOME INCREASINGLY INCONVENIENT. IF YOU'D BUT LEFT ME ALONE, NO ONE WOULD HAVE BEEN HURT.
BUT NOW IT APPEARS THAT I'LL BE THE ONE WHO KILLS CAPTAIN AMERICA.
GOT NEWS FOR YOU, LADY--YOU CAN'T KILL CAPTAIN AMERICA. NO ONE CAN.
AND BETTER THAN YOU HAVE TRIED!
BLAM
HHLG
YOU DAMNABLE--!
LANGUAGE! LANGUAGE!
I'LL START TO THINK YOU'RE A DELINQUENT, NOT A DEBUTANTE!

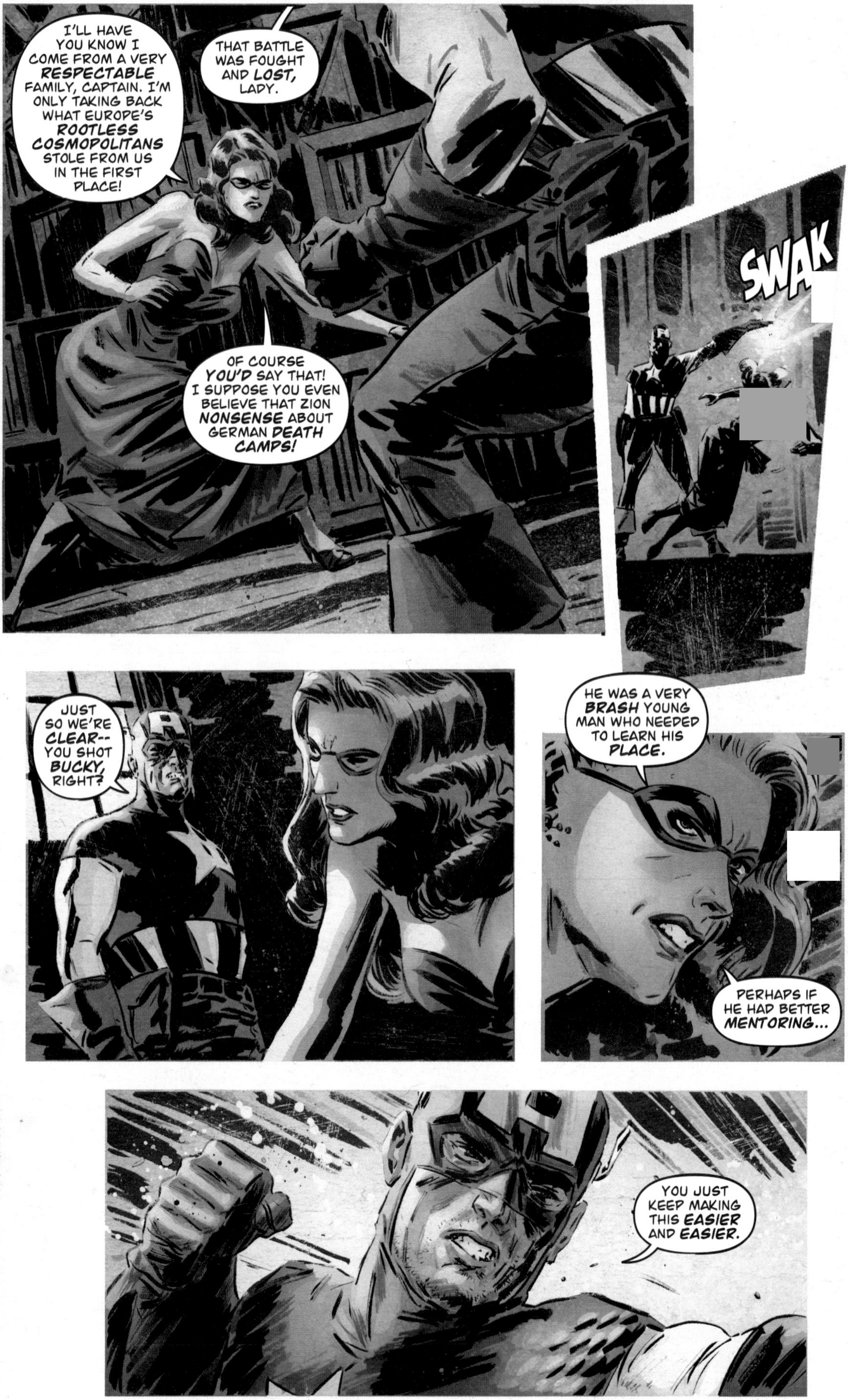
I'LL HAVE YOU KNOW I COME FROM A VERY RESPECTABLE FAMILY, CAPTAIN. I'M ONLY TAKING BACK WHAT EUROPE'S ROOTLESS COSMOPOLITANS STOLE FROM US IN THE FIRST PLACE!
THAT BATTLE WAS FOUGHT AND LOST, LADY.
OF COURSE YOU'D SAY THAT! I SUPPOSE YOU EVEN BELIEVE THAT ZION NONSENSE ABOUT GERMAN DEATH CAMPS!
SWAK
JUST SO WE'RE CLEAR-- YOU SHOT BUCKY, RIGHT?
HE WAS A VERY BRASH YOUNG MAN WHO NEEDED TO LEARN HIS PLACE.
PERHAPS IF HE HAD BETTER MENTORING...
YOU JUST KEEP MAKING THIS EASIER AND EASIER.

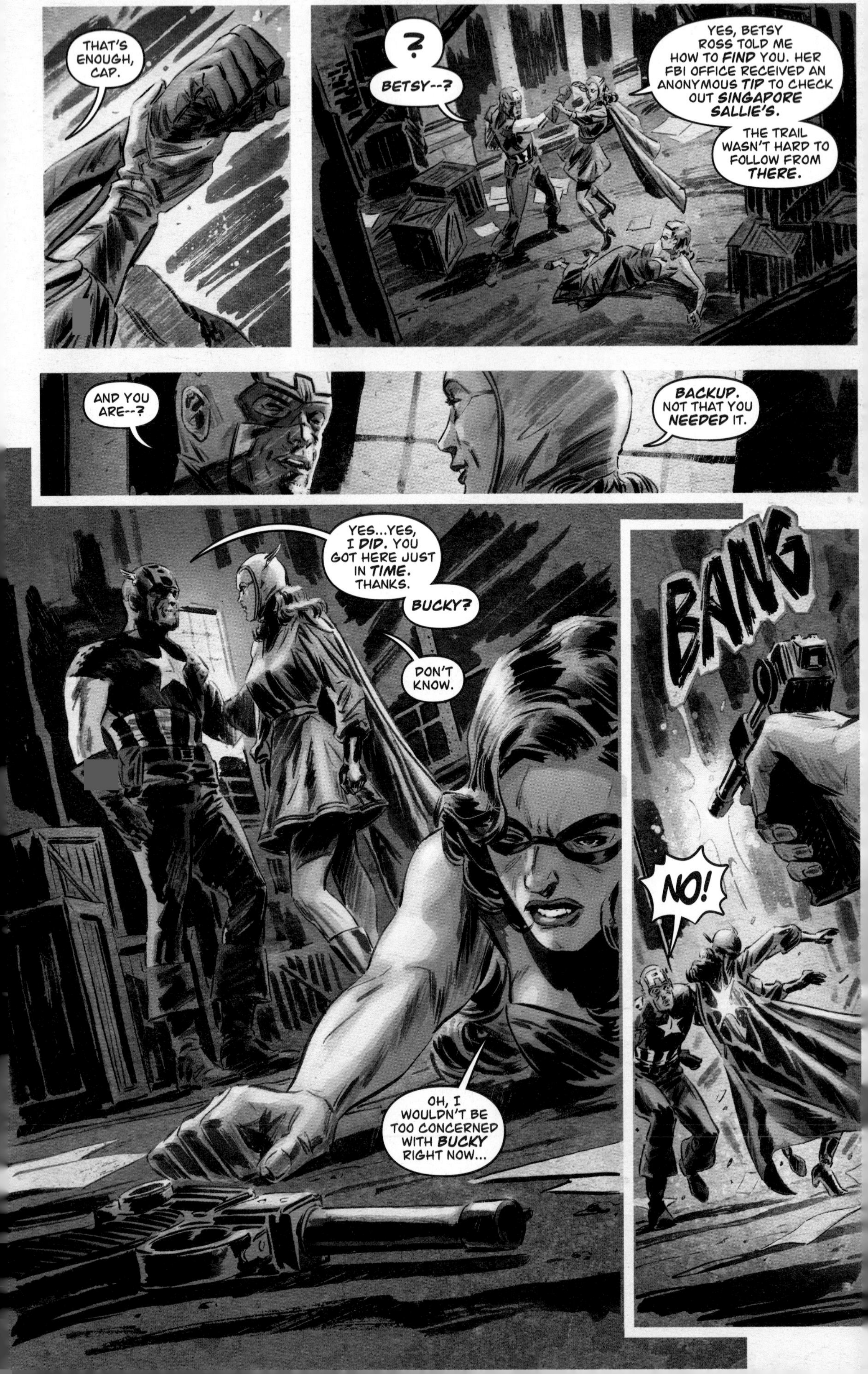
THAT'S ENOUGH, CAP.
?
BETSY--?
YES, BETSY ROSS TOLD ME HOW TO FIND YOU. HER FBI OFFICE RECEIVED AN ANONYMOUS TIP TO CHECK OUT SINGAPORE SALLIE'S.
THE TRAIL WASN'T HARD TO FOLLOW FROM THERE.
AND YOU ARE--?
BACKUP. NOT THAT YOU NEEDED IT.
YES...YES, I DID. YOU GOT HERE JUST IN TIME. THANKS.
BUCKY?
DON'T KNOW.
OH, I WOULDN'T BE TOO CONCERNED WITH BUCKY RIGHT NOW...
BANG
NO!

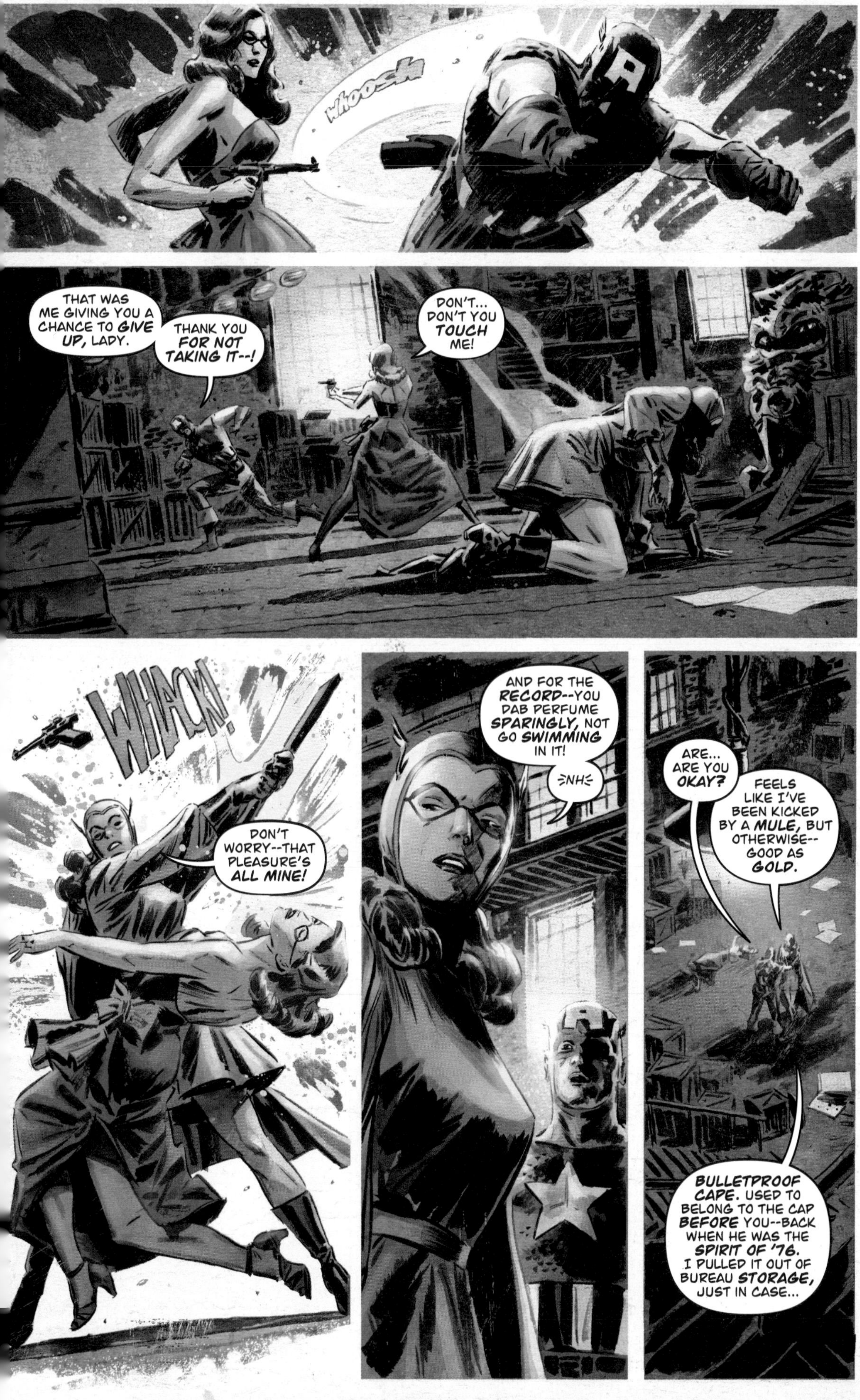

WHOOSH
THAT WAS ME GIVING YOU A CHANCE TO GIVE UP, LADY.
THANK YOU FOR NOT TAKING IT--!
DON'T... DON'T YOU TOUCH ME!
WHACK!
DON'T WORRY--THAT PLEASURE'S ALL MINE!
AND FOR THE RECORD--YOU DAB PERFUME SPARINGLY, NOT GO SWIMMING IN IT!
NH
ARE... ARE YOU OKAY?
FEELS LIKE I'VE BEEN KICKED BY A MULE, BUT OTHERWISE--GOOD AS GOLD.
BULLETPROOF CAPE. USED TO BELONG TO THE CAP BEFORE YOU--BACK WHEN HE WAS THE SPIRIT OF '76. I PULLED IT OUT OF BUREAU STORAGE, JUST IN CASE...

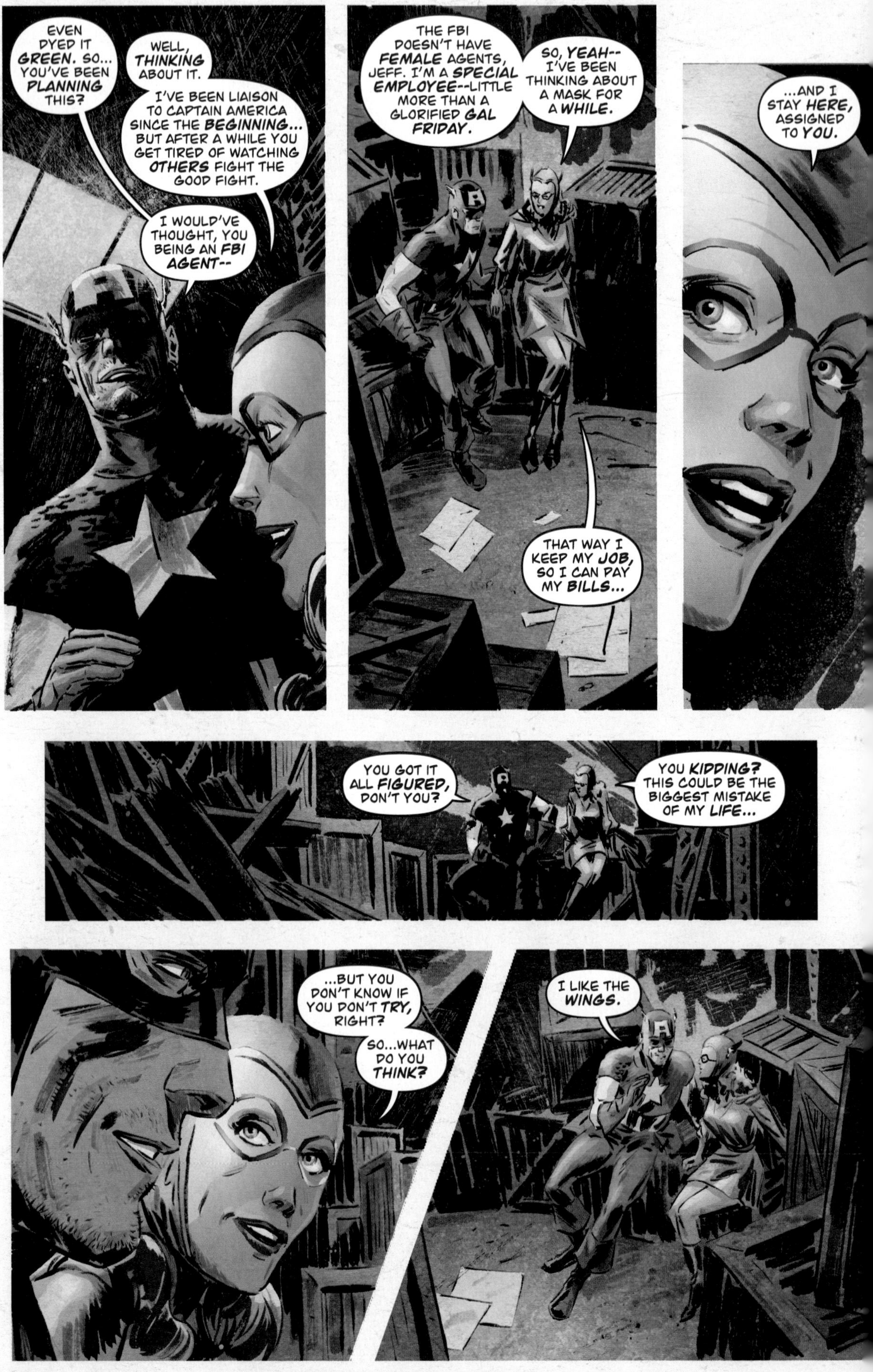
EVEN DYED IT GREEN. SO... YOU'VE BEEN PLANNING THIS?
WELL, THINKING ABOUT IT.
I'VE BEEN LIAISON TO CAPTAIN AMERICA SINCE THE BEGINNING... BUT AFTER A WHILE YOU GET TIRED OF WATCHING OTHERS FIGHT THE GOOD FIGHT.
I WOULD'VE THOUGHT, YOU BEING AN FBI AGENT--
THE FBI DOESN'T HAVE FEMALE AGENTS, JEFF. I'M A SPECIAL EMPLOYEE--LITTLE MORE THAN A GLORIFIED GAL FRIDAY.
SO, YEAH-- I'VE BEEN THINKING ABOUT A MASK FOR A WHILE.
THAT WAY I KEEP MY JOB, SO I CAN PAY MY BILLS...
...AND I STAY HERE, ASSIGNED TO YOU.
YOU GOT IT ALL FIGURED, DON'T YOU?
YOU KIDDING? THIS COULD BE THE BIGGEST MISTAKE OF MY LIFE...
...BUT YOU DON'T KNOW IF YOU DON'T TRY, RIGHT?
SO...WHAT DO YOU THINK?
I LIKE THE WINGS.

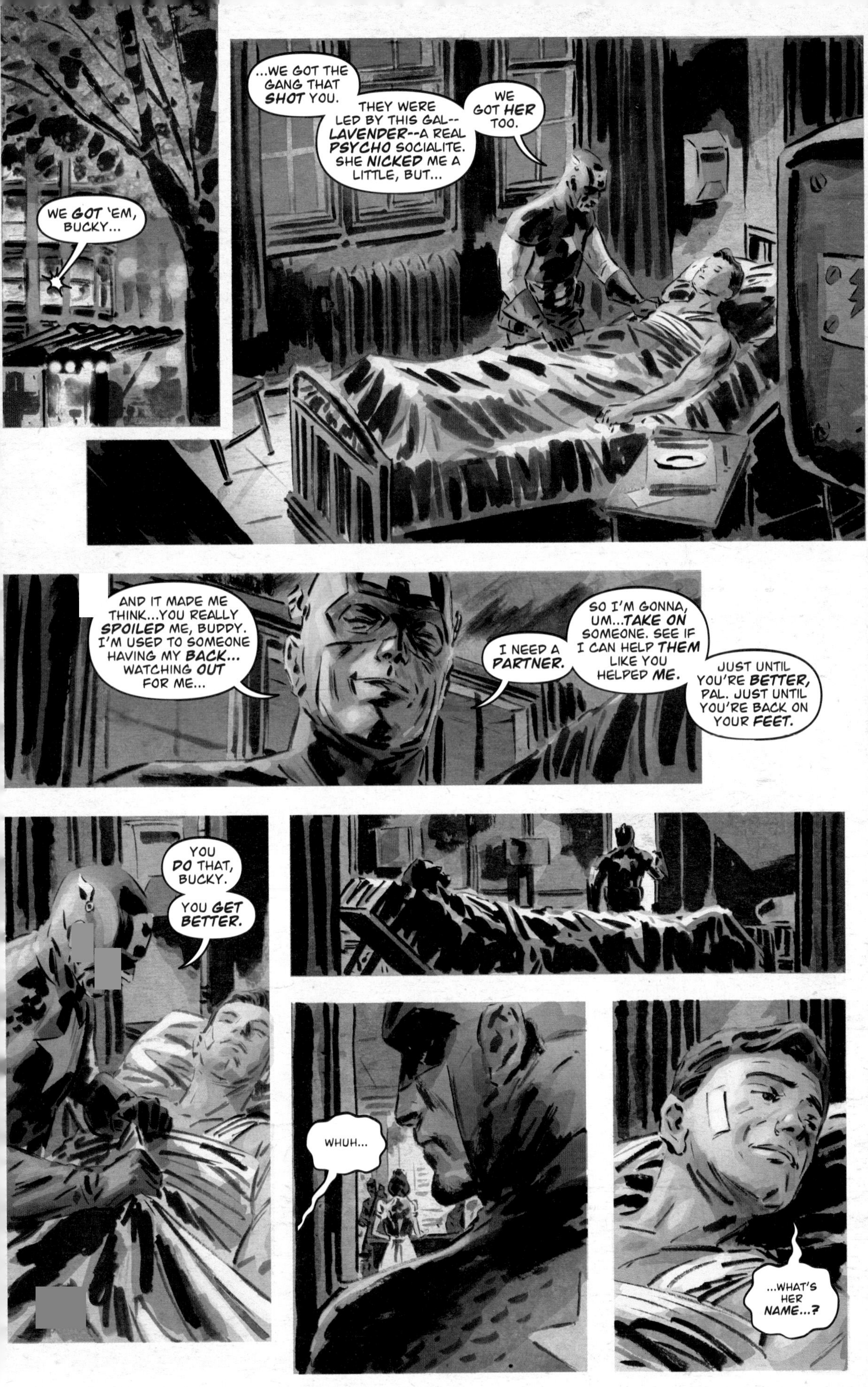
WE GOT 'EM, BUCKY...
...WE GOT THE GANG THAT SHOT YOU.
THEY WERE LED BY THIS GAL-- LAVENDER--A REAL PSYCHO SOCIALITE. SHE NICKED ME A LITTLE, BUT...
WE GOT HER TOO.
AND IT MADE ME THINK...YOU REALLY SPOILED ME, BUDDY. I'M USED TO SOMEONE HAVING MY BACK... WATCHING OUT FOR ME...
I NEED A PARTNER.
SO I'M GONNA, UM...TAKE ON SOMEONE. SEE IF I CAN HELP THEM LIKE YOU HELPED ME.
JUST UNTIL YOU'RE BETTER, PAL. JUST UNTIL YOU'RE BACK ON YOUR FEET.
YOU DO THAT, BUCKY.
YOU GET BETTER.
WHUH...
...WHAT'S HER NAME...?

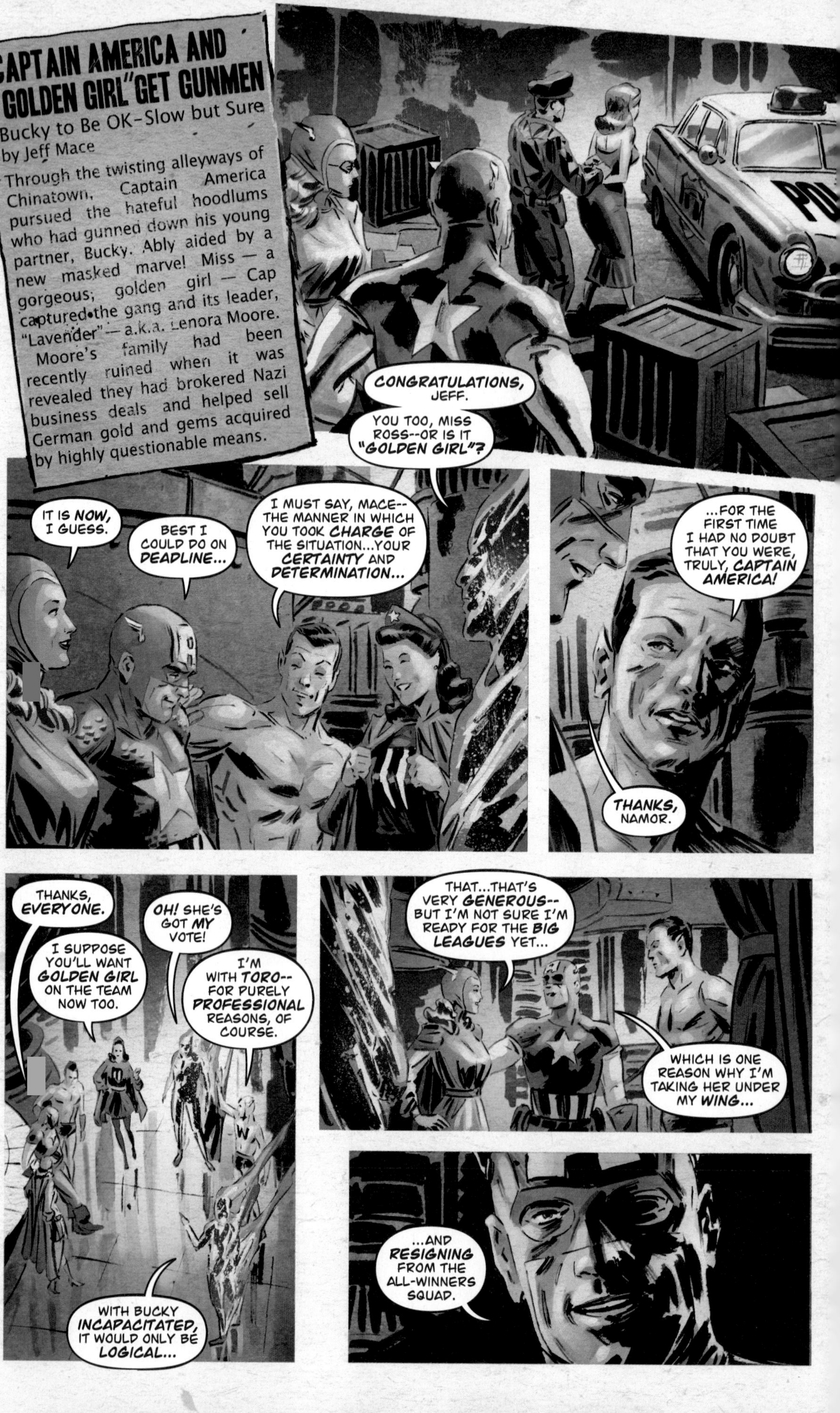
CAPTAIN AMERICA AND "GOLDEN GIRL" GET GUNMEN
Bucky to Be OK–Slow but Sure
by Jeff Mace
Through the twisting alleyways of Chinatown, Captain America pursued the hateful hoodlums who had gunned down his young partner, Bucky. Ably aided by a new masked marvel! Miss — a gorgeous; golden girl — Cap captured the gang and its leader, "Lavender" — a.k.a. Lenora Moore. Moore's family had been recently ruined when it was revealed they had brokered Nazi business deals and helped sell German gold and gems acquired by highly questionable means.
CONGRATULATIONS, JEFF.
YOU TOO, MISS ROSS--OR IS IT "GOLDEN GIRL"?
IT IS NOW, I GUESS.
BEST I COULD DO ON DEADLINE...
I MUST SAY, MACE--THE MANNER IN WHICH YOU TOOK CHARGE OF THE SITUATION...YOUR CERTAINTY AND DETERMINATION...
...FOR THE FIRST TIME I HAD NO DOUBT THAT YOU WERE, TRULY, CAPTAIN AMERICA!
THANKS, NAMOR.
THANKS, EVERYONE.
I SUPPOSE YOU'LL WANT GOLDEN GIRL ON THE TEAM NOW TOO.
OH! SHE'S GOT MY VOTE!
I'M WITH TORO--FOR PURELY PROFESSIONAL REASONS, OF COURSE.
WITH BUCKY INCAPACITATED, IT WOULD ONLY BE LOGICAL...
THAT...THAT'S VERY GENEROUS--BUT I'M NOT SURE I'M READY FOR THE BIG LEAGUES YET...
WHICH IS ONE REASON WHY I'M TAKING HER UNDER MY WING...
...AND RESIGNING FROM THE ALL-WINNERS SQUAD.

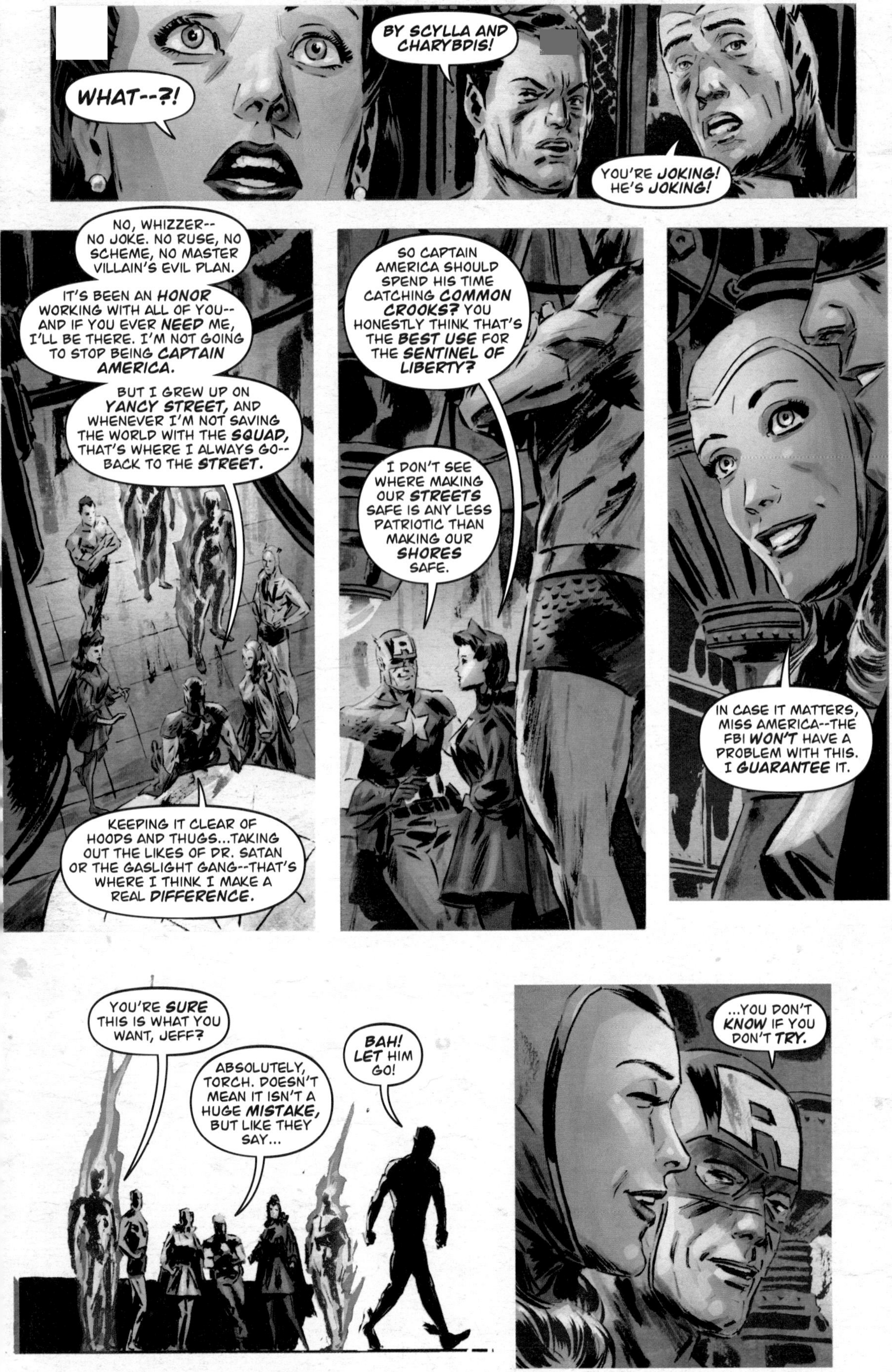
WHAT--?!
BY SCYLLA AND CHARYBDIS!
YOU'RE JOKING! HE'S JOKING!
NO, WHIZZER-- NO JOKE. NO RUSE, NO SCHEME, NO MASTER VILLAIN'S EVIL PLAN.
IT'S BEEN AN HONOR WORKING WITH ALL OF YOU-- AND IF YOU EVER NEED ME, I'LL BE THERE. I'M NOT GOING TO STOP BEING CAPTAIN AMERICA.
BUT I GREW UP ON YANCY STREET, AND WHENEVER I'M NOT SAVING THE WORLD WITH THE SQUAD, THAT'S WHERE I ALWAYS GO-- BACK TO THE STREET.
KEEPING IT CLEAR OF HOODS AND THUGS...TAKING OUT THE LIKES OF DR. SATAN OR THE GASLIGHT GANG--THAT'S WHERE I THINK I MAKE A REAL DIFFERENCE.
SO CAPTAIN AMERICA SHOULD SPEND HIS TIME CATCHING COMMON CROOKS? YOU HONESTLY THINK THAT'S THE BEST USE FOR THE SENTINEL OF LIBERTY?
I DON'T SEE WHERE MAKING OUR STREETS SAFE IS ANY LESS PATRIOTIC THAN MAKING OUR SHORES SAFE.
IN CASE IT MATTERS, MISS AMERICA--THE FBI WON'T HAVE A PROBLEM WITH THIS. I GUARANTEE IT.
YOU'RE SURE THIS IS WHAT YOU WANT, JEFF?
ABSOLUTELY, TORCH. DOESN'T MEAN IT ISN'T A HUGE MISTAKE, BUT LIKE THEY SAY...
BAH! LET HIM GO!
...YOU DON'T KNOW IF YOU DON'T TRY.

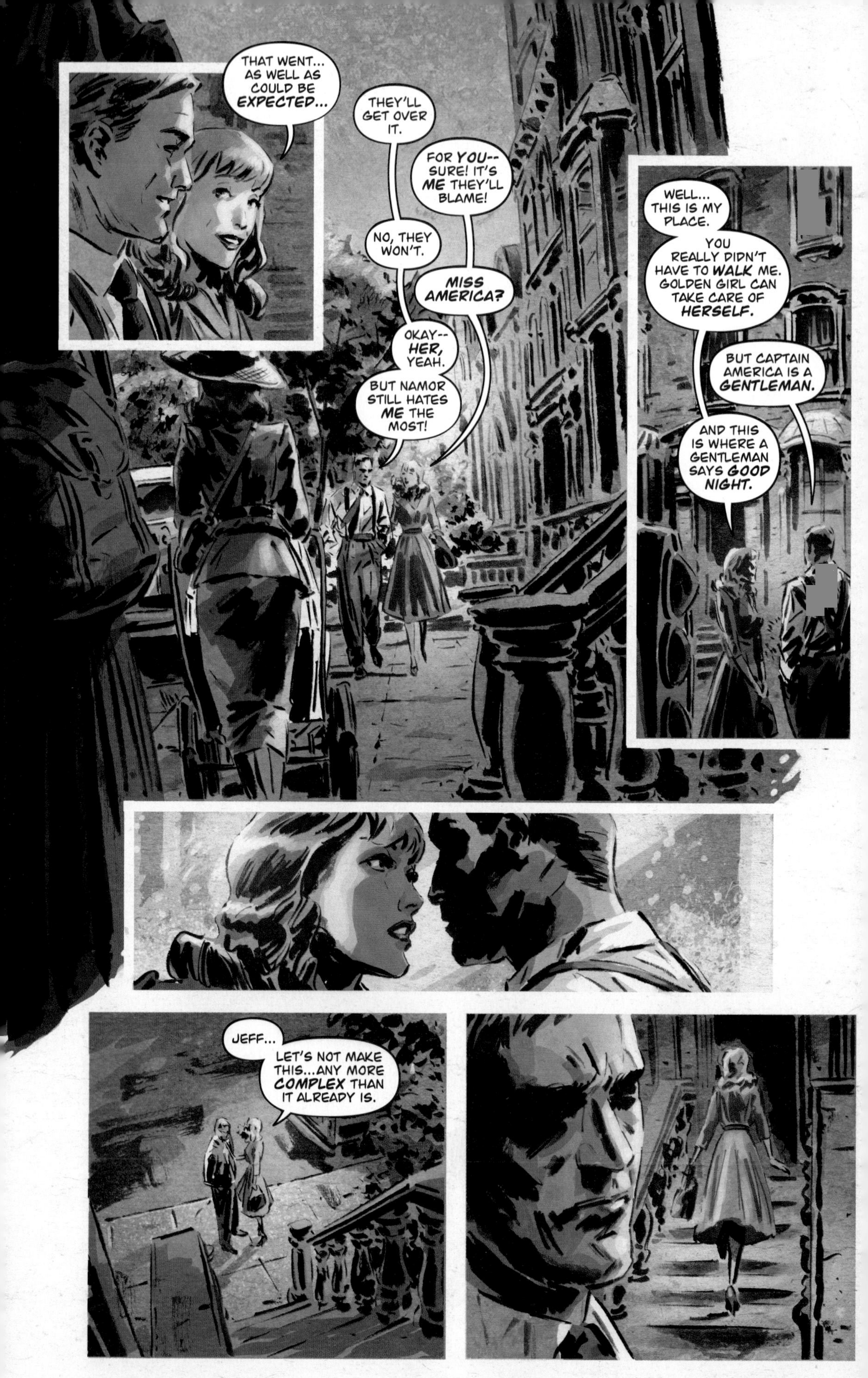
THAT WENT... AS WELL AS COULD BE EXPECTED...
THEY'LL GET OVER IT.
FOR YOU-- SURE! IT'S ME THEY'LL BLAME!
NO, THEY WON'T.
MISS AMERICA?
OKAY-- HER, YEAH.
BUT NAMOR STILL HATES ME THE MOST!
WELL... THIS IS MY PLACE.
YOU REALLY DIDN'T HAVE TO WALK ME. GOLDEN GIRL CAN TAKE CARE OF HERSELF.
BUT CAPTAIN AMERICA IS A GENTLEMAN.
AND THIS IS WHERE A GENTLEMAN SAYS GOOD NIGHT.
JEFF...
LET'S NOT MAKE THIS...ANY MORE COMPLEX THAN IT ALREADY IS.

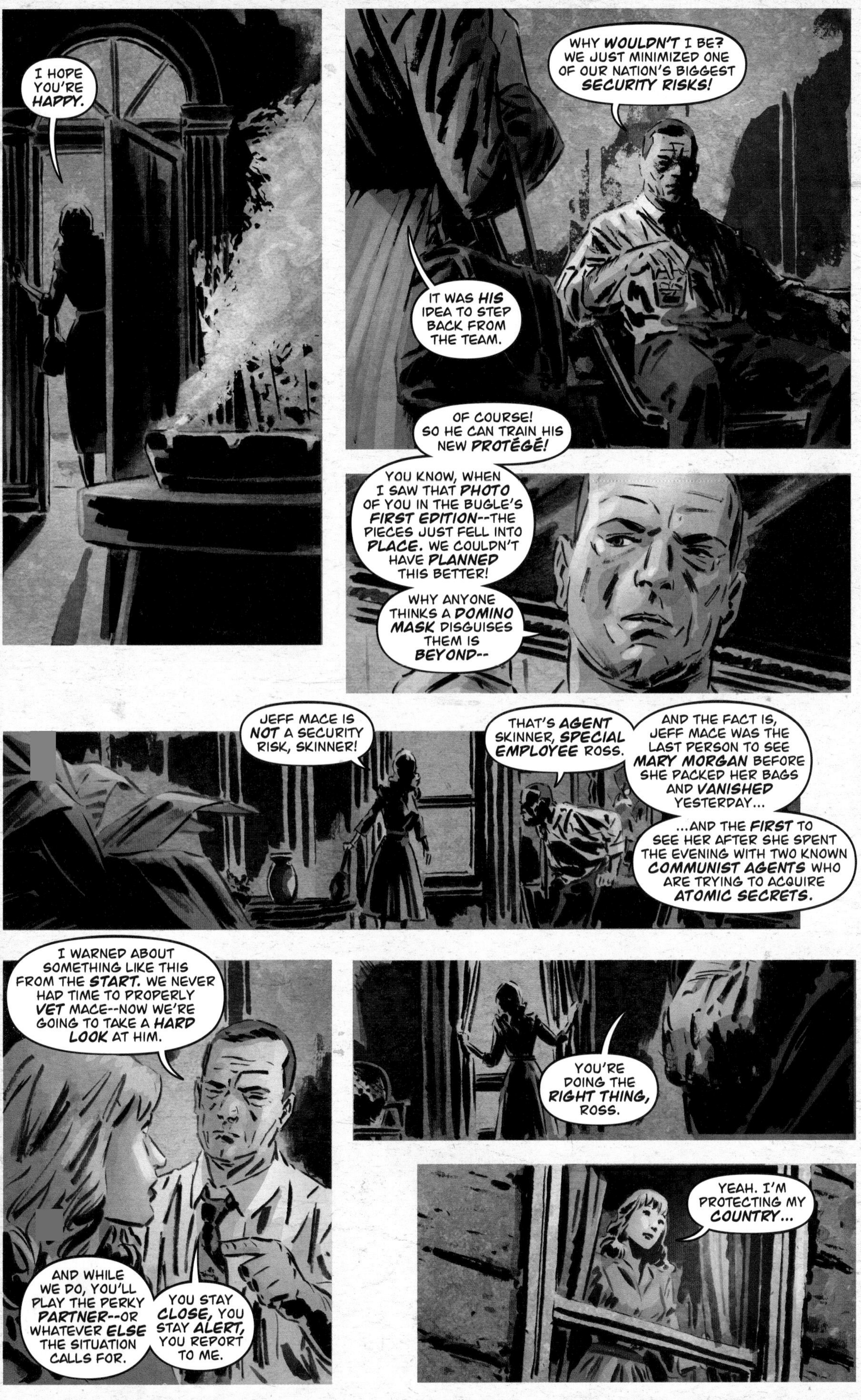
I HOPE YOU'RE HAPPY.
WHY WOULDN'T I BE? WE JUST MINIMIZED ONE OF OUR NATION'S BIGGEST SECURITY RISKS!
IT WAS HIS IDEA TO STEP BACK FROM THE TEAM.
OF COURSE! SO HE CAN TRAIN HIS NEW PROTÉGÉ!
YOU KNOW, WHEN I SAW THAT PHOTO OF YOU IN THE BUGLE'S FIRST EDITION--THE PIECES JUST FELL INTO PLACE. WE COULDN'T HAVE PLANNED THIS BETTER!
WHY ANYONE THINKS A DOMINO MASK DISGUISES THEM IS BEYOND--
JEFF MACE IS NOT A SECURITY RISK, SKINNER!
THAT'S AGENT SKINNER, SPECIAL EMPLOYEE ROSS.
AND THE FACT IS, JEFF MACE WAS THE LAST PERSON TO SEE MARY MORGAN BEFORE SHE PACKED HER BAGS AND VANISHED YESTERDAY...
...AND THE FIRST TO SEE HER AFTER SHE SPENT THE EVENING WITH TWO KNOWN COMMUNIST AGENTS WHO ARE TRYING TO ACQUIRE ATOMIC SECRETS.
I WARNED ABOUT SOMETHING LIKE THIS FROM THE START. WE NEVER HAD TIME TO PROPERLY VET MACE--NOW WE'RE GOING TO TAKE A HARD LOOK AT HIM.
AND WHILE WE DO, YOU'LL PLAY THE PERKY PARTNER--OR WHATEVER ELSE THE SITUATION CALLS FOR.
YOU STAY CLOSE, YOU STAY ALERT, YOU REPORT TO ME.
YOU'RE DOING THE RIGHT THING, ROSS.
YEAH. I'M PROTECTING MY COUNTRY...

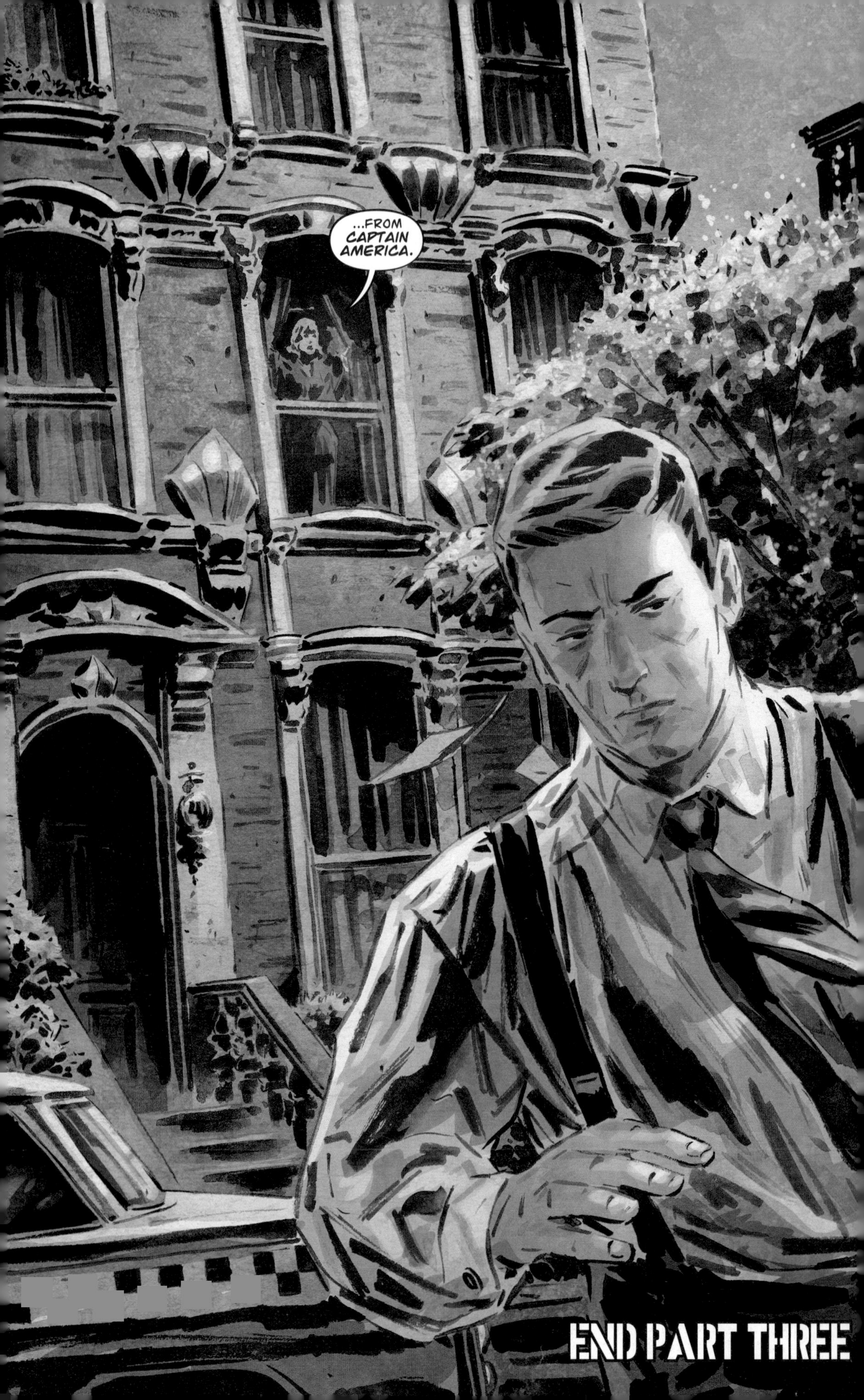
...FROM CAPTAIN AMERICA.
END PART THREE

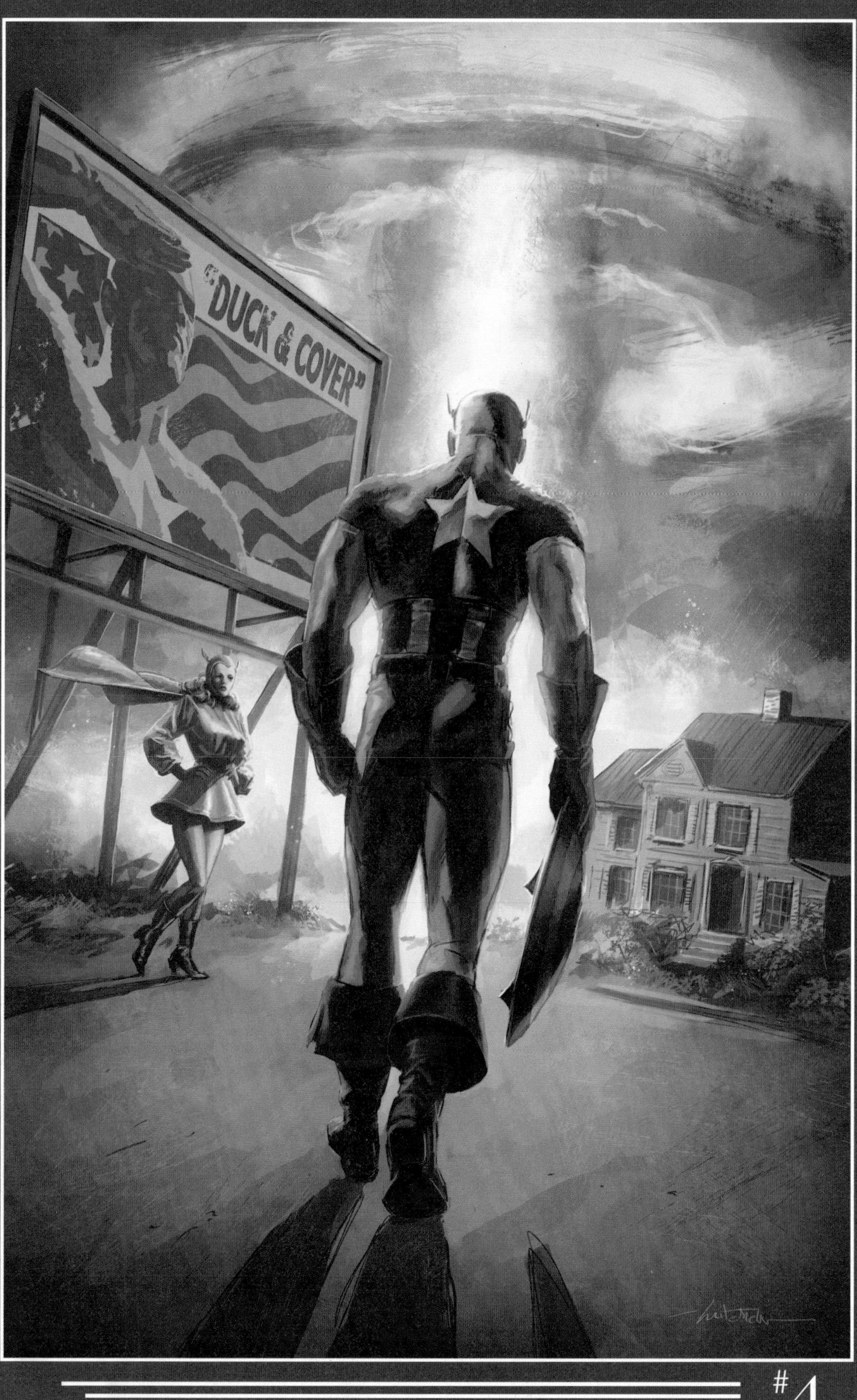
"DUCK & COVER"

#4

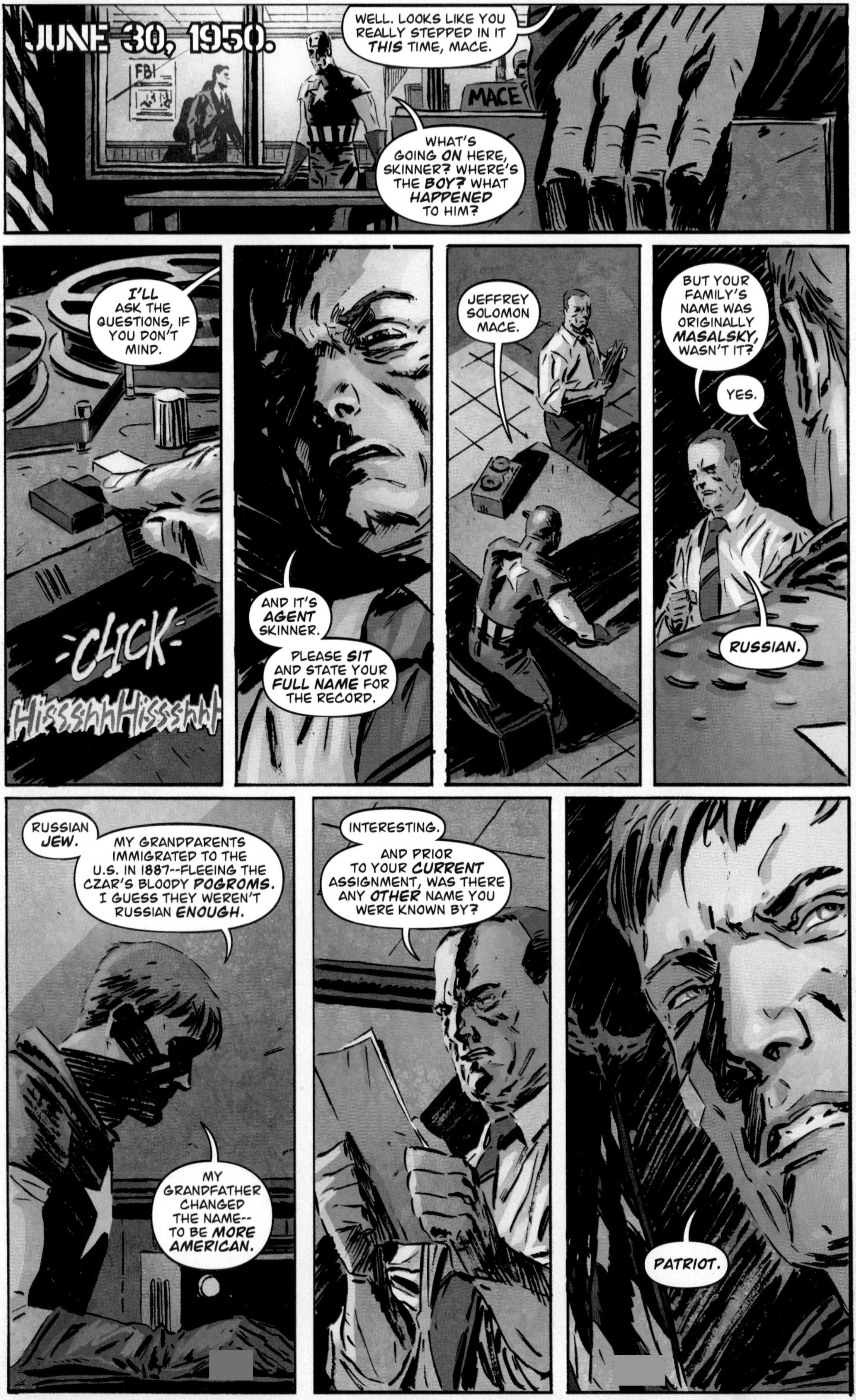
JUNE 30, 1950.
FBI
MACE
WELL. LOOKS LIKE YOU REALLY STEPPED IN IT THIS TIME, MACE.
WHAT'S GOING ON HERE, SKINNER? WHERE'S THE BOY? WHAT HAPPENED TO HIM?
I'LL ASK THE QUESTIONS, IF YOU DON'T MIND.
CLICK
HISSSHHHISSSHHH
AND IT'S AGENT SKINNER.
PLEASE SIT AND STATE YOUR FULL NAME FOR THE RECORD.
JEFFREY SOLOMON MACE.
BUT YOUR FAMILY'S NAME WAS ORIGINALLY MASALSKY, WASN'T IT?
YES.
RUSSIAN.
RUSSIAN JEW.
MY GRANDPARENTS IMMIGRATED TO THE U.S. IN 1887--FLEEING THE CZAR'S BLOODY POGROMS. I GUESS THEY WEREN'T RUSSIAN ENOUGH.
MY GRANDFATHER CHANGED THE NAME-- TO BE MORE AMERICAN.
INTERESTING.
AND PRIOR TO YOUR CURRENT ASSIGNMENT, WAS THERE ANY OTHER NAME YOU WERE KNOWN BY?
PATRIOT.

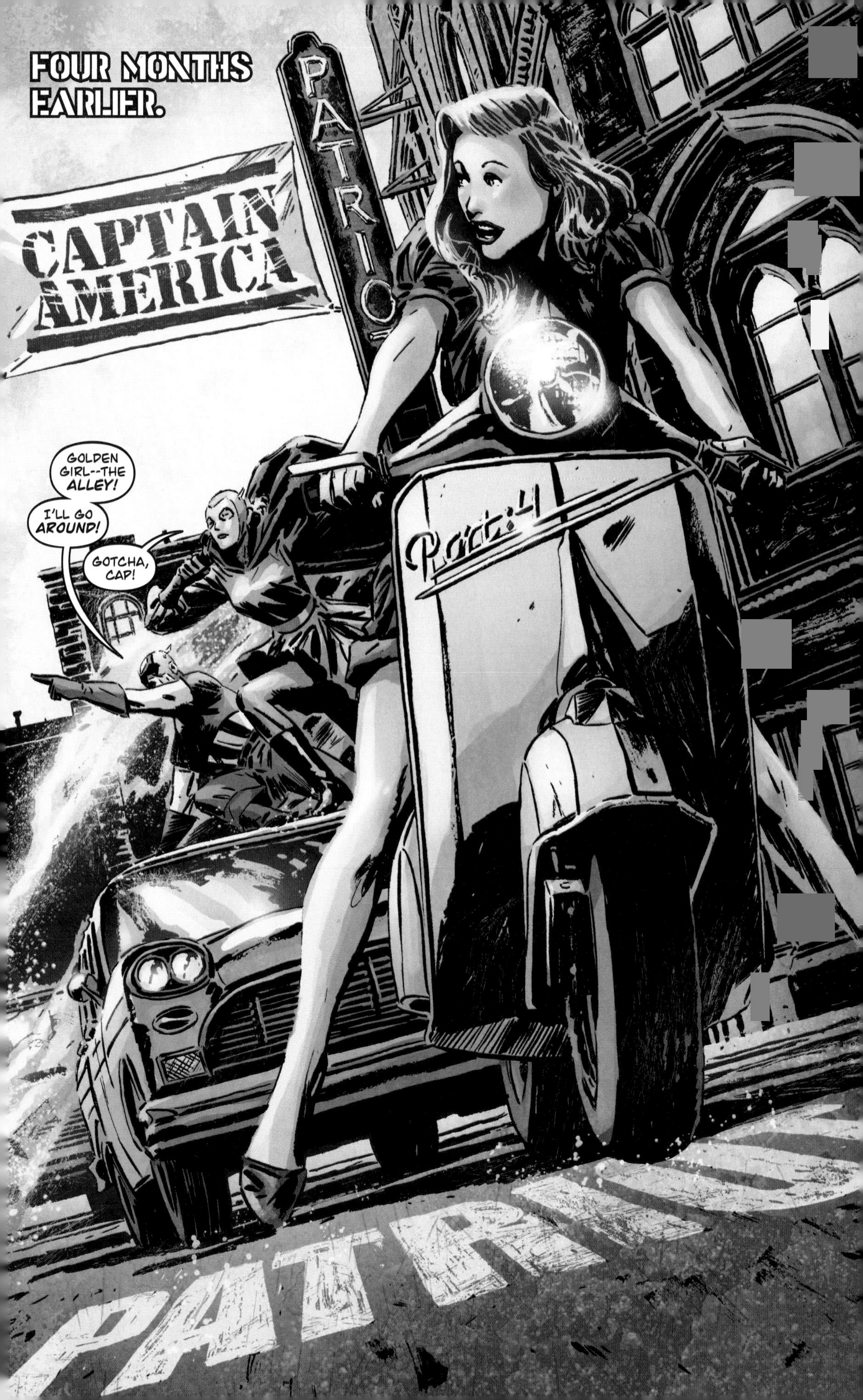
FOUR MONTHS EARLIER.
CAPTAIN AMERICA
GOLDEN GIRL--THE ALLEY!
I'LL GO AROUND!
GOTCHA, CAP!

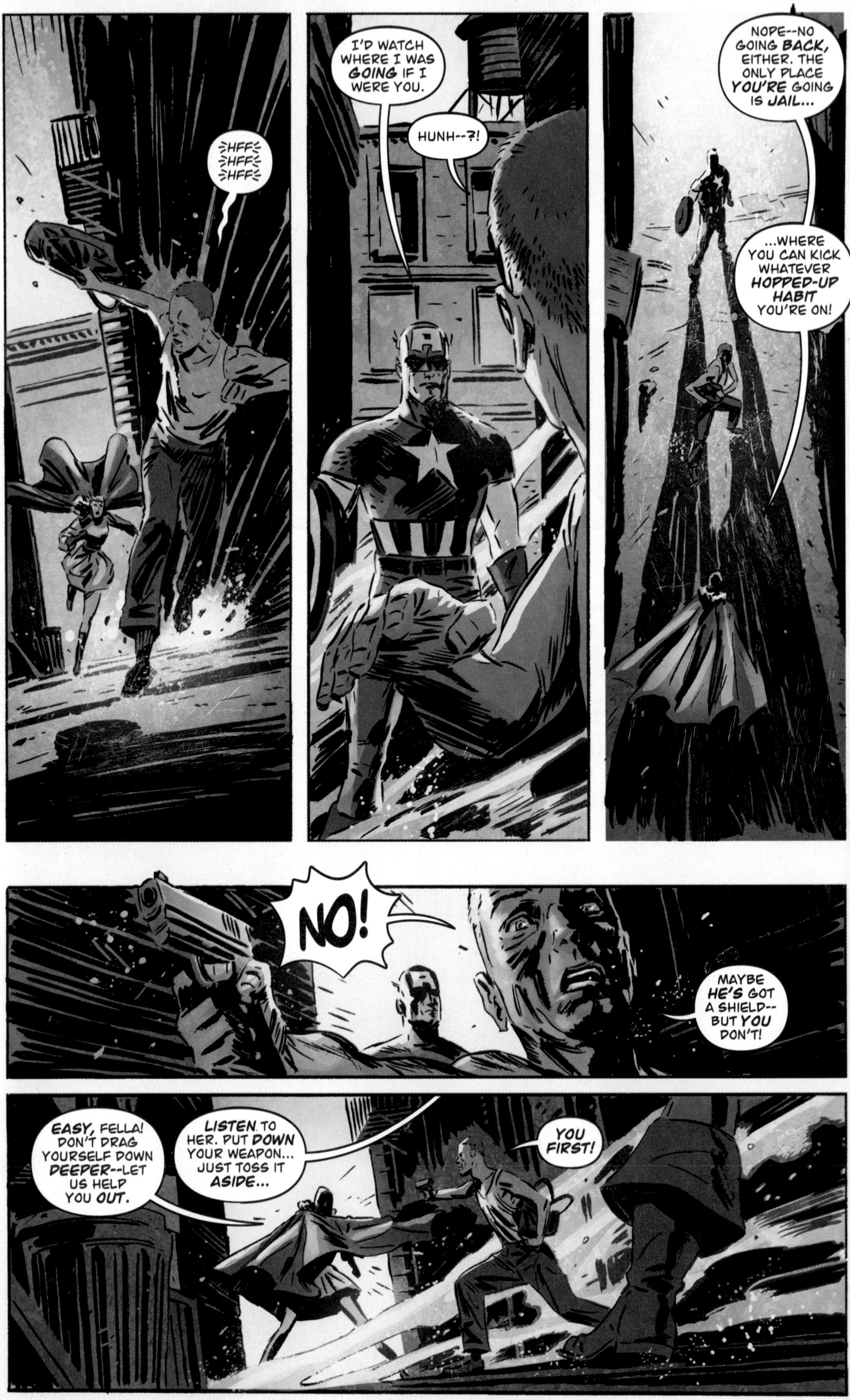

HFF HFF HFF
I'D WATCH WHERE I WAS GOING IF I WERE YOU.
HUNH--?!
NOPE--NO GOING BACK, EITHER. THE ONLY PLACE YOU'RE GOING IS JAIL...
...WHERE YOU CAN KICK WHATEVER HOPPED-UP HABIT YOU'RE ON!
NO!
MAYBE HE'S GOT A SHIELD-- BUT YOU DON'T!
EASY, FELLA! DON'T DRAG YOURSELF DOWN DEEPER--LET US HELP YOU OUT.
LISTEN TO HER. PUT DOWN YOUR WEAPON... JUST TOSS IT ASIDE...
YOU FIRST!

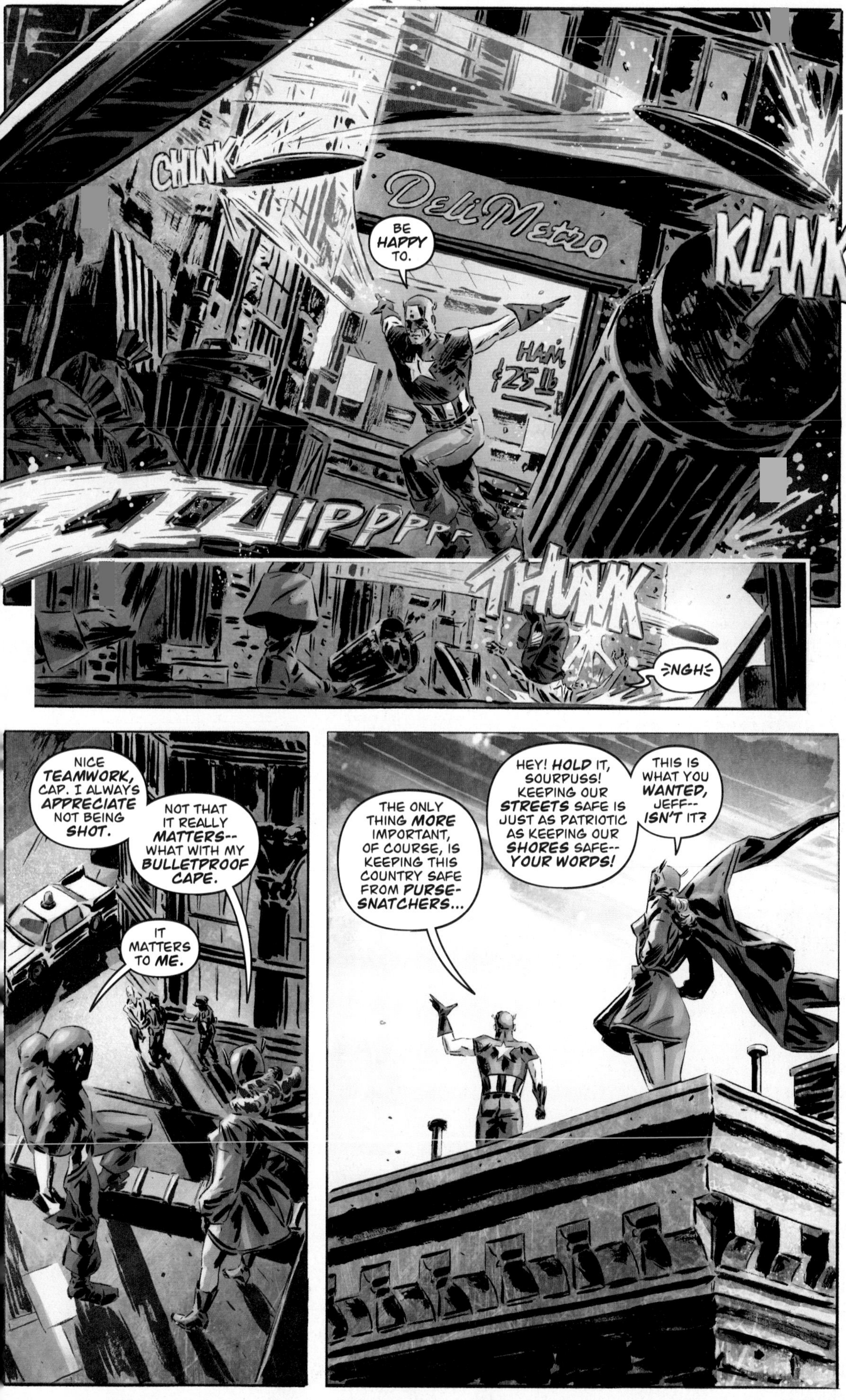

CHINK
DeliMetro
BE HAPPY TO.
HAM ¢25 lb
KLANK
ZZZIIPPPPPP
THUNK
NGH
NICE TEAMWORK, CAP. I ALWAYS APPRECIATE NOT BEING SHOT.
NOT THAT IT REALLY MATTERS-- WHAT WITH MY BULLETPROOF CAPE.
IT MATTERS TO ME.
THE ONLY THING MORE IMPORTANT, OF COURSE, IS KEEPING THIS COUNTRY SAFE FROM PURSE-SNATCHERS...
HEY! HOLD IT, SOURPUSS! KEEPING OUR STREETS SAFE IS JUST AS PATRIOTIC AS KEEPING OUR SHORES SAFE-- YOUR WORDS!
THIS IS WHAT YOU WANTED, JEFF-- ISN'T IT?

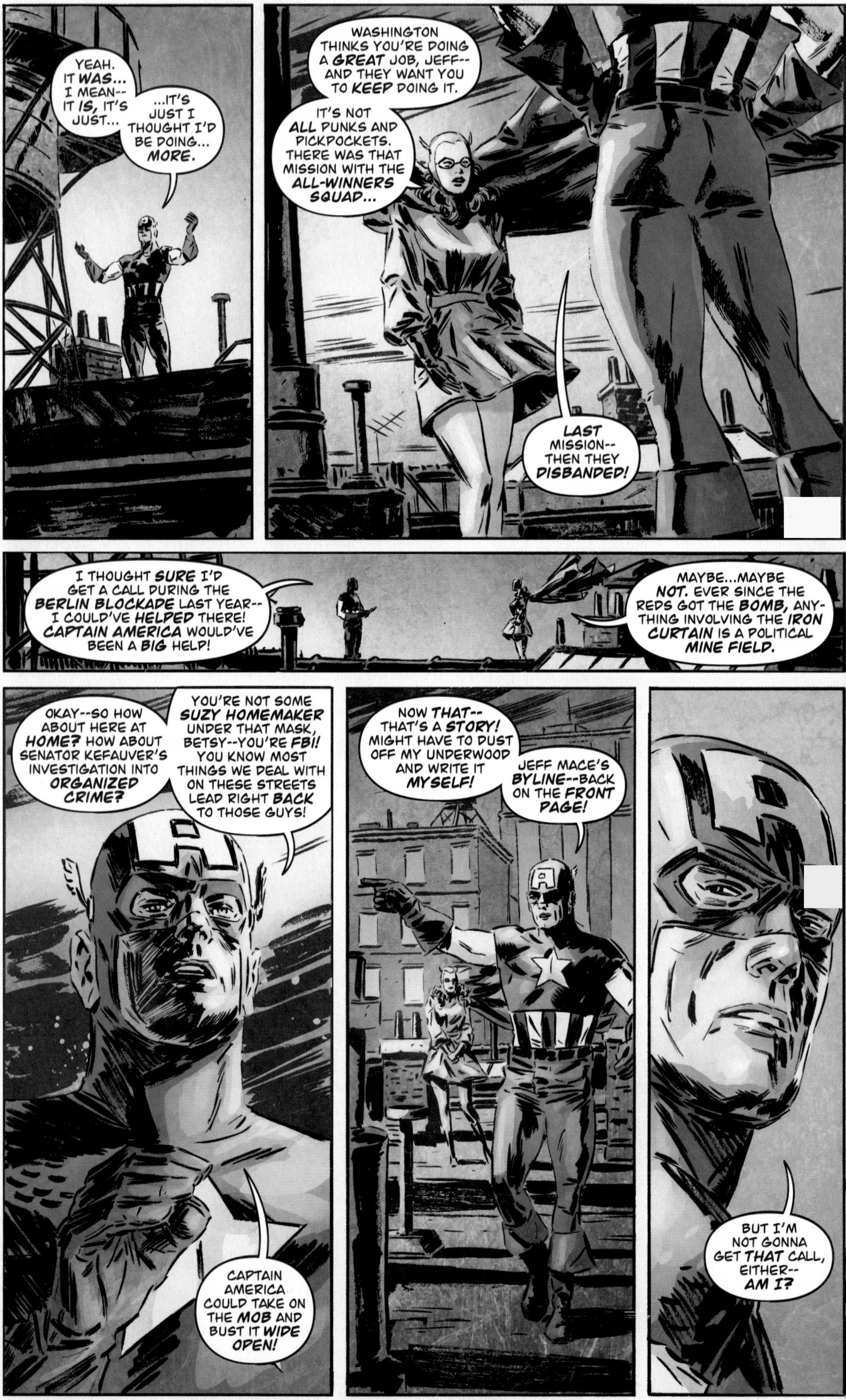
YEAH. IT WAS... I MEAN-- IT IS, IT'S JUST...
...IT'S JUST I THOUGHT I'D BE DOING... MORE.
WASHINGTON THINKS YOU'RE DOING A GREAT JOB, JEFF-- AND THEY WANT YOU TO KEEP DOING IT.
IT'S NOT ALL PUNKS AND PICKPOCKETS. THERE WAS THAT MISSION WITH THE ALL-WINNERS SQUAD...
LAST MISSION-- THEN THEY DISBANDED!
I THOUGHT SURE I'D GET A CALL DURING THE BERLIN BLOCKADE LAST YEAR-- I COULD'VE HELPED THERE! CAPTAIN AMERICA WOULD'VE BEEN A BIG HELP!
MAYBE...MAYBE NOT. EVER SINCE THE REDS GOT THE BOMB, ANYTHING INVOLVING THE IRON CURTAIN IS A POLITICAL MINE FIELD.
OKAY--SO HOW ABOUT HERE AT HOME? HOW ABOUT SENATOR KEFAUVER'S INVESTIGATION INTO ORGANIZED CRIME?
YOU'RE NOT SOME SUZY HOMEMAKER UNDER THAT MASK, BETSY--YOU'RE FBI! YOU KNOW MOST THINGS WE DEAL WITH ON THESE STREETS LEAD RIGHT BACK TO THOSE GUYS!
CAPTAIN AMERICA COULD TAKE ON THE MOB AND BUST IT WIDE OPEN!
NOW THAT-- THAT'S A STORY! MIGHT HAVE TO DUST OFF MY UNDERWOOD AND WRITE IT MYSELF!
JEFF MACE'S BYLINE--BACK ON THE FRONT PAGE!
BUT I'M NOT GONNA GET THAT CALL, EITHER-- AM I?

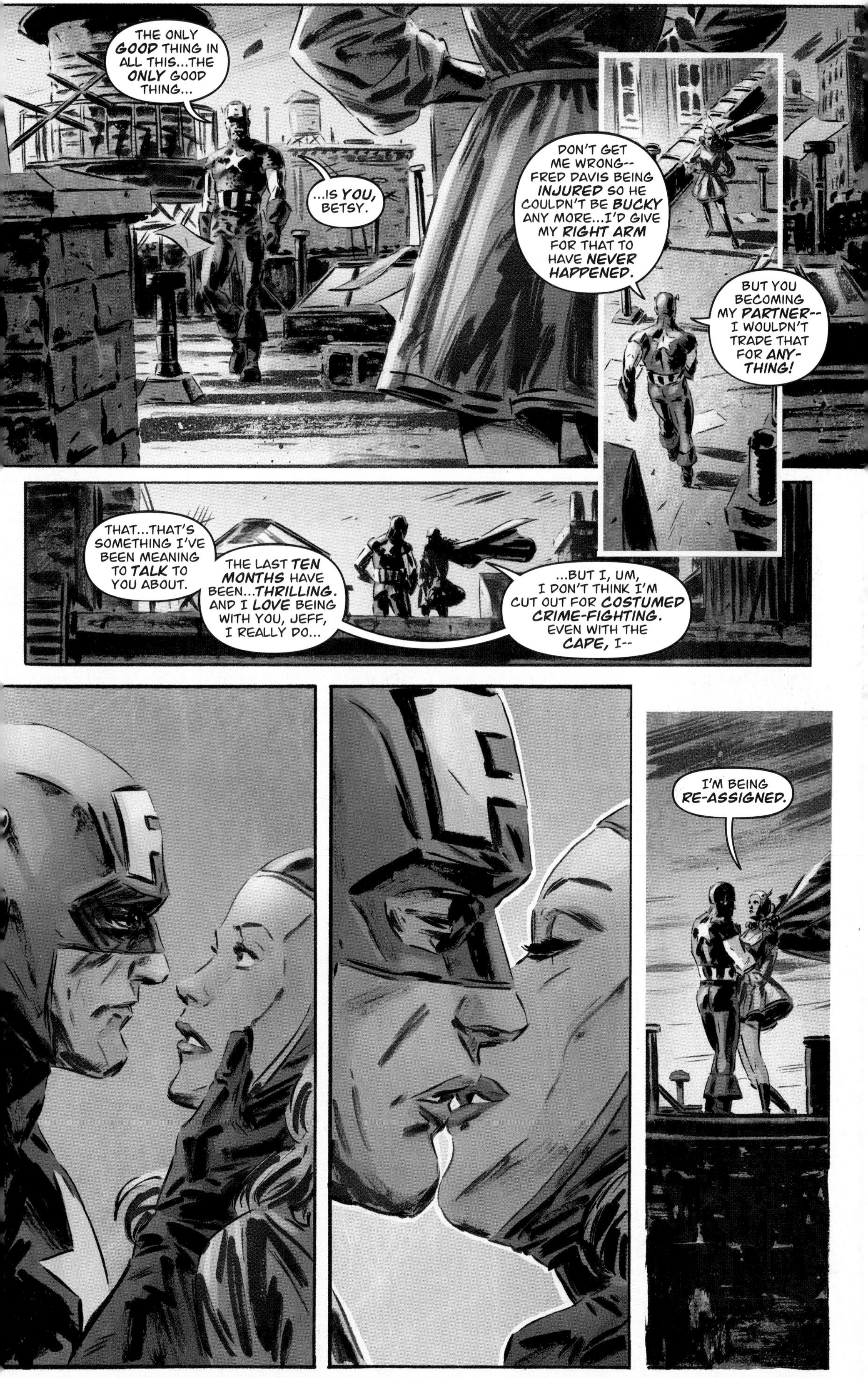

THE ONLY GOOD THING IN ALL THIS...THE ONLY GOOD THING...
...IS YOU, BETSY.
DON'T GET ME WRONG-- FRED DAVIS BEING INJURED SO HE COULDN'T BE BUCKY ANY MORE...I'D GIVE MY RIGHT ARM FOR THAT TO HAVE NEVER HAPPENED.
BUT YOU BECOMING MY PARTNER-- I WOULDN'T TRADE THAT FOR ANY-THING!
THAT...THAT'S SOMETHING I'VE BEEN MEANING TO TALK TO YOU ABOUT.
THE LAST TEN MONTHS HAVE BEEN...THRILLING. AND I LOVE BEING WITH YOU, JEFF, I REALLY DO...
...BUT I, UM, I DON'T THINK I'M CUT OUT FOR COSTUMED CRIME-FIGHTING. EVEN WITH THE CAPE, I--
I'M BEING RE-ASSIGNED.

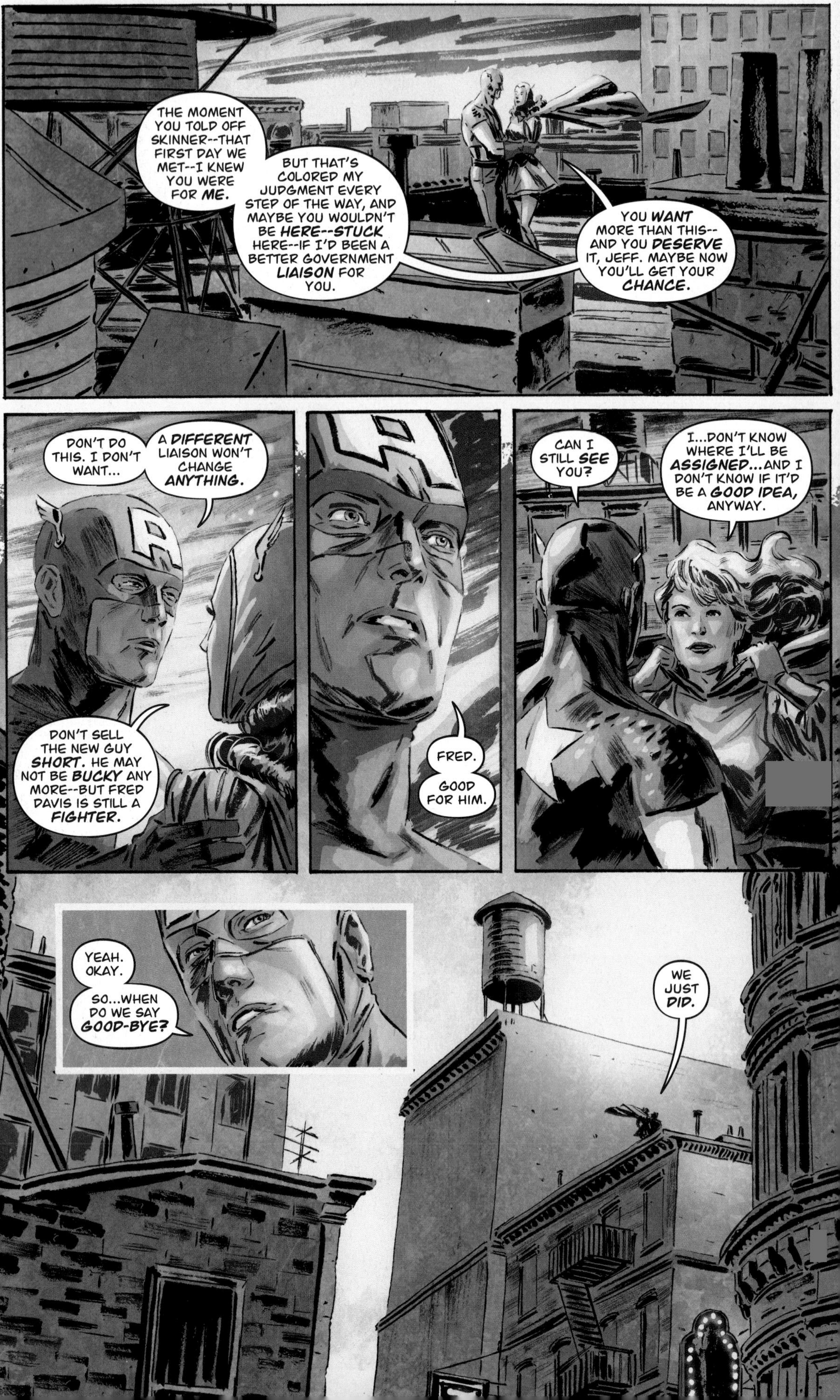
THE MOMENT YOU TOLD OFF SKINNER--THAT FIRST DAY WE MET--I KNEW YOU WERE FOR ME.
BUT THAT'S COLORED MY JUDGMENT EVERY STEP OF THE WAY, AND MAYBE YOU WOULDN'T BE HERE--STUCK HERE--IF I'D BEEN A BETTER GOVERNMENT LIAISON FOR YOU.
YOU WANT MORE THAN THIS--AND YOU DESERVE IT, JEFF. MAYBE NOW YOU'LL GET YOUR CHANCE.
DON'T DO THIS. I DON'T WANT...
A DIFFERENT LIAISON WON'T CHANGE ANYTHING.
DON'T SELL THE NEW GUY SHORT. HE MAY NOT BE BUCKY ANY MORE--BUT FRED DAVIS IS STILL A FIGHTER.
FRED.
GOOD FOR HIM.
CAN I STILL SEE YOU?
I...DON'T KNOW WHERE I'LL BE ASSIGNED...AND I DON'T KNOW IF IT'D BE A GOOD IDEA, ANYWAY.
YEAH. OKAY.
SO...WHEN DO WE SAY GOOD-BYE?
WE JUST DID.

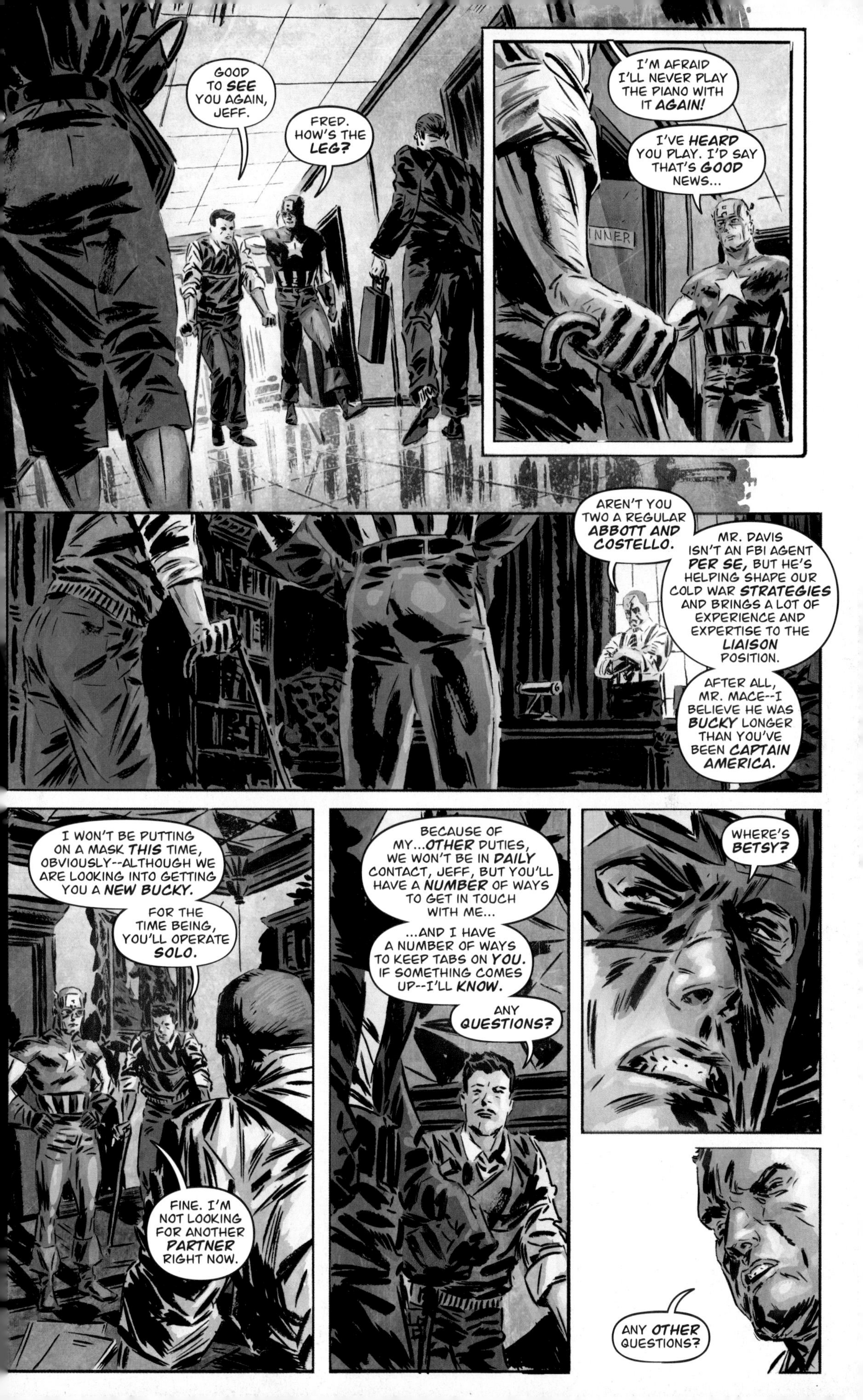
GOOD TO SEE YOU AGAIN, JEFF.
FRED. HOW'S THE LEG?
I'M AFRAID I'LL NEVER PLAY THE PIANO WITH IT AGAIN!
I'VE HEARD YOU PLAY. I'D SAY THAT'S GOOD NEWS...
INNER
AREN'T YOU TWO A REGULAR ABBOTT AND COSTELLO.
MR. DAVIS ISN'T AN FBI AGENT PER SE, BUT HE'S HELPING SHAPE OUR COLD WAR STRATEGIES AND BRINGS A LOT OF EXPERIENCE AND EXPERTISE TO THE LIAISON POSITION.
AFTER ALL, MR. MACE--I BELIEVE HE WAS BUCKY LONGER THAN YOU'VE BEEN CAPTAIN AMERICA.
I WON'T BE PUTTING ON A MASK THIS TIME, OBVIOUSLY--ALTHOUGH WE ARE LOOKING INTO GETTING YOU A NEW BUCKY.
FOR THE TIME BEING, YOU'LL OPERATE SOLO.
FINE. I'M NOT LOOKING FOR ANOTHER PARTNER RIGHT NOW.
BECAUSE OF MY...OTHER DUTIES, WE WON'T BE IN DAILY CONTACT, JEFF, BUT YOU'LL HAVE A NUMBER OF WAYS TO GET IN TOUCH WITH ME...
...AND I HAVE A NUMBER OF WAYS TO KEEP TABS ON YOU. IF SOMETHING COMES UP--I'LL KNOW.
ANY QUESTIONS?
WHERE'S BETSY?
ANY OTHER QUESTIONS?

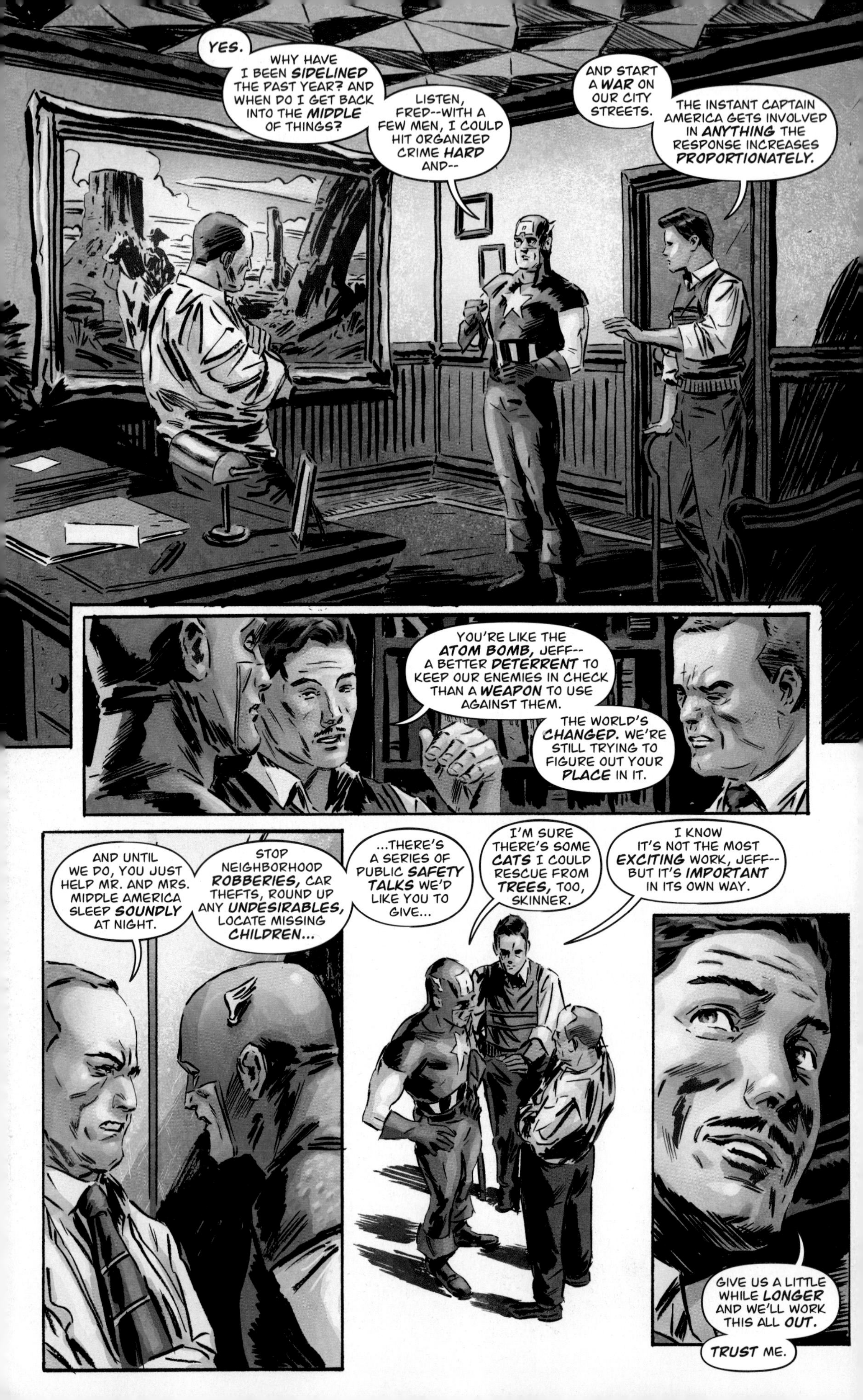
YES.
WHY HAVE I BEEN SIDELINED THE PAST YEAR? AND WHEN DO I GET BACK INTO THE MIDDLE OF THINGS?
LISTEN, FRED--WITH A FEW MEN, I COULD HIT ORGANIZED CRIME HARD AND--
AND START A WAR ON OUR CITY STREETS.
THE INSTANT CAPTAIN AMERICA GETS INVOLVED IN ANYTHING THE RESPONSE INCREASES PROPORTIONATELY.
YOU'RE LIKE THE ATOM BOMB, JEFF-- A BETTER DETERRENT TO KEEP OUR ENEMIES IN CHECK THAN A WEAPON TO USE AGAINST THEM.
THE WORLD'S CHANGED. WE'RE STILL TRYING TO FIGURE OUT YOUR PLACE IN IT.
AND UNTIL WE DO, YOU JUST HELP MR. AND MRS. MIDDLE AMERICA SLEEP SOUNDLY AT NIGHT.
STOP NEIGHBORHOOD ROBBERIES, CAR THEFTS, ROUND UP ANY UNDESIRABLES, LOCATE MISSING CHILDREN...
...THERE'S A SERIES OF PUBLIC SAFETY TALKS WE'D LIKE YOU TO GIVE...
I'M SURE THERE'S SOME CATS I COULD RESCUE FROM TREES, TOO, SKINNER.
I KNOW IT'S NOT THE MOST EXCITING WORK, JEFF-- BUT IT'S IMPORTANT IN ITS OWN WAY.
GIVE US A LITTLE WHILE LONGER AND WE'LL WORK THIS ALL OUT.
TRUST ME.

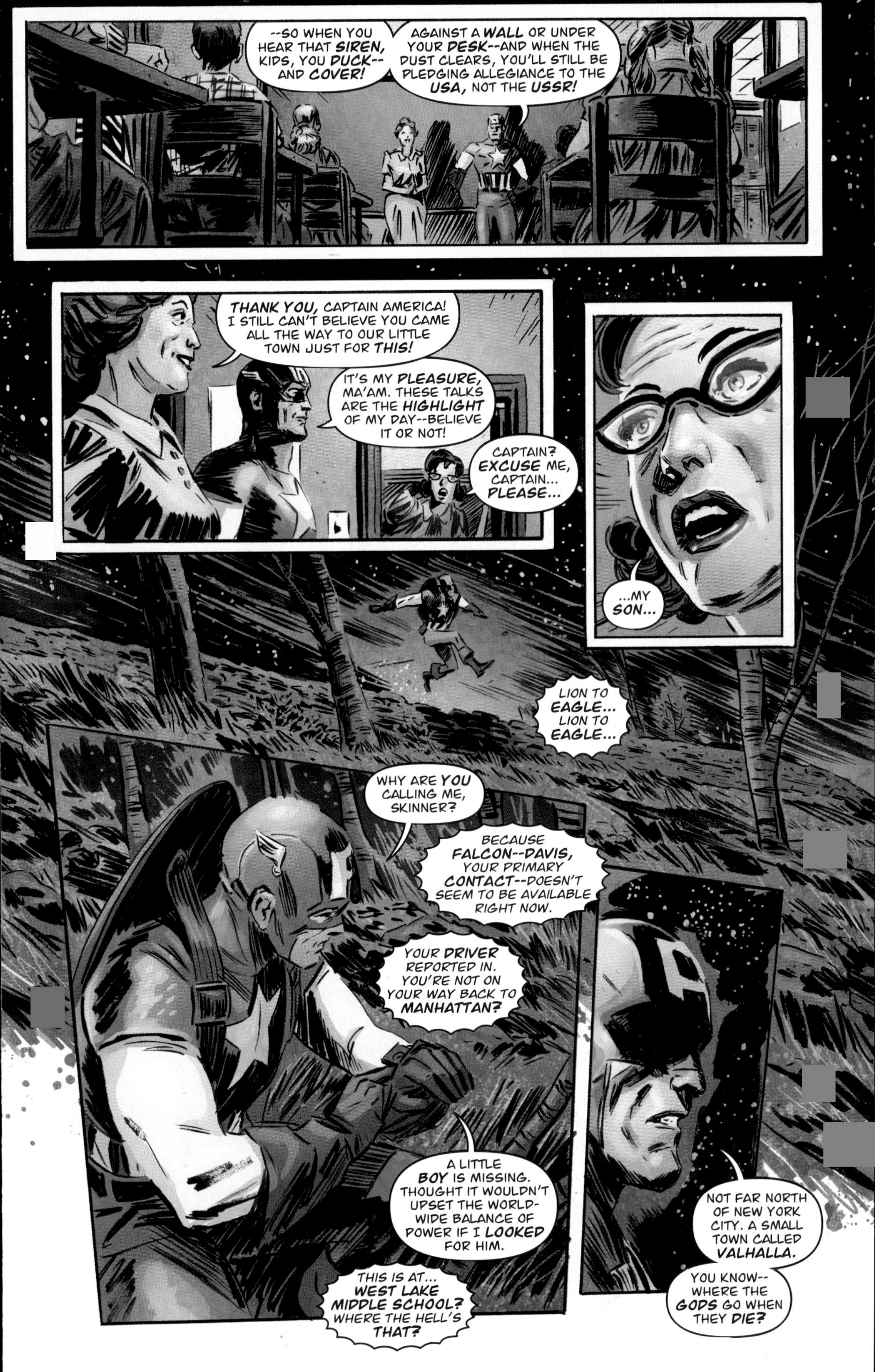
--SO WHEN YOU HEAR THAT SIREN, KIDS, YOU DUCK-- AND COVER!
AGAINST A WALL OR UNDER YOUR DESK--AND WHEN THE DUST CLEARS, YOU'LL STILL BE PLEDGING ALLEGIANCE TO THE USA, NOT THE USSR!
THANK YOU, CAPTAIN AMERICA! I STILL CAN'T BELIEVE YOU CAME ALL THE WAY TO OUR LITTLE TOWN JUST FOR THIS!
IT'S MY PLEASURE, MA'AM. THESE TALKS ARE THE HIGHLIGHT OF MY DAY--BELIEVE IT OR NOT!
CAPTAIN? EXCUSE ME, CAPTAIN... PLEASE...
...MY SON...
LION TO EAGLE... LION TO EAGLE...
WHY ARE YOU CALLING ME, SKINNER?
BECAUSE FALCON--DAVIS, YOUR PRIMARY CONTACT--DOESN'T SEEM TO BE AVAILABLE RIGHT NOW.
YOUR DRIVER REPORTED IN. YOU'RE NOT ON YOUR WAY BACK TO MANHATTAN?
A LITTLE BOY IS MISSING. THOUGHT IT WOULDN'T UPSET THE WORLD-WIDE BALANCE OF POWER IF I LOOKED FOR HIM.
THIS IS AT... WEST LAKE MIDDLE SCHOOL? WHERE THE HELL'S THAT?
NOT FAR NORTH OF NEW YORK CITY. A SMALL TOWN CALLED VALHALLA.
YOU KNOW-- WHERE THE GODS GO WHEN THEY DIE?

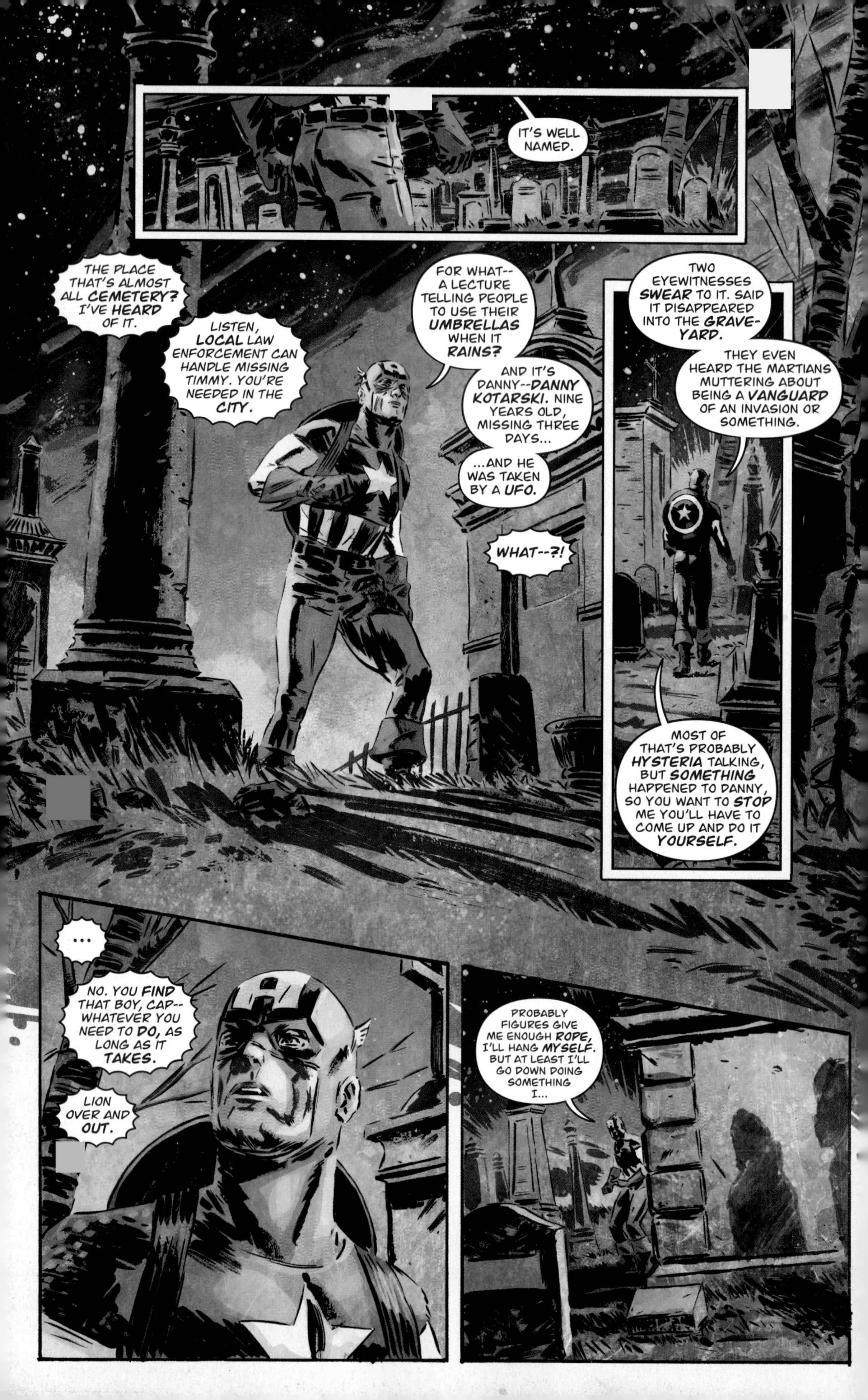
IT'S WELL NAMED.
THE PLACE THAT'S ALMOST ALL CEMETERY? I'VE HEARD OF IT.
LISTEN, LOCAL LAW ENFORCEMENT CAN HANDLE MISSING TIMMY. YOU'RE NEEDED IN THE CITY.
FOR WHAT-- A LECTURE TELLING PEOPLE TO USE THEIR UMBRELLAS WHEN IT RAINS?
AND IT'S DANNY--DANNY KOTARSKI. NINE YEARS OLD, MISSING THREE DAYS...
...AND HE WAS TAKEN BY A UFO.
WHAT--?!
TWO EYEWITNESSES SWEAR TO IT. SAID IT DISAPPEARED INTO THE GRAVE-YARD.
THEY EVEN HEARD THE MARTIANS MUTTERING ABOUT BEING A VANGUARD OF AN INVASION OR SOMETHING.
MOST OF THAT'S PROBABLY HYSTERIA TALKING, BUT SOMETHING HAPPENED TO DANNY, SO YOU WANT TO STOP ME YOU'LL HAVE TO COME UP AND DO IT YOURSELF.
...
NO. YOU FIND THAT BOY, CAP-- WHATEVER YOU NEED TO DO, AS LONG AS IT TAKES.
LION OVER AND OUT.
PROBABLY FIGURES GIVE ME ENOUGH ROPE, I'LL HANG MYSELF. BUT AT LEAST I'LL GO DOWN DOING SOMETHING I...

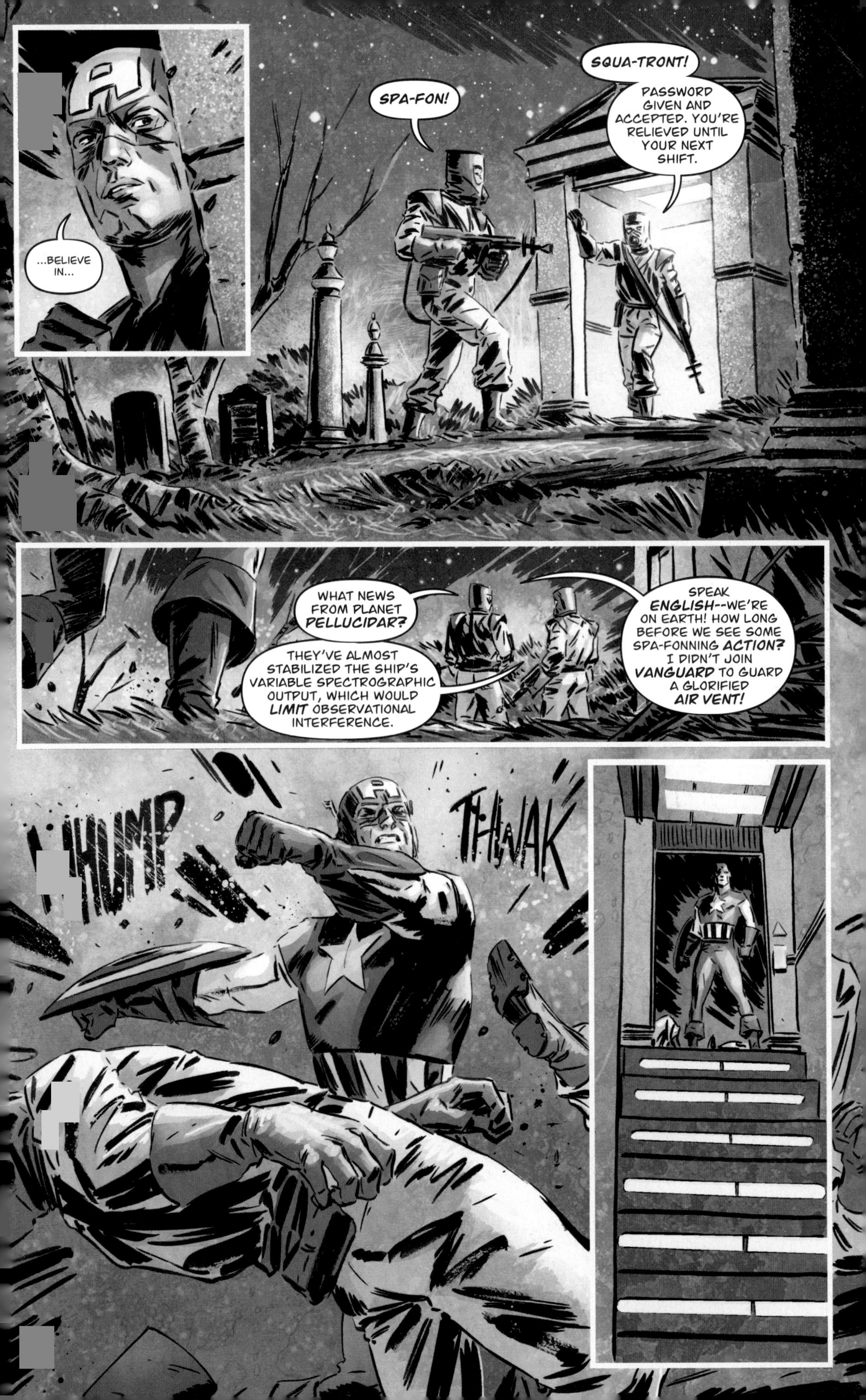
...BELIEVE IN...
SPA-FON!
SQUA-TRONT!
PASSWORD GIVEN AND ACCEPTED. YOU'RE RELIEVED UNTIL YOUR NEXT SHIFT.
WHAT NEWS FROM PLANET PELLUCIDAR?
THEY'VE ALMOST STABILIZED THE SHIP'S VARIABLE SPECTROGRAPHIC OUTPUT, WHICH WOULD LIMIT OBSERVATIONAL INTERFERENCE.
SPEAK ENGLISH--WE'RE ON EARTH! HOW LONG BEFORE WE SEE SOME SPA-FONNING ACTION? I DIDN'T JOIN VANGUARD TO GUARD A GLORIFIED AIR VENT!
THUMP
THWAK

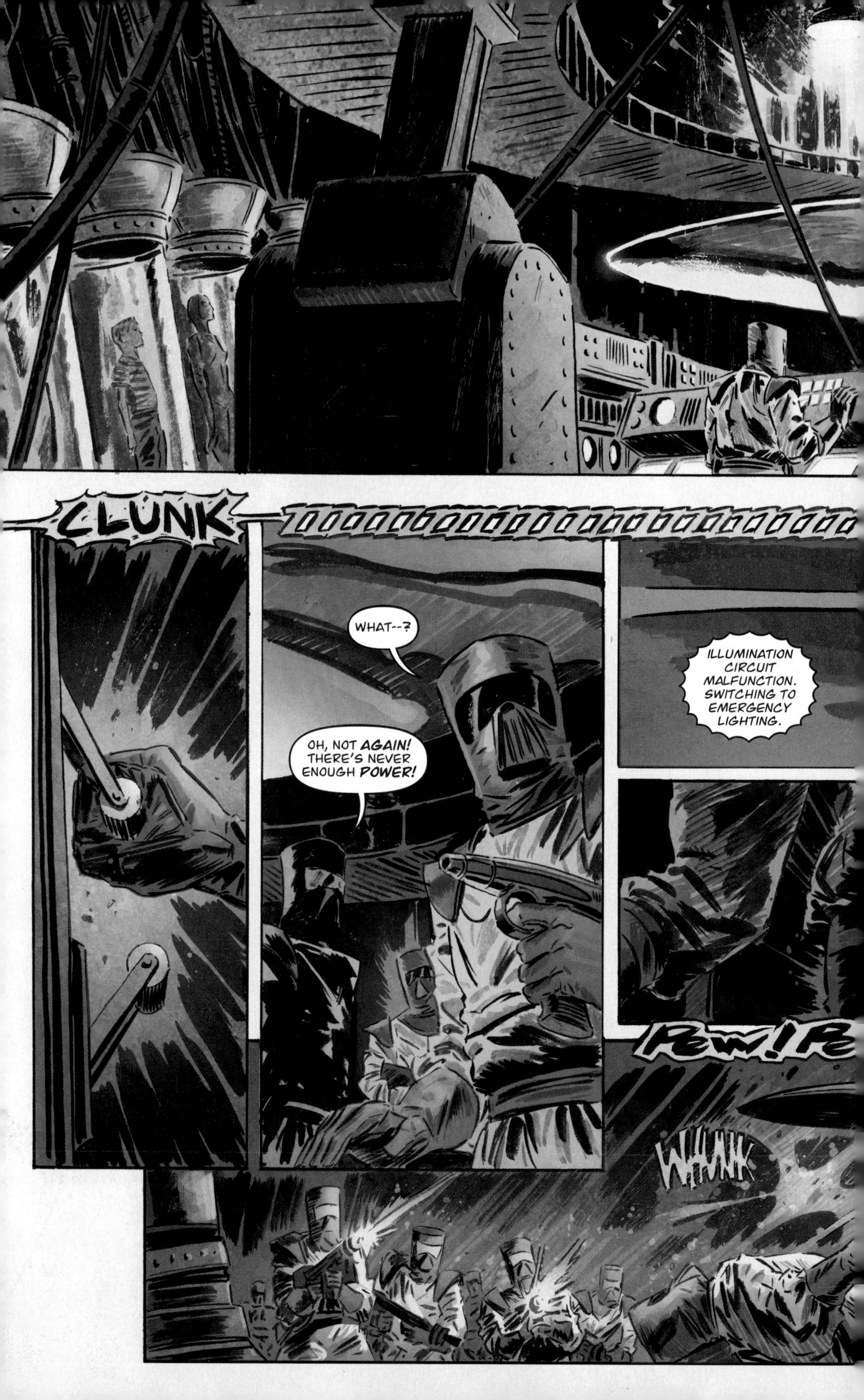
CLUNK
WHAT--?
OH, NOT AGAIN! THERE'S NEVER ENOUGH POWER!
ILLUMINATION CIRCUIT MALFUNCTION. SWITCHING TO EMERGENCY LIGHTING.
WHUNK

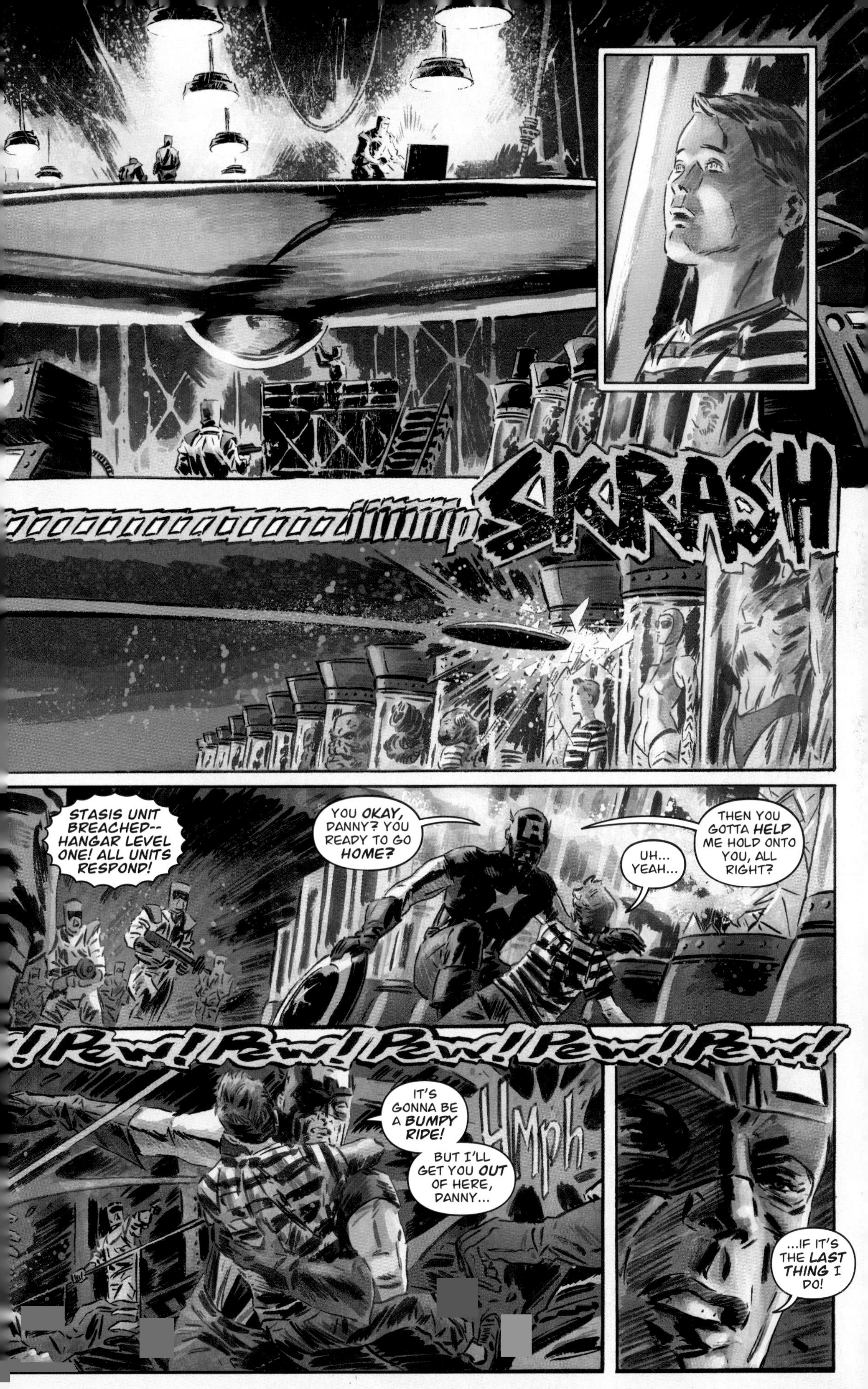
SKRASH
STASIS UNIT BREACHED-- HANGAR LEVEL ONE! ALL UNITS RESPOND!
YOU OKAY, DANNY? YOU READY TO GO HOME?
UH... YEAH...
THEN YOU GOTTA HELP ME HOLD ONTO YOU, ALL RIGHT?
Pew! Pew! Pew! Pew! Pew!
IT'S GONNA BE A BUMPY RIDE!
BUT I'LL GET YOU OUT OF HERE, DANNY...
...IF IT'S THE LAST THING I DO!

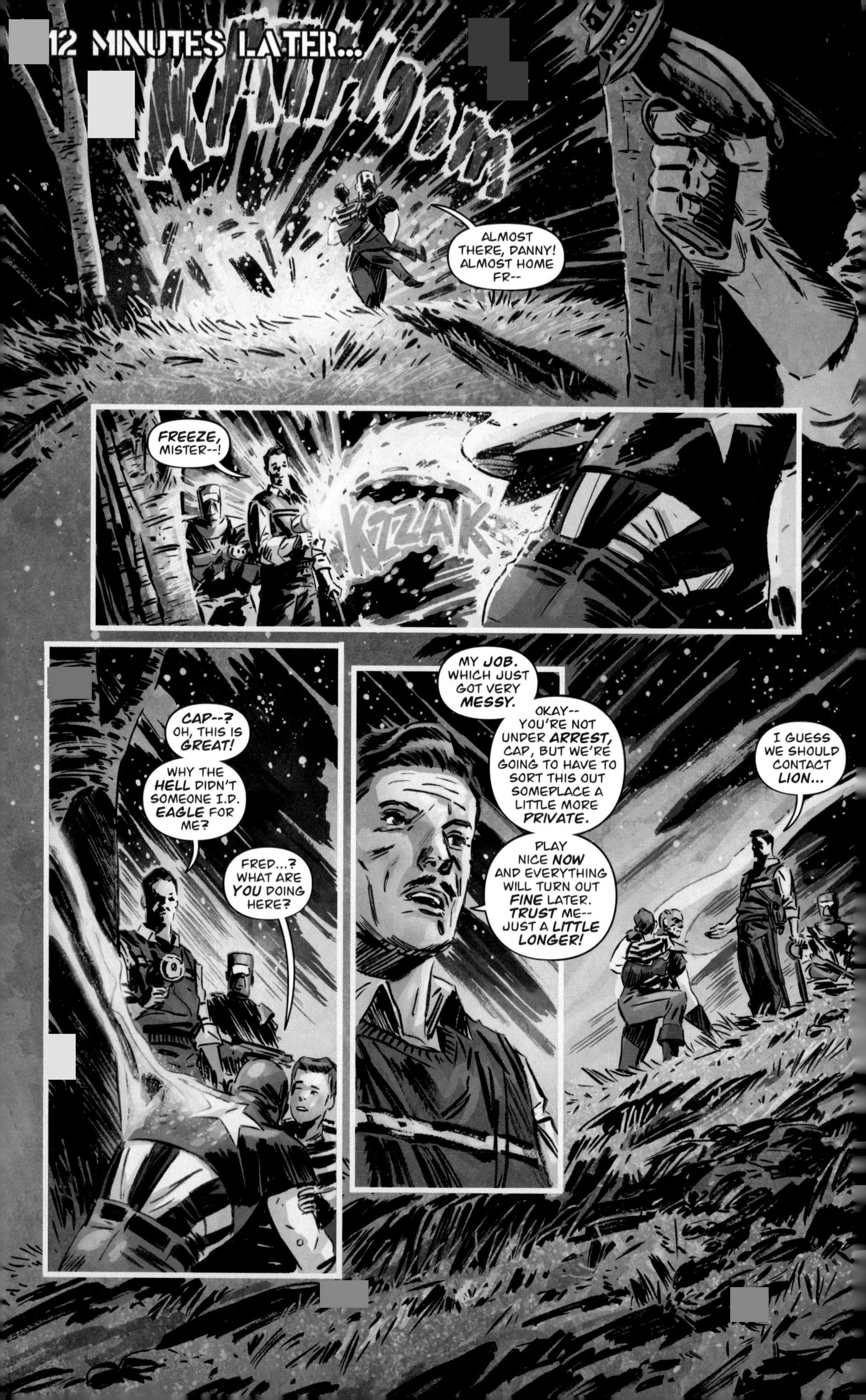
12 MINUTES LATER...
ALMOST THERE, DANNY! ALMOST HOME FR--
FREEZE, MISTER--!
KZZAK
CAP--? OH, THIS IS GREAT!
WHY THE HELL DIDN'T SOMEONE I.D. EAGLE FOR ME?
FRED...? WHAT ARE YOU DOING HERE?
MY JOB. WHICH JUST GOT VERY MESSY.
OKAY-- YOU'RE NOT UNDER ARREST, CAP, BUT WE'RE GOING TO HAVE TO SORT THIS OUT SOMEPLACE A LITTLE MORE PRIVATE.
PLAY NICE NOW AND EVERYTHING WILL TURN OUT FINE LATER. TRUST ME-- JUST A LITTLE LONGER!
I GUESS WE SHOULD CONTACT LION...

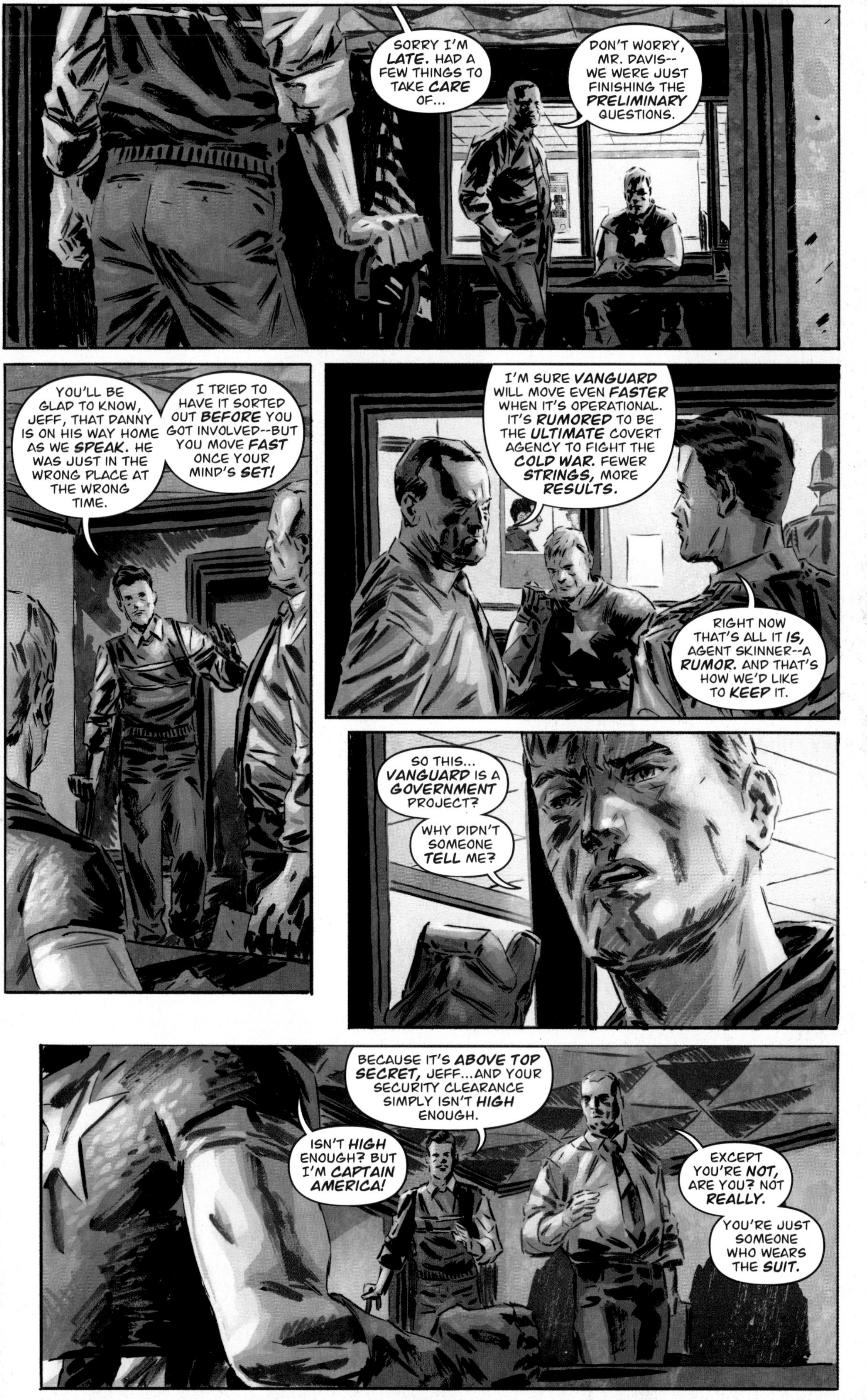
SORRY I'M LATE. HAD A FEW THINGS TO TAKE CARE OF...
DON'T WORRY, MR. DAVIS-- WE WERE JUST FINISHING THE PRELIMINARY QUESTIONS.
YOU'LL BE GLAD TO KNOW, JEFF, THAT DANNY IS ON HIS WAY HOME AS WE SPEAK. HE WAS JUST IN THE WRONG PLACE AT THE WRONG TIME.
I TRIED TO HAVE IT SORTED OUT BEFORE YOU GOT INVOLVED--BUT YOU MOVE FAST ONCE YOUR MIND'S SET!
I'M SURE VANGUARD WILL MOVE EVEN FASTER WHEN IT'S OPERATIONAL. IT'S RUMORED TO BE THE ULTIMATE COVERT AGENCY TO FIGHT THE COLD WAR. FEWER STRINGS, MORE RESULTS.
RIGHT NOW THAT'S ALL IT IS, AGENT SKINNER--A RUMOR. AND THAT'S HOW WE'D LIKE TO KEEP IT.
SO THIS... VANGUARD IS A GOVERNMENT PROJECT?
WHY DIDN'T SOMEONE TELL ME?
BECAUSE IT'S ABOVE TOP SECRET, JEFF...AND YOUR SECURITY CLEARANCE SIMPLY ISN'T HIGH ENOUGH.
ISN'T HIGH ENOUGH? BUT I'M CAPTAIN AMERICA!
EXCEPT YOU'RE NOT, ARE YOU? NOT REALLY.
YOU'RE JUST SOMEONE WHO WEARS THE SUIT.

AND IF I'D HAD *MY* WAY--IF WE'D LOOKED INTO YOUR PAST *PROPERLY* AND HADN'T *RUSHED* YOU OUT IN FRONT OF GOD AND EVERYONE--IF WE KNEW *THEN* WHAT WE KNOW *NOW*...

...YOU'D HAVE *NEVER* BECOME CAPTAIN AMERICA!

YOUR PRE-WAR REPORTING IS NOTICEABLY *LEFTIST,* AND SOME OF THE LABOR MOVEMENTS YOU CHAMPIONED HAD *KNOWN COMMUNISTS* AS MEMBERS.

I DIDN'T KNOW THAT *THEN*--I WAS JUST FOLLOWING THE *NEWS.* MARY HAD THE *CONNECTIONS* AND ALWAYS KNEW WHERE THINGS WOULD GET *HOT.*

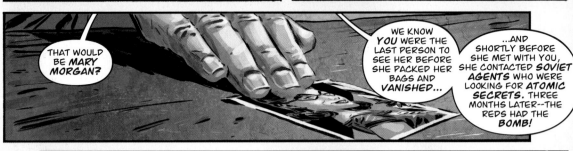

THAT WOULD BE *MARY MORGAN*?

WE KNOW *YOU* WERE THE LAST PERSON TO SEE HER BEFORE SHE PACKED HER BAGS AND *VANISHED*...

...AND SHORTLY BEFORE SHE MET WITH YOU, SHE CONTACTED *SOVIET AGENTS* WHO WERE LOOKING FOR *ATOMIC SECRETS.* THREE MONTHS LATER--THE REDS HAD THE *BOMB*!

THAT'S QUITE A *LEAP*--AND ONE I CAN'T BELIEVE MARY WOULD *MAKE.*

LOOK, I WAS AFTER THE PERSON WHO *SHOT BUCKY* THAT DAY. I WOULDN'T HAVE *FOUND* THAT PERSON WITHOUT *MARY'S* HELP.

SURE, IF SHE DIDN'T LIKE SOMETHING SHE *SPOKE UP*--BUT THAT'S BECAUSE SHE *LOVED* THIS COUNTRY AND WANTED TO MAKE IT *BETTER.*

I THINK THERE WAS ONE THING SHE LOVED *MORE,* JEFF-- *YOU.* AND YOU BROKE HER *HEART.*

CAPTAIN AMERICA BROKE HER HEART.

YEAH...

YEAH, I KNOW I COULDN'T GIVE HER WHAT SHE *WANTED,* AND I CAN SEE HER GOING SOMEPLACE SO SHE NEVER RUNS INTO ME *AGAIN,* BUT...

TREASON? BECAUSE OF *ME*?

THAT'S JUST TOO...*INDIRECT* FOR MARY. IF SHE HAD A *BEEF* WITH YOU, YOU *KNEW* IT!

WE'LL SEE WHAT SHE SAYS WHEN WE *FIND* HER.

THAT'S A *LAUGH.* YOU'LL *NEVER* FIND HER.

THEN *YOUR* NAME WILL NEVER BE *CLEARED.*

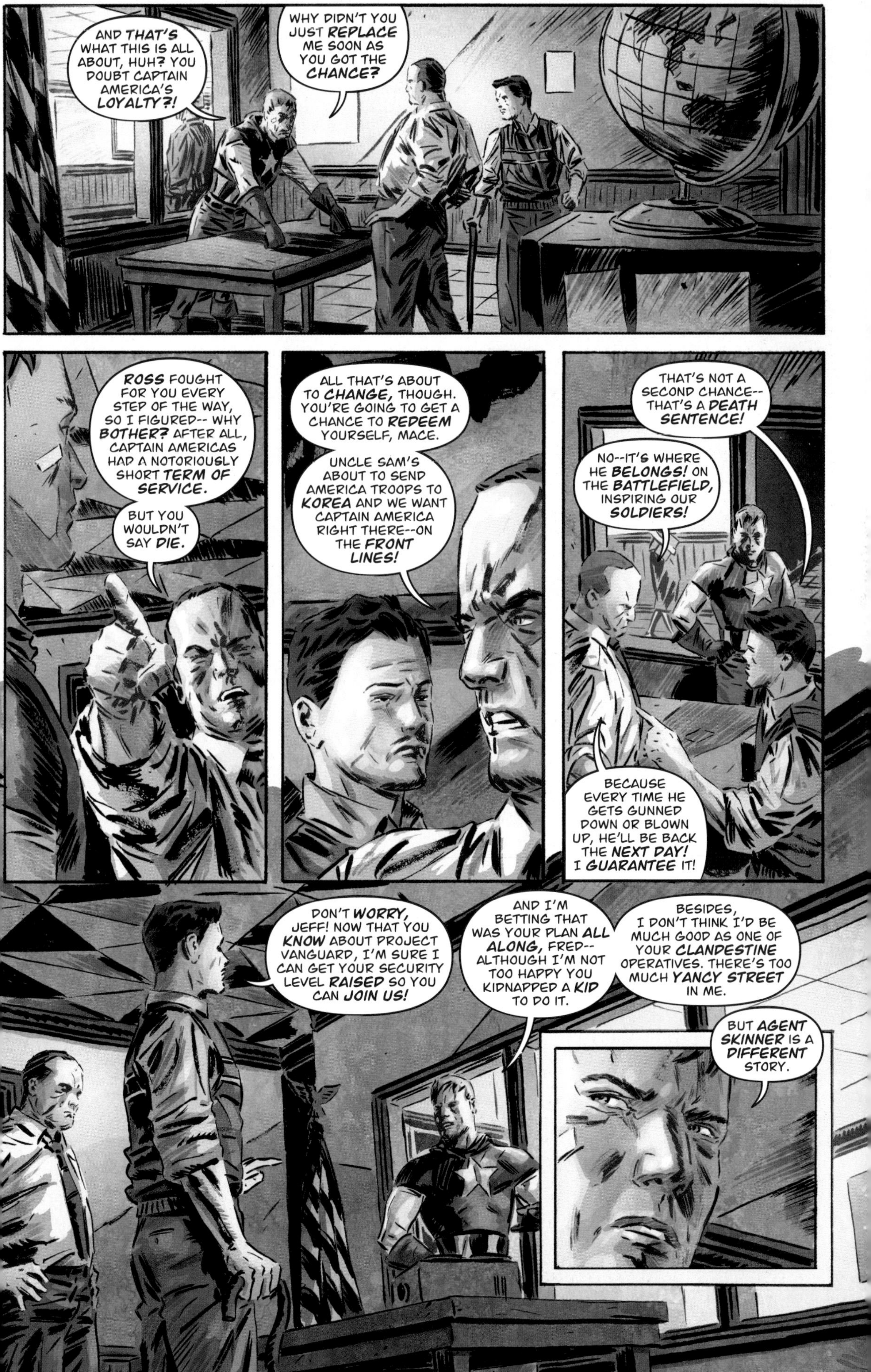
AND THAT'S WHAT THIS IS ALL ABOUT, HUH? YOU DOUBT CAPTAIN AMERICA'S LOYALTY?!
WHY DIDN'T YOU JUST REPLACE ME SOON AS YOU GOT THE CHANCE?
ROSS FOUGHT FOR YOU EVERY STEP OF THE WAY, SO I FIGURED-- WHY BOTHER? AFTER ALL, CAPTAIN AMERICAS HAD A NOTORIOUSLY SHORT TERM OF SERVICE.
BUT YOU WOULDN'T SAY DIE.
ALL THAT'S ABOUT TO CHANGE, THOUGH. YOU'RE GOING TO GET A CHANCE TO REDEEM YOURSELF, MACE.
UNCLE SAM'S ABOUT TO SEND AMERICA TROOPS TO KOREA AND WE WANT CAPTAIN AMERICA RIGHT THERE--ON THE FRONT LINES!
THAT'S NOT A SECOND CHANCE-- THAT'S A DEATH SENTENCE!
NO--IT'S WHERE HE BELONGS! ON THE BATTLEFIELD, INSPIRING OUR SOLDIERS!
BECAUSE EVERY TIME HE GETS GUNNED DOWN OR BLOWN UP, HE'LL BE BACK THE NEXT DAY! I GUARANTEE IT!
DON'T WORRY, JEFF! NOW THAT YOU KNOW ABOUT PROJECT VANGUARD, I'M SURE I CAN GET YOUR SECURITY LEVEL RAISED SO YOU CAN JOIN US!
AND I'M BETTING THAT WAS YOUR PLAN ALL ALONG, FRED-- ALTHOUGH I'M NOT TOO HAPPY YOU KIDNAPPED A KID TO DO IT.
BESIDES, I DON'T THINK I'D BE MUCH GOOD AS ONE OF YOUR CLANDESTINE OPERATIVES. THERE'S TOO MUCH YANCY STREET IN ME.
BUT AGENT SKINNER IS A DIFFERENT STORY.

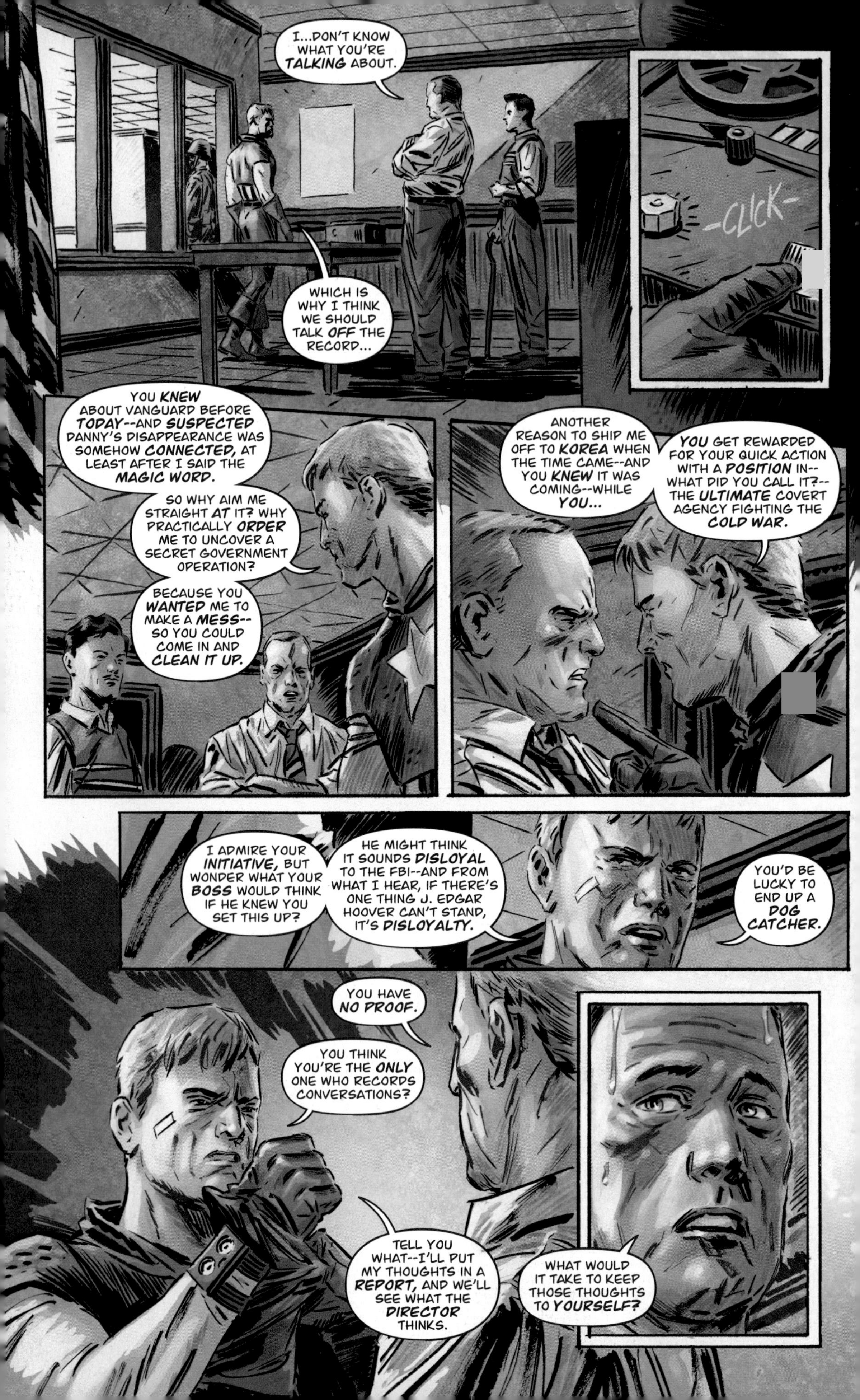
I...DON'T KNOW WHAT YOU'RE TALKING ABOUT.
WHICH IS WHY I THINK WE SHOULD TALK OFF THE RECORD...
-CLICK-
YOU KNEW ABOUT VANGUARD BEFORE TODAY--AND SUSPECTED DANNY'S DISAPPEARANCE WAS SOMEHOW CONNECTED, AT LEAST AFTER I SAID THE MAGIC WORD.
SO WHY AIM ME STRAIGHT AT IT? WHY PRACTICALLY ORDER ME TO UNCOVER A SECRET GOVERNMENT OPERATION?
BECAUSE YOU WANTED ME TO MAKE A MESS--SO YOU COULD COME IN AND CLEAN IT UP.
ANOTHER REASON TO SHIP ME OFF TO KOREA WHEN THE TIME CAME--AND YOU KNEW IT WAS COMING--WHILE YOU...
YOU GET REWARDED FOR YOUR QUICK ACTION WITH A POSITION IN--WHAT DID YOU CALL IT?--THE ULTIMATE COVERT AGENCY FIGHTING THE COLD WAR.
I ADMIRE YOUR INITIATIVE, BUT WONDER WHAT YOUR BOSS WOULD THINK IF HE KNEW YOU SET THIS UP?
HE MIGHT THINK IT SOUNDS DISLOYAL TO THE FBI--AND FROM WHAT I HEAR, IF THERE'S ONE THING J. EDGAR HOOVER CAN'T STAND, IT'S DISLOYALTY.
YOU'D BE LUCKY TO END UP A DOG CATCHER.
YOU HAVE NO PROOF.
YOU THINK YOU'RE THE ONLY ONE WHO RECORDS CONVERSATIONS?
TELL YOU WHAT--I'LL PUT MY THOUGHTS IN A REPORT, AND WE'LL SEE WHAT THE DIRECTOR THINKS.
WHAT WOULD IT TAKE TO KEEP THOSE THOUGHTS TO YOURSELF?

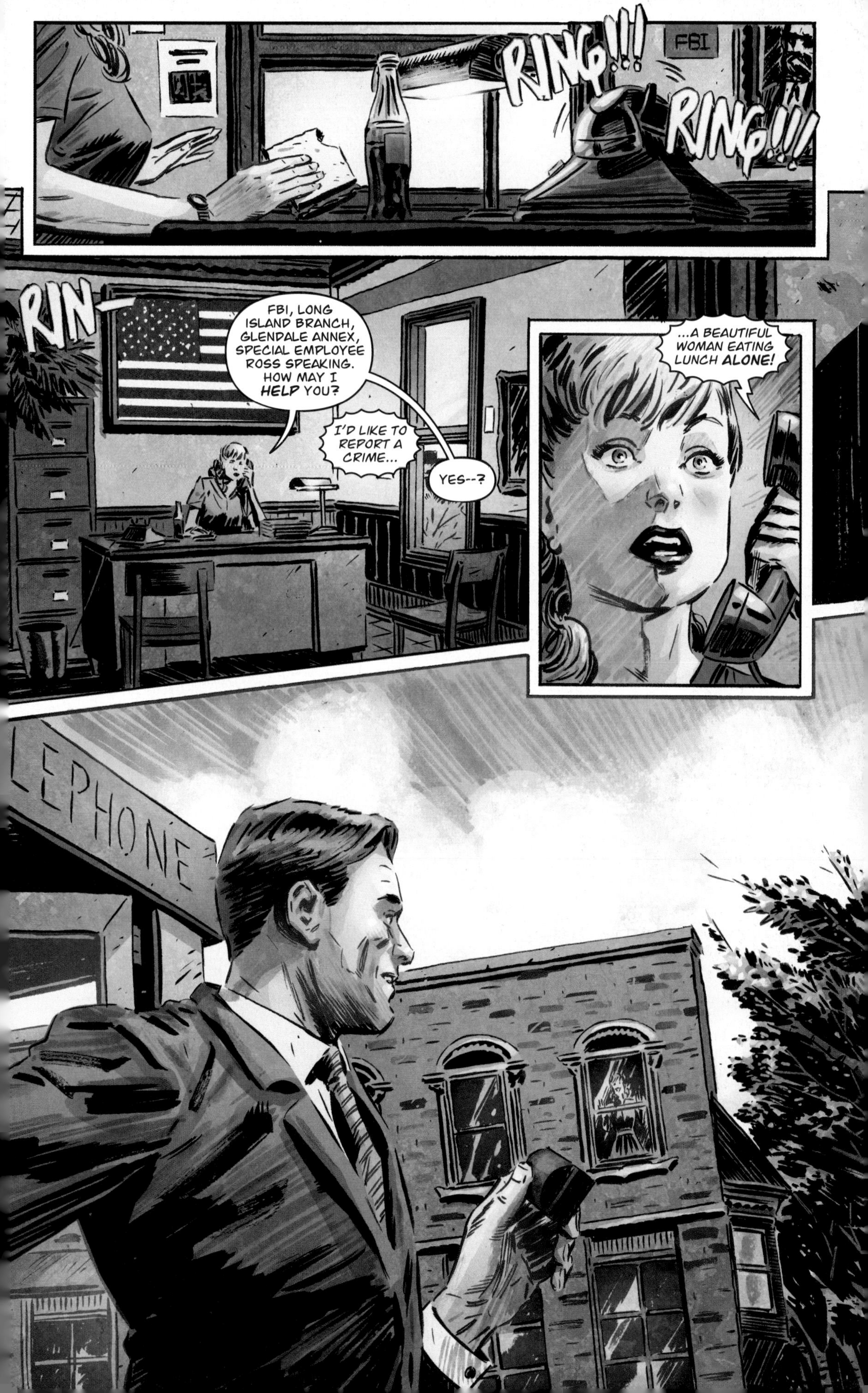
RING!!!
RING!!!
RIN--
FBI, LONG ISLAND BRANCH, GLENDALE ANNEX, SPECIAL EMPLOYEE ROSS SPEAKING. HOW MAY I HELP YOU?
I'D LIKE TO REPORT A CRIME...
YES--?
...A BEAUTIFUL WOMAN EATING LUNCH ALONE!
LEPHONE

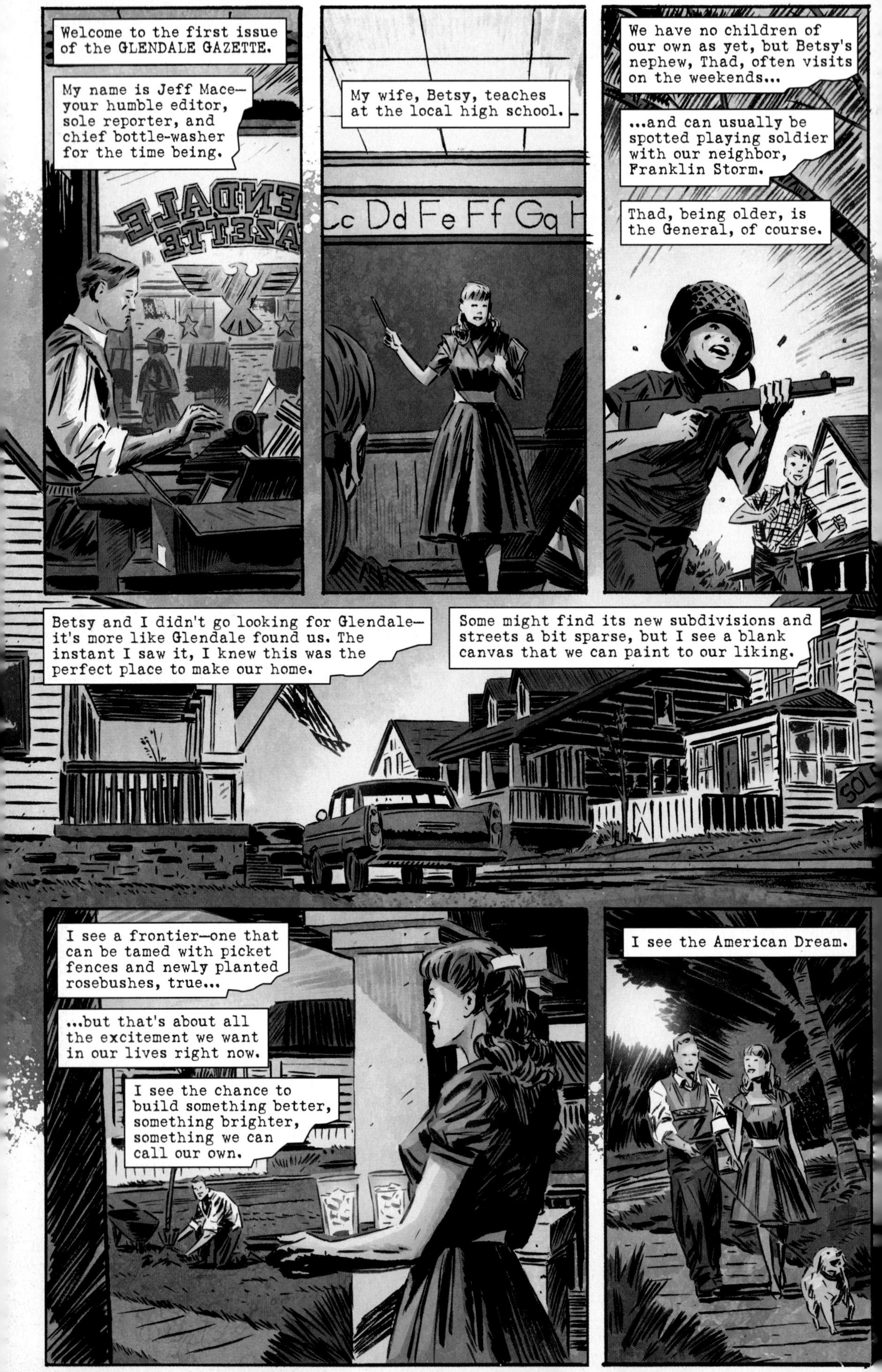

Welcome to the first issue of the GLENDALE GAZETTE.
My name is Jeff Mace—your humble editor, sole reporter, and chief bottle-washer for the time being.
My wife, Betsy, teaches at the local high school.
We have no children of our own as yet, but Betsy's nephew, Thad, often visits on the weekends...
...and can usually be spotted playing soldier with our neighbor, Franklin Storm.
Thad, being older, is the General, of course.
Betsy and I didn't go looking for Glendale—it's more like Glendale found us. The instant I saw it, I knew this was the perfect place to make our home.
Some might find its new subdivisions and streets a bit sparse, but I see a blank canvas that we can paint to our liking.
I see a frontier—one that can be tamed with picket fences and newly planted rosebushes, true...
...but that's about all the excitement we want in our lives right now.
I see the chance to build something better, something brighter, something we can call our own.
I see the American Dream.

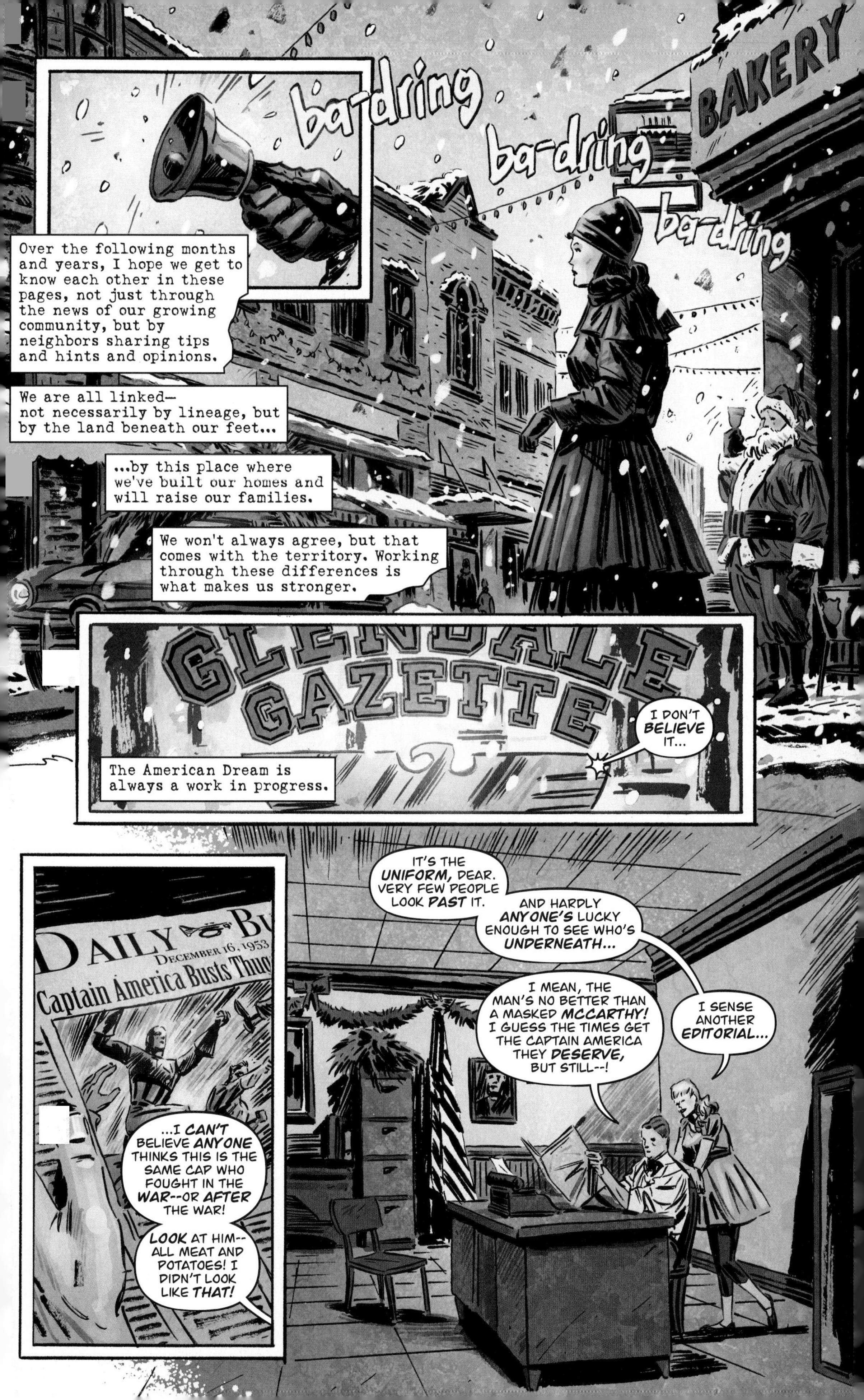

ba-dring
ba-dring
BAKERY
ba-dring
Over the following months and years, I hope we get to know each other in these pages, not just through the news of our growing community, but by neighbors sharing tips and hints and opinions.
We are all linked—not necessarily by lineage, but by the land beneath our feet...
...by this place where we've built our homes and will raise our families.
We won't always agree, but that comes with the territory. Working through these differences is what makes us stronger.
GLENDALE GAZETTE
The American Dream is always a work in progress.
I DON'T BELIEVE IT...
December 16, 1953
Captain America Busts
...I CAN'T BELIEVE ANYONE THINKS THIS IS THE SAME CAP WHO FOUGHT IN THE WAR--OR AFTER THE WAR!
LOOK AT HIM--ALL MEAT AND POTATOES! I DIDN'T LOOK LIKE THAT!
IT'S THE UNIFORM, DEAR. VERY FEW PEOPLE LOOK PAST IT.
AND HARDLY ANYONE'S LUCKY ENOUGH TO SEE WHO'S UNDERNEATH...
I MEAN, THE MAN'S NO BETTER THAN A MASKED MCCARTHY! I GUESS THE TIMES GET THE CAPTAIN AMERICA THEY DESERVE, BUT STILL--!
I SENSE ANOTHER EDITORIAL...

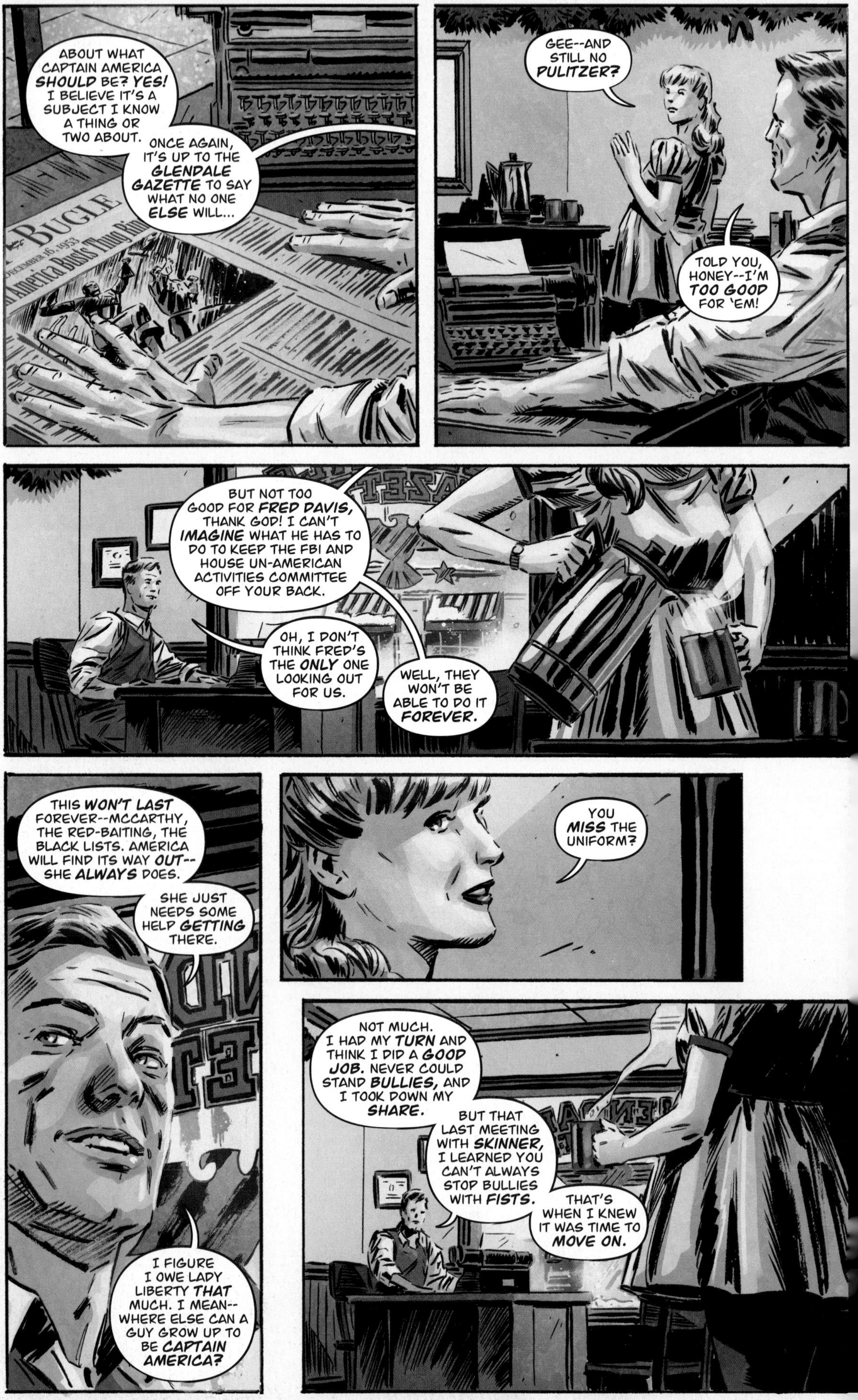
ABOUT WHAT CAPTAIN AMERICA SHOULD BE? YES! I BELIEVE IT'S A SUBJECT I KNOW A THING OR TWO ABOUT.
ONCE AGAIN, IT'S UP TO THE GLENDALE GAZETTE TO SAY WHAT NO ONE ELSE WILL...
BUGLE
GEE--AND STILL NO PULITZER?
TOLD YOU, HONEY--I'M TOO GOOD FOR 'EM!
BUT NOT TOO GOOD FOR FRED DAVIS, THANK GOD! I CAN'T IMAGINE WHAT HE HAS TO DO TO KEEP THE FBI AND HOUSE UN-AMERICAN ACTIVITIES COMMITTEE OFF YOUR BACK.
OH, I DON'T THINK FRED'S THE ONLY ONE LOOKING OUT FOR US.
WELL, THEY WON'T BE ABLE TO DO IT FOREVER.
THIS WON'T LAST FOREVER--MCCARTHY, THE RED-BAITING, THE BLACK LISTS. AMERICA WILL FIND ITS WAY OUT--SHE ALWAYS DOES.
SHE JUST NEEDS SOME HELP GETTING THERE.
I FIGURE I OWE LADY LIBERTY THAT MUCH. I MEAN--WHERE ELSE CAN A GUY GROW UP TO BE CAPTAIN AMERICA?
YOU MISS THE UNIFORM?
NOT MUCH. I HAD MY TURN AND THINK I DID A GOOD JOB. NEVER COULD STAND BULLIES, AND I TOOK DOWN MY SHARE.
BUT THAT LAST MEETING WITH SKINNER, I LEARNED YOU CAN'T ALWAYS STOP BULLIES WITH FISTS.
THAT'S WHEN I KNEW IT WAS TIME TO MOVE ON.

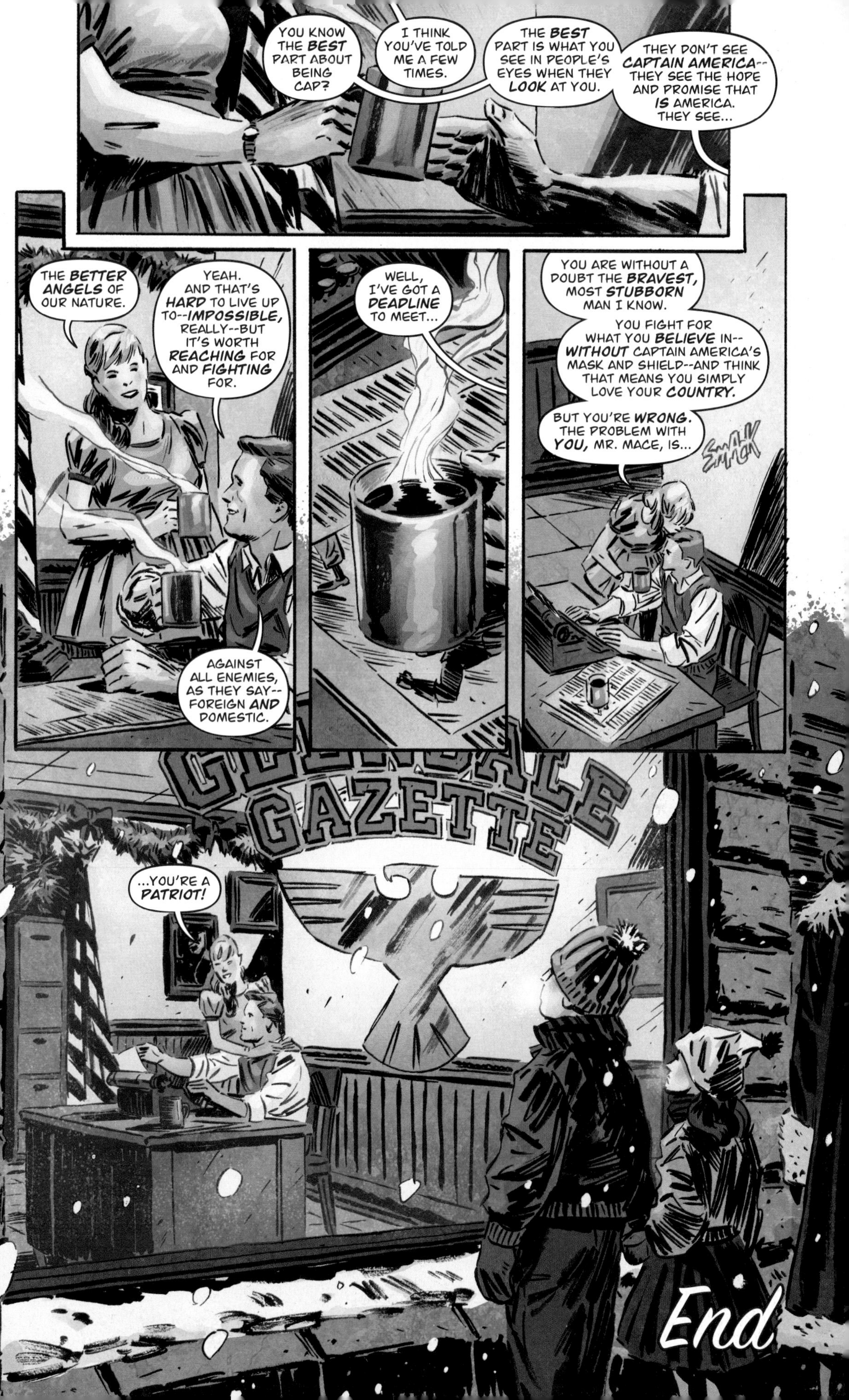
YOU KNOW THE BEST PART ABOUT BEING CAP?
I THINK YOU'VE TOLD ME A FEW TIMES.
THE BEST PART IS WHAT YOU SEE IN PEOPLE'S EYES WHEN THEY LOOK AT YOU.
THEY DON'T SEE CAPTAIN AMERICA--THEY SEE THE HOPE AND PROMISE THAT IS AMERICA. THEY SEE...
THE BETTER ANGELS OF OUR NATURE.
YEAH. AND THAT'S HARD TO LIVE UP TO--IMPOSSIBLE, REALLY--BUT IT'S WORTH REACHING FOR AND FIGHTING FOR.
AGAINST ALL ENEMIES, AS THEY SAY--FOREIGN AND DOMESTIC.
WELL, I'VE GOT A DEADLINE TO MEET...
YOU ARE WITHOUT A DOUBT THE BRAVEST, MOST STUBBORN MAN I KNOW.
YOU FIGHT FOR WHAT YOU BELIEVE IN--WITHOUT CAPTAIN AMERICA'S MASK AND SHIELD--AND THINK THAT MEANS YOU SIMPLY LOVE YOUR COUNTRY.
BUT YOU'RE WRONG. THE PROBLEM WITH YOU, MR. MACE, IS...
SMACK
GAZETTE
...YOU'RE A PATRIOT!
End

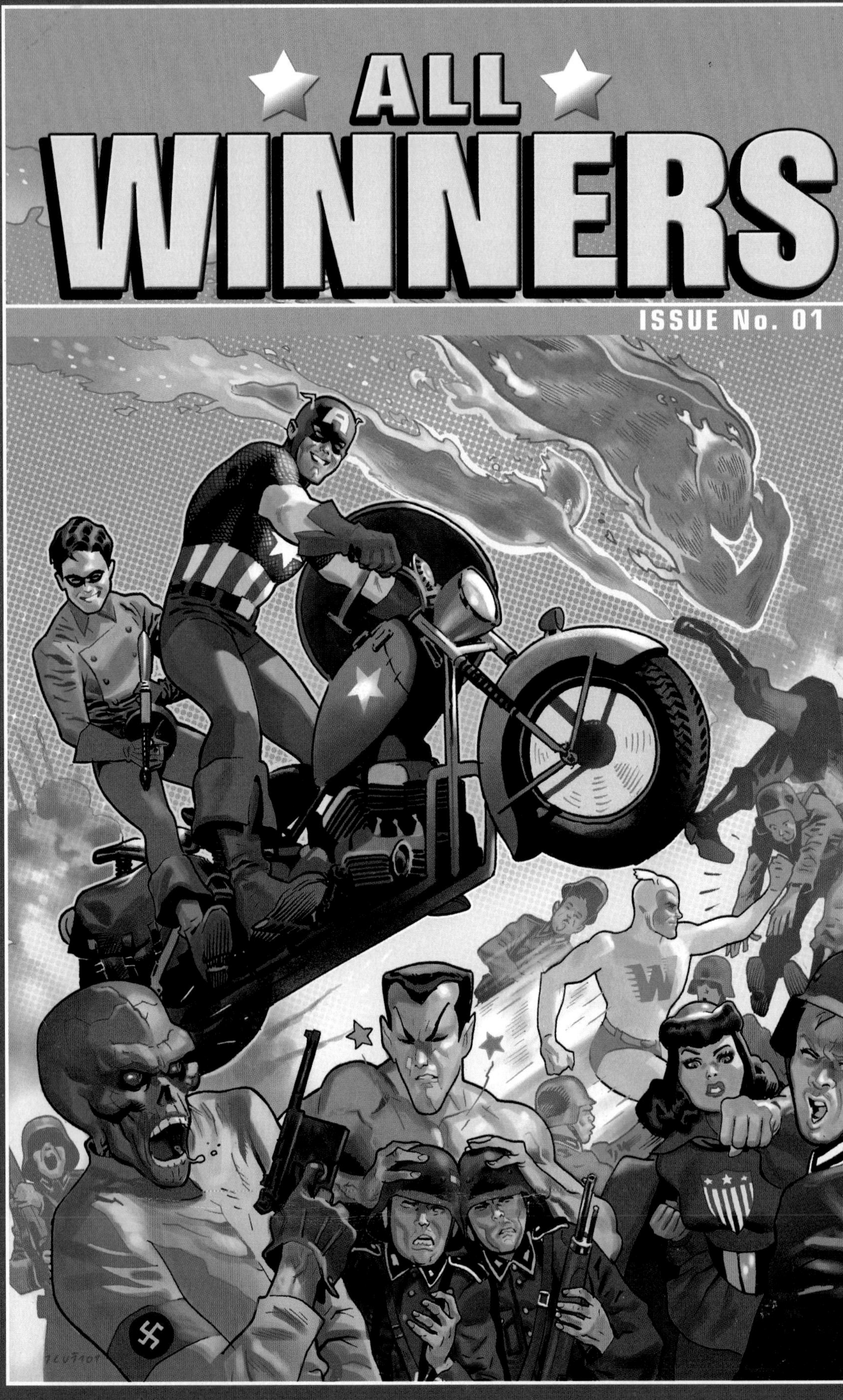
ALL WINNERS
ISSUE No. 01

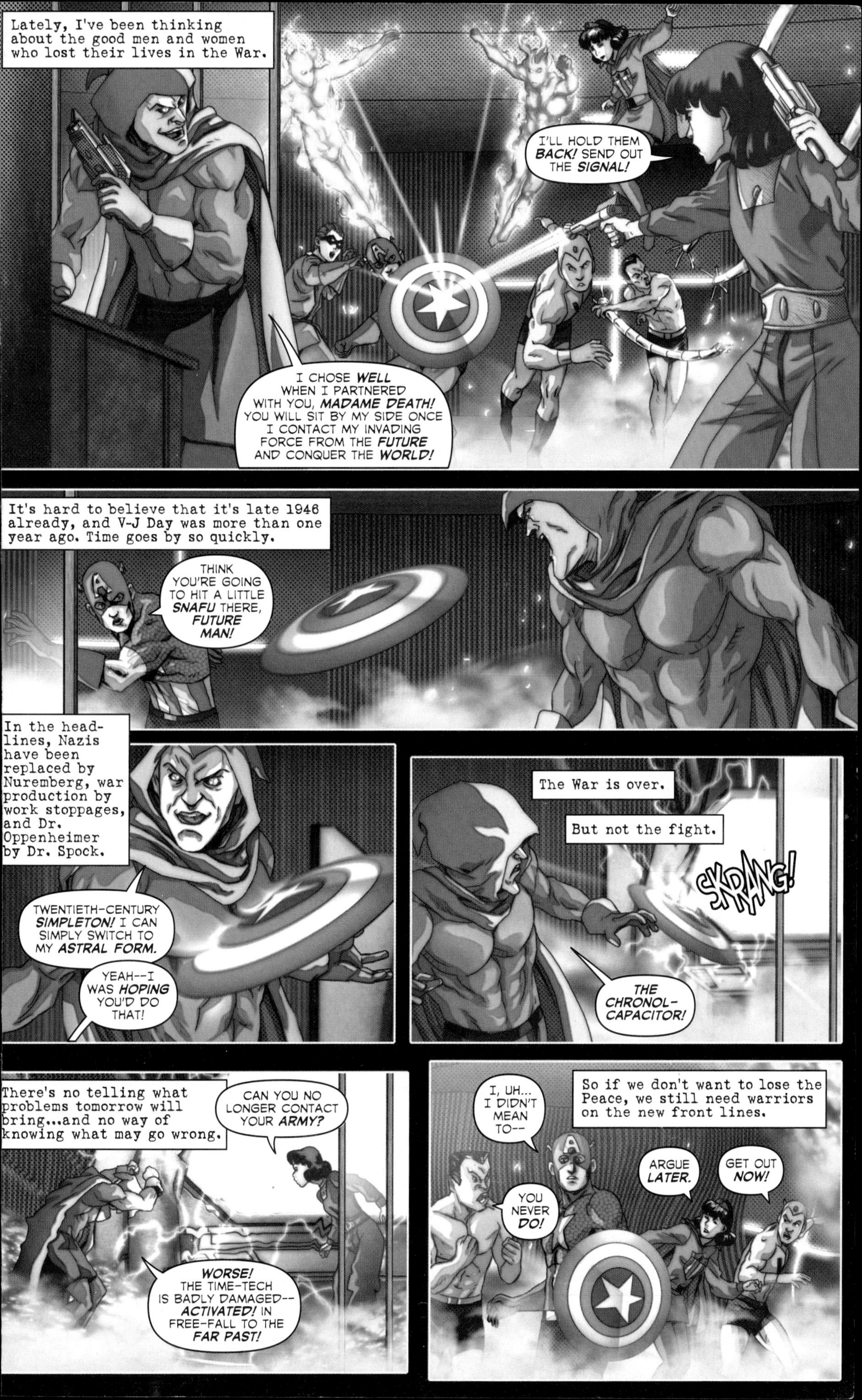
Lately, I've been thinking about the good men and women who lost their lives in the War.
I'LL HOLD THEM BACK! SEND OUT THE SIGNAL!
I CHOSE WELL WHEN I PARTNERED WITH YOU, MADAME DEATH! YOU WILL SIT BY MY SIDE ONCE I CONTACT MY INVADING FORCE FROM THE FUTURE AND CONQUER THE WORLD!
It's hard to believe that it's late 1946 already, and V-J Day was more than one year ago. Time goes by so quickly.
THINK YOU'RE GOING TO HIT A LITTLE SNAFU THERE, FUTURE MAN!
In the head-lines, Nazis have been replaced by Nuremberg, war production by work stoppages, and Dr. Oppenheimer by Dr. Spock.
TWENTIETH-CENTURY SIMPLETON! I CAN SIMPLY SWITCH TO MY ASTRAL FORM.
YEAH--I WAS HOPING YOU'D DO THAT!
The War is over.
But not the fight.
SKRANG!
THE CHRONOL-CAPACITOR!
There's no telling what problems tomorrow will bring...and no way of knowing what may go wrong.
CAN YOU NO LONGER CONTACT YOUR ARMY?
WORSE! THE TIME-TECH IS BADLY DAMAGED--ACTIVATED! IN FREE-FALL TO THE FAR PAST!
So if we don't want to lose the Peace, we still need warriors on the new front lines.
I, UH... I DIDN'T MEAN TO--
YOU NEVER DO!
ARGUE LATER.
GET OUT NOW!

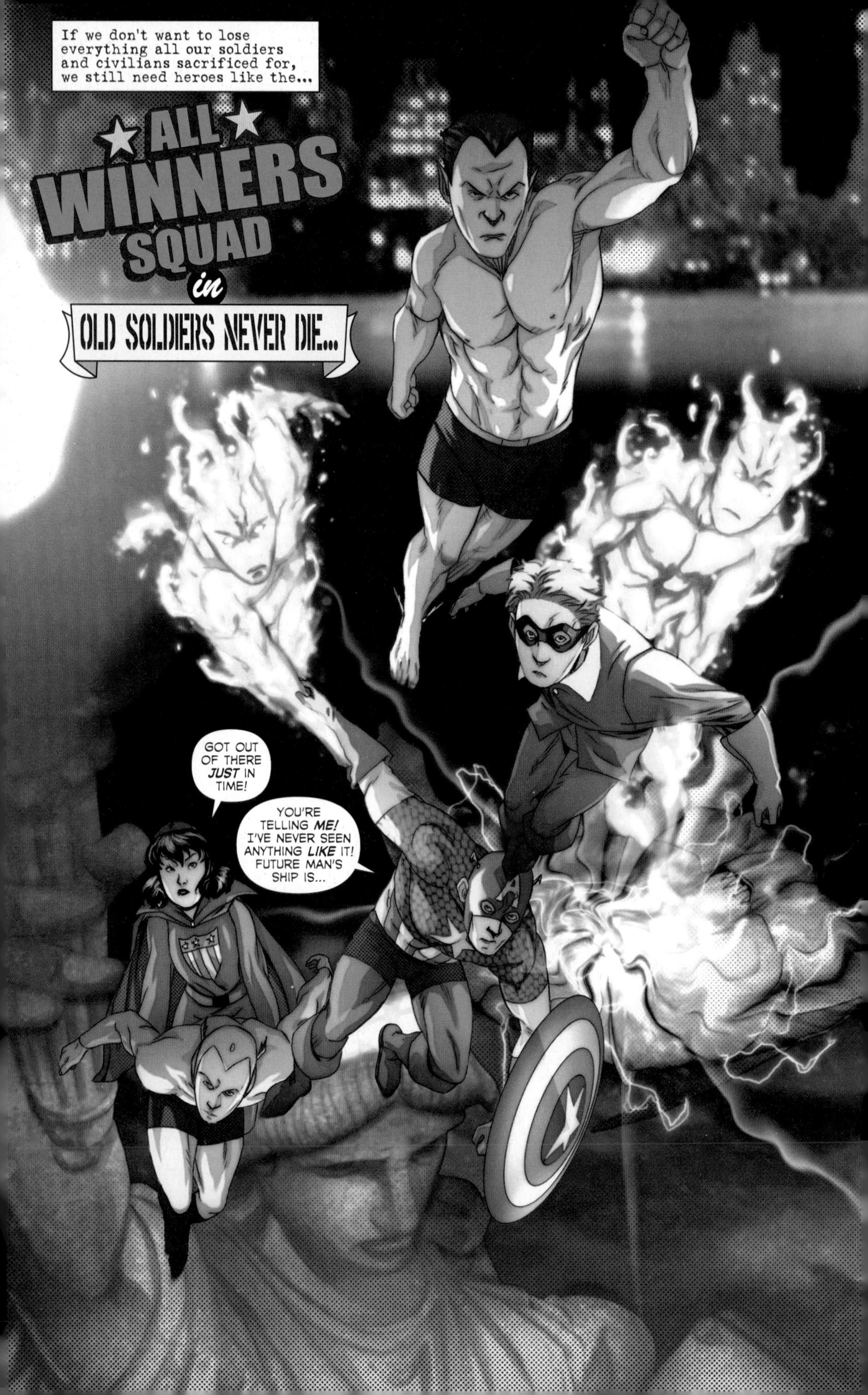
If we don't want to lose everything all our soldiers and civilians sacrificed for, we still need heroes like the...
ALL WINNERS SQUAD
in
OLD SOLDIERS NEVER DIE...
GOT OUT OF THERE JUST IN TIME!
YOU'RE TELLING ME! I'VE NEVER SEEN ANYTHING LIKE IT! FUTURE MAN'S SHIP IS...

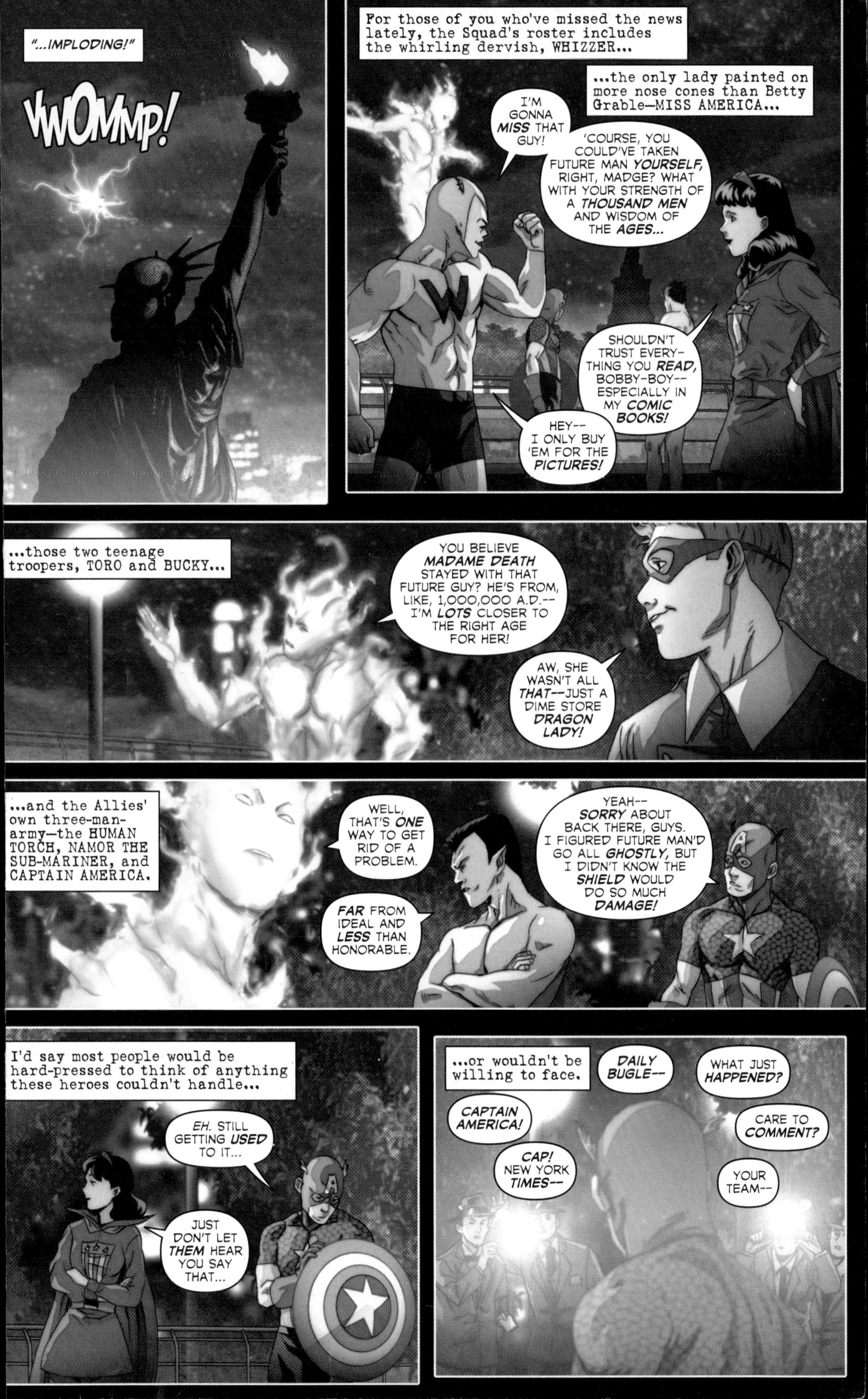

"...IMPLODING!"
VWOMMP!
For those of you who've missed the news lately, the Squad's roster includes the whirling dervish, WHIZZER...
...the only lady painted on more nose cones than Betty Grable—MISS AMERICA...
I'M GONNA MISS THAT GUY!
'COURSE, YOU COULD'VE TAKEN FUTURE MAN YOURSELF, RIGHT, MADGE? WHAT WITH YOUR STRENGTH OF A THOUSAND MEN AND WISDOM OF THE AGES...
SHOULDN'T TRUST EVERY-THING YOU READ, BOBBY-BOY-- ESPECIALLY IN MY COMIC BOOKS!
HEY-- I ONLY BUY 'EM FOR THE PICTURES!
...those two teenage troopers, TORO and BUCKY...
YOU BELIEVE MADAME DEATH STAYED WITH THAT FUTURE GUY? HE'S FROM, LIKE, 1,000,000 A.D.-- I'M LOTS CLOSER TO THE RIGHT AGE FOR HER!
AW, SHE WASN'T ALL THAT--JUST A DIME STORE DRAGON LADY!
...and the Allies' own three-man-army—the HUMAN TORCH, NAMOR THE SUB-MARINER, and CAPTAIN AMERICA.
WELL, THAT'S ONE WAY TO GET RID OF A PROBLEM.
FAR FROM IDEAL AND LESS THAN HONORABLE.
YEAH-- SORRY ABOUT BACK THERE, GUYS. I FIGURED FUTURE MAN'D GO ALL GHOSTLY, BUT I DIDN'T KNOW THE SHIELD WOULD DO SO MUCH DAMAGE!
I'd say most people would be hard-pressed to think of anything these heroes couldn't handle...
EH. STILL GETTING USED TO IT...
JUST DON'T LET THEM HEAR YOU SAY THAT...
...or wouldn't be willing to face.
DAILY BUGLE--
WHAT JUST HAPPENED?
CAPTAIN AMERICA!
CARE TO COMMENT?
CAP! NEW YORK TIMES--
YOUR TEAM--

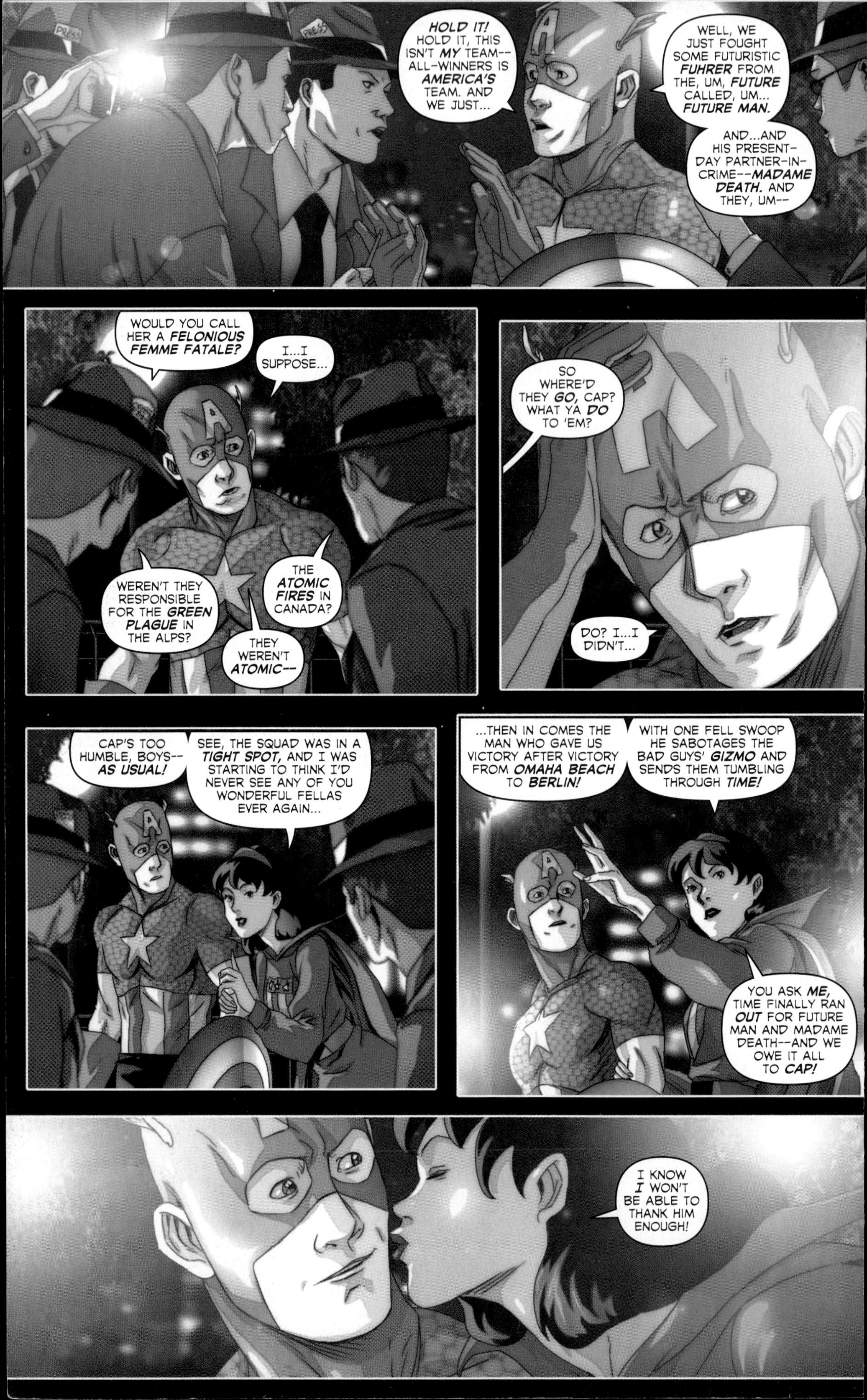
HOLD IT! HOLD IT, THIS ISN'T MY TEAM-- ALL-WINNERS IS AMERICA'S TEAM. AND WE JUST...
WELL, WE JUST FOUGHT SOME FUTURISTIC FUHRER FROM THE, UM, FUTURE CALLED, UM... FUTURE MAN.
AND...AND HIS PRESENT-DAY PARTNER-IN-CRIME--MADAME DEATH. AND THEY, UM--
WOULD YOU CALL HER A FELONIOUS FEMME FATALE?
I...I SUPPOSE...
WEREN'T THEY RESPONSIBLE FOR THE GREEN PLAGUE IN THE ALPS?
THE ATOMIC FIRES IN CANADA?
THEY WEREN'T ATOMIC--
SO WHERE'D THEY GO, CAP? WHAT YA DO TO 'EM?
DO? I...I DIDN'T...
CAP'S TOO HUMBLE, BOYS-- AS USUAL!
SEE, THE SQUAD WAS IN A TIGHT SPOT, AND I WAS STARTING TO THINK I'D NEVER SEE ANY OF YOU WONDERFUL FELLAS EVER AGAIN...
...THEN IN COMES THE MAN WHO GAVE US VICTORY AFTER VICTORY FROM OMAHA BEACH TO BERLIN!
WITH ONE FELL SWOOP HE SABOTAGES THE BAD GUYS' GIZMO AND SENDS THEM TUMBLING THROUGH TIME!
YOU ASK ME, TIME FINALLY RAN OUT FOR FUTURE MAN AND MADAME DEATH--AND WE OWE IT ALL TO CAP!
I KNOW I WON'T BE ABLE TO THANK HIM ENOUGH!

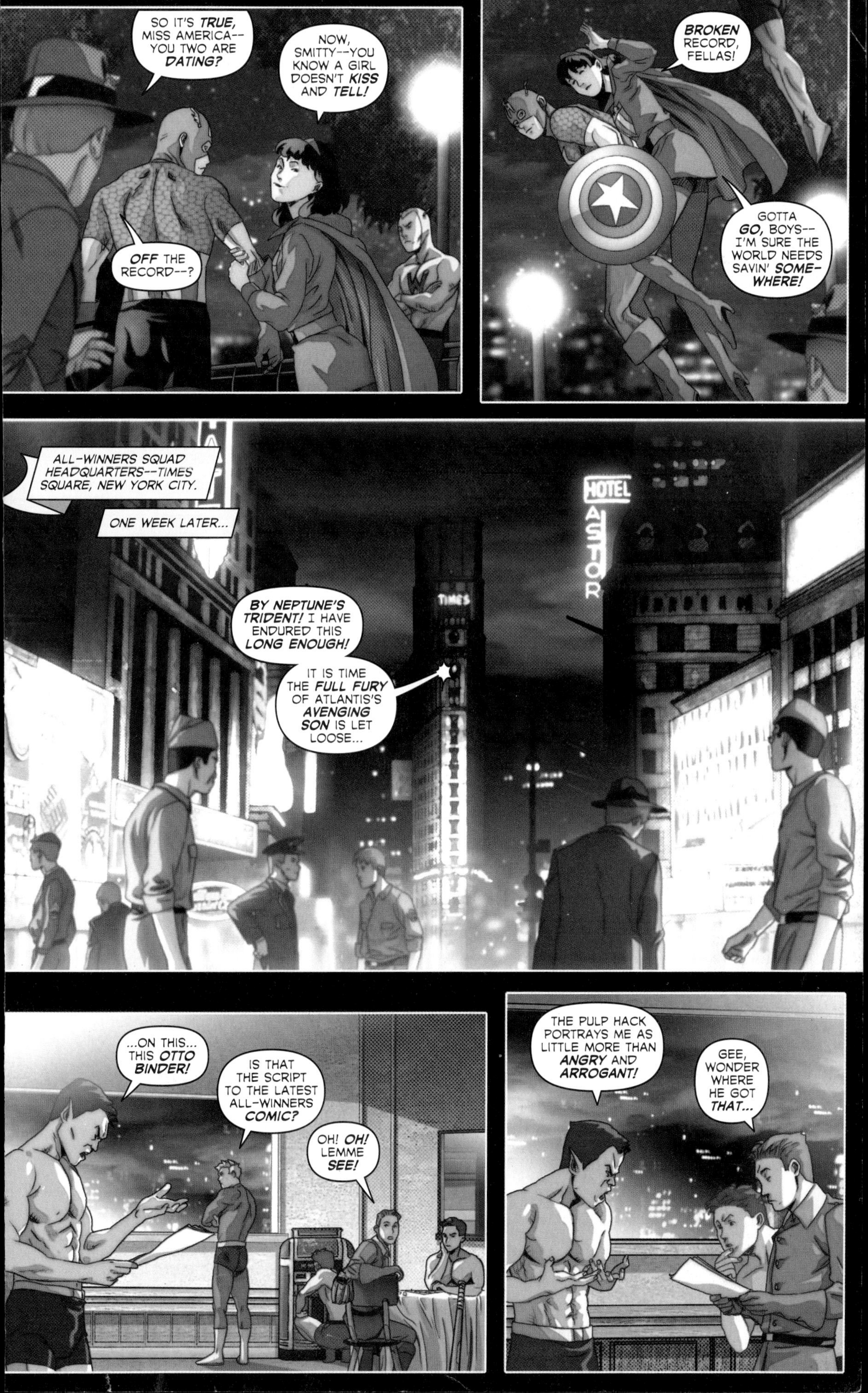
SO IT'S TRUE, MISS AMERICA-- YOU TWO ARE DATING?
NOW, SMITTY--YOU KNOW A GIRL DOESN'T KISS AND TELL!
OFF THE RECORD--?
BROKEN RECORD, FELLAS!
GOTTA GO, BOYS-- I'M SURE THE WORLD NEEDS SAVIN' SOME-WHERE!
ALL-WINNERS SQUAD HEADQUARTERS--TIMES SQUARE, NEW YORK CITY.
ONE WEEK LATER...
HOTEL ASTOR
TIMES
BY NEPTUNE'S TRIDENT! I HAVE ENDURED THIS LONG ENOUGH!
IT IS TIME THE FULL FURY OF ATLANTIS'S AVENGING SON IS LET LOOSE...
...ON THIS... THIS OTTO BINDER!
IS THAT THE SCRIPT TO THE LATEST ALL-WINNERS COMIC?
OH! OH! LEMME SEE!
THE PULP HACK PORTRAYS ME AS LITTLE MORE THAN ANGRY AND ARROGANT!
GEE, WONDER WHERE HE GOT THAT...

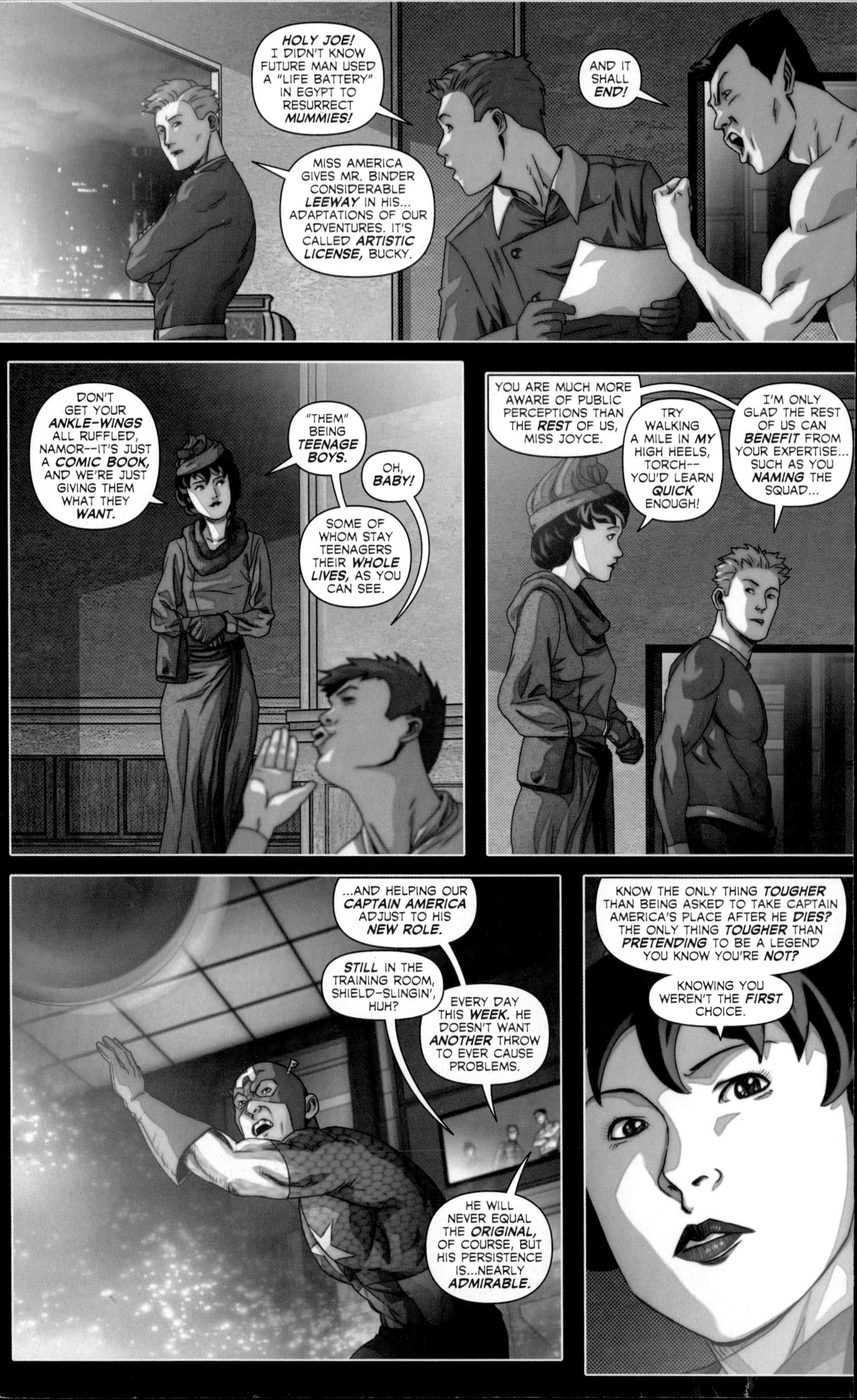
HOLY JOE! I DIDN'T KNOW FUTURE MAN USED A "LIFE BATTERY" IN EGYPT TO RESURRECT MUMMIES!
MISS AMERICA GIVES MR. BINDER CONSIDERABLE LEEWAY IN HIS... ADAPTATIONS OF OUR ADVENTURES. IT'S CALLED ARTISTIC LICENSE, BUCKY.
AND IT SHALL END!
DON'T GET YOUR ANKLE-WINGS ALL RUFFLED, NAMOR--IT'S JUST A COMIC BOOK, AND WE'RE JUST GIVING THEM WHAT THEY WANT.
"THEM" BEING TEENAGE BOYS.
OH, BABY!
SOME OF WHOM STAY TEENAGERS THEIR WHOLE LIVES, AS YOU CAN SEE.
YOU ARE MUCH MORE AWARE OF PUBLIC PERCEPTIONS THAN THE REST OF US, MISS JOYCE.
TRY WALKING A MILE IN MY HIGH HEELS, TORCH-- YOU'D LEARN QUICK ENOUGH!
I'M ONLY GLAD THE REST OF US CAN BENEFIT FROM YOUR EXPERTISE... SUCH AS YOU NAMING THE SQUAD...
...AND HELPING OUR CAPTAIN AMERICA ADJUST TO HIS NEW ROLE.
STILL IN THE TRAINING ROOM, SHIELD-SLINGIN', HUH?
EVERY DAY THIS WEEK. HE DOESN'T WANT ANOTHER THROW TO EVER CAUSE PROBLEMS.
HE WILL NEVER EQUAL THE ORIGINAL, OF COURSE, BUT HIS PERSISTENCE IS...NEARLY ADMIRABLE.
KNOW THE ONLY THING TOUGHER THAN BEING ASKED TO TAKE CAPTAIN AMERICA'S PLACE AFTER HE DIES? THE ONLY THING TOUGHER THAN PRETENDING TO BE A LEGEND YOU KNOW YOU'RE NOT?
KNOWING YOU WEREN'T THE FIRST CHOICE.

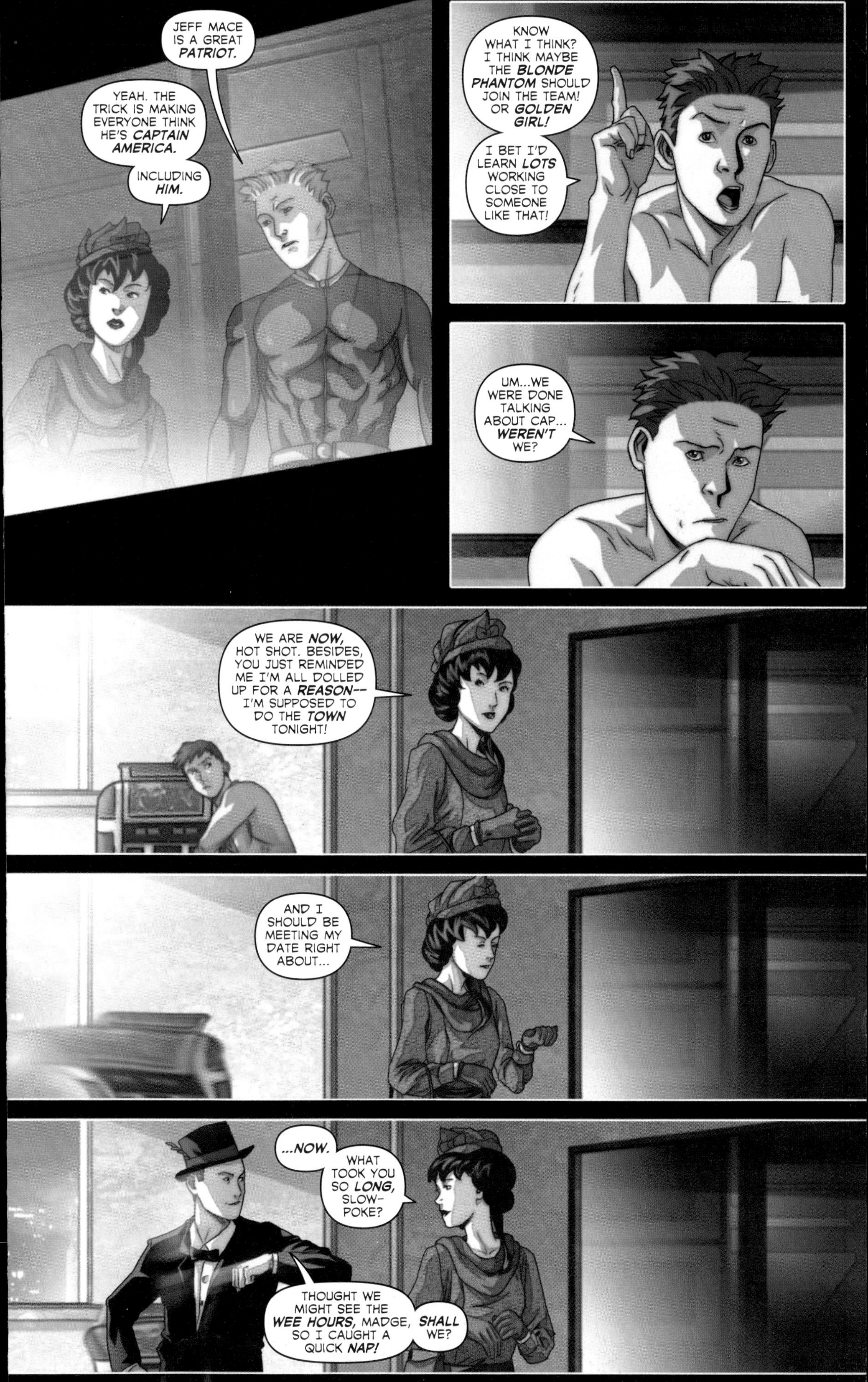

JEFF MACE IS A GREAT *PATRIOT.*
YEAH. THE TRICK IS MAKING EVERYONE THINK HE'S *CAPTAIN AMERICA.*
INCLUDING *HIM.*
KNOW WHAT I THINK? I THINK MAYBE THE *BLONDE PHANTOM* SHOULD JOIN THE TEAM! OR *GOLDEN GIRL!*
I BET I'D LEARN *LOTS* WORKING CLOSE TO SOMEONE LIKE THAT!
UM...WE WERE DONE TALKING ABOUT CAP... *WEREN'T* WE?
WE ARE *NOW,* HOT SHOT. BESIDES, YOU JUST REMINDED ME I'M ALL DOLLED UP FOR A *REASON--* I'M SUPPOSED TO DO THE *TOWN* TONIGHT!
AND I SHOULD BE MEETING MY DATE RIGHT ABOUT...
...NOW.
WHAT TOOK YOU SO *LONG,* SLOW-POKE?
THOUGHT WE MIGHT SEE THE *WEE HOURS,* MADGE, SO I CAUGHT A QUICK *NAP!*
SHALL WE?

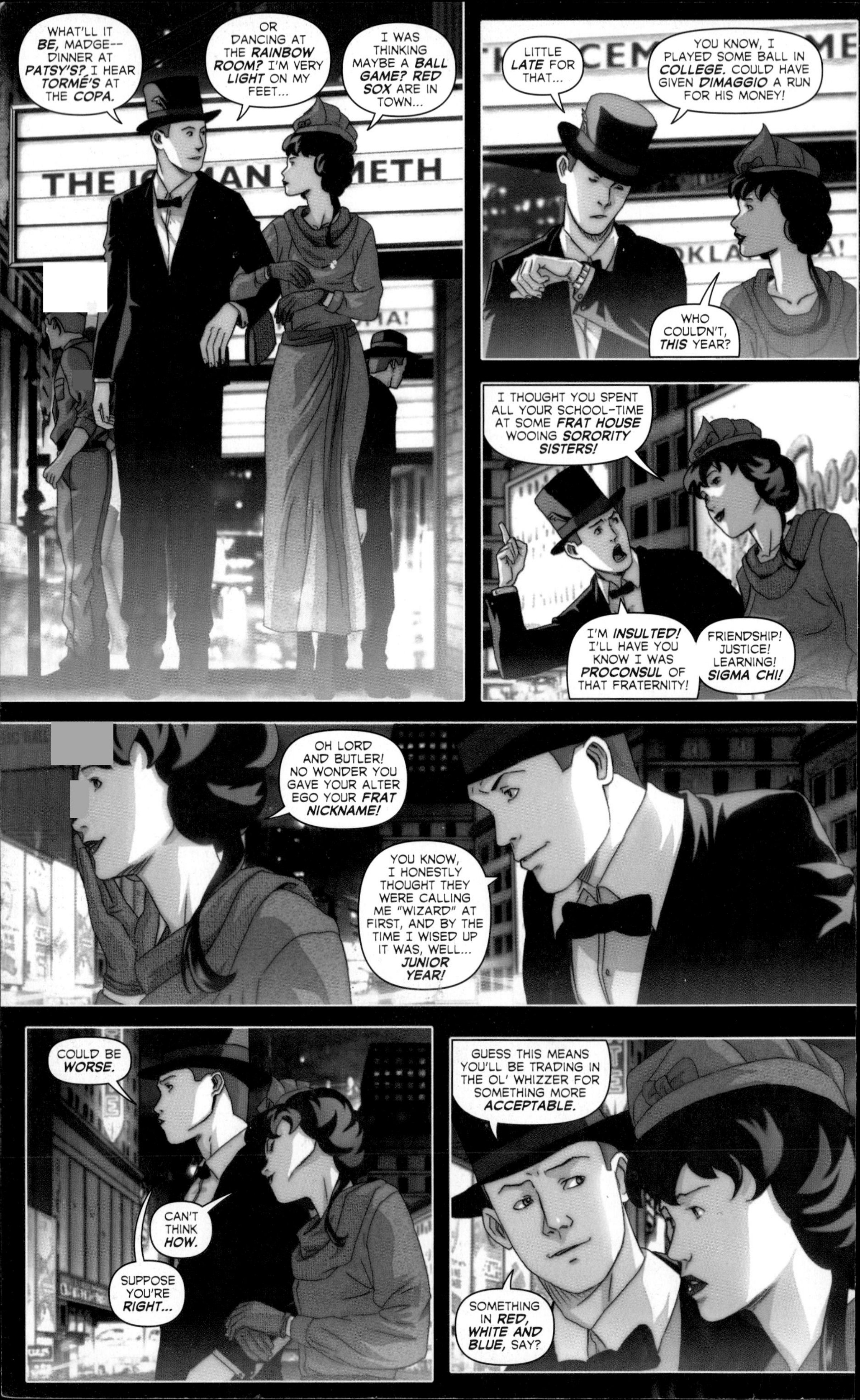
WHAT'LL IT BE, MADGE-- DINNER AT PATSY'S? I HEAR TORMÉ'S AT THE COPA.
OR DANCING AT THE RAINBOW ROOM? I'M VERY LIGHT ON MY FEET...
I WAS THINKING MAYBE A BALL GAME? RED SOX ARE IN TOWN...
THE IC MAN METH
LITTLE LATE FOR THAT...
YOU KNOW, I PLAYED SOME BALL IN COLLEGE. COULD HAVE GIVEN DIMAGGIO A RUN FOR HIS MONEY!
WHO COULDN'T, THIS YEAR?
I THOUGHT YOU SPENT ALL YOUR SCHOOL-TIME AT SOME FRAT HOUSE WOOING SORORITY SISTERS!
I'M INSULTED! I'LL HAVE YOU KNOW I WAS PROCONSUL OF THAT FRATERNITY!
FRIENDSHIP! JUSTICE! LEARNING! SIGMA CHI!
OH LORD AND BUTLER! NO WONDER YOU GAVE YOUR ALTER EGO YOUR FRAT NICKNAME!
YOU KNOW, I HONESTLY THOUGHT THEY WERE CALLING ME "WIZARD" AT FIRST, AND BY THE TIME I WISED UP IT WAS, WELL... JUNIOR YEAR!
COULD BE WORSE.
CAN'T THINK HOW.
SUPPOSE YOU'RE RIGHT...
GUESS THIS MEANS YOU'LL BE TRADING IN THE OL' WHIZZER FOR SOMETHING MORE ACCEPTABLE.
SOMETHING IN RED, WHITE AND BLUE, SAY?

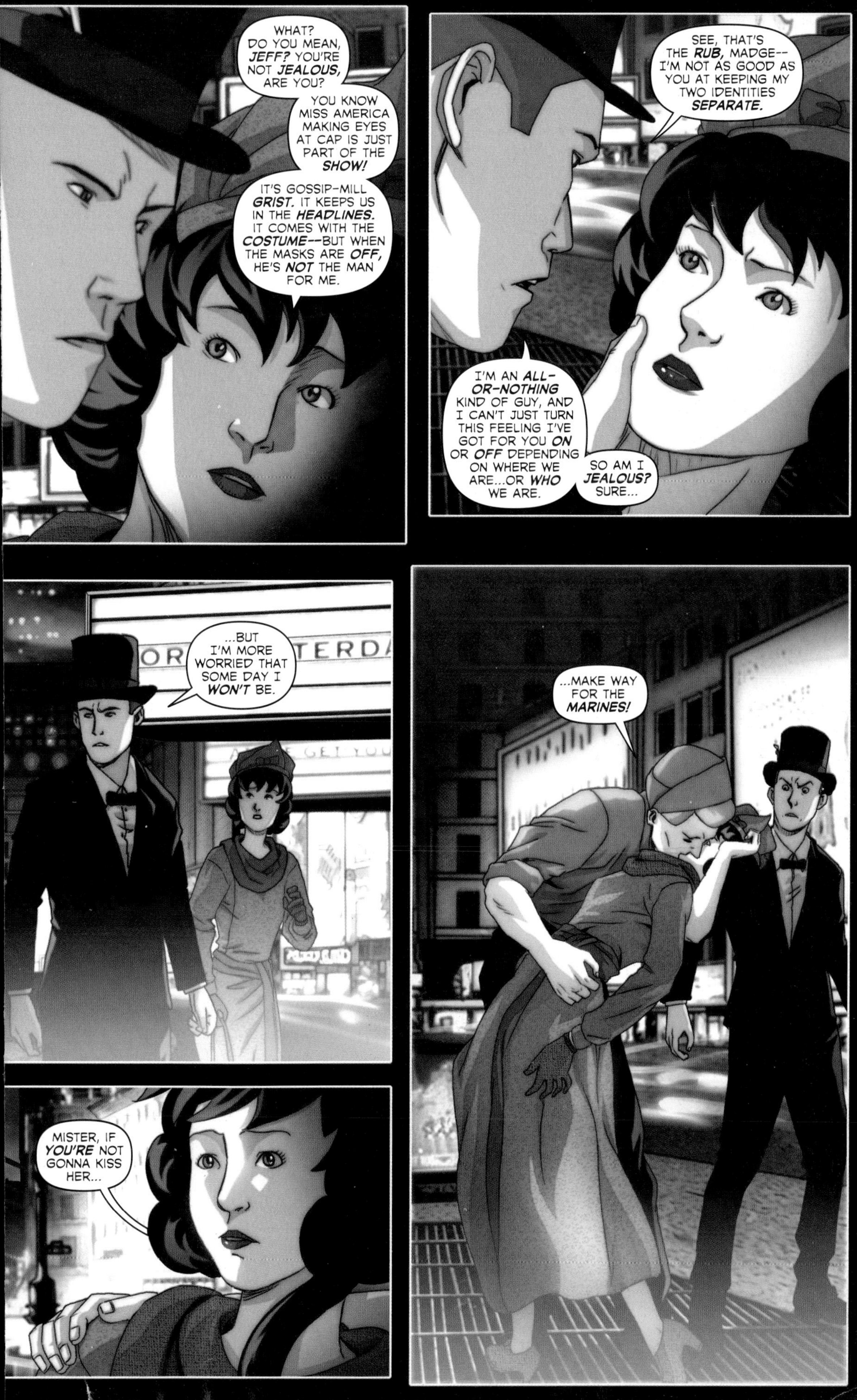
WHAT? DO YOU MEAN, JEFF? YOU'RE NOT JEALOUS, ARE YOU?
YOU KNOW MISS AMERICA MAKING EYES AT CAP IS JUST PART OF THE SHOW!
IT'S GOSSIP-MILL GRIST. IT KEEPS US IN THE HEADLINES. IT COMES WITH THE COSTUME--BUT WHEN THE MASKS ARE OFF, HE'S NOT THE MAN FOR ME.
SEE, THAT'S THE RUB, MADGE--I'M NOT AS GOOD AS YOU AT KEEPING MY TWO IDENTITIES SEPARATE.
I'M AN ALL-OR-NOTHING KIND OF GUY, AND I CAN'T JUST TURN THIS FEELING I'VE GOT FOR YOU ON OR OFF DEPENDING ON WHERE WE ARE...OR WHO WE ARE.
SO AM I JEALOUS? SURE...
...BUT I'M MORE WORRIED THAT SOME DAY I WON'T BE.
MISTER, IF YOU'RE NOT GONNA KISS HER...
...MAKE WAY FOR THE MARINES!

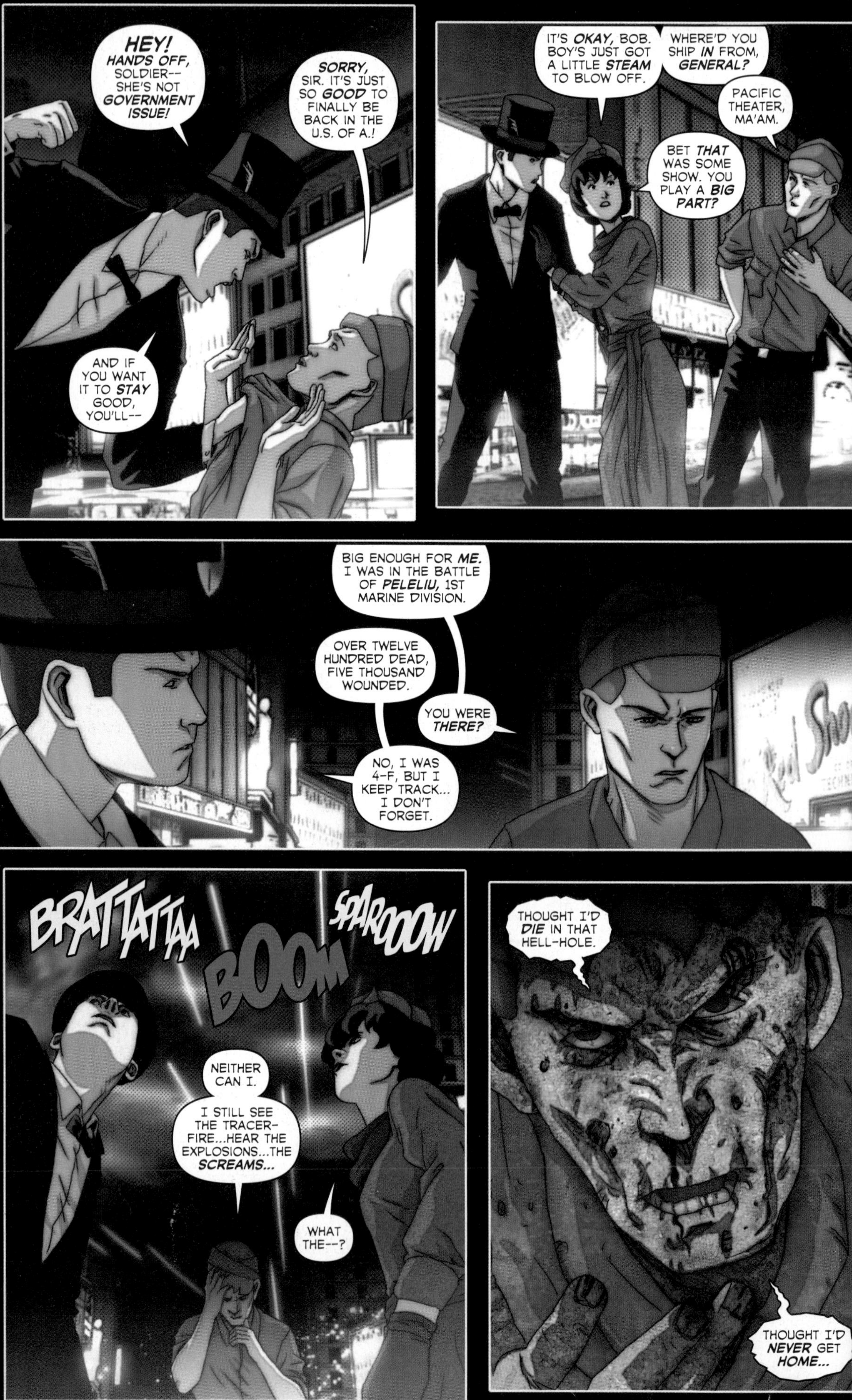
HEY! HANDS OFF, SOLDIER-- SHE'S NOT GOVERNMENT ISSUE!
SORRY, SIR. IT'S JUST SO GOOD TO FINALLY BE BACK IN THE U.S. OF A.!
AND IF YOU WANT IT TO STAY GOOD, YOU'LL--
IT'S OKAY, BOB. BOY'S JUST GOT A LITTLE STEAM TO BLOW OFF.
WHERE'D YOU SHIP IN FROM, GENERAL?
PACIFIC THEATER, MA'AM.
BET THAT WAS SOME SHOW. YOU PLAY A BIG PART?
BIG ENOUGH FOR ME. I WAS IN THE BATTLE OF PELELIU, 1ST MARINE DIVISION.
OVER TWELVE HUNDRED DEAD, FIVE THOUSAND WOUNDED.
YOU WERE THERE?
NO, I WAS 4-F, BUT I KEEP TRACK... I DON'T FORGET.
BRATTATTAA
BOOM
SPAROOOW
NEITHER CAN I.
I STILL SEE THE TRACER-FIRE...HEAR THE EXPLOSIONS...THE SCREAMS...
WHAT THE--?
THOUGHT I'D DIE IN THAT HELL-HOLE.
THOUGHT I'D NEVER GET HOME...

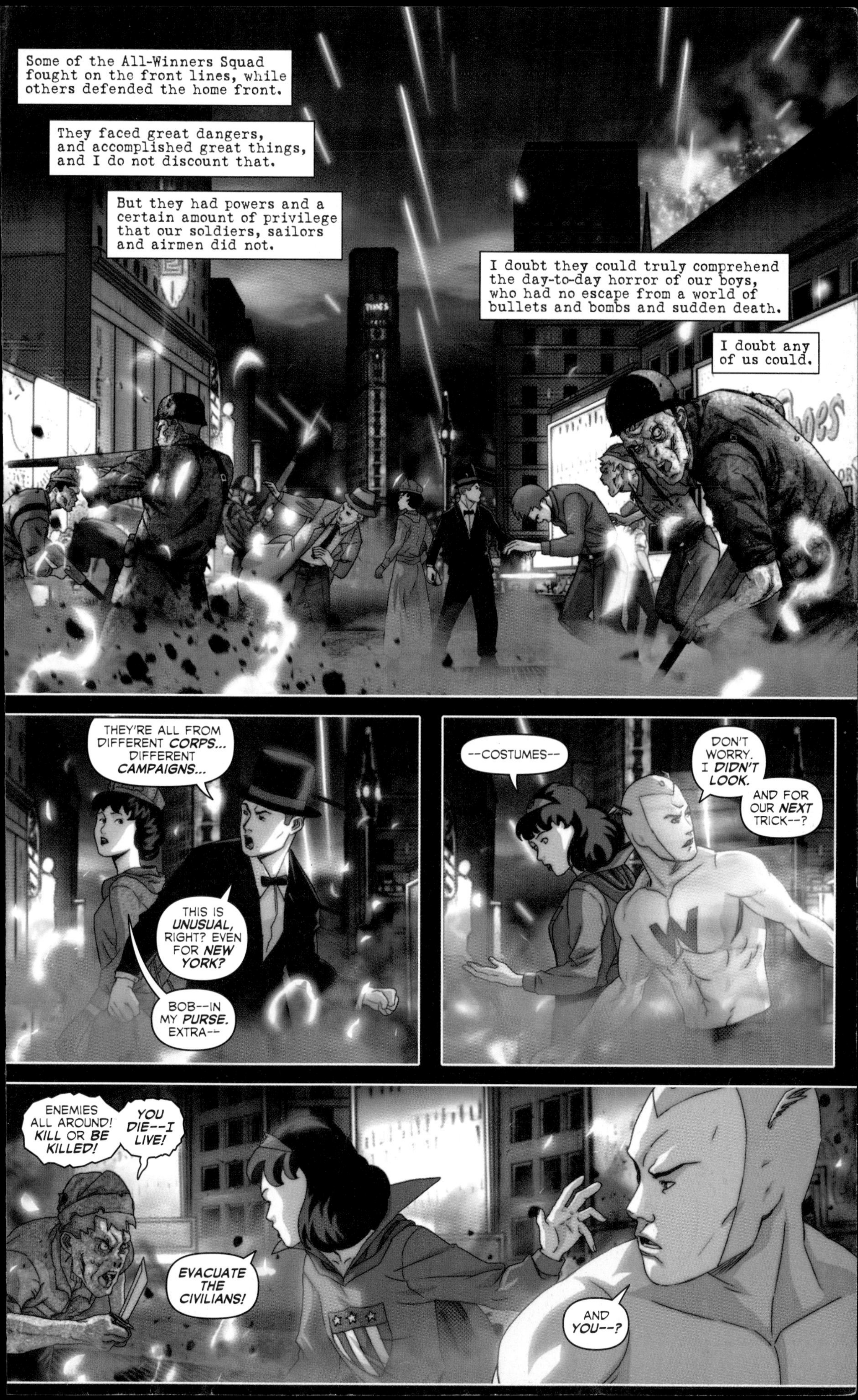
Some of the All-Winners Squad fought on the front lines, while others defended the home front.
They faced great dangers, and accomplished great things, and I do not discount that.
But they had powers and a certain amount of privilege that our soldiers, sailors and airmen did not.
I doubt they could truly comprehend the day-to-day horror of our boys, who had no escape from a world of bullets and bombs and sudden death.
I doubt any of us could.
THEY'RE ALL FROM DIFFERENT CORPS... DIFFERENT CAMPAIGNS...
THIS IS UNUSUAL, RIGHT? EVEN FOR NEW YORK?
BOB--IN MY PURSE. EXTRA--
--COSTUMES--
DON'T WORRY. I DIDN'T LOOK.
AND FOR OUR NEXT TRICK--?
ENEMIES ALL AROUND! KILL OR BE KILLED!
YOU DIE--I LIVE!
EVACUATE THE CIVILIANS!
AND YOU--?

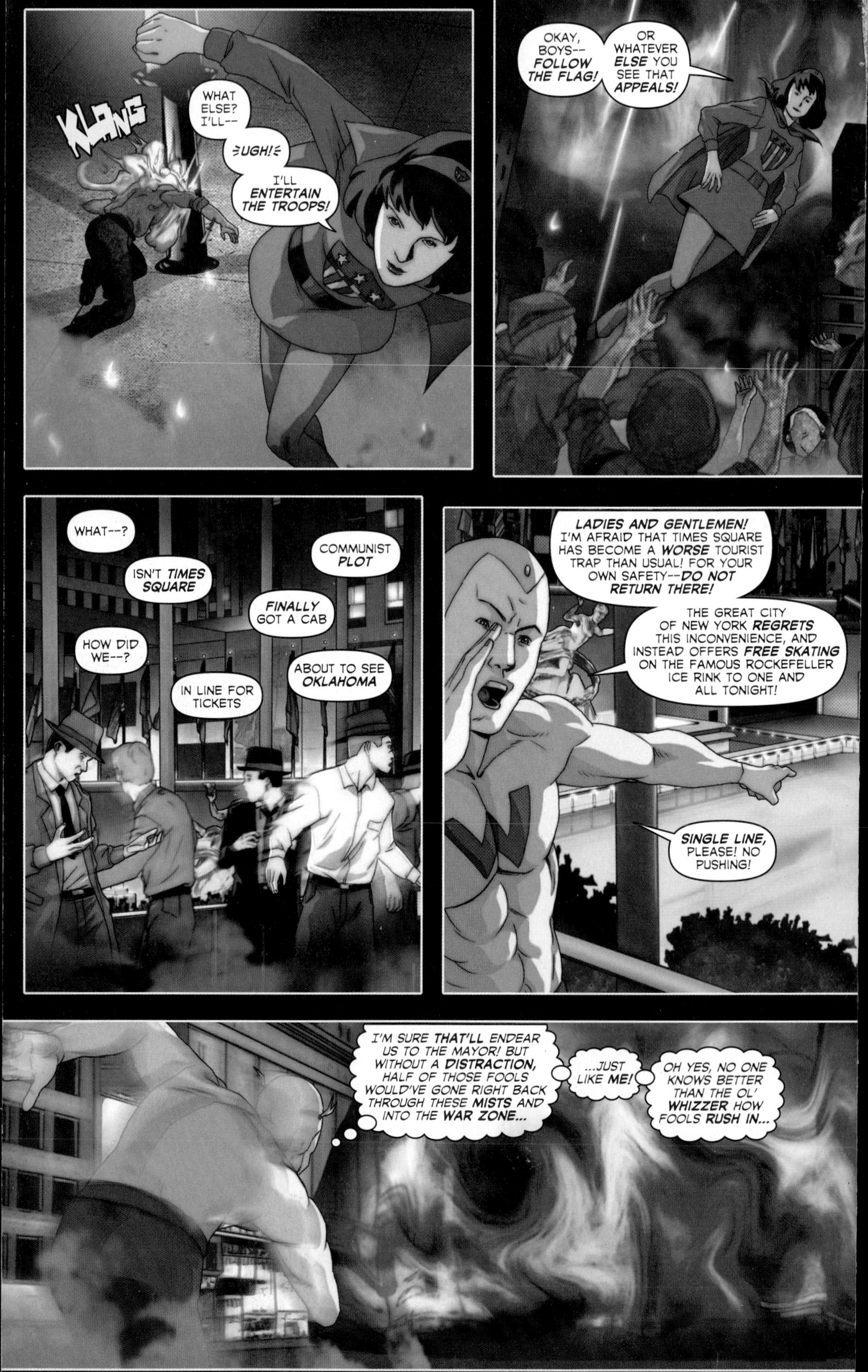
KLANG
WHAT ELSE? I'LL--
UGH!
I'LL ENTERTAIN THE TROOPS!
OKAY, BOYS-- FOLLOW THE FLAG!
OR WHATEVER ELSE YOU SEE THAT APPEALS!
WHAT--?
ISN'T TIMES SQUARE
COMMUNIST PLOT
FINALLY GOT A CAB
HOW DID WE--?
ABOUT TO SEE OKLAHOMA
IN LINE FOR TICKETS
LADIES AND GENTLEMEN! I'M AFRAID THAT TIMES SQUARE HAS BECOME A WORSE TOURIST TRAP THAN USUAL! FOR YOUR OWN SAFETY--DO NOT RETURN THERE!
THE GREAT CITY OF NEW YORK REGRETS THIS INCONVENIENCE, AND INSTEAD OFFERS FREE SKATING ON THE FAMOUS ROCKEFELLER ICE RINK TO ONE AND ALL TONIGHT!
SINGLE LINE, PLEASE! NO PUSHING!
I'M SURE THAT'LL ENDEAR US TO THE MAYOR! BUT WITHOUT A DISTRACTION, HALF OF THOSE FOOLS WOULD'VE GONE RIGHT BACK THROUGH THESE MISTS AND INTO THE WAR ZONE...
...JUST LIKE ME!
OH YES, NO ONE KNOWS BETTER THAN THE OL' WHIZZER HOW FOOLS RUSH IN...

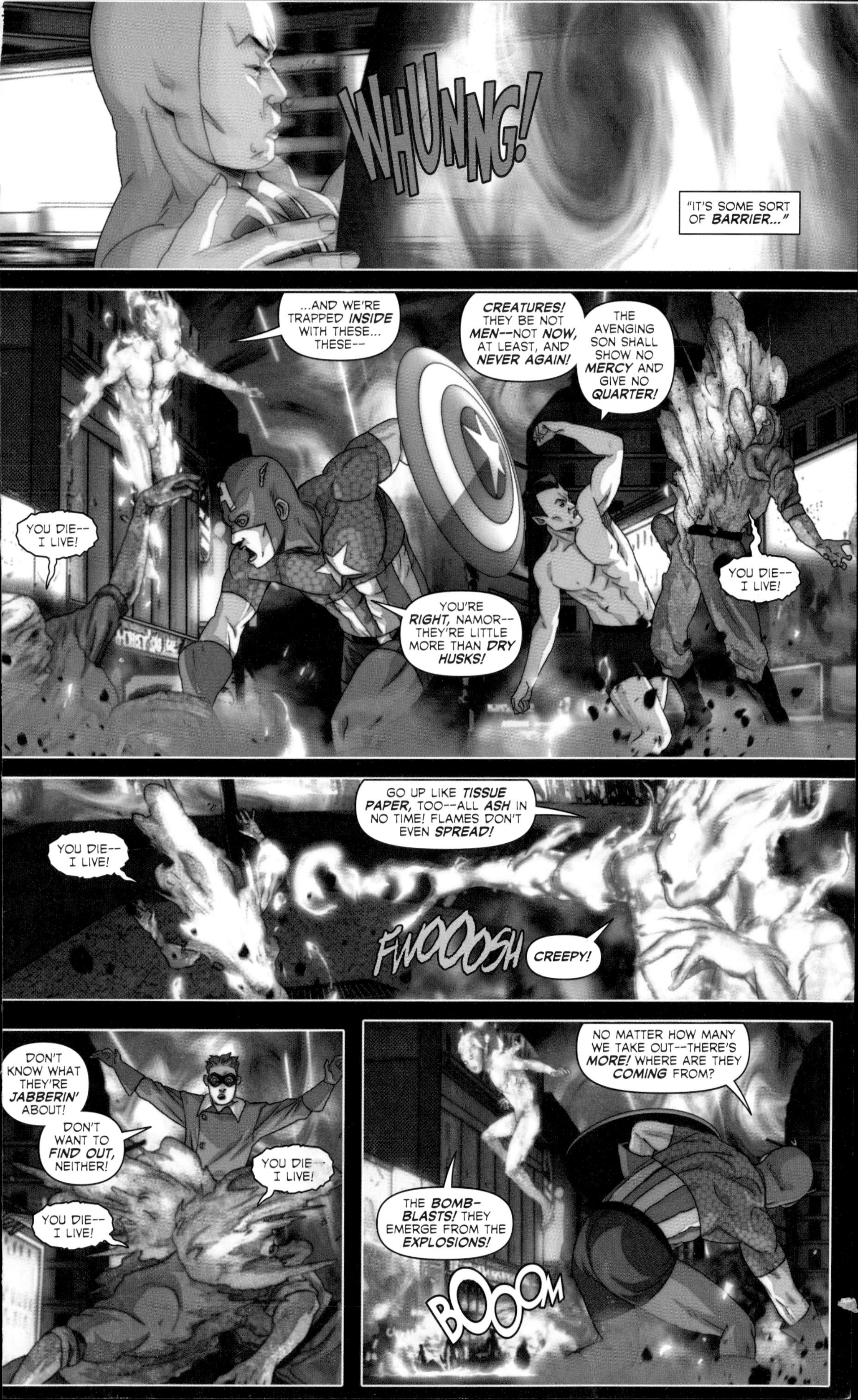
WHUNNG!
"IT'S SOME SORT OF BARRIER..."
...AND WE'RE TRAPPED INSIDE WITH THESE... THESE--
CREATURES! THEY BE NOT MEN--NOT NOW, AT LEAST, AND NEVER AGAIN!
THE AVENGING SON SHALL SHOW NO MERCY AND GIVE NO QUARTER!
YOU DIE-- I LIVE!
YOU'RE RIGHT, NAMOR-- THEY'RE LITTLE MORE THAN DRY HUSKS!
YOU DIE-- I LIVE!
GO UP LIKE TISSUE PAPER, TOO--ALL ASH IN NO TIME! FLAMES DON'T EVEN SPREAD!
YOU DIE-- I LIVE!
FWOOOSH
CREEPY!
DON'T KNOW WHAT THEY'RE JABBERIN' ABOUT!
DON'T WANT TO FIND OUT, NEITHER!
YOU DIE-- I LIVE!
YOU DIE-- I LIVE!
NO MATTER HOW MANY WE TAKE OUT--THERE'S MORE! WHERE ARE THEY COMING FROM?
THE BOMB-BLASTS! THEY EMERGE FROM THE EXPLOSIONS!
BOOOOM

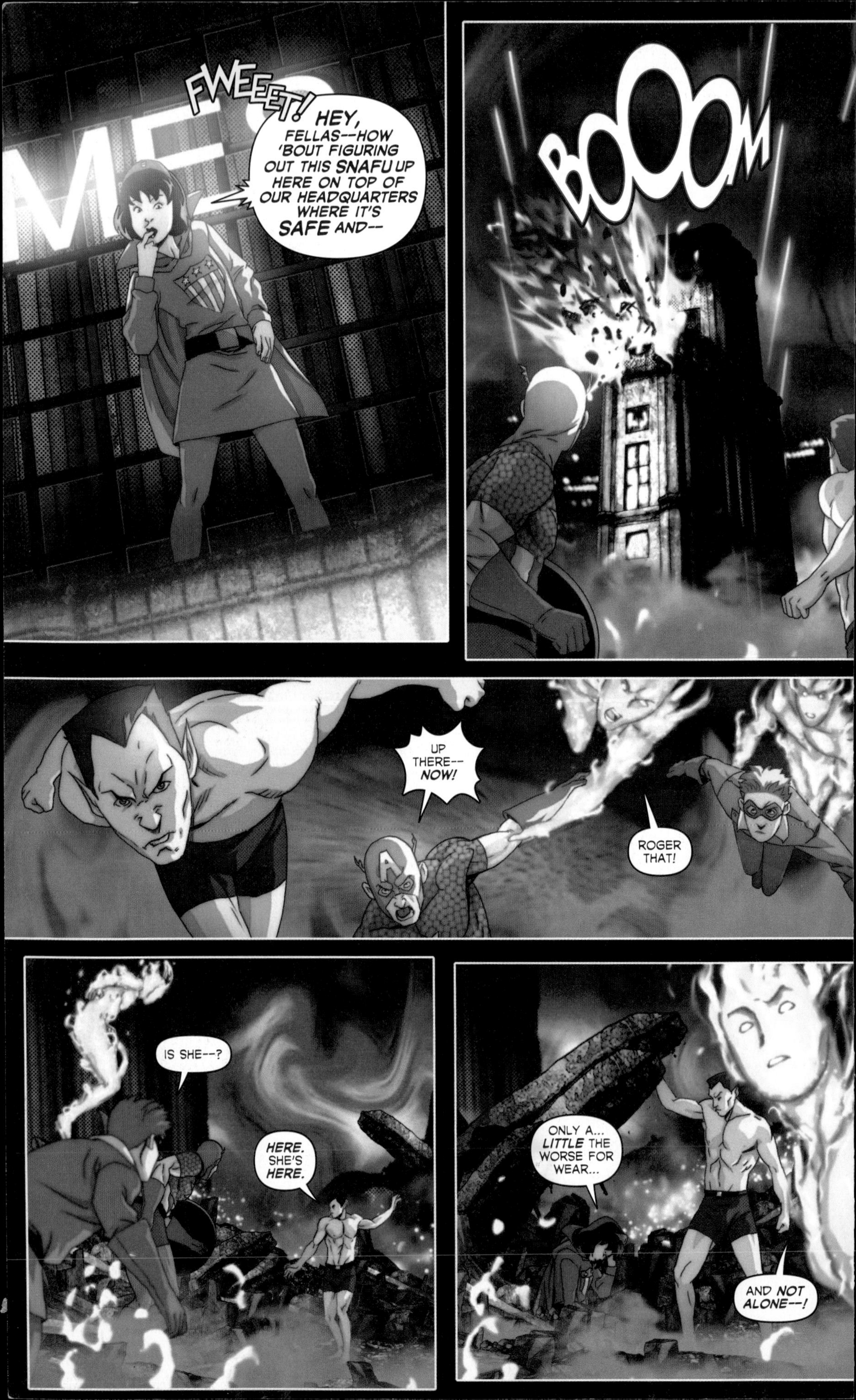
FWEEET!
HEY, FELLAS--HOW 'BOUT FIGURING OUT THIS SNAFU UP HERE ON TOP OF OUR HEADQUARTERS WHERE IT'S SAFE AND--
BOOOOM
UP THERE-- NOW!
ROGER THAT!
IS SHE--?
HERE. SHE'S HERE.
ONLY A... LITTLE THE WORSE FOR WEAR...
AND NOT ALONE--!

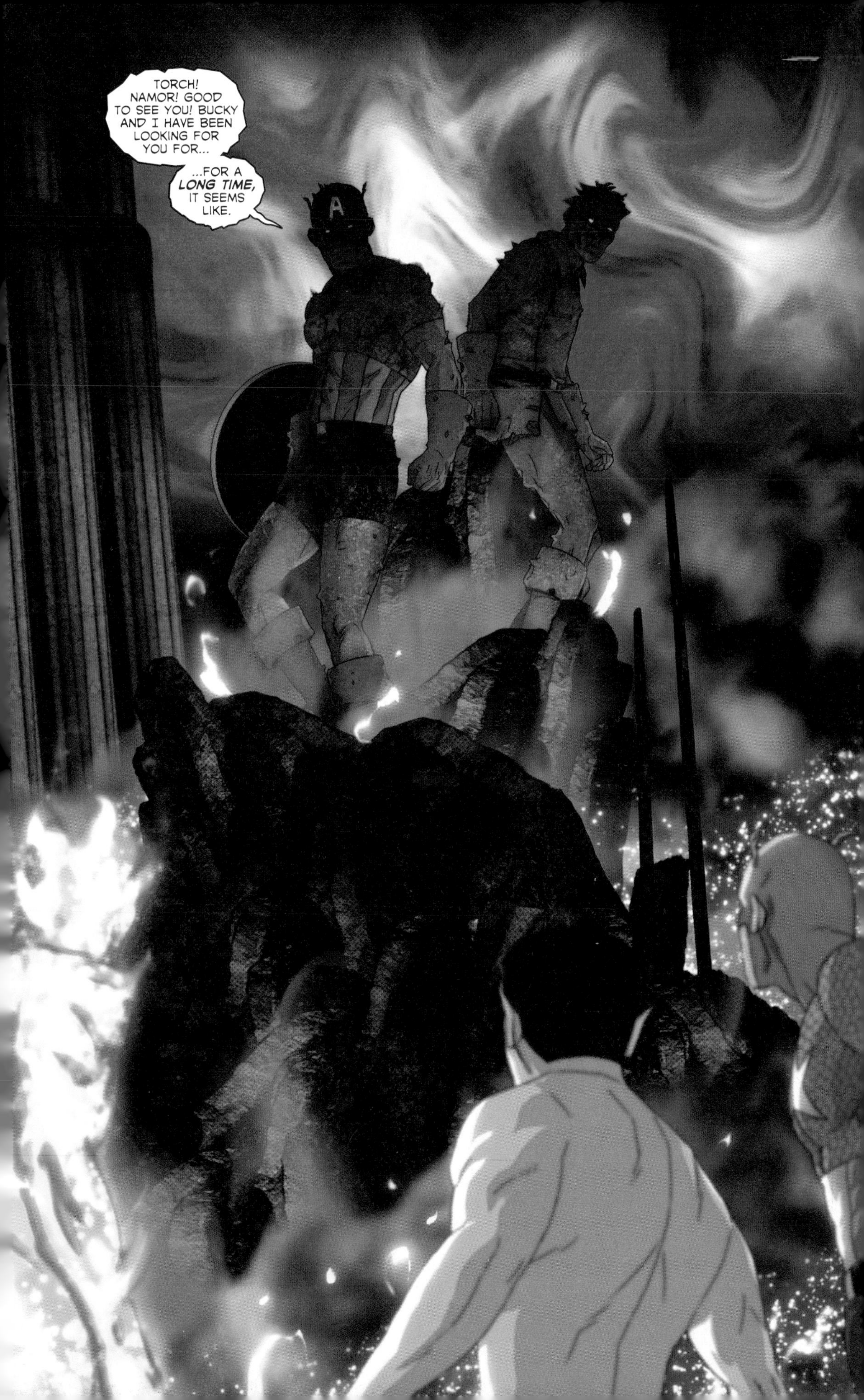
TORCH! NAMOR! GOOD TO SEE YOU! BUCKY AND I HAVE BEEN LOOKING FOR YOU FOR...
...FOR A *LONG TIME,* IT SEEMS LIKE.

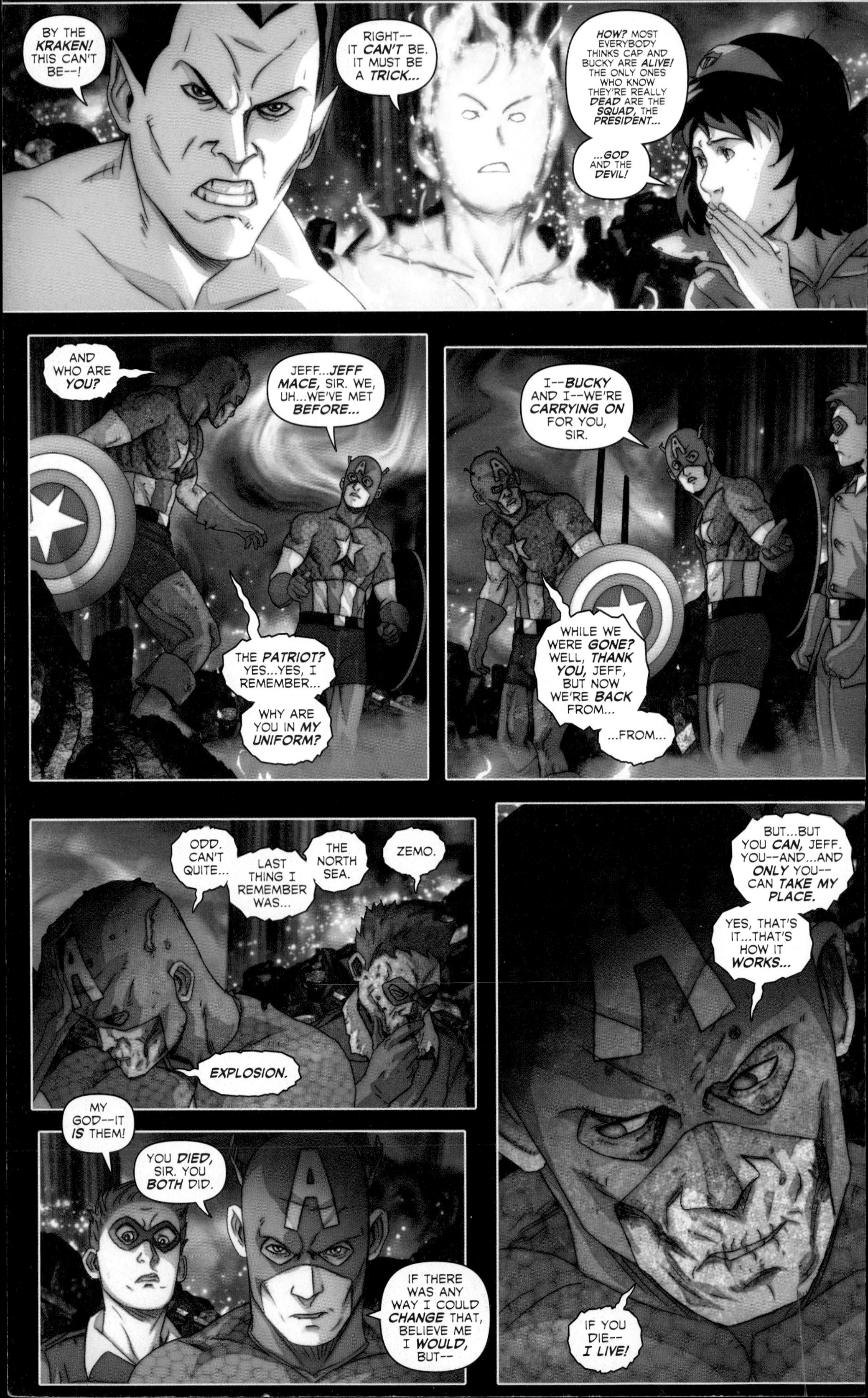
BY THE KRAKEN! THIS CAN'T BE--!
RIGHT-- IT CAN'T BE. IT MUST BE A TRICK...
HOW? MOST EVERYBODY THINKS CAP AND BUCKY ARE ALIVE! THE ONLY ONES WHO KNOW THEY'RE REALLY DEAD ARE THE SQUAD, THE PRESIDENT...
...GOD AND THE DEVIL!
AND WHO ARE YOU?
JEFF...JEFF MACE, SIR. WE, UH...WE'VE MET BEFORE...
THE PATRIOT? YES...YES, I REMEMBER...
WHY ARE YOU IN MY UNIFORM?
I--BUCKY AND I--WE'RE CARRYING ON FOR YOU, SIR.
WHILE WE WERE GONE? WELL, THANK YOU, JEFF, BUT NOW WE'RE BACK FROM...
...FROM...
ODD. CAN'T QUITE...
LAST THING I REMEMBER WAS...
THE NORTH SEA.
ZEMO.
EXPLOSION.
MY GOD--IT IS THEM!
YOU DIED, SIR. YOU BOTH DID.
IF THERE WAS ANY WAY I COULD CHANGE THAT, BELIEVE ME I WOULD, BUT--
BUT...BUT YOU CAN, JEFF. YOU--AND...AND ONLY YOU--CAN TAKE MY PLACE.
YES, THAT'S IT...THAT'S HOW IT WORKS...
IF YOU DIE-- I LIVE!

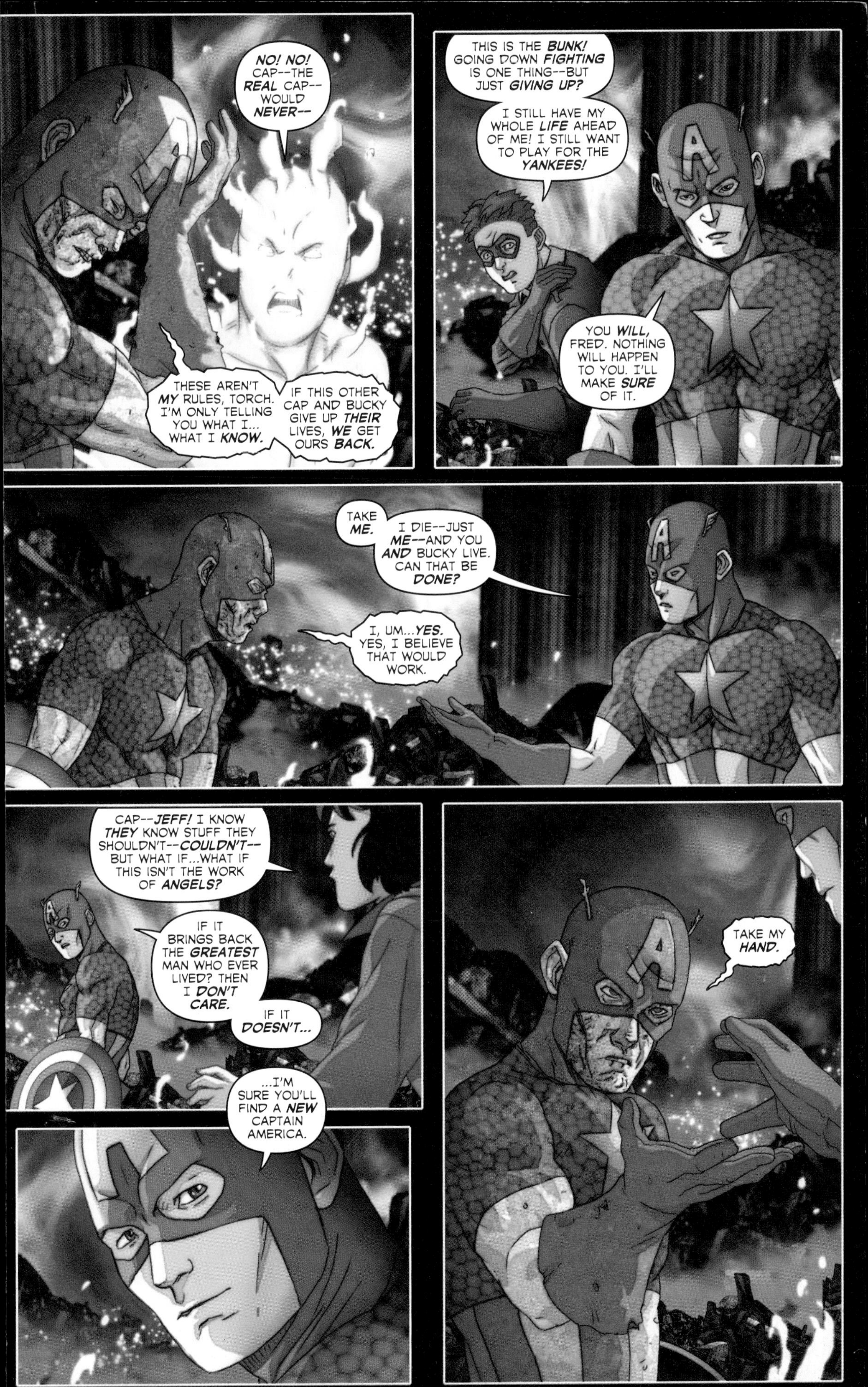

NO! NO! CAP--THE REAL CAP--WOULD NEVER--
THESE AREN'T MY RULES, TORCH. I'M ONLY TELLING YOU WHAT I... WHAT I KNOW.
IF THIS OTHER CAP AND BUCKY GIVE UP THEIR LIVES, WE GET OURS BACK.
THIS IS THE BUNK! GOING DOWN FIGHTING IS ONE THING--BUT JUST GIVING UP?
I STILL HAVE MY WHOLE LIFE AHEAD OF ME! I STILL WANT TO PLAY FOR THE YANKEES!
YOU WILL, FRED. NOTHING WILL HAPPEN TO YOU. I'LL MAKE SURE OF IT.
TAKE ME.
I DIE--JUST ME--AND YOU AND BUCKY LIVE. CAN THAT BE DONE?
I, UM...YES. YES, I BELIEVE THAT WOULD WORK.
CAP--JEFF! I KNOW THEY KNOW STUFF THEY SHOULDN'T--COULDN'T--BUT WHAT IF...WHAT IF THIS ISN'T THE WORK OF ANGELS?
IF IT BRINGS BACK THE GREATEST MAN WHO EVER LIVED? THEN I DON'T CARE.
IF IT DOESN'T...
...I'M SURE YOU'LL FIND A NEW CAPTAIN AMERICA.
TAKE MY HAND.

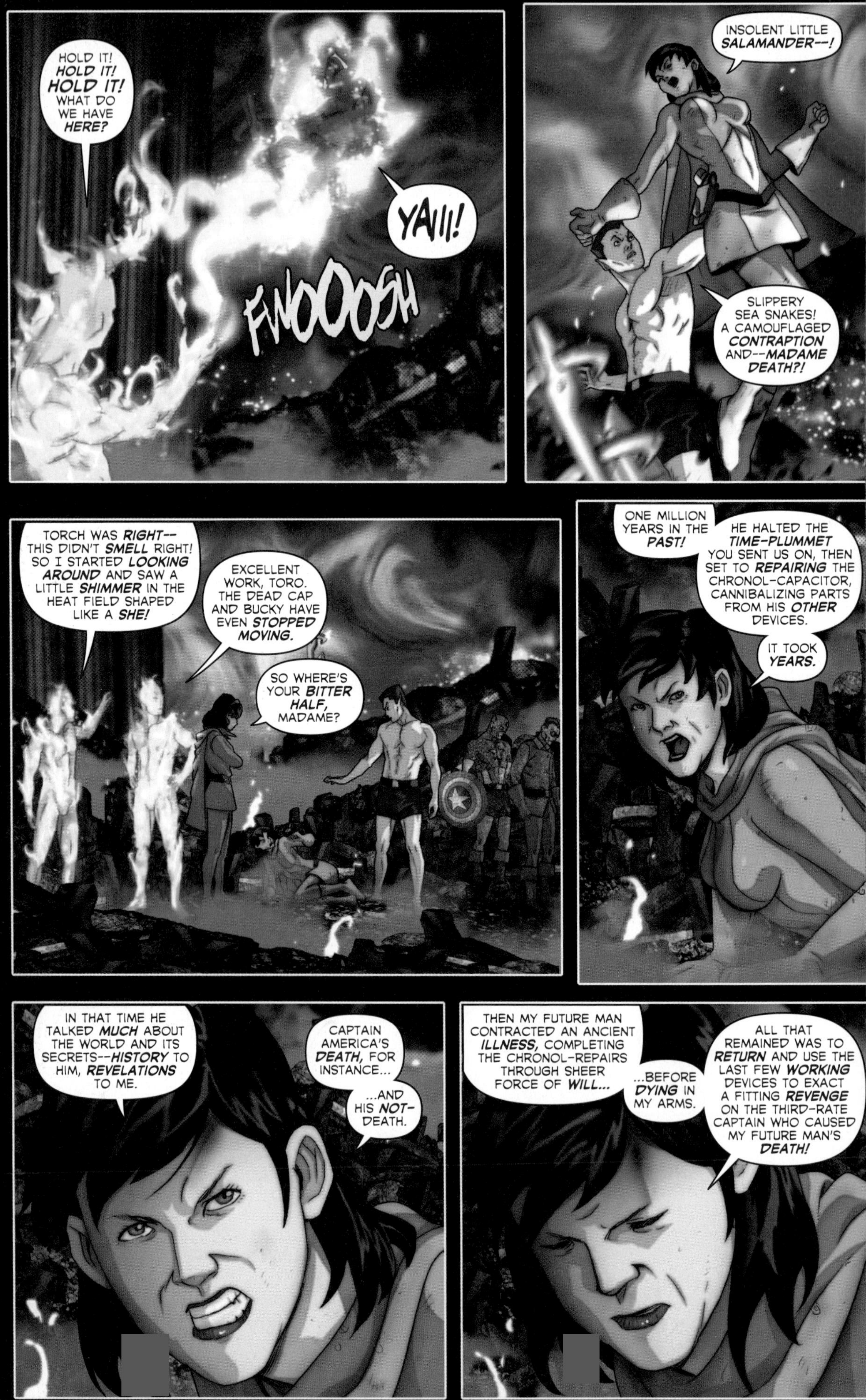

HOLD IT! HOLD IT! HOLD IT! WHAT DO WE HAVE HERE?
YAIII!
FWOOOSH
INSOLENT LITTLE SALAMANDER--!
SLIPPERY SEA SNAKES! A CAMOUFLAGED CONTRAPTION AND--MADAME DEATH?!
TORCH WAS RIGHT-- THIS DIDN'T SMELL RIGHT! SO I STARTED LOOKING AROUND AND SAW A LITTLE SHIMMER IN THE HEAT FIELD SHAPED LIKE A SHE!
EXCELLENT WORK, TORO. THE DEAD CAP AND BUCKY HAVE EVEN STOPPED MOVING.
SO WHERE'S YOUR BITTER HALF, MADAME?
ONE MILLION YEARS IN THE PAST!
HE HALTED THE TIME-PLUMMET YOU SENT US ON, THEN SET TO REPAIRING THE CHRONOL-CAPACITOR, CANNIBALIZING PARTS FROM HIS OTHER DEVICES.
IT TOOK YEARS.
IN THAT TIME HE TALKED MUCH ABOUT THE WORLD AND ITS SECRETS--HISTORY TO HIM, REVELATIONS TO ME.
CAPTAIN AMERICA'S DEATH, FOR INSTANCE...
...AND HIS NOT-DEATH.
THEN MY FUTURE MAN CONTRACTED AN ANCIENT ILLNESS, COMPLETING THE CHRONOL-REPAIRS THROUGH SHEER FORCE OF WILL...
...BEFORE DYING IN MY ARMS.
ALL THAT REMAINED WAS TO RETURN AND USE THE LAST FEW WORKING DEVICES TO EXACT A FITTING REVENGE ON THE THIRD-RATE CAPTAIN WHO CAUSED MY FUTURE MAN'S DEATH!

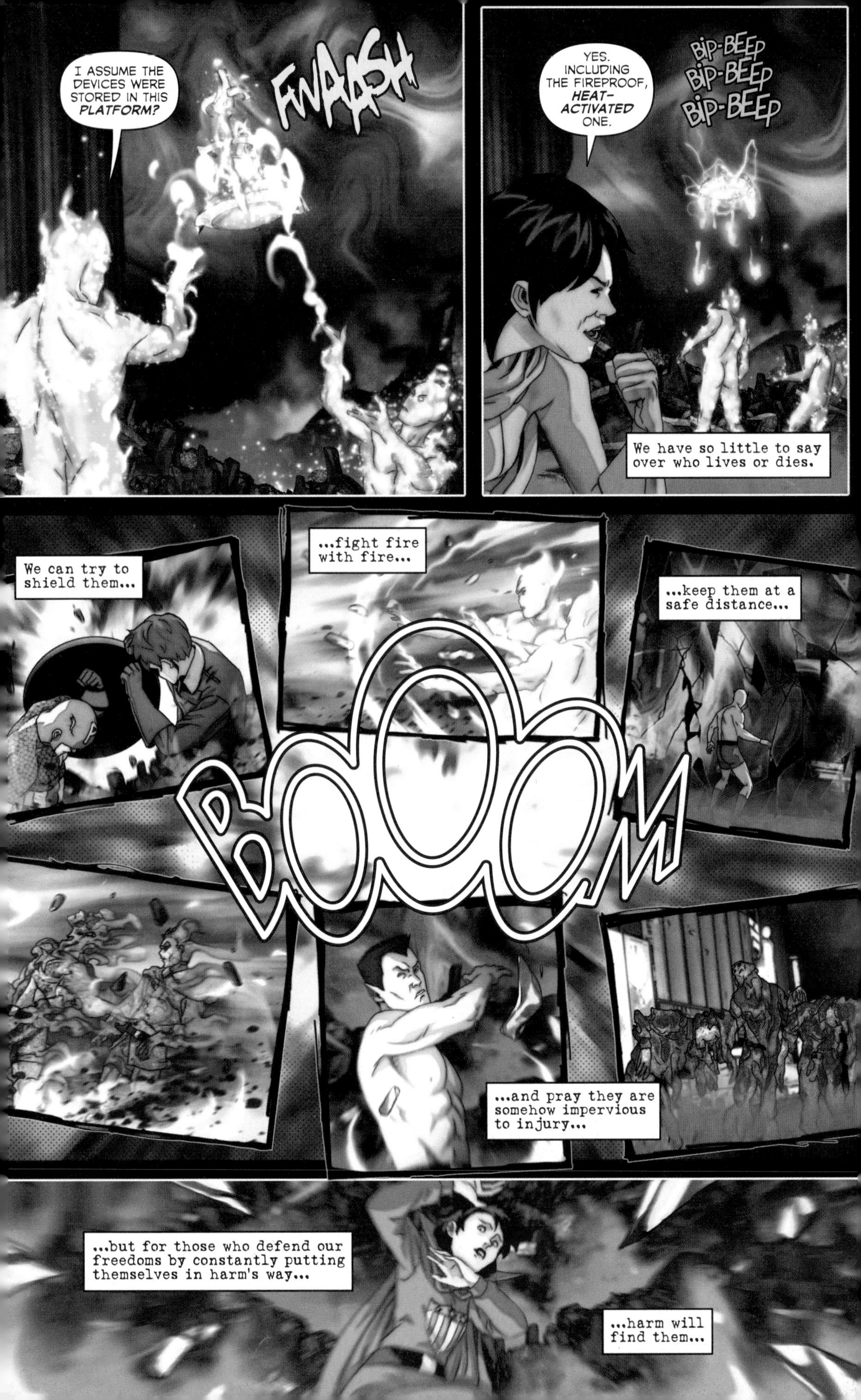

I ASSUME THE DEVICES WERE STORED IN THIS *PLATFORM?*
FWASH
YES. INCLUDING THE FIREPROOF, *HEAT-ACTIVATED* ONE.
BIP-BEEP BIP-BEEP BIP-BEEP
We have so little to say over who lives or dies.
We can try to shield them...
...fight fire with fire...
...keep them at a safe distance...
BOOOM
...and pray they are somehow impervious to injury...
...but for those who defend our freedoms by constantly putting themselves in harm's way...
...harm will find them...

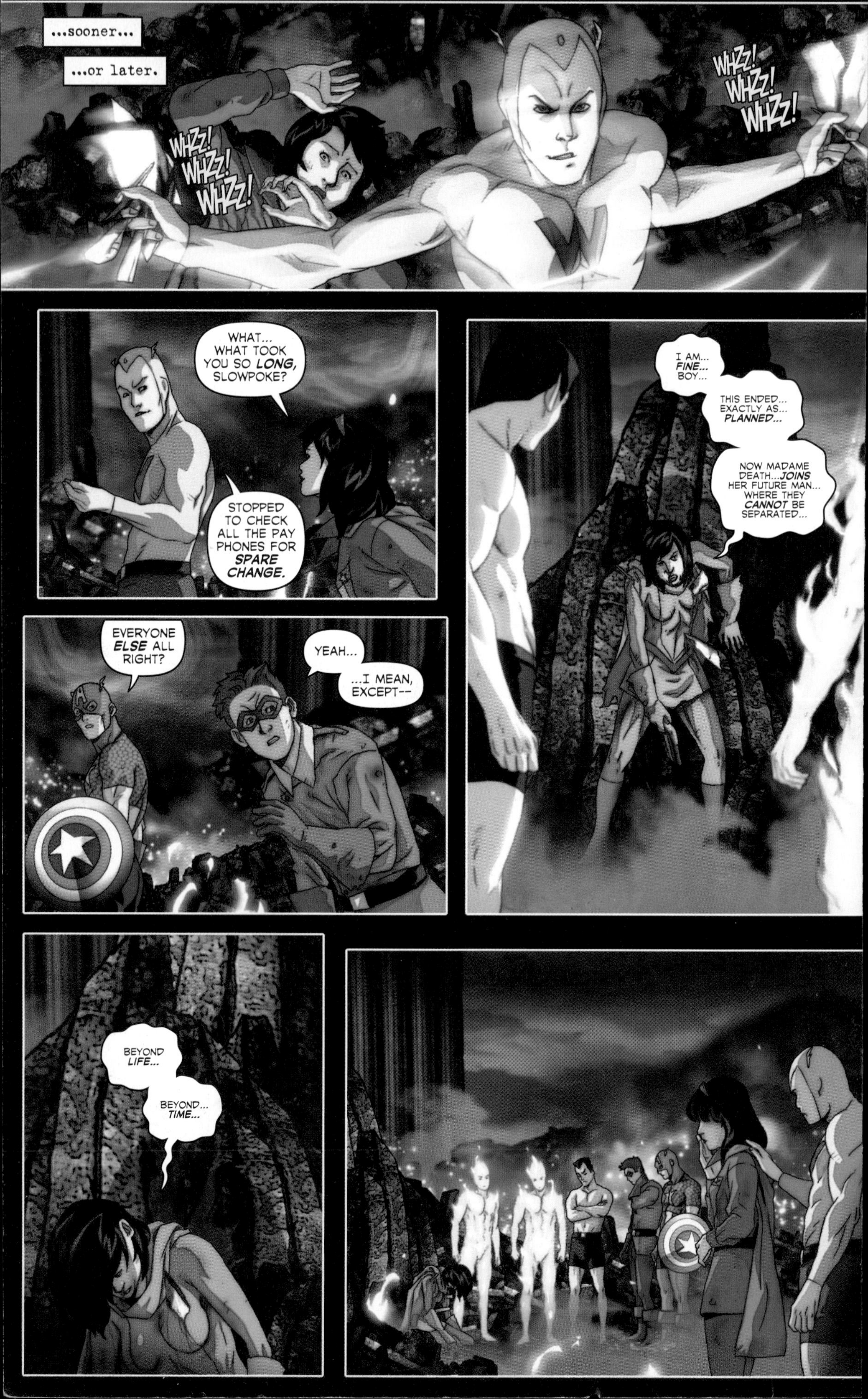
...sooner...
...or later.
WHZZ! WHZZ! WHZZ!
WHZZ! WHZZ! WHZZ!
WHAT... WHAT TOOK YOU SO LONG, SLOWPOKE?
STOPPED TO CHECK ALL THE PAY PHONES FOR SPARE CHANGE.
EVERYONE ELSE ALL RIGHT?
YEAH...
...I MEAN, EXCEPT--
I AM... FINE... BOY...
THIS ENDED... EXACTLY AS... PLANNED...
NOW MADAME DEATH...JOINS HER FUTURE MAN... WHERE THEY CANNOT BE SEPARATED...
BEYOND LIFE...
BEYOND... TIME...

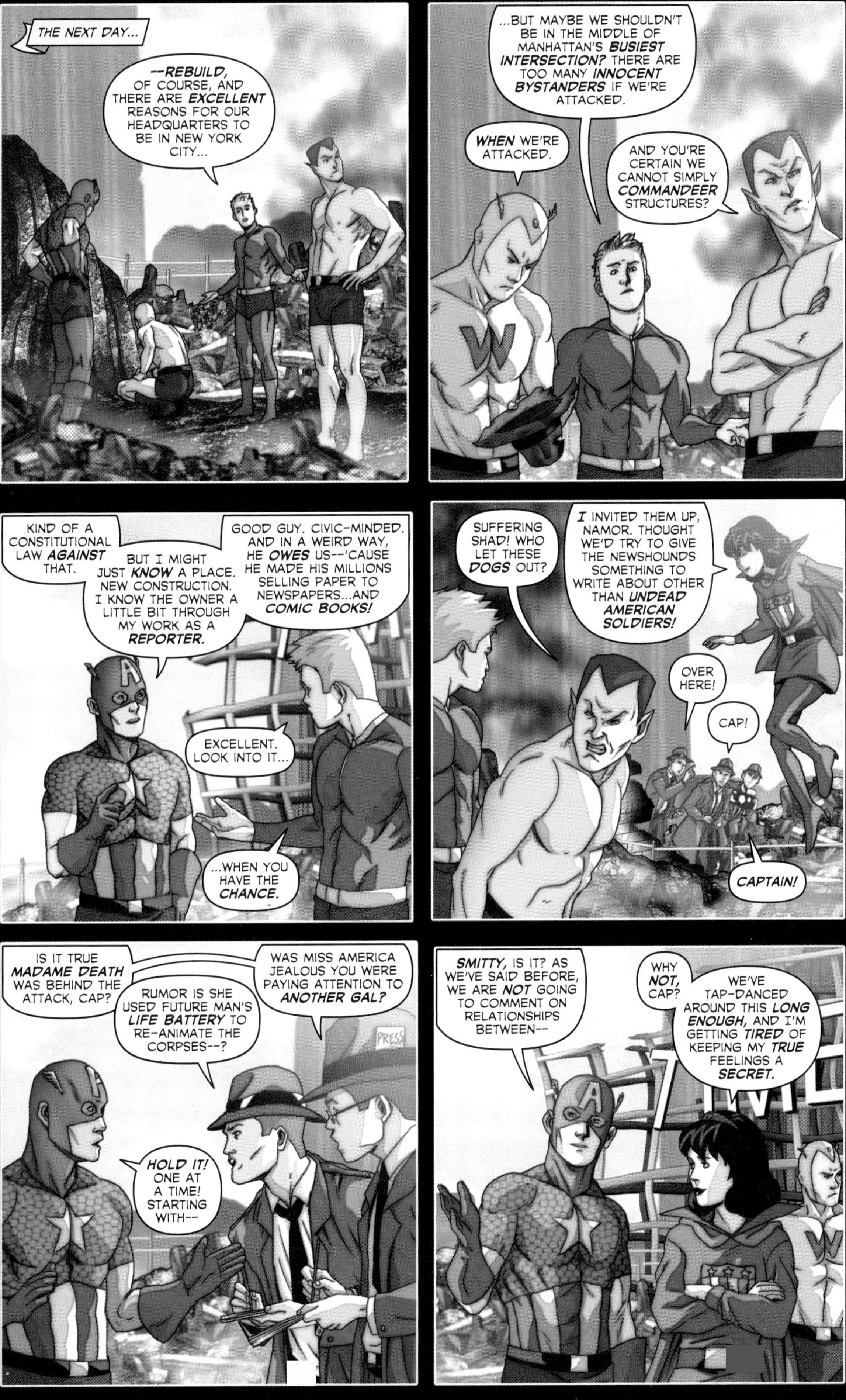
THE NEXT DAY...
--REBUILD, OF COURSE, AND THERE ARE EXCELLENT REASONS FOR OUR HEADQUARTERS TO BE IN NEW YORK CITY...
...BUT MAYBE WE SHOULDN'T BE IN THE MIDDLE OF MANHATTAN'S BUSIEST INTERSECTION? THERE ARE TOO MANY INNOCENT BYSTANDERS IF WE'RE ATTACKED.
WHEN WE'RE ATTACKED.
AND YOU'RE CERTAIN WE CANNOT SIMPLY COMMANDEER STRUCTURES?
KIND OF A CONSTITUTIONAL LAW AGAINST THAT.
BUT I MIGHT JUST KNOW A PLACE. NEW CONSTRUCTION. I KNOW THE OWNER A LITTLE BIT THROUGH MY WORK AS A REPORTER.
GOOD GUY. CIVIC-MINDED. AND IN A WEIRD WAY, HE OWES US--'CAUSE HE MADE HIS MILLIONS SELLING PAPER TO NEWSPAPERS...AND COMIC BOOKS!
EXCELLENT. LOOK INTO IT...
...WHEN YOU HAVE THE CHANCE.
SUFFERING SHAD! WHO LET THESE DOGS OUT?
I INVITED THEM UP, NAMOR. THOUGHT WE'D TRY TO GIVE THE NEWSHOUNDS SOMETHING TO WRITE ABOUT OTHER THAN UNDEAD AMERICAN SOLDIERS!
OVER HERE!
CAP!
CAPTAIN!
IS IT TRUE MADAME DEATH WAS BEHIND THE ATTACK, CAP?
RUMOR IS SHE USED FUTURE MAN'S LIFE BATTERY TO RE-ANIMATE THE CORPSES--?
WAS MISS AMERICA JEALOUS YOU WERE PAYING ATTENTION TO ANOTHER GAL?
PRESS
HOLD IT! ONE AT A TIME! STARTING WITH--
SMITTY, IS IT? AS WE'VE SAID BEFORE, WE ARE NOT GOING TO COMMENT ON RELATIONSHIPS BETWEEN--
WHY NOT, CAP?
WE'VE TAP-DANCED AROUND THIS LONG ENOUGH, AND I'M GETTING TIRED OF KEEPING MY TRUE FEELINGS A SECRET.

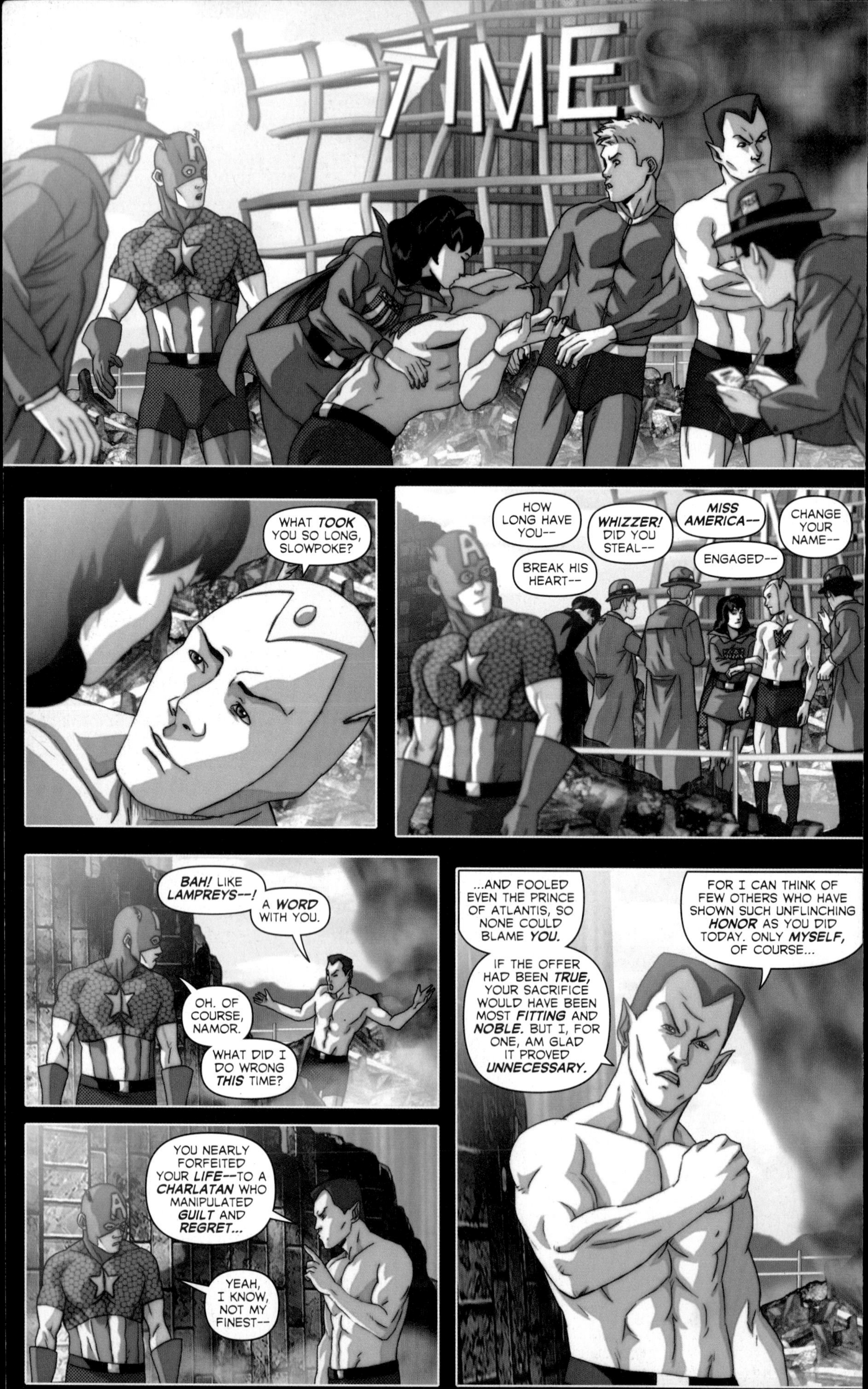
TIMES
WHAT TOOK YOU SO LONG, SLOWPOKE?
HOW LONG HAVE YOU--
BREAK HIS HEART--
WHIZZER! DID YOU STEAL--
MISS AMERICA--
ENGAGED--
CHANGE YOUR NAME--
BAH! LIKE LAMPREYS--!
A WORD WITH YOU.
OH. OF COURSE, NAMOR.
WHAT DID I DO WRONG THIS TIME?
YOU NEARLY FORFEITED YOUR LIFE--TO A CHARLATAN WHO MANIPULATED GUILT AND REGRET...
YEAH, I KNOW, NOT MY FINEST--
...AND FOOLED EVEN THE PRINCE OF ATLANTIS, SO NONE COULD BLAME YOU.
IF THE OFFER HAD BEEN TRUE, YOUR SACRIFICE WOULD HAVE BEEN MOST FITTING AND NOBLE. BUT I, FOR ONE, AM GLAD IT PROVED UNNECESSARY.
FOR I CAN THINK OF FEW OTHERS WHO HAVE SHOWN SUCH UNFLINCHING HONOR AS YOU DID TODAY. ONLY MYSELF, OF COURSE...

...AND THE *ORIGINAL* CAPTAIN AMERICA.

We all follow in the footsteps of those who came before us...

...and while we should not forget the past, we should not be haunted by it, either.

KLAK-KLEK-KLIKLAK-KLEK

We should remember that their sacrifice--their blood, toil, tears, and sweat, as Winston Churchill put it--is what makes us all winners today.

KLAK-KLEK-KLIKLAK-KLEK

JEFF MACE

TZZZZIK!

The best way to honor them--the only way, if you ask me--is by doing your very best, every single day...

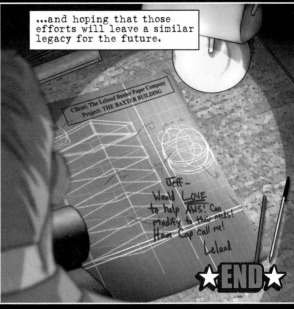

...and hoping that those efforts will leave a similar legacy for the future.

Client: The Leland Baxter Paper Company
Project: THE BAXTER BUILDING

Jeff--
Would LOVE to help AWS! Can modify to their needs! Have Cap call me!
Leland

★END★

PATRIOT ACTS

ACT ONE.

It all started when Tom Brevoort asked if I'd like to write a new All-Winners Squad story. A simple 22-page one-shot that quickly took on a life of its own...

As I put together the All-Winners story I became very fond of the Whizzer, saw untapped potential in Miss America, loved writing every word Namor proclaimed... and became very intrigued by the man in the Captain America uniform. Jeff Mace was the third person to wear the uniform and the first — and, I'm pretty sure only — to actually take it off and walk away from what is arguably the top super hero job in the world. What was the story there? I wanted to know and, thankfully, so did Marvel. So I started writing...

ACT TWO.

They say, "Write what you know" — and I certainly don't know anything about fighting Nazis or Commies, but I did find a strong connection with Jeff Mace on another level. In the early 1990s I was given the opportunity to write one of the Superman books. Overnight, I went from relative obscurity to being front-and-center in one of the biggest publishing events in comic history — The Death (and Return) of Superman. It was a wonderful, exciting time and I worked with some of the most talented people in the business. And while they were all extremely welcoming to me — I never had to prove myself the way Jeff did to, say, Namor — I'll admit to having felt a bit out of my depth. Plus, as much as I love my job, it has never come easy to me. Whether I'm writing or drawing, I have to work at it, hard, every single day. So I knew exactly what Jeff had to be going through.

The last piece of the writing puzzle was my wonderful wife, Myrna. I hope to write and draw comics for the rest of my life, but meeting, marrying and loving Myrna is the only thing that ever made — and still makes — me want to work less. Being with her is just so much more important to me. Without Myrna, this story could have ended quite differently.

ACT THREE.

And then there's the art! I like to think my scripts were solid — but what Mitch and Elizabeth Breitweiser did artistically took them to a whole other level. Mitch's naturalistic style could not have been better suited to the subject. It brought a deep humanity to every character, pulled you into the story and never let go. Elizabeth's colors only highlighted her husband's abilities and literally set the tone for the entire mini-series. Every new page I saw from either of them left me breathless. It was one of the best experiences of my entire career.

Which isn't to slight Steve Uy who drew the All-Winners story, and certainly not Roy Thomas and Frank Robbins who unknowingly laid the foundation for this entire collection when they put together their issue of *What If?* some 30 years ago. (The only "What If?" that should probably be called "And Then..." since it actually *did* happen in the mainstream Marvel Universe!) They're all amazing, all talented, and All-Winners in my book!

Karl Kesel
Portland, Oregon
December 2010

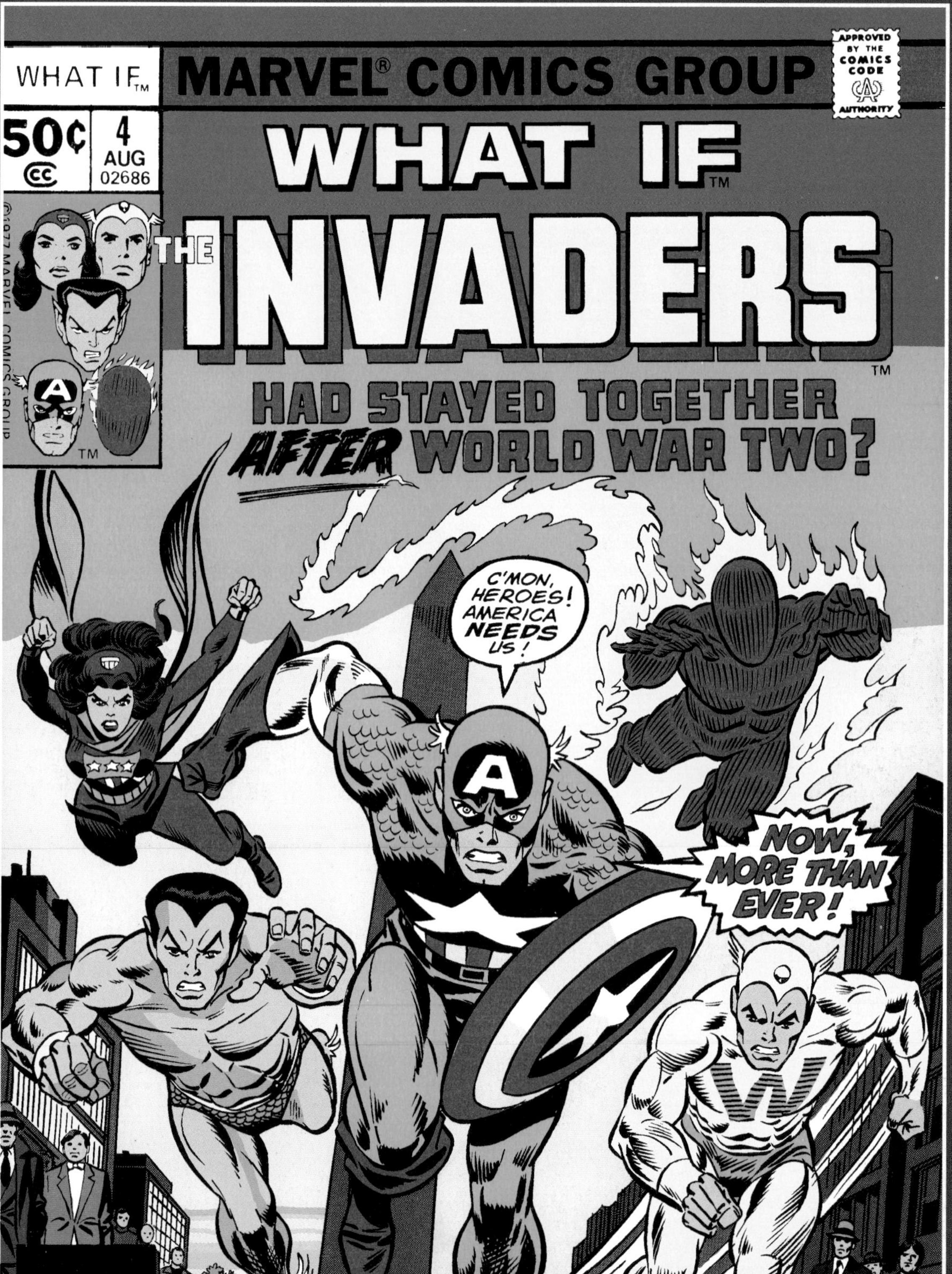
WHAT IF™
MARVEL® COMICS GROUP
APPROVED BY THE COMICS CODE AUTHORITY
50¢
4
AUG
02686
WHAT IF™
THE INVADERS™
HAD STAYED TOGETHER AFTER WORLD WAR TWO?
C'MON, HEROES! AMERICA NEEDS US!
NOW, MORE THAN EVER!

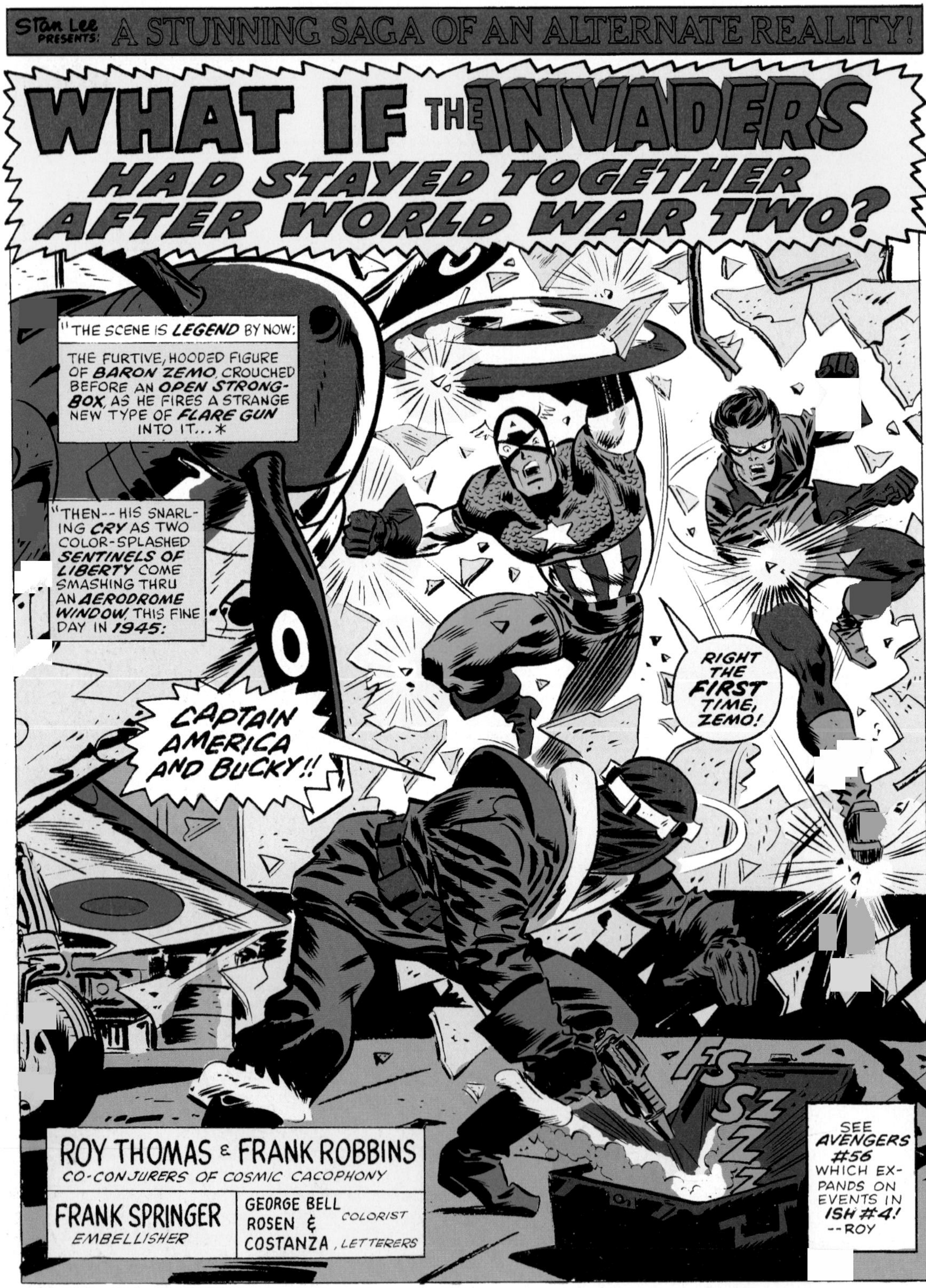

STAN LEE PRESENTS:
A STUNNING SAGA OF AN ALTERNATE REALITY!
WHAT IF THE INVADERS HAD STAYED TOGETHER AFTER WORLD WAR TWO?
"THE SCENE IS LEGEND BY NOW:
THE FURTIVE, HOODED FIGURE OF BARON ZEMO, CROUCHED BEFORE AN OPEN STRONG-BOX, AS HE FIRES A STRANGE NEW TYPE OF FLARE GUN INTO IT...*
"THEN--HIS SNARLING CRY AS TWO COLOR-SPLASHED SENTINELS OF LIBERTY COME SMASHING THRU AN AERODROME WINDOW, THIS FINE DAY IN 1945:
CAPTAIN AMERICA AND BUCKY!!
RIGHT THE FIRST TIME, ZEMO!
FSSZZZ
ROY THOMAS & FRANK ROBBINS
CO-CONJURERS OF COSMIC CACOPHONY
FRANK SPRINGER
EMBELLISHER
GEORGE BELL COLORIST
ROSEN & COSTANZA, LETTERERS
*SEE AVENGERS #56 WHICH EXPANDS ON EVENTS IN ISH #4! --ROY

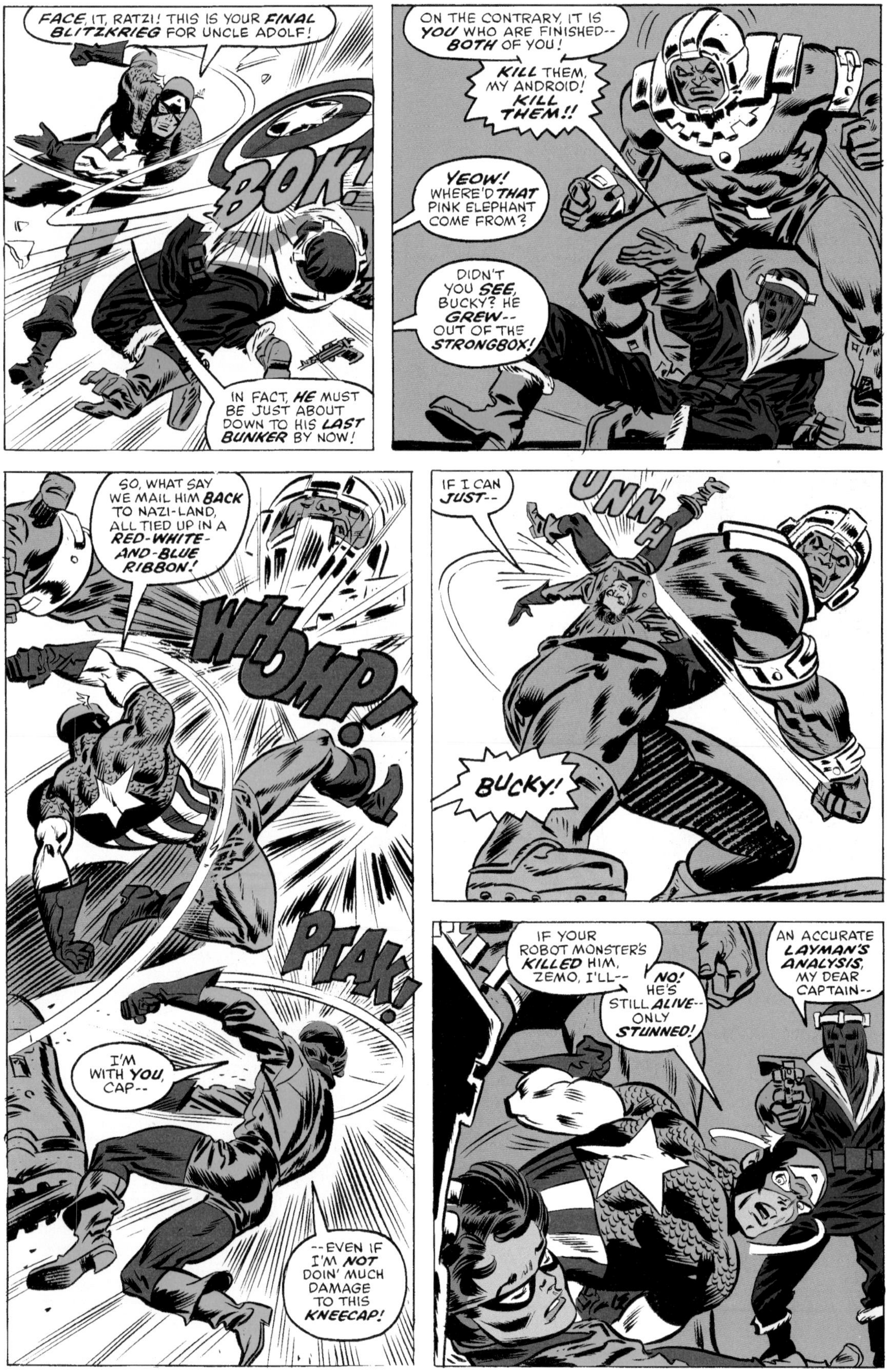

FACE IT, RATZI! THIS IS YOUR FINAL BLITZKRIEG FOR UNCLE ADOLF!
BOK!
IN FACT, HE MUST BE JUST ABOUT DOWN TO HIS LAST BUNKER BY NOW!
ON THE CONTRARY, IT IS YOU WHO ARE FINISHED-- BOTH OF YOU!
KILL THEM, MY ANDROID! KILL THEM!!
YEOW! WHERE'D THAT PINK ELEPHANT COME FROM?
DIDN'T YOU SEE, BUCKY? HE GREW-- OUT OF THE STRONGBOX!
SO, WHAT SAY WE MAIL HIM BACK TO NAZI-LAND, ALL TIED UP IN A RED-WHITE-AND-BLUE RIBBON!
WHOMP!
PTAK!
I'M WITH YOU, CAP--
--EVEN IF I'M NOT DOIN' MUCH DAMAGE TO THIS KNEECAP!
IF I CAN JUST--
UNNH
BUCKY!
IF YOUR ROBOT MONSTER'S KILLED HIM, ZEMO, I'LL--
NO! HE'S STILL ALIVE-- ONLY STUNNED!
AN ACCURATE LAYMAN'S ANALYSIS, MY DEAR CAPTAIN--

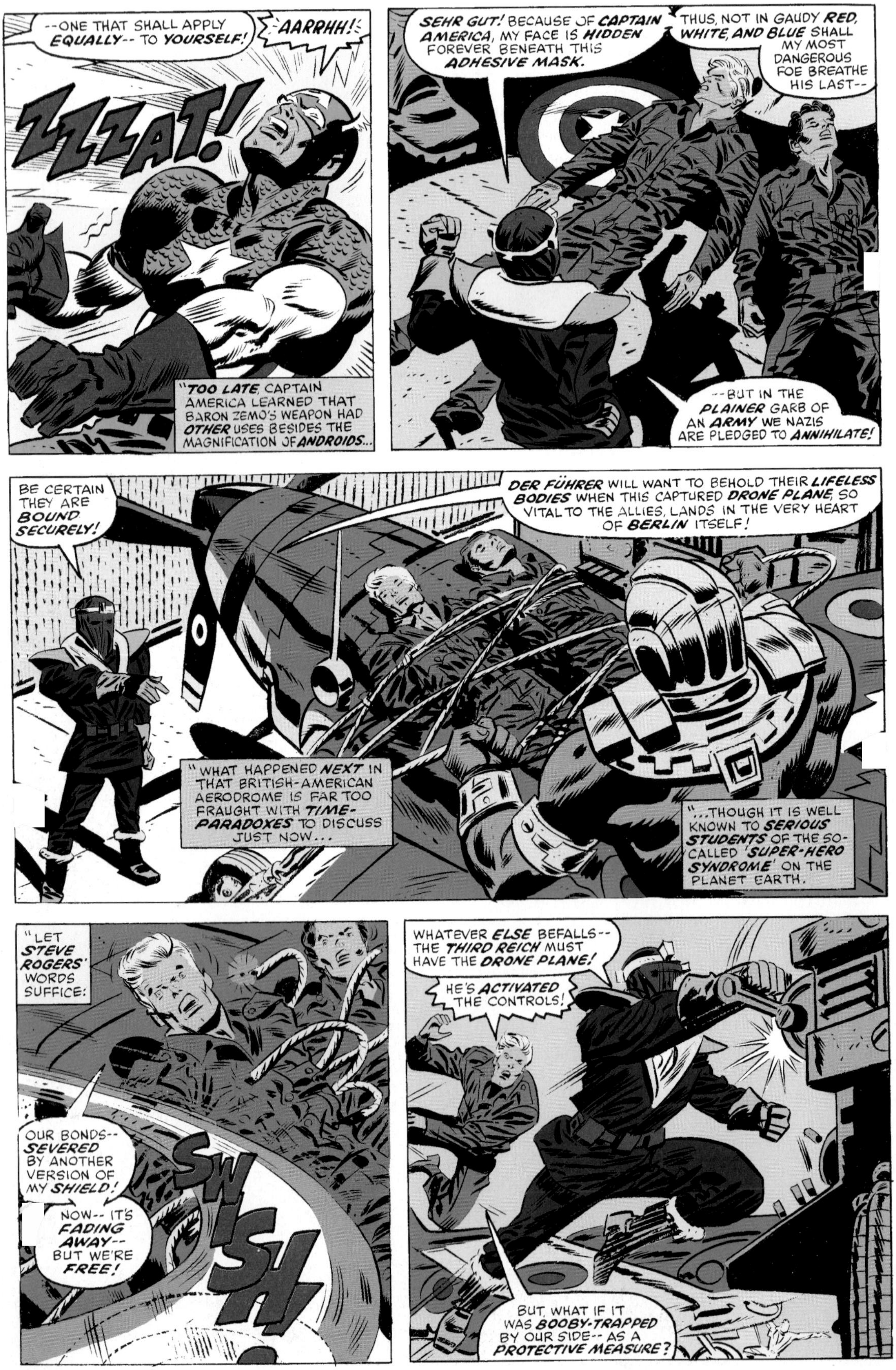
--ONE THAT SHALL APPLY EQUALLY-- TO YOURSELF!
AARRHH!
ZZZAT!
"TOO LATE, CAPTAIN AMERICA LEARNED THAT BARON ZEMO'S WEAPON HAD OTHER USES BESIDES THE MAGNIFICATION OF ANDROIDS...
SEHR GUT! BECAUSE OF CAPTAIN AMERICA, MY FACE IS HIDDEN FOREVER BENEATH THIS ADHESIVE MASK.
THUS, NOT IN GAUDY RED, WHITE, AND BLUE SHALL MY MOST DANGEROUS FOE BREATHE HIS LAST--
--BUT IN THE PLAINER GARB OF AN ARMY WE NAZIS ARE PLEDGED TO ANNIHILATE!
BE CERTAIN THEY ARE BOUND SECURELY!
DER FÜHRER WILL WANT TO BEHOLD THEIR LIFELESS BODIES WHEN THIS CAPTURED DRONE PLANE, SO VITAL TO THE ALLIES, LANDS IN THE VERY HEART OF BERLIN ITSELF!
"WHAT HAPPENED NEXT IN THAT BRITISH-AMERICAN AERODROME IS FAR TOO FRAUGHT WITH TIME-PARADOXES TO DISCUSS JUST NOW...
"...THOUGH IT IS WELL KNOWN TO SERIOUS STUDENTS OF THE SO-CALLED 'SUPER-HERO SYNDROME' ON THE PLANET EARTH.
"LET STEVE ROGERS' WORDS SUFFICE:
OUR BONDS-- SEVERED BY ANOTHER VERSION OF MY SHIELD!
NOW-- IT'S FADING AWAY-- BUT WE'RE FREE!
SWISH
WHATEVER ELSE BEFALLS-- THE THIRD REICH MUST HAVE THE DRONE PLANE!
HE'S ACTIVATED THE CONTROLS!
BUT, WHAT IF IT WAS BOOBY-TRAPPED BY OUR SIDE-- AS A PROTECTIVE MEASURE?

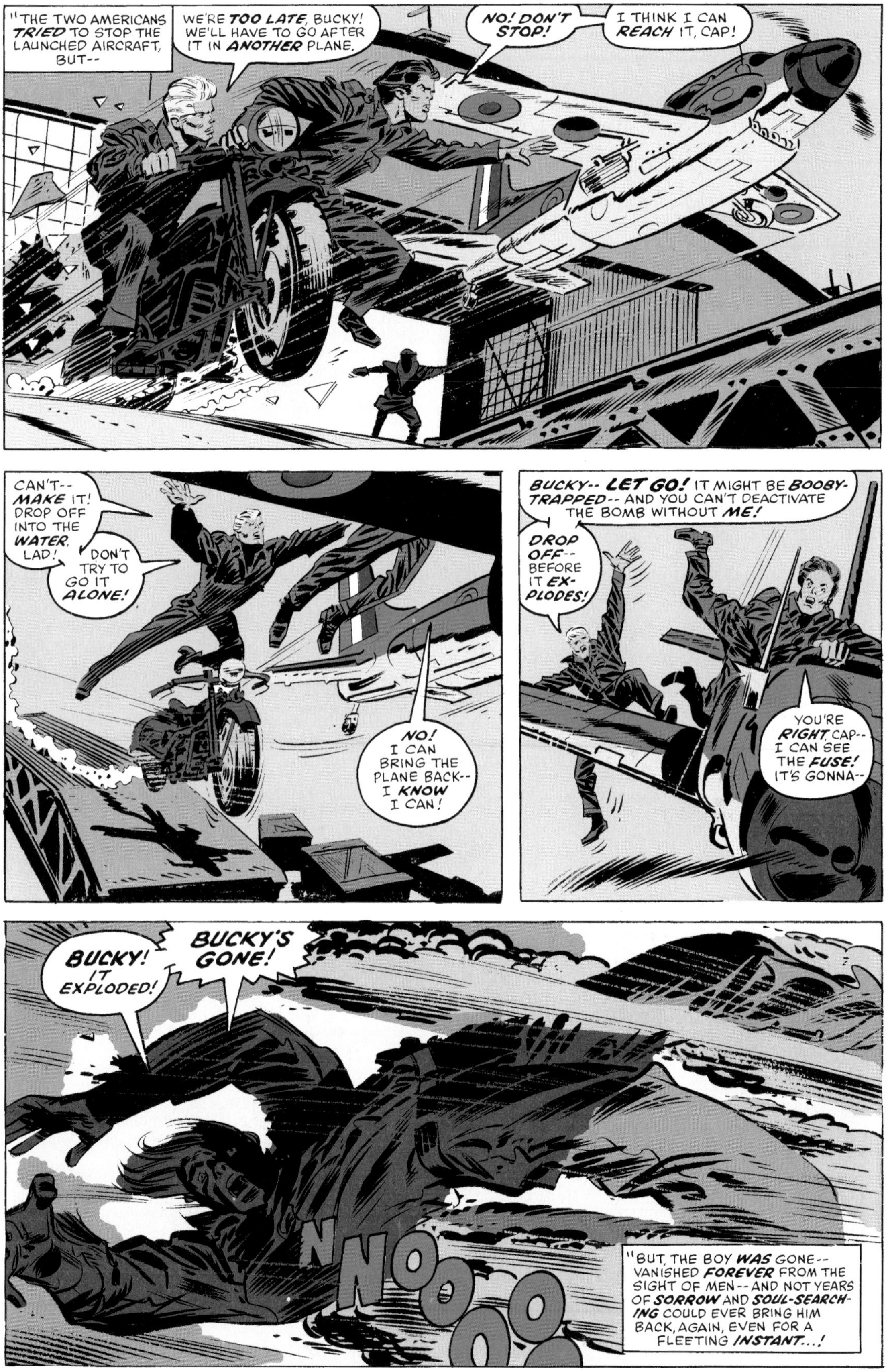

"THE TWO AMERICANS TRIED TO STOP THE LAUNCHED AIRCRAFT, BUT--
WE'RE TOO LATE, BUCKY! WE'LL HAVE TO GO AFTER IT IN ANOTHER PLANE.
NO! DON'T STOP!
I THINK I CAN REACH IT, CAP!
CAN'T-- MAKE IT! DROP OFF INTO THE WATER, LAD!
DON'T TRY TO GO IT ALONE!
NO! I CAN BRING THE PLANE BACK-- I KNOW I CAN!
BUCKY-- LET GO! IT MIGHT BE BOOBY-TRAPPED-- AND YOU CAN'T DEACTIVATE THE BOMB WITHOUT ME!
DROP OFF-- BEFORE IT EX-PLODES!
YOU'RE RIGHT, CAP-- I CAN SEE THE FUSE! IT'S GONNA--
BUCKY! IT EXPLODED!
BUCKY'S GONE!
NNOOOOO
"BUT, THE BOY WAS GONE-- VANISHED FOREVER FROM THE SIGHT OF MEN-- AND NOT YEARS OF SORROW AND SOUL-SEARCHING COULD EVER BRING HIM BACK, AGAIN, EVEN FOR A FLEETING INSTANT...!

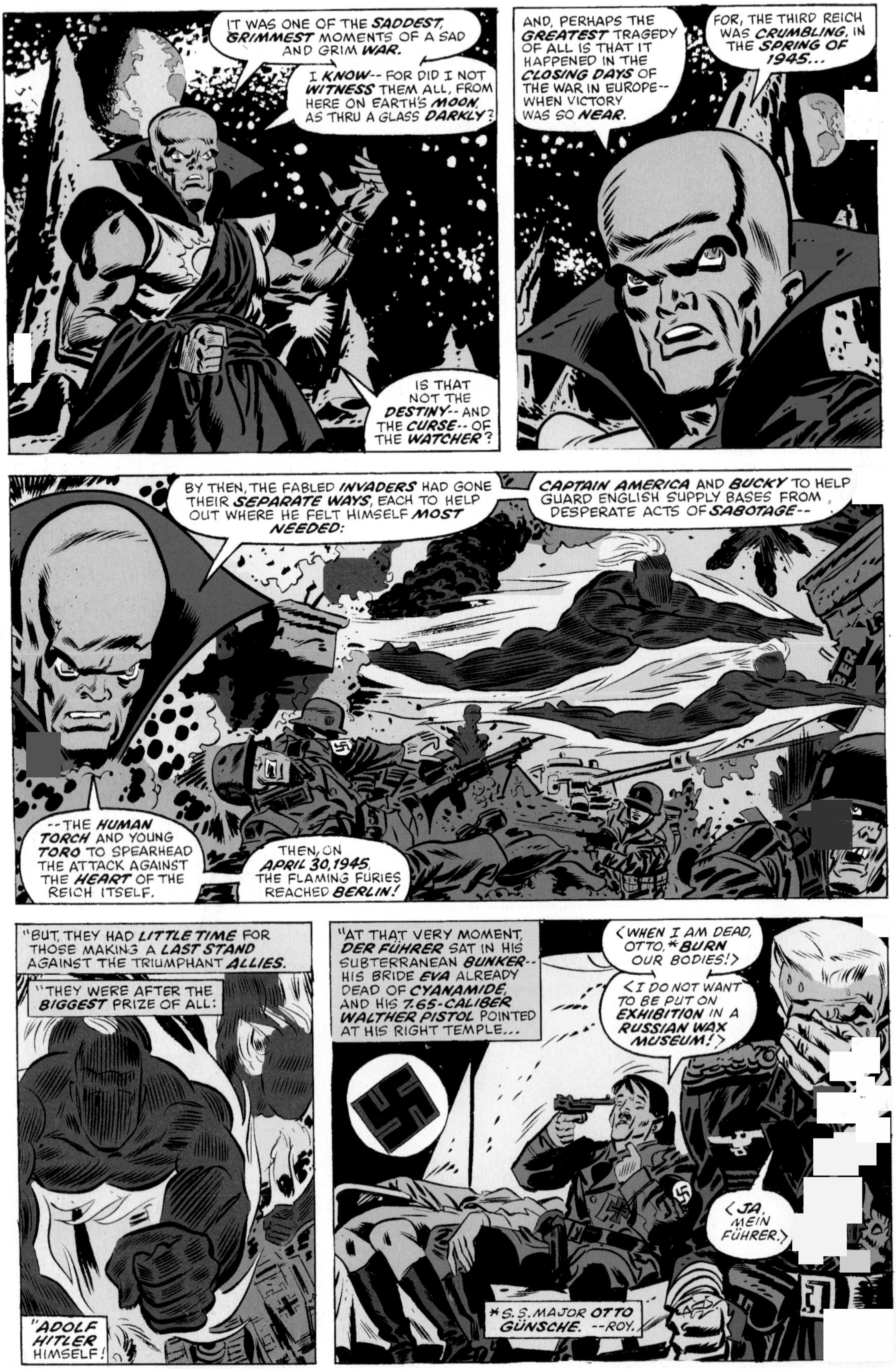
IT WAS ONE OF THE SADDEST, GRIMMEST MOMENTS OF A SAD AND GRIM WAR.
I KNOW-- FOR DID I NOT WITNESS THEM ALL, FROM HERE ON EARTH'S MOON, AS THRU A GLASS DARKLY?
IS THAT NOT THE DESTINY-- AND THE CURSE-- OF THE WATCHER?
AND, PERHAPS THE GREATEST TRAGEDY OF ALL IS THAT IT HAPPENED IN THE CLOSING DAYS OF THE WAR IN EUROPE-- WHEN VICTORY WAS SO NEAR.
FOR, THE THIRD REICH WAS CRUMBLING, IN THE SPRING OF 1945...
BY THEN, THE FABLED INVADERS HAD GONE THEIR SEPARATE WAYS, EACH TO HELP OUT WHERE HE FELT HIMSELF MOST NEEDED:
CAPTAIN AMERICA AND BUCKY TO HELP GUARD ENGLISH SUPPLY BASES FROM DESPERATE ACTS OF SABOTAGE--
--THE HUMAN TORCH AND YOUNG TORO TO SPEARHEAD THE ATTACK AGAINST THE HEART OF THE REICH ITSELF.
THEN, ON APRIL 30, 1945, THE FLAMING FURIES REACHED BERLIN!
"BUT, THEY HAD LITTLE TIME FOR THOSE MAKING A LAST STAND AGAINST THE TRIUMPHANT ALLIES.
"THEY WERE AFTER THE BIGGEST PRIZE OF ALL:
"ADOLF HITLER HIMSELF!
"AT THAT VERY MOMENT, DER FÜHRER SAT IN HIS SUBTERRANEAN BUNKER-- HIS BRIDE EVA ALREADY DEAD OF CYANAMIDE, AND HIS 7.65-CALIBER WALTHER PISTOL POINTED AT HIS RIGHT TEMPLE...
<WHEN I AM DEAD, OTTO,* BURN OUR BODIES!>
<I DO NOT WANT TO BE PUT ON EXHIBITION IN A RUSSIAN WAX MUSEUM!>
<JA, MEIN FÜHRER.>
*S.S. MAJOR OTTO GÜNSCHE. --ROY.

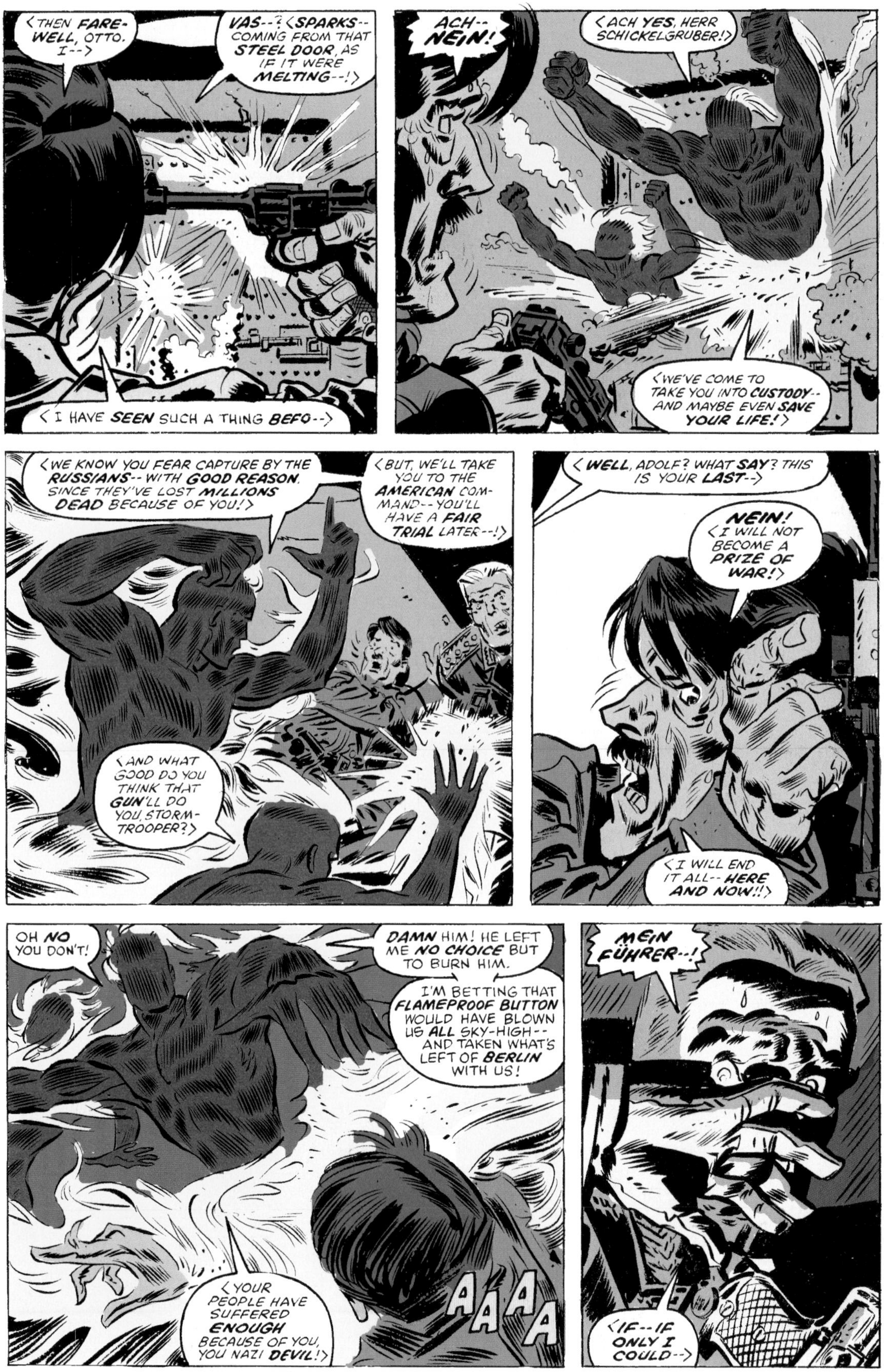
<THEN FARE-WELL, OTTO. I-->
VAS--? <SPARKS--COMING FROM THAT STEEL DOOR, AS IF IT WERE MELTING--!>
<I HAVE SEEN SUCH A THING BEFO-->
ACH--NEIN!
<ACH YES, HERR SCHICKELGRUBER!>
<WE'VE COME TO TAKE YOU INTO CUSTODY--AND MAYBE EVEN SAVE YOUR LIFE!>
<WE KNOW YOU FEAR CAPTURE BY THE RUSSIANS--WITH GOOD REASON, SINCE THEY'VE LOST MILLIONS DEAD BECAUSE OF YOU!>
<BUT, WE'LL TAKE YOU TO THE AMERICAN COMMAND--YOU'LL HAVE A FAIR TRIAL LATER--!>
<AND WHAT GOOD DO YOU THINK THAT GUN'LL DO YOU, STORM-TROOPER?>
<WELL, ADOLF? WHAT SAY? THIS IS YOUR LAST-->
NEIN! <I WILL NOT BECOME A PRIZE OF WAR!>
<I WILL END IT ALL--HERE AND NOW!!>
OH NO YOU DON'T!
DAMN HIM! HE LEFT ME NO CHOICE BUT TO BURN HIM.
I'M BETTING THAT FLAMEPROOF BUTTON WOULD HAVE BLOWN US ALL SKY-HIGH--AND TAKEN WHAT'S LEFT OF BERLIN WITH US!
<YOUR PEOPLE HAVE SUFFERED ENOUGH BECAUSE OF YOU, YOU NAZI DEVIL!>
AAAA
MEIN FÜHRER--!
<IF--IF ONLY I COULD-->

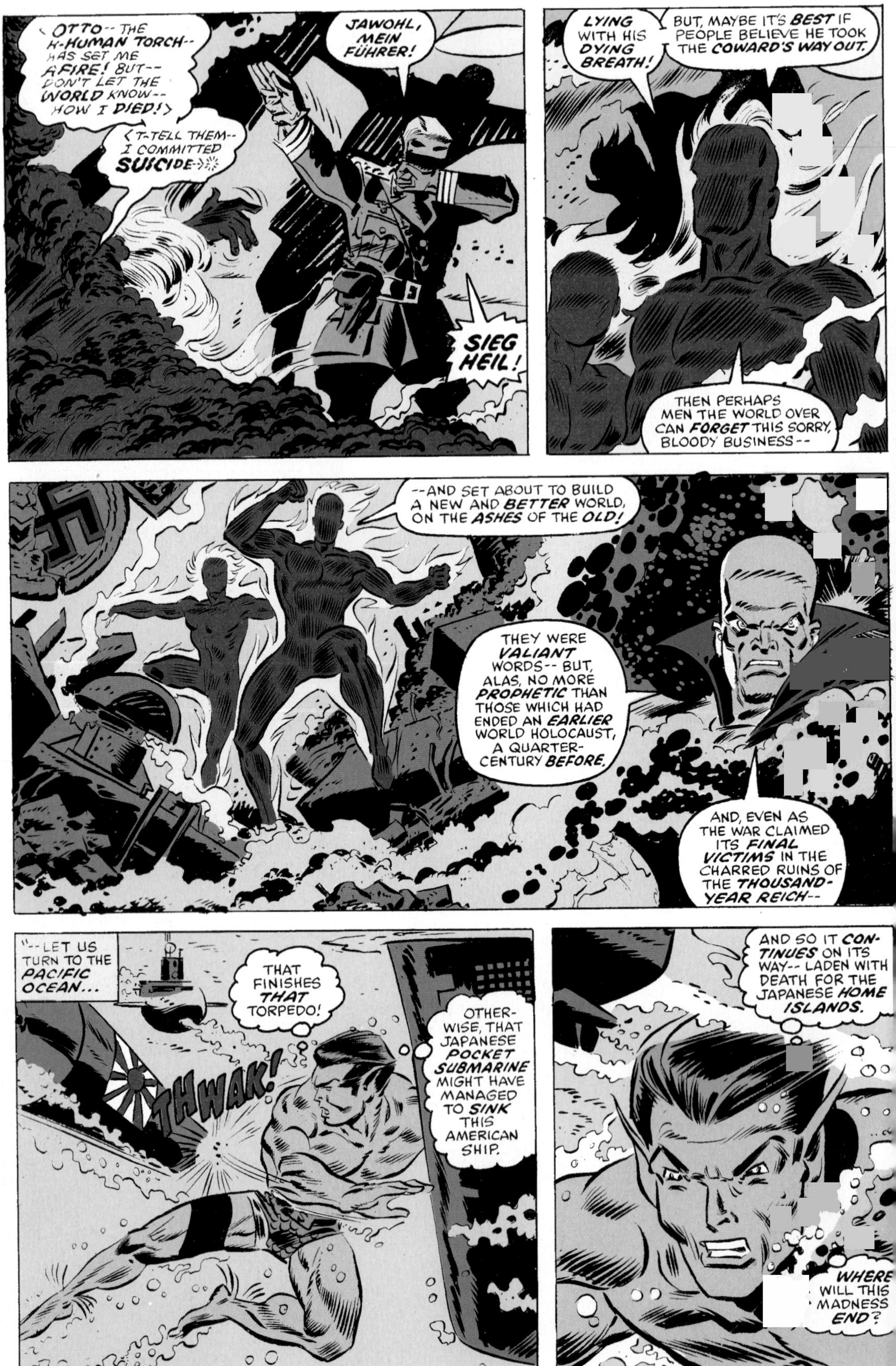

<OTTO-- THE H-HUMAN TORCH-- HAS SET ME AFIRE! BUT-- DON'T LET THE WORLD KNOW-- HOW I DIED!>
JAWOHL, MEIN FÜHRER!
<T-TELL THEM-- I COMMITTED SUICIDE->
SIEG HEIL!
LYING WITH HIS DYING BREATH!
BUT, MAYBE IT'S BEST IF PEOPLE BELIEVE HE TOOK THE COWARD'S WAY OUT.
THEN PERHAPS MEN THE WORLD OVER CAN FORGET THIS SORRY, BLOODY BUSINESS--
--AND SET ABOUT TO BUILD A NEW AND BETTER WORLD, ON THE ASHES OF THE OLD!
THEY WERE VALIANT WORDS-- BUT, ALAS, NO MORE PROPHETIC THAN THOSE WHICH HAD ENDED AN EARLIER WORLD HOLOCAUST, A QUARTER-CENTURY BEFORE.
AND, EVEN AS THE WAR CLAIMED ITS FINAL VICTIMS IN THE CHARRED RUINS OF THE THOUSAND-YEAR REICH--
"--LET US TURN TO THE PACIFIC OCEAN...
THAT FINISHES THAT TORPEDO!
OTHER-WISE, THAT JAPANESE POCKET SUBMARINE MIGHT HAVE MANAGED TO SINK THIS AMERICAN SHIP.
THWAK!
AND SO IT CONTINUES ON ITS WAY-- LADEN WITH DEATH FOR THE JAPANESE HOME ISLANDS.
WHERE WILL THIS MADNESS END?

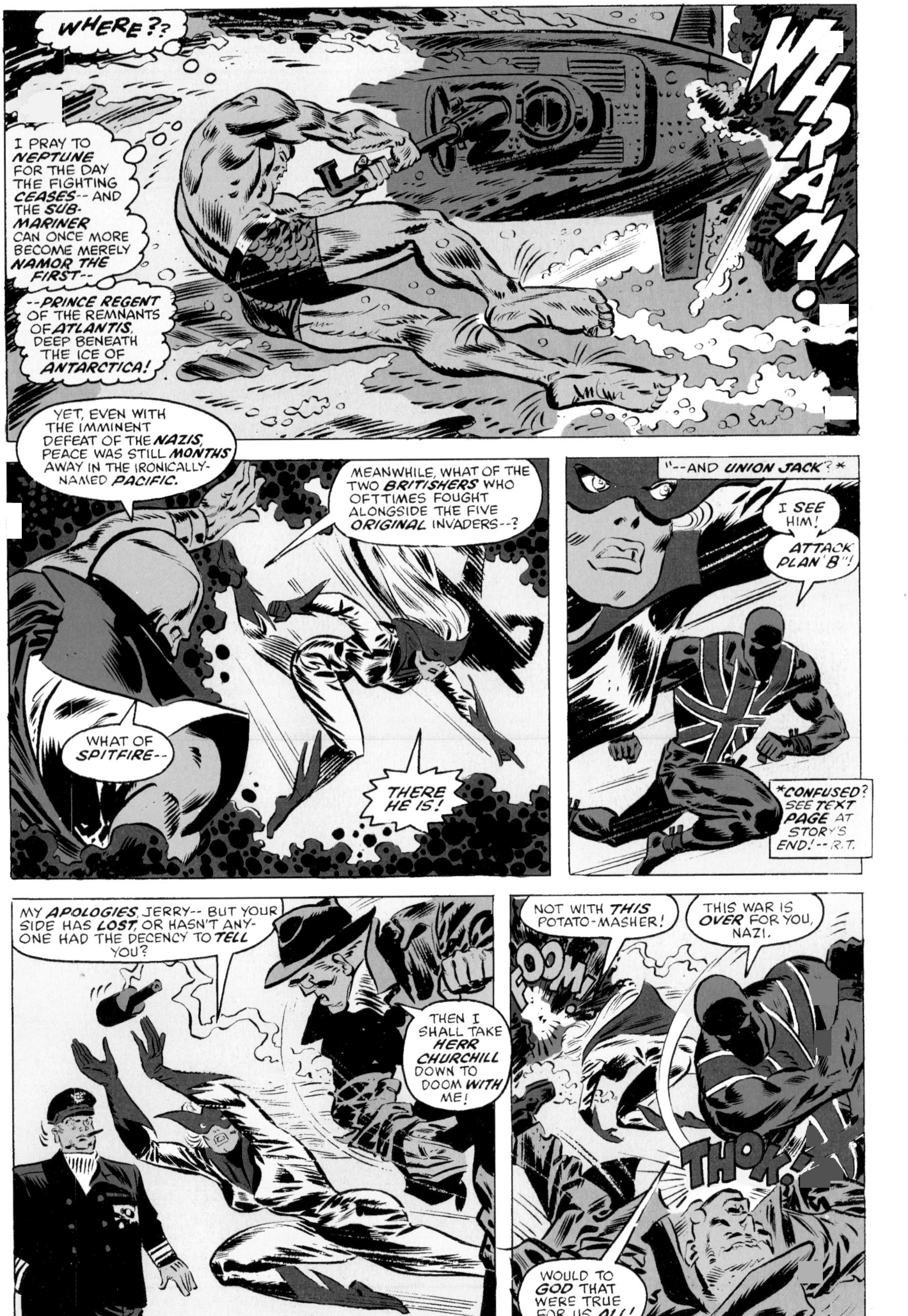
WHERE??
I PRAY TO NEPTUNE FOR THE DAY THE FIGHTING CEASES-- AND THE SUB-MARINER CAN ONCE MORE BECOME MERELY NAMOR THE FIRST--
--PRINCE REGENT OF THE REMNANTS OF ATLANTIS, DEEP BENEATH THE ICE OF ANTARCTICA!
WHRAM!
YET, EVEN WITH THE IMMINENT DEFEAT OF THE NAZIS, PEACE WAS STILL MONTHS AWAY IN THE IRONICALLY-NAMED PACIFIC.
MEANWHILE, WHAT OF THE TWO BRITISHERS WHO OFTTIMES FOUGHT ALONGSIDE THE FIVE ORIGINAL INVADERS--?
WHAT OF SPITFIRE--
THERE HE IS!
"--AND UNION JACK"?*
I SEE HIM!
ATTACK PLAN 'B'!
*CONFUSED? SEE TEXT PAGE AT STORY'S END! --R.T.
MY APOLOGIES, JERRY-- BUT YOUR SIDE HAS LOST, OR HASN'T ANY-ONE HAD THE DECENCY TO TELL YOU?
THEN I SHALL TAKE HERR CHURCHILL DOWN TO DOOM WITH ME!
NOT WITH THIS POTATO-MASHER!
FOOM!
THIS WAR IS OVER FOR YOU, NAZI.
THOK!
WOULD TO GOD THAT WERE TRUE FOR US ALL!

"LATER THAT NIGHT, IN THE HEART OF LONDON..." ✱

AH, *UNION JACK*-- AND, ER, *MISS SPITFIRE*-- THANK YOU FOR COMING SO *PROMPTLY!*

✱ *THIS* WILL BE EXPLAINED ON THE TEXT PAGE, *ALSO*-- AS WILL THE GENTS *INSIDE.* --ROY.

WE CAME AS QUICKLY AS WE *COULD*, MAJOR RAWLINGS.

I FEAR *I* SLOW HER DOWN QUITE A BIT, GENTLEMEN.

IN MANY WAYS, I WISH YOU HAD BEEN *SLOWER!*

WHAT DO YOU *MEAN*, MAJOR? WHY WERE WE *CALLED* HERE?

AYE! AND WHERE ARE *CAPTAIN AMERICA* AND HIS YOUNG ALLY?

THAT, I FEAR, IS *WHY* YOU WERE SUMMONED! COLONEL FARROW?

THE FOLLOWING *TOP SECRET* DISPATCH IS DATED *APRIL 18, 1945:*

"*CAPTAIN AMERICA* AND BUCKY *KILLED IN ACTION*-- DEFENDING SECRET WEAPON ON *ENGLISH BASE.*"

I'M AFRAID-- THAT SAYS IT *ALL.*

THE CAPTAIN-- *DEAD??*

YOU'RE LYING!

I WISH TO GOD I *WERE*, MISS.

HOW DID IT HAPPEN? *HOW?*

AN *AERIAL EXPLOSION* -- THE BODIES WERE NOT RECOVERED--!

NO BODIES!? THEN HOW DO YOU *KNOW* THEY'RE DEAD? THEY--

EASY, TORO! I'M SURE THE OFFICERS HAVE *MORE* TO SAY.

THE EXPLOSION WAS *WITNESSED* BY *R.A.F.* PERSONNEL. *BUCKY* WAS STILL ABOARD THE CRAFT...

THE *CAPTAIN'S* BODY FELL INTO THE *CHANNEL*. IT DID *NOT* SURFACE.

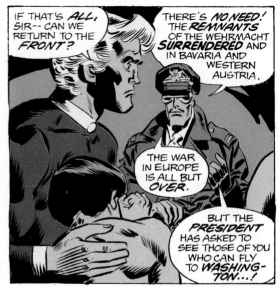

IF THAT'S *ALL*, SIR-- CAN WE RETURN TO THE *FRONT?*

THERE'S *NO NEED!* THE *REMNANTS* OF THE WEHRMACHT *SURRENDERED* AND IN BAVARIA AND WESTERN AUSTRIA.

THE WAR IN EUROPE IS ALL BUT *OVER.*

BUT THE *PRESIDENT* HAS ASKED TO SEE THOSE OF YOU WHO CAN FLY TO *WASHINGTON*...!

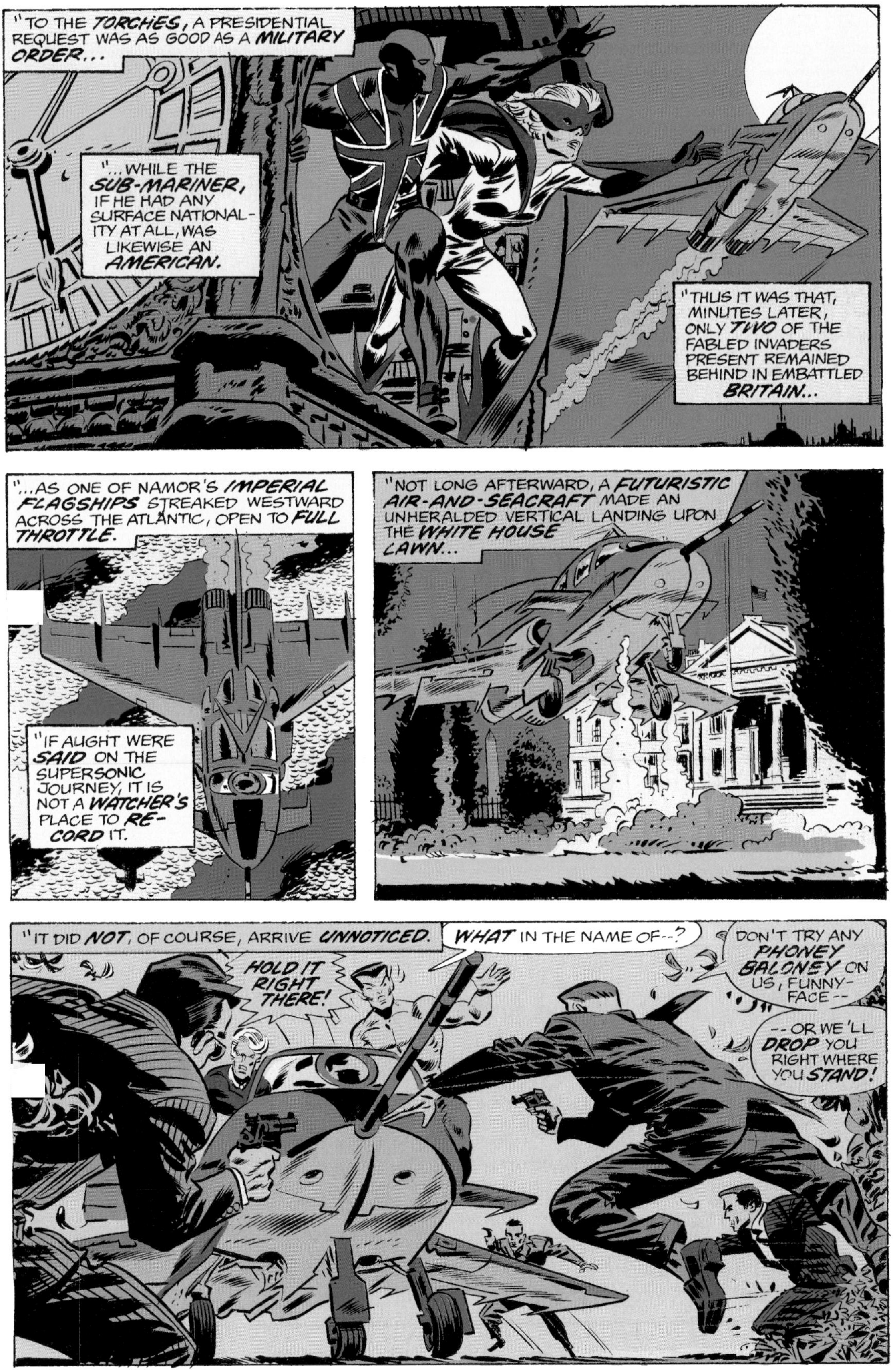
"TO THE TORCHES, A PRESIDENTIAL REQUEST WAS AS GOOD AS A MILITARY ORDER...
"...WHILE THE SUB-MARINER, IF HE HAD ANY SURFACE NATIONALITY AT ALL, WAS LIKEWISE AN AMERICAN.
"THUS IT WAS THAT, MINUTES LATER, ONLY TWO OF THE FABLED INVADERS PRESENT REMAINED BEHIND IN EMBATTLED BRITAIN...
"...AS ONE OF NAMOR'S IMPERIAL FLAGSHIPS STREAKED WESTWARD ACROSS THE ATLANTIC, OPEN TO FULL THROTTLE.
"IF AUGHT WERE SAID ON THE SUPERSONIC JOURNEY, IT IS NOT A WATCHER'S PLACE TO RECORD IT.
"NOT LONG AFTERWARD, A FUTURISTIC AIR-AND-SEACRAFT MADE AN UNHERALDED VERTICAL LANDING UPON THE WHITE HOUSE LAWN...
"IT DID NOT, OF COURSE, ARRIVE UNNOTICED.
WHAT IN THE NAME OF--?
HOLD IT RIGHT THERE!
DON'T TRY ANY PHONEY BALONEY ON US, FUNNY-FACE --
-- OR WE'LL DROP YOU RIGHT WHERE YOU STAND!

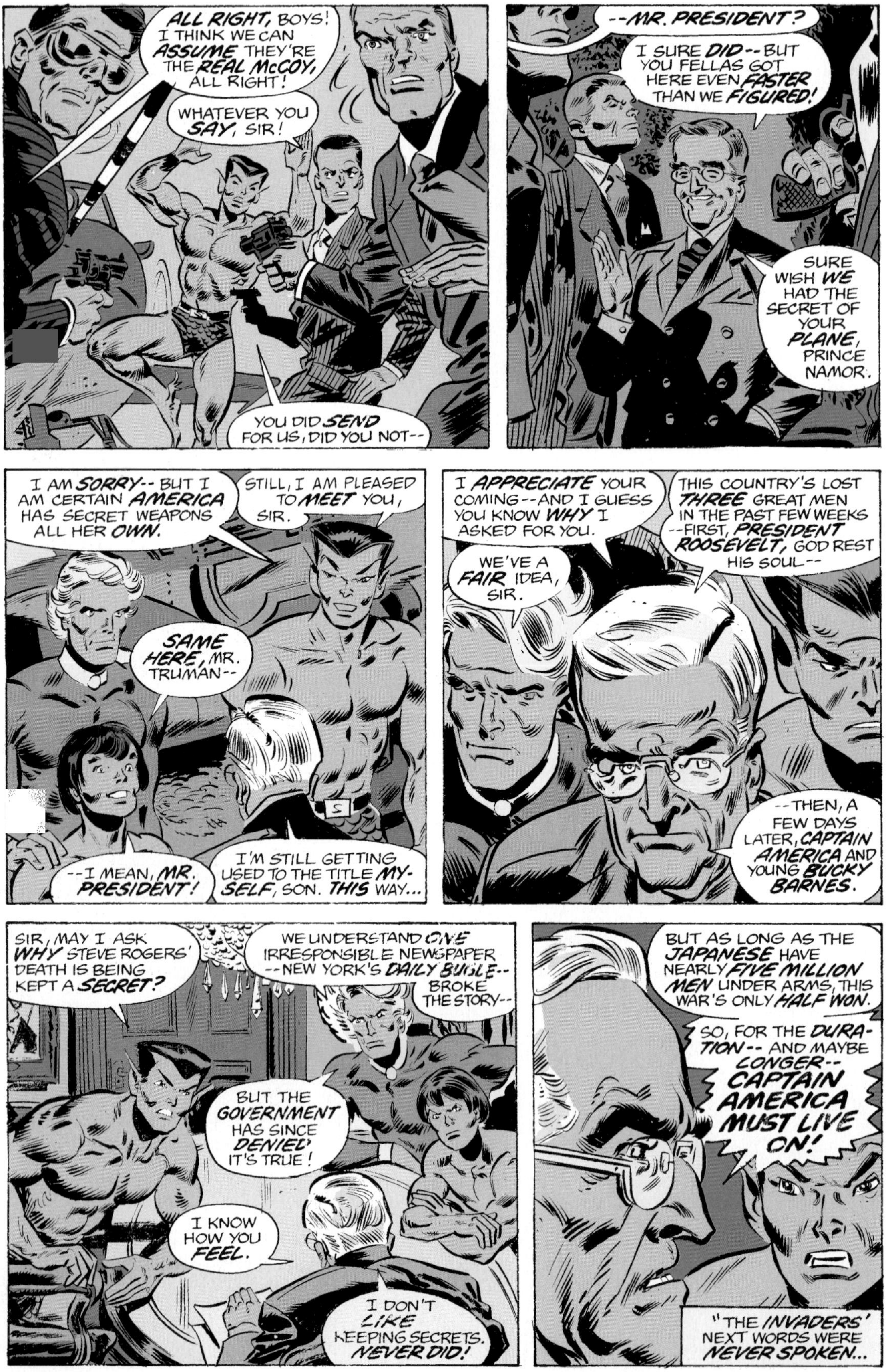
ALL RIGHT, BOYS! I THINK WE CAN ASSUME THEY'RE THE REAL McCOY, ALL RIGHT!
WHATEVER YOU SAY, SIR!
YOU DID SEND FOR US, DID YOU NOT--
--MR. PRESIDENT?
I SURE DID--BUT YOU FELLAS GOT HERE EVEN FASTER THAN WE FIGURED!
SURE WISH WE HAD THE SECRET OF YOUR PLANE, PRINCE NAMOR.
I AM SORRY--BUT I AM CERTAIN AMERICA HAS SECRET WEAPONS ALL HER OWN.
STILL, I AM PLEASED TO MEET YOU, SIR.
SAME HERE, MR. TRUMAN--
--I MEAN, MR. PRESIDENT!
I'M STILL GETTING USED TO THE TITLE MY-SELF, SON. THIS WAY...
I APPRECIATE YOUR COMING--AND I GUESS YOU KNOW WHY I ASKED FOR YOU.
WE'VE A FAIR IDEA, SIR.
THIS COUNTRY'S LOST THREE GREAT MEN IN THE PAST FEW WEEKS --FIRST, PRESIDENT ROOSEVELT, GOD REST HIS SOUL--
--THEN, A FEW DAYS LATER, CAPTAIN AMERICA AND YOUNG BUCKY BARNES.
SIR, MAY I ASK WHY STEVE ROGERS' DEATH IS BEING KEPT A SECRET?
WE UNDERSTAND ONE IRRESPONSIBLE NEWSPAPER --NEW YORK'S DAILY BUGLE--BROKE THE STORY--
BUT THE GOVERNMENT HAS SINCE DENIED IT'S TRUE!
I KNOW HOW YOU FEEL.
I DON'T LIKE KEEPING SECRETS. NEVER DID!
BUT AS LONG AS THE JAPANESE HAVE NEARLY FIVE MILLION MEN UNDER ARMS, THIS WAR'S ONLY HALF WON.
SO, FOR THE DURA-TION--AND MAYBE LONGER--CAPTAIN AMERICA MUST LIVE ON!
"THE INVADERS' NEXT WORDS WERE NEVER SPOKEN...

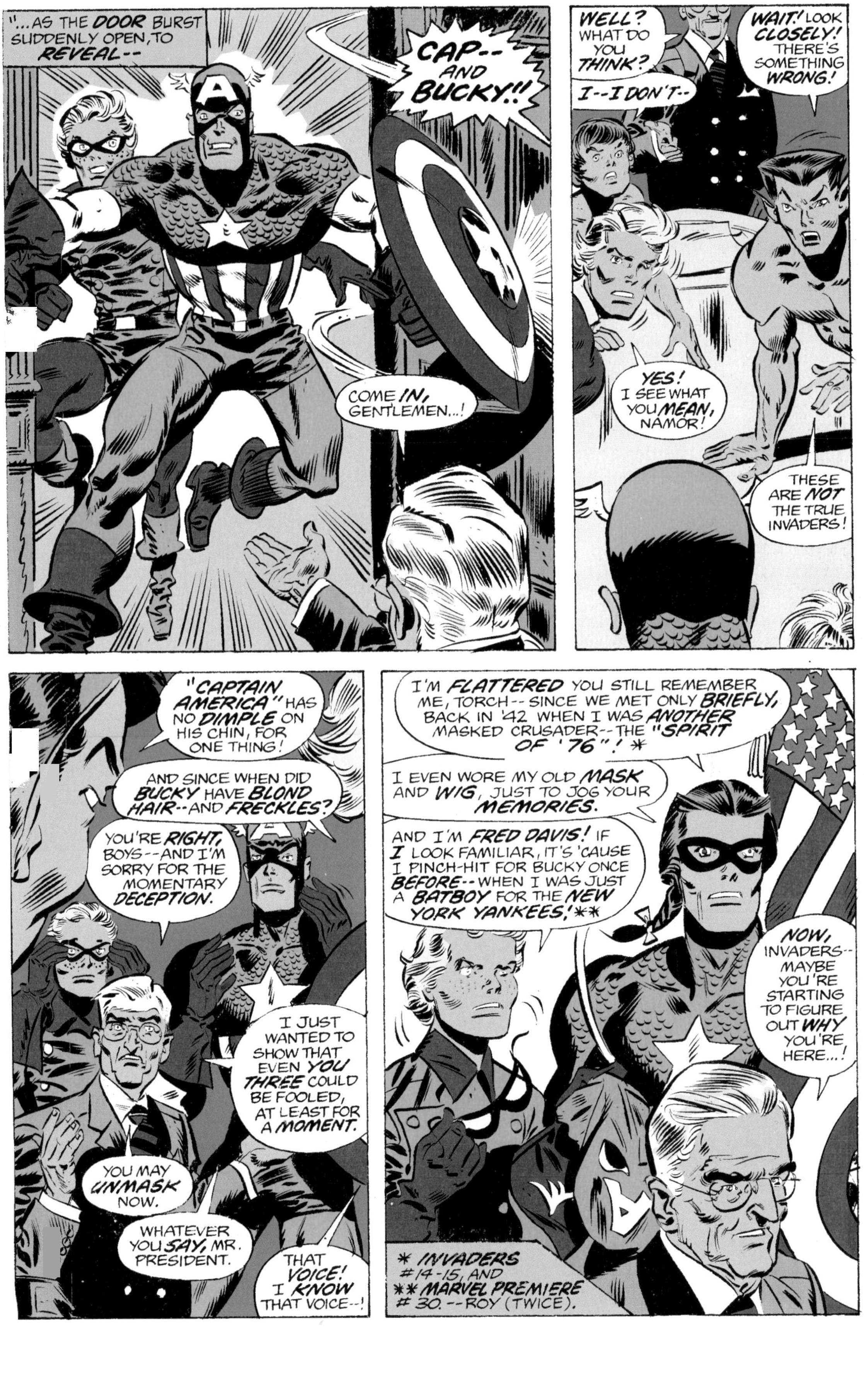
"...AS THE DOOR BURST SUDDENLY OPEN, TO REVEAL--
CAP-- AND BUCKY!!
COME IN, GENTLEMEN...!
WELL? WHAT DO YOU THINK?
I--I DON'T--
WAIT! LOOK CLOSELY! THERE'S SOMETHING WRONG!
YES! I SEE WHAT YOU MEAN, NAMOR!
THESE ARE NOT THE TRUE INVADERS!
"CAPTAIN AMERICA" HAS NO DIMPLE ON HIS CHIN, FOR ONE THING!
AND SINCE WHEN DID BUCKY HAVE BLOND HAIR--AND FRECKLES?
YOU'RE RIGHT, BOYS--AND I'M SORRY FOR THE MOMENTARY DECEPTION.
I JUST WANTED TO SHOW THAT EVEN YOU THREE COULD BE FOOLED, AT LEAST FOR A MOMENT.
YOU MAY UNMASK NOW.
WHATEVER YOU SAY, MR. PRESIDENT.
THAT VOICE! I KNOW THAT VOICE--!
I'M FLATTERED YOU STILL REMEMBER ME, TORCH--SINCE WE MET ONLY BRIEFLY, BACK IN '42 WHEN I WAS ANOTHER MASKED CRUSADER--THE "SPIRIT OF '76"! *
I EVEN WORE MY OLD MASK AND WIG, JUST TO JOG YOUR MEMORIES.
AND I'M FRED DAVIS! IF I LOOK FAMILIAR, IT'S 'CAUSE I PINCH-HIT FOR BUCKY ONCE BEFORE--WHEN I WAS JUST A BATBOY FOR THE NEW YORK YANKEES! **
NOW, INVADERS--MAYBE YOU'RE STARTING TO FIGURE OUT WHY YOU'RE HERE...!
* INVADERS #14-15, AND ** MARVEL PREMIERE # 30. --ROY (TWICE).

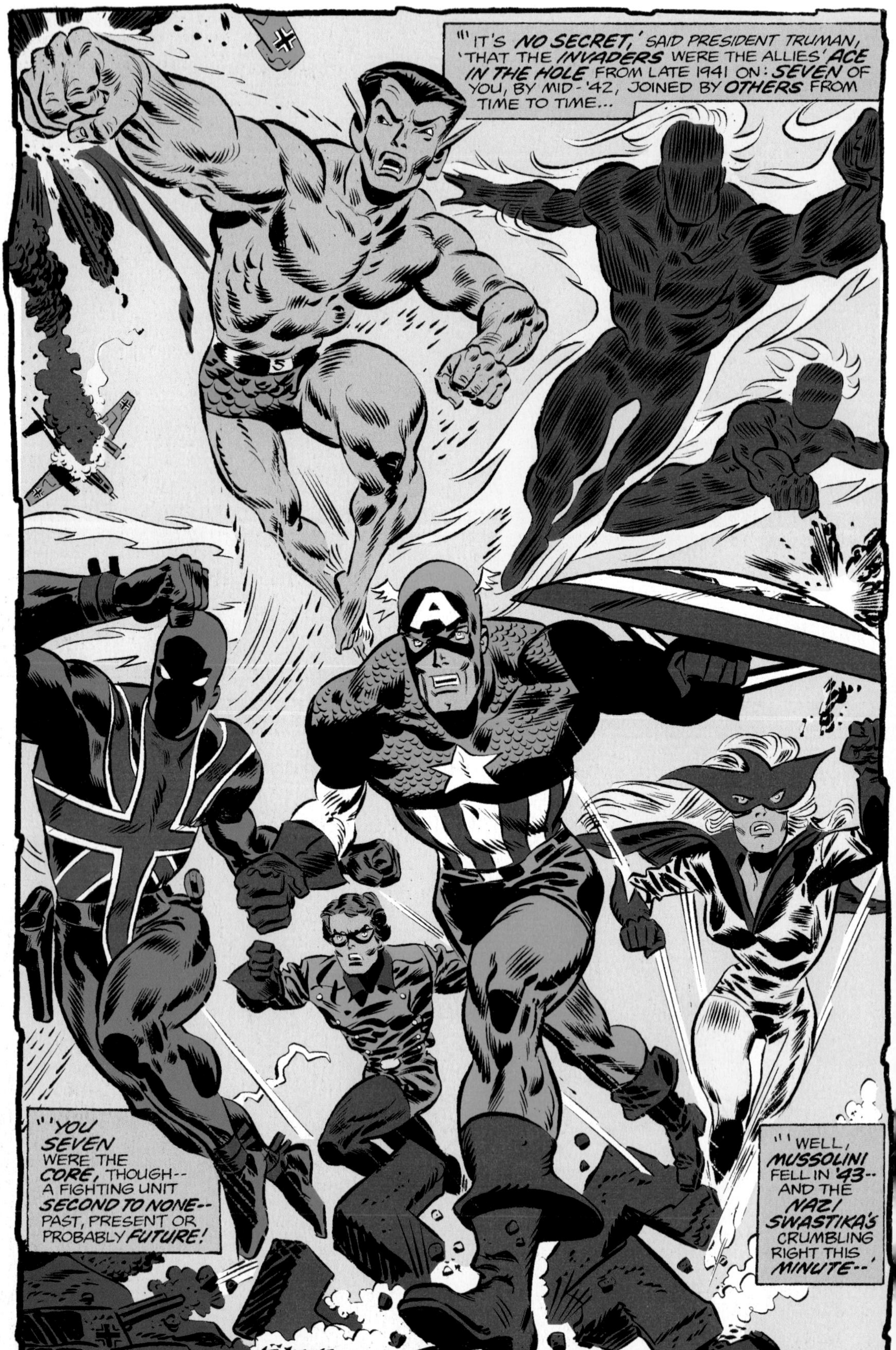
"'IT'S NO SECRET,' SAID PRESIDENT TRUMAN, 'THAT THE INVADERS WERE THE ALLIES' ACE IN THE HOLE FROM LATE 1941 ON: SEVEN OF YOU, BY MID-'42, JOINED BY OTHERS FROM TIME TO TIME...
"'YOU SEVEN WERE THE CORE, THOUGH-- A FIGHTING UNIT SECOND TO NONE-- PAST, PRESENT OR PROBABLY FUTURE!
"'WELL, MUSSOLINI FELL IN '43-- AND THE NAZI SWASTIKA'S CRUMBLING RIGHT THIS MINUTE--'

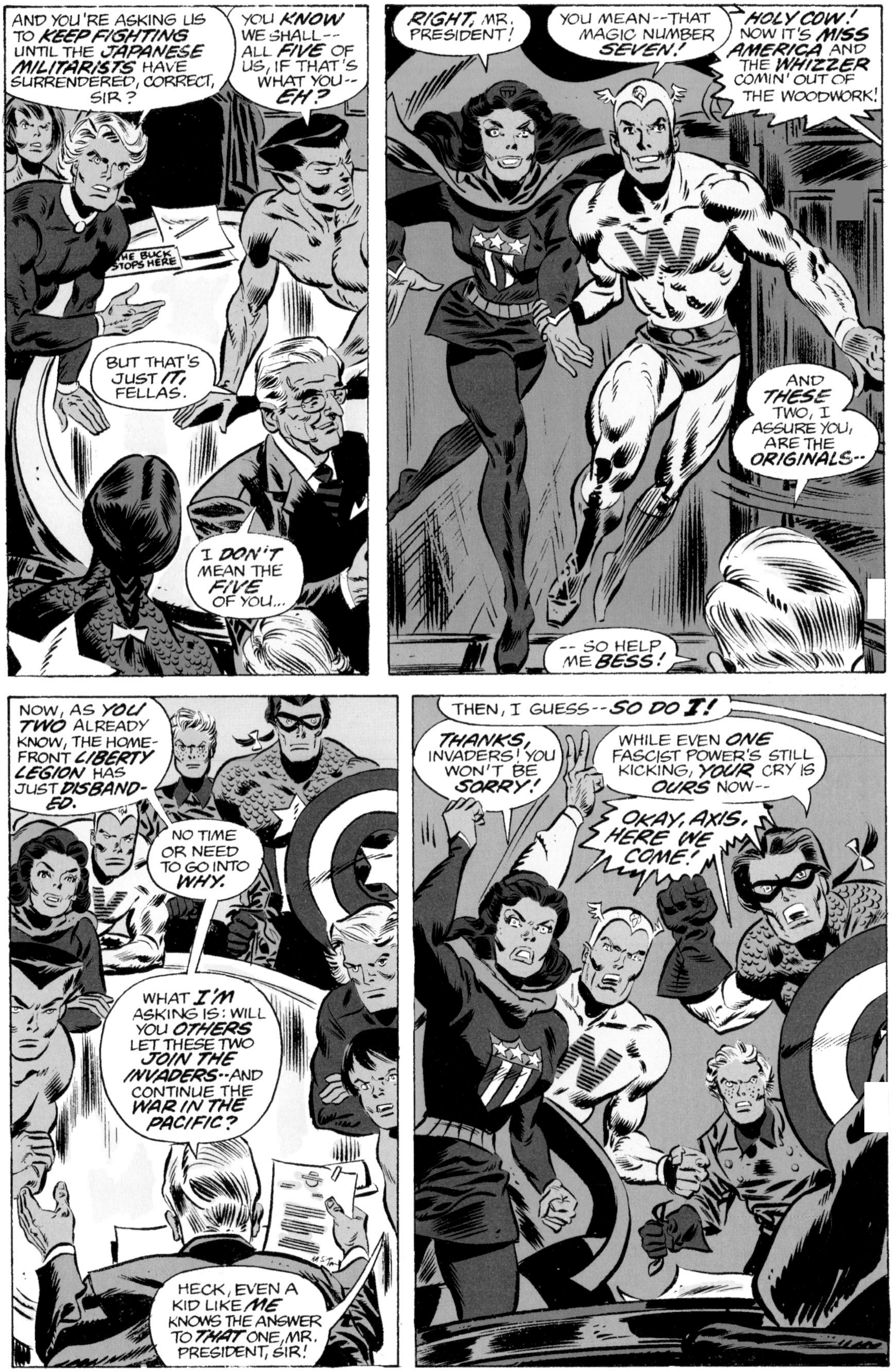

AND YOU'RE ASKING US TO KEEP FIGHTING UNTIL THE JAPANESE MILITARISTS HAVE SURRENDERED, CORRECT, SIR?
YOU KNOW WE SHALL-- ALL FIVE OF US, IF THAT'S WHAT YOU-- EH?
THE BUCK STOPS HERE
BUT THAT'S JUST IT, FELLAS.
I DON'T MEAN THE FIVE OF YOU...
RIGHT, MR. PRESIDENT!
YOU MEAN--THAT MAGIC NUMBER SEVEN!
HOLY COW! NOW IT'S MISS AMERICA AND THE WHIZZER COMIN' OUT OF THE WOODWORK!
AND THESE TWO, I ASSURE YOU, ARE THE ORIGINALS--
-- SO HELP ME BESS!
NOW, AS YOU TWO ALREADY KNOW, THE HOME-FRONT LIBERTY LEGION HAS JUST DISBANDED.
NO TIME OR NEED TO GO INTO WHY.
WHAT I'M ASKING IS: WILL YOU OTHERS LET THESE TWO JOIN THE INVADERS--AND CONTINUE THE WAR IN THE PACIFIC?
HECK, EVEN A KID LIKE ME KNOWS THE ANSWER TO THAT ONE, MR. PRESIDENT, SIR!
THEN, I GUESS--SO DO I!
THANKS, INVADERS! YOU WON'T BE SORRY!
WHILE EVEN ONE FASCIST POWER'S STILL KICKING, YOUR CRY IS OURS NOW--
OKAY, AXIS, HERE WE COME!

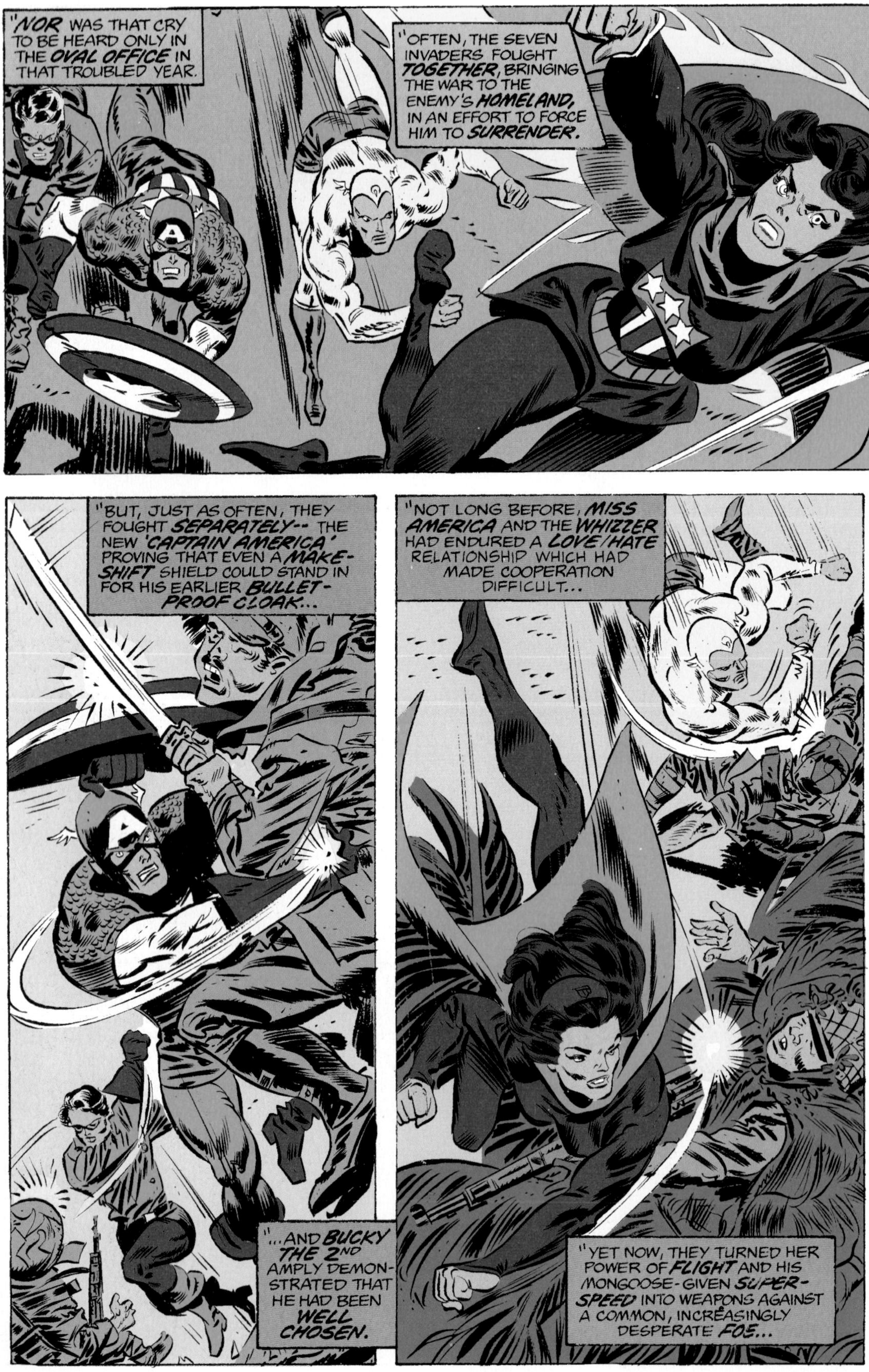
"NOR WAS THAT CRY TO BE HEARD ONLY IN THE OVAL OFFICE IN THAT TROUBLED YEAR.
"OFTEN, THE SEVEN INVADERS FOUGHT TOGETHER, BRINGING THE WAR TO THE ENEMY'S HOMELAND, IN AN EFFORT TO FORCE HIM TO SURRENDER.
"BUT, JUST AS OFTEN, THEY FOUGHT SEPARATELY-- THE NEW 'CAPTAIN AMERICA' PROVING THAT EVEN A MAKE-SHIFT SHIELD COULD STAND IN FOR HIS EARLIER BULLET-PROOF CLOAK...
"...AND BUCKY THE 2ND AMPLY DEMONSTRATED THAT HE HAD BEEN WELL CHOSEN.
"NOT LONG BEFORE, MISS AMERICA AND THE WHIZZER HAD ENDURED A LOVE/HATE RELATIONSHIP WHICH HAD MADE COOPERATION DIFFICULT...
"YET NOW, THEY TURNED HER POWER OF FLIGHT AND HIS MONGOOSE-GIVEN SUPER-SPEED INTO WEAPONS AGAINST A COMMON, INCREASINGLY DESPERATE FOE...

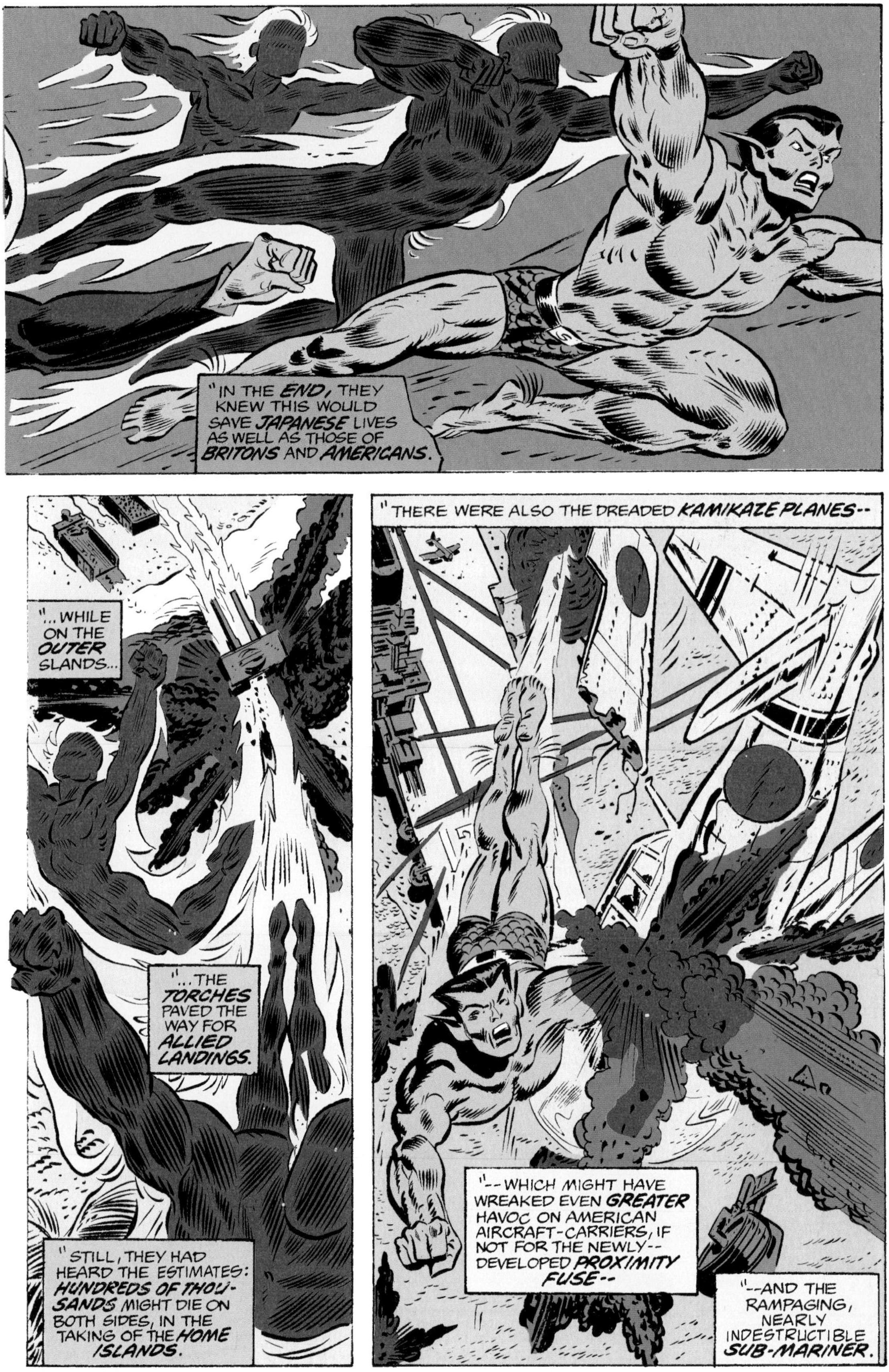
"IN THE END, THEY KNEW THIS WOULD SAVE JAPANESE LIVES AS WELL AS THOSE OF BRITONS AND AMERICANS.
"...WHILE ON THE OUTER SLANDS...
"...THE TORCHES PAVED THE WAY FOR ALLIED LANDINGS.
"STILL, THEY HAD HEARD THE ESTIMATES: HUNDREDS OF THOU-SANDS MIGHT DIE ON BOTH SIDES, IN THE TAKING OF THE HOME ISLANDS.
"THERE WERE ALSO THE DREADED KAMIKAZE PLANES--
"--WHICH MIGHT HAVE WREAKED EVEN GREATER HAVOC ON AMERICAN AIRCRAFT-CARRIERS, IF NOT FOR THE NEWLY--DEVELOPED PROXIMITY FUSE--
"--AND THE RAMPAGING, NEARLY INDESTRUCTIBLE SUB-MARINER.

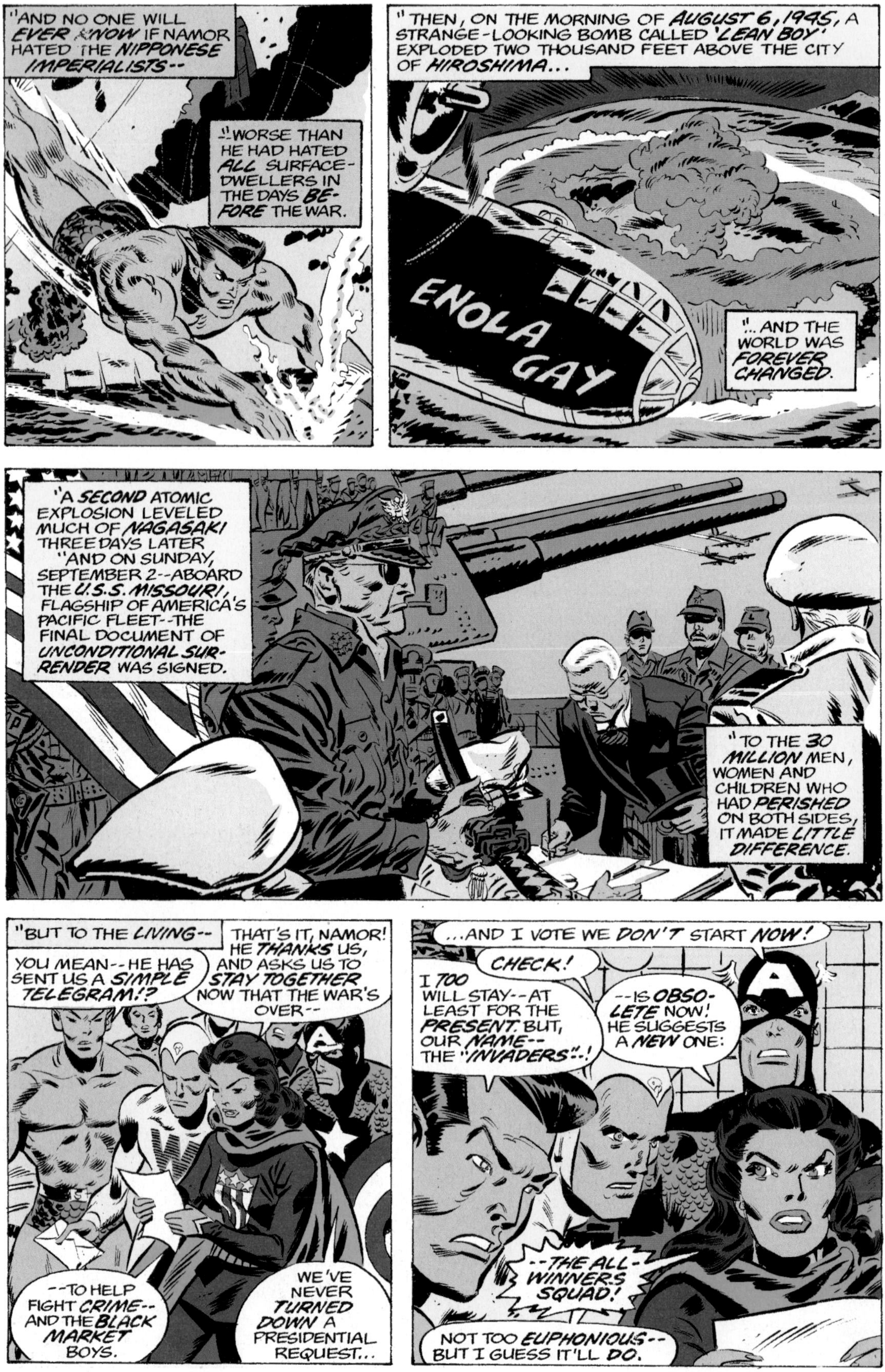
"AND NO ONE WILL EVER KNOW IF NAMOR HATED THE NIPPONESE IMPERIALISTS--
"--WORSE THAN HE HAD HATED ALL SURFACE-DWELLERS IN THE DAYS BEFORE THE WAR.
"THEN, ON THE MORNING OF AUGUST 6, 1945, A STRANGE-LOOKING BOMB CALLED 'LEAN BOY' EXPLODED TWO THOUSAND FEET ABOVE THE CITY OF HIROSHIMA...
ENOLA GAY
"...AND THE WORLD WAS FOREVER CHANGED.
"A SECOND ATOMIC EXPLOSION LEVELED MUCH OF NAGASAKI THREE DAYS LATER
"AND ON SUNDAY, SEPTEMBER 2--ABOARD THE U.S.S. MISSOURI, FLAGSHIP OF AMERICA'S PACIFIC FLEET--THE FINAL DOCUMENT OF UNCONDITIONAL SURRENDER WAS SIGNED.
"TO THE 30 MILLION MEN, WOMEN AND CHILDREN WHO HAD PERISHED ON BOTH SIDES, IT MADE LITTLE DIFFERENCE.
"BUT TO THE LIVING--
YOU MEAN--HE HAS SENT US A SIMPLE TELEGRAM!?
THAT'S IT, NAMOR! HE THANKS US, AND ASKS US TO STAY TOGETHER NOW THAT THE WAR'S OVER--
--TO HELP FIGHT CRIME--AND THE BLACK MARKET BOYS.
WE'VE NEVER TURNED DOWN A PRESIDENTIAL REQUEST...
...AND I VOTE WE DON'T START NOW!
CHECK!
I TOO WILL STAY--AT LEAST FOR THE PRESENT. BUT, OUR NAME--THE "INVADERS"--!
--IS OBSOLETE NOW! HE SUGGESTS A NEW ONE:
--THE ALL-WINNERS SQUAD!
NOT TOO EUPHONIOUS--BUT I GUESS IT'LL DO.

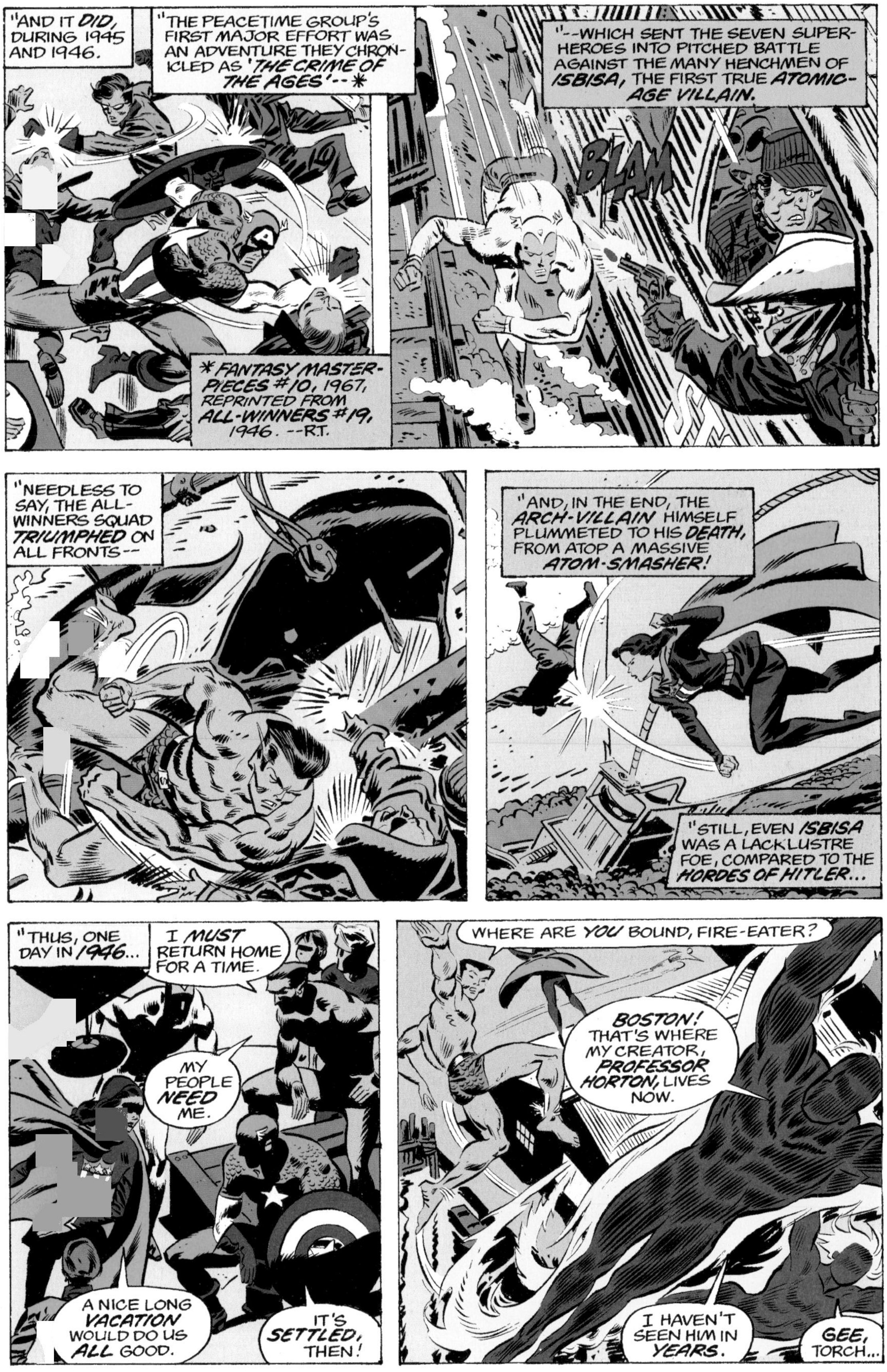
"AND IT DID, DURING 1945 AND 1946.
"THE PEACETIME GROUP'S FIRST MAJOR EFFORT WAS AN ADVENTURE THEY CHRONICLED AS 'THE CRIME OF THE AGES'-- *
* FANTASY MASTERPIECES #10, 1967, REPRINTED FROM ALL-WINNERS #19, 1946. --R.T.
"--WHICH SENT THE SEVEN SUPER-HEROES INTO PITCHED BATTLE AGAINST THE MANY HENCHMEN OF ISBISA, THE FIRST TRUE ATOMIC-AGE VILLAIN.
BLAM
"NEEDLESS TO SAY, THE ALL-WINNERS SQUAD TRIUMPHED ON ALL FRONTS--
"AND, IN THE END, THE ARCH-VILLAIN HIMSELF PLUMMETED TO HIS DEATH, FROM ATOP A MASSIVE ATOM-SMASHER!
"STILL, EVEN ISBISA WAS A LACKLUSTRE FOE, COMPARED TO THE HORDES OF HITLER...
"THUS, ONE DAY IN 1946...
I MUST RETURN HOME FOR A TIME.
MY PEOPLE NEED ME.
A NICE LONG VACATION WOULD DO US ALL GOOD.
IT'S SETTLED, THEN!
WHERE ARE YOU BOUND, FIRE-EATER?
BOSTON! THAT'S WHERE MY CREATOR, PROFESSOR HORTON, LIVES NOW.
I HAVEN'T SEEN HIM IN YEARS.
GEE, TORCH...

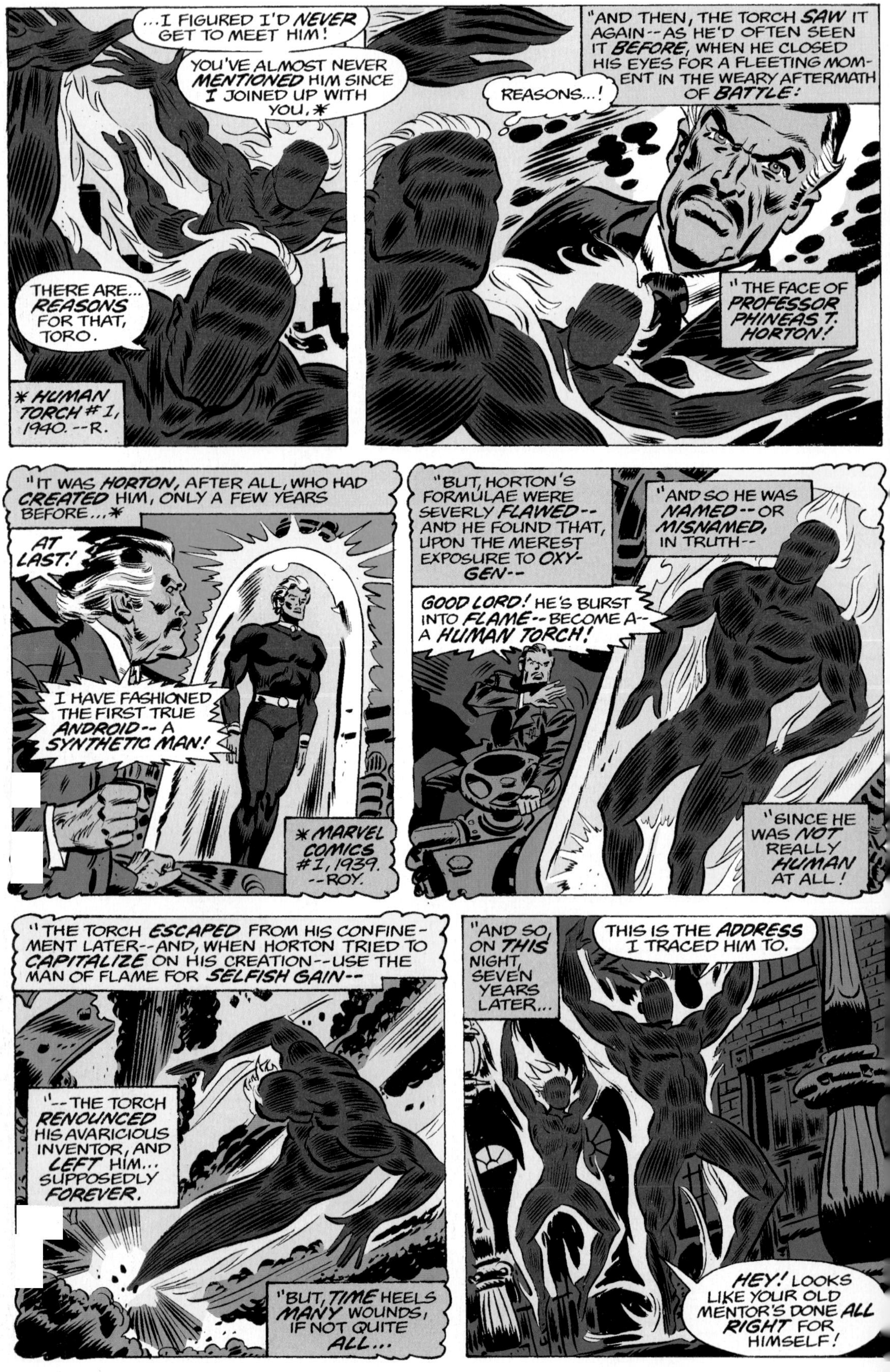
...I FIGURED I'D NEVER GET TO MEET HIM!
YOU'VE ALMOST NEVER MENTIONED HIM SINCE I JOINED UP WITH YOU.*
THERE ARE... REASONS FOR THAT, TORO.
* HUMAN TORCH #1, 1940. --R.
"AND THEN, THE TORCH SAW IT AGAIN--AS HE'D OFTEN SEEN IT BEFORE, WHEN HE CLOSED HIS EYES FOR A FLEETING MOMENT IN THE WEARY AFTERMATH OF BATTLE:
REASONS...!
"THE FACE OF PROFESSOR PHINEAS T. HORTON!
"IT WAS HORTON, AFTER ALL, WHO HAD CREATED HIM, ONLY A FEW YEARS BEFORE...*
AT LAST!
I HAVE FASHIONED THE FIRST TRUE ANDROID-- A SYNTHETIC MAN!
* MARVEL COMICS #1, 1939. --ROY.
"BUT, HORTON'S FORMULAE WERE SEVERLY FLAWED--AND HE FOUND THAT, UPON THE MEREST EXPOSURE TO OXYGEN--
GOOD LORD! HE'S BURST INTO FLAME--BECOME A--A HUMAN TORCH!
"AND SO HE WAS NAMED--OR MISNAMED, IN TRUTH--
"SINCE HE WAS NOT REALLY HUMAN AT ALL!
"THE TORCH ESCAPED FROM HIS CONFINEMENT LATER--AND, WHEN HORTON TRIED TO CAPITALIZE ON HIS CREATION--USE THE MAN OF FLAME FOR SELFISH GAIN--
"--THE TORCH RENOUNCED HIS AVARICIOUS INVENTOR, AND LEFT HIM... SUPPOSEDLY FOREVER.
"BUT, TIME HEELS MANY WOUNDS, IF NOT QUITE ALL...
"AND SO, ON THIS NIGHT, SEVEN YEARS LATER...
THIS IS THE ADDRESS I TRACED HIM TO.
HEY! LOOKS LIKE YOUR OLD MENTOR'S DONE ALL RIGHT FOR HIMSELF!

HE IS A *BRILLIANT* MAN, LAD... THOUGH MARRED BY ALL-TOO-HUMAN *GREED* WHEN I LAST KNEW HIM.

I HEAR SOMEBODY COMING.

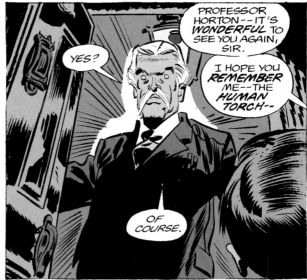

YES?

PROFESSOR HORTON--IT'S *WONDERFUL* TO SEE YOU AGAIN, SIR.

I HOPE YOU *REMEMBER* ME--THE *HUMAN TORCH*--

OF COURSE.

AND *THIS* IS MY YOUNG FRIEND *TORO.*

PUT 'ER *THERE,* PROF! GLAD TO *MEETCHA!*

LIKEWISE.

GOSH, SIR, I'VE ALWAYS BEEN *WANTING* TO--

ER, *'SCUZE* ME, BUT--I'M AFRAID YOUR *GRIP* IS HURTING MY *HAND!* I--

YEEEOWW!

HEY, *TORCH*--WHAT'S *WRONG* WITH HIM?

HE WON'T LET GO.!!

FLAME ON!

LIKEWISE.

WH-WHAT'S THE *BIG IDEA,* TORCH? WHY IS THE *PROF*--?

THAT'S *NOT* PROFESSOR HORTON, TORO!

YOU'VE GOT TO *FLAME ON*-- *FAST!*

IF YOU S-SAY SO--

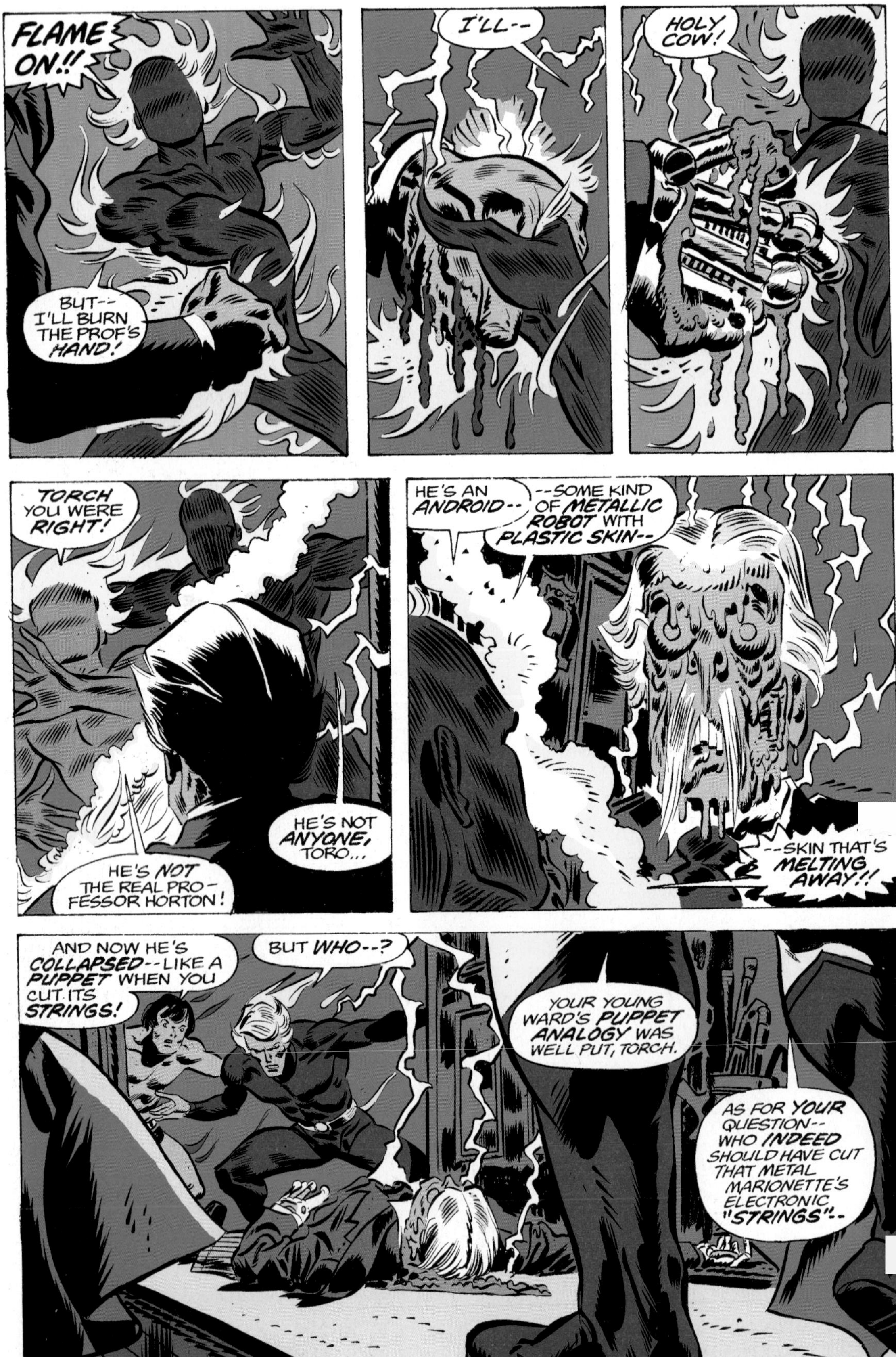
FLAME ON!!
BUT-- I'LL BURN THE PROF'S HAND!
I'LL--
HOLY COW!
TORCH YOU WERE RIGHT!
HE'S NOT THE REAL PRO- FESSOR HORTON!
HE'S NOT ANYONE, TORO...
HE'S AN ANDROID--
--SOME KIND OF METALLIC ROBOT WITH PLASTIC SKIN--
--SKIN THAT'S MELTING AWAY!!
AND NOW HE'S COLLAPSED--LIKE A PUPPET WHEN YOU CUT ITS STRINGS!
BUT WHO--?
YOUR YOUNG WARD'S PUPPET ANALOGY WAS WELL PUT, TORCH.
AS FOR YOUR QUESTION-- WHO INDEED SHOULD HAVE CUT THAT METAL MARIONETTE'S ELECTRONIC "STRINGS"--

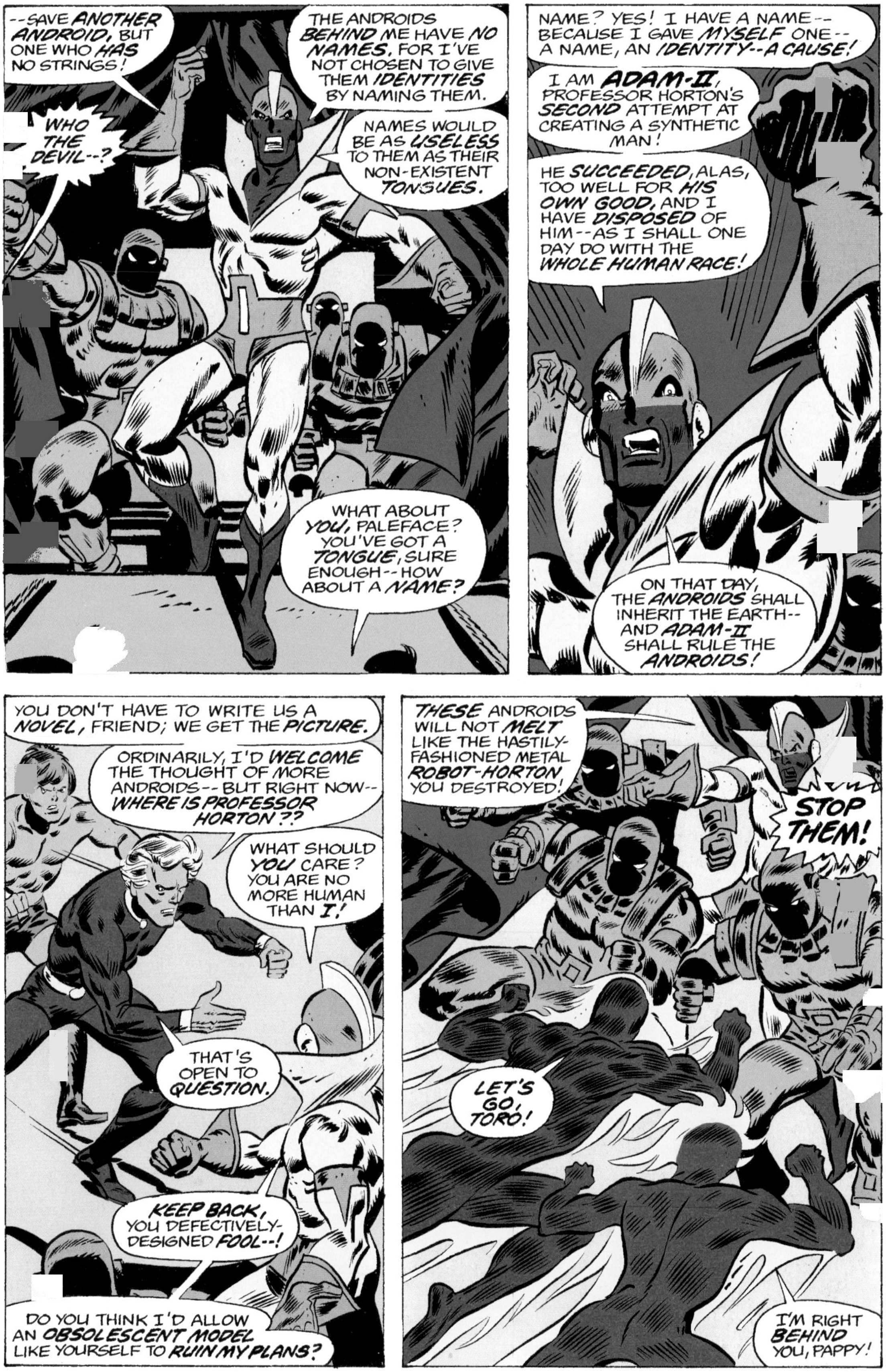
--SAVE ANOTHER ANDROID, BUT ONE WHO HAS NO STRINGS!
WHO THE DEVIL--?
THE ANDROIDS BEHIND ME HAVE NO NAMES, FOR I'VE NOT CHOSEN TO GIVE THEM IDENTITIES BY NAMING THEM.
NAMES WOULD BE AS USELESS TO THEM AS THEIR NON-EXISTENT TONGUES.
WHAT ABOUT YOU, PALEFACE? YOU'VE GOT A TONGUE, SURE ENOUGH--HOW ABOUT A NAME?
NAME? YES! I HAVE A NAME--BECAUSE I GAVE MYSELF ONE--A NAME, AN IDENTITY--A CAUSE!
I AM ADAM-II, PROFESSOR HORTON'S SECOND ATTEMPT AT CREATING A SYNTHETIC MAN!
HE SUCCEEDED, ALAS, TOO WELL FOR HIS OWN GOOD, AND I HAVE DISPOSED OF HIM--AS I SHALL ONE DAY DO WITH THE WHOLE HUMAN RACE!
ON THAT DAY, THE ANDROIDS SHALL INHERIT THE EARTH--AND ADAM-II SHALL RULE THE ANDROIDS!
YOU DON'T HAVE TO WRITE US A NOVEL, FRIEND; WE GET THE PICTURE.
ORDINARILY, I'D WELCOME THE THOUGHT OF MORE ANDROIDS--BUT RIGHT NOW--WHERE IS PROFESSOR HORTON??
WHAT SHOULD YOU CARE? YOU ARE NO MORE HUMAN THAN I!
THAT'S OPEN TO QUESTION.
KEEP BACK, YOU DEFECTIVELY-DESIGNED FOOL--!
DO YOU THINK I'D ALLOW AN OBSOLESCENT MODEL LIKE YOURSELF TO RUIN MY PLANS?
THESE ANDROIDS WILL NOT MELT LIKE THE HASTILY-FASHIONED METAL ROBOT-HORTON YOU DESTROYED!
STOP THEM!
LET'S GO, TORO!
I'M RIGHT BEHIND YOU, PAPPY!

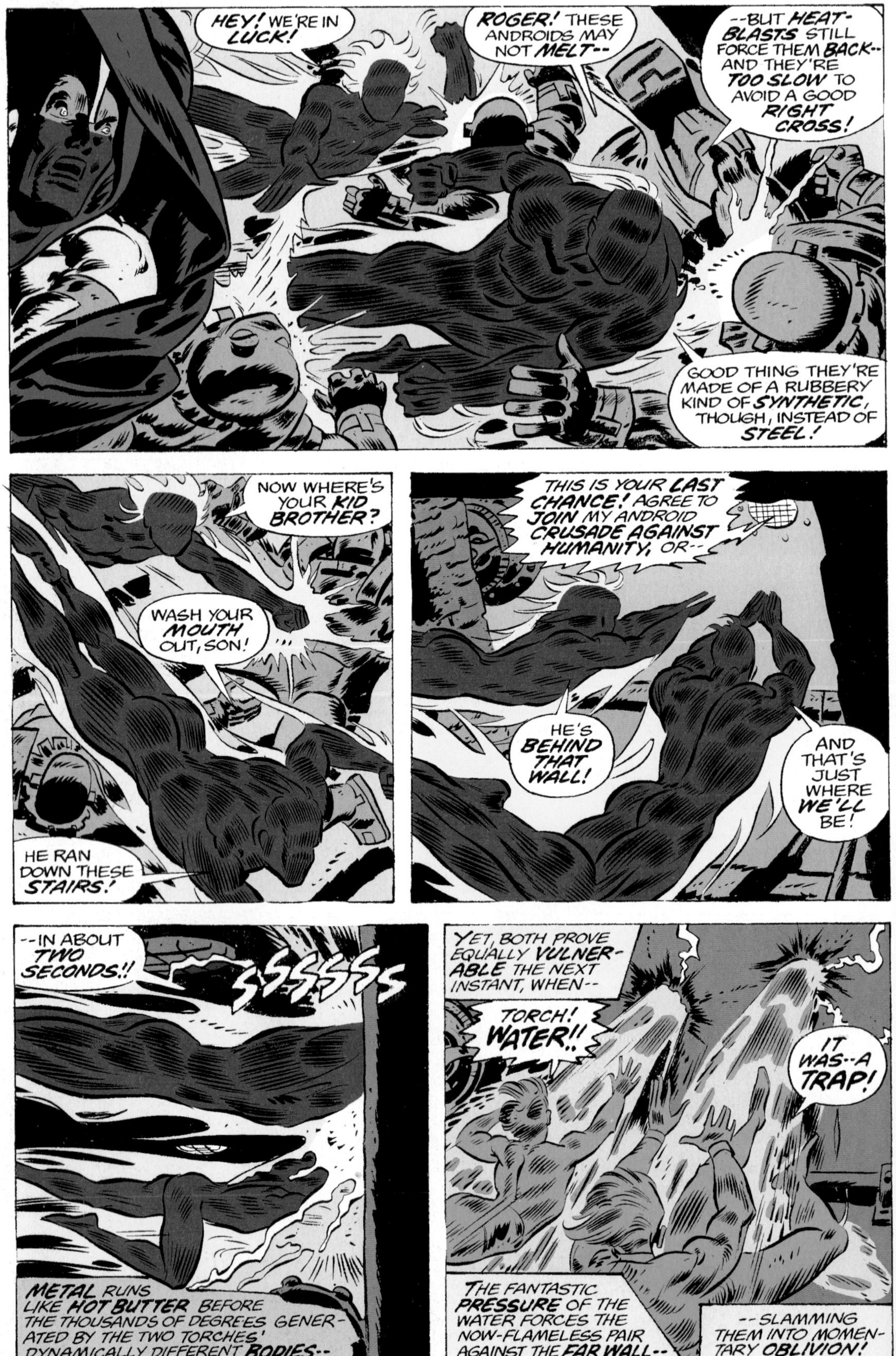
HEY! WE'RE IN LUCK!
ROGER! THESE ANDROIDS MAY NOT MELT--
--BUT HEAT-BLASTS STILL FORCE THEM BACK--AND THEY'RE TOO SLOW TO AVOID A GOOD RIGHT CROSS!
GOOD THING THEY'RE MADE OF A RUBBERY KIND OF SYNTHETIC, THOUGH, INSTEAD OF STEEL!
NOW WHERE'S YOUR KID BROTHER?
WASH YOUR MOUTH OUT, SON!
HE RAN DOWN THESE STAIRS!
THIS IS YOUR LAST CHANCE! AGREE TO JOIN MY ANDROID CRUSADE AGAINST HUMANITY, OR--
HE'S BEHIND THAT WALL!
AND THAT'S JUST WHERE WE'LL BE!
--IN ABOUT TWO SECONDS!!
SSSSSSS
METAL RUNS LIKE HOT BUTTER BEFORE THE THOUSANDS OF DEGREES GENERATED BY THE TWO TORCHES' DYNAMICALLY DIFFERENT BODIES--
YET, BOTH PROVE EQUALLY VULNERABLE THE NEXT INSTANT, WHEN--
TORCH! WATER!!
IT WAS--A TRAP!
THE FANTASTIC PRESSURE OF THE WATER FORCES THE NOW-FLAMELESS PAIR AGAINST THE FAR WALL--
--SLAMMING THEM INTO MOMENTARY OBLIVION!

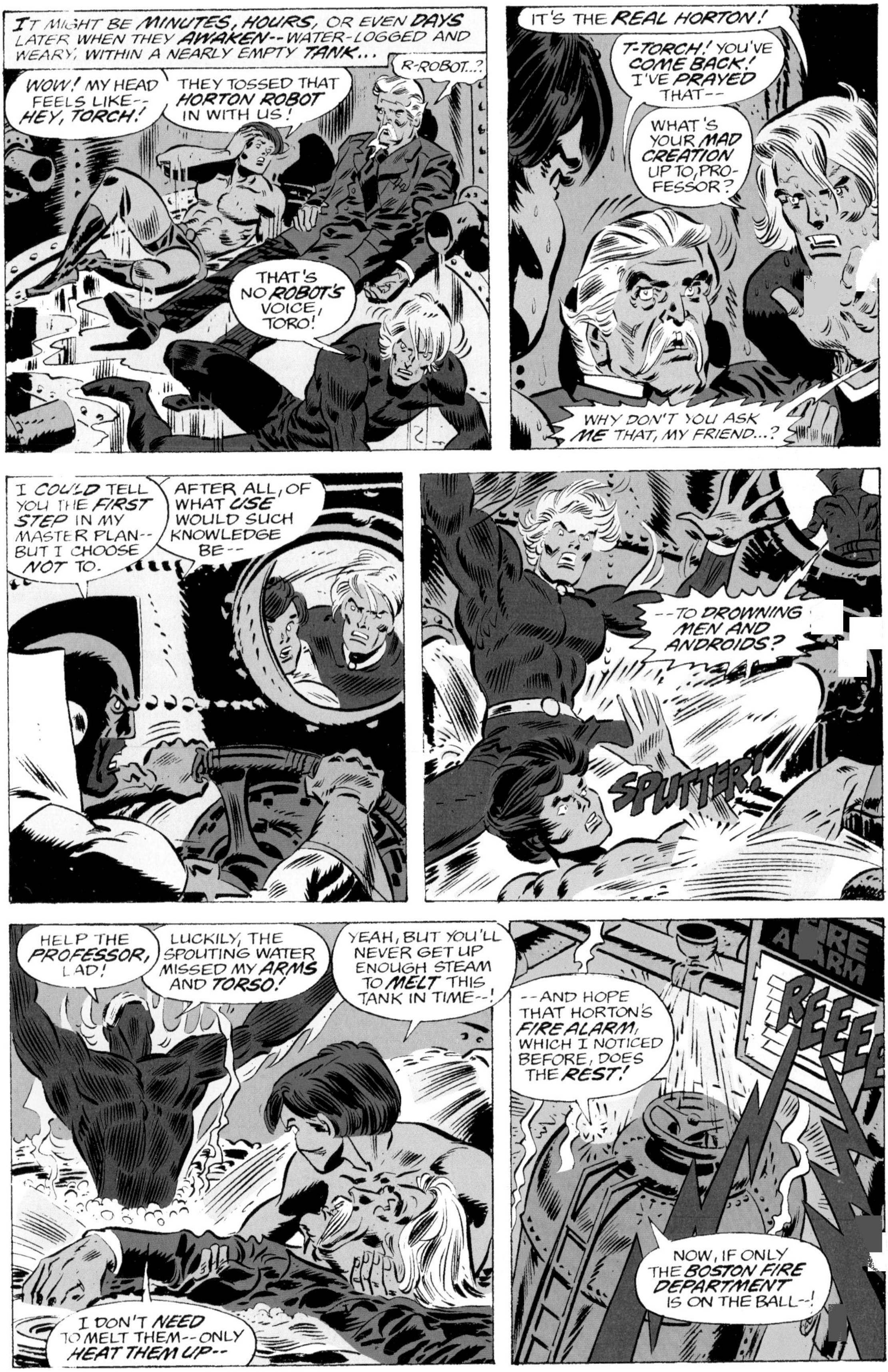
IT MIGHT BE MINUTES, HOURS, OR EVEN DAYS LATER WHEN THEY AWAKEN--WATER-LOGGED AND WEARY, WITHIN A NEARLY EMPTY TANK...
WOW! MY HEAD FEELS LIKE-- HEY, TORCH!
THEY TOSSED THAT HORTON ROBOT IN WITH US!
R-ROBOT...?
THAT'S NO ROBOT'S VOICE, TORO!
IT'S THE REAL HORTON!
T-TORCH! YOU'VE COME BACK! I'VE PRAYED THAT--
WHAT'S YOUR MAD CREATION UP TO, PROFESSOR?
WHY DON'T YOU ASK ME THAT, MY FRIEND...?
I COULD TELL YOU THE FIRST STEP IN MY MASTER PLAN-- BUT I CHOOSE NOT TO.
AFTER ALL, OF WHAT USE WOULD SUCH KNOWLEDGE BE--
--TO DROWNING MEN AND ANDROIDS?
SPUTTER!
HELP THE PROFESSOR, LAD!
LUCKILY, THE SPOUTING WATER MISSED MY ARMS AND TORSO!
YEAH, BUT YOU'LL NEVER GET UP ENOUGH STEAM TO MELT THIS TANK IN TIME--!
I DON'T NEED TO MELT THEM--ONLY HEAT THEM UP--
--AND HOPE THAT HORTON'S FIRE ALARM, WHICH I NOTICED BEFORE, DOES THE REST!
FIRE ALARM
REEEE
NOW, IF ONLY THE BOSTON FIRE DEPARTMENT IS ON THE BALL--!

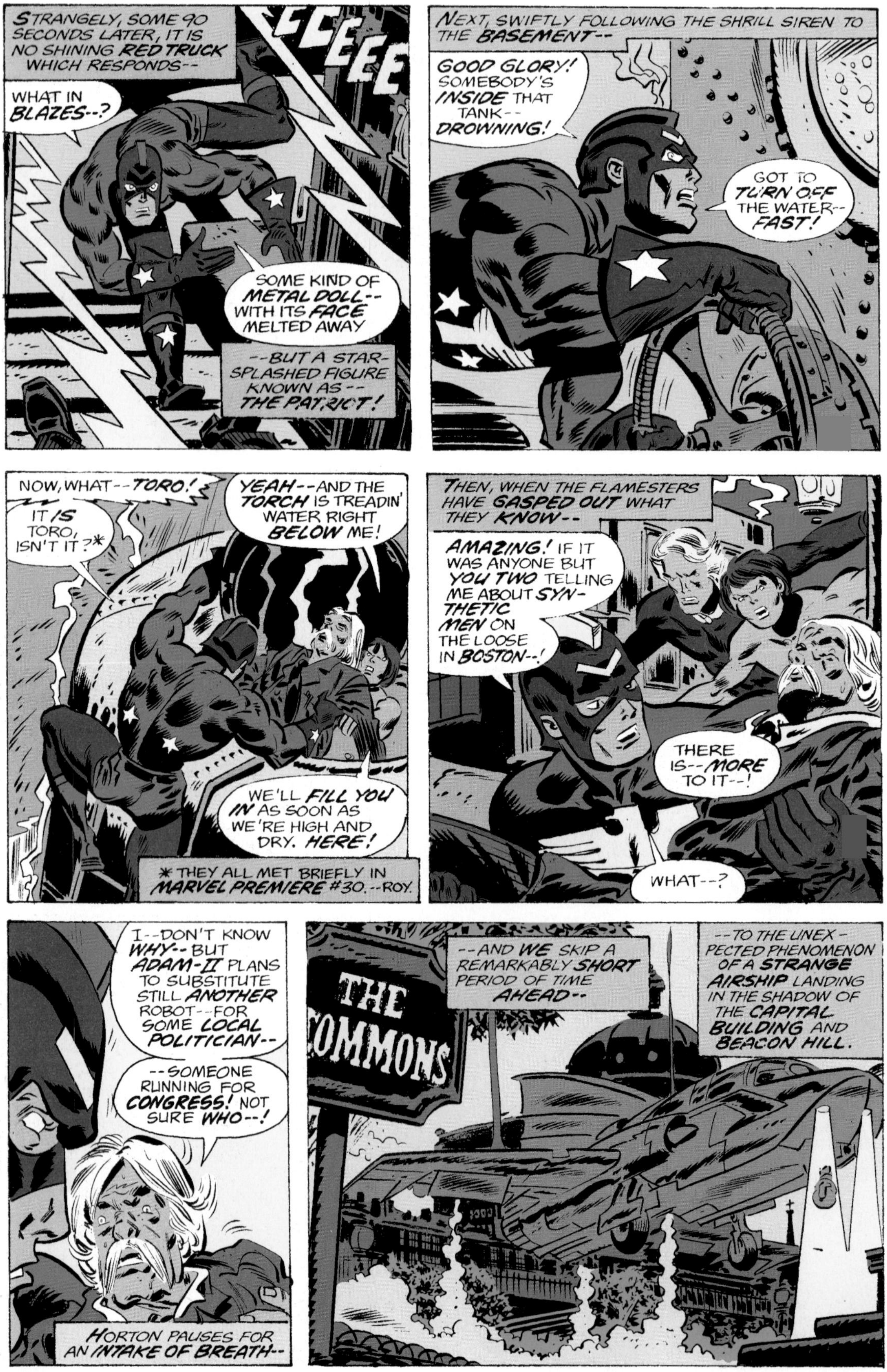
STRANGELY, SOME 90 SECONDS LATER, IT IS NO SHINING RED TRUCK WHICH RESPONDS--
EEEE
WHAT IN BLAZES--?
SOME KIND OF METAL DOLL--WITH ITS FACE MELTED AWAY
--BUT A STAR-SPLASHED FIGURE KNOWN AS--THE PATRIOT!
NEXT, SWIFTLY FOLLOWING THE SHRILL SIREN TO THE BASEMENT--
GOOD GLORY! SOMEBODY'S INSIDE THAT TANK--DROWNING!
GOT TO TURN OFF THE WATER--FAST!
NOW, WHAT--TORO!
IT IS TORO, ISN'T IT?*
YEAH--AND THE TORCH IS TREADIN' WATER RIGHT BELOW ME!
WE'LL FILL YOU IN AS SOON AS WE'RE HIGH AND DRY. HERE!
* THEY ALL MET BRIEFLY IN MARVEL PREMIERE #30. --ROY.
THEN, WHEN THE FLAMESTERS HAVE GASPED OUT WHAT THEY KNOW--
AMAZING! IF IT WAS ANYONE BUT YOU TWO TELLING ME ABOUT SYN-THETIC MEN ON THE LOOSE IN BOSTON--!
THERE IS--MORE TO IT--!
WHAT--?
I--DON'T KNOW WHY--BUT ADAM-II PLANS TO SUBSTITUTE STILL ANOTHER ROBOT--FOR SOME LOCAL POLITICIAN--
--SOMEONE RUNNING FOR CONGRESS! NOT SURE WHO--!
HORTON PAUSES FOR AN INTAKE OF BREATH--
THE COMMONS
--AND WE SKIP A REMARKABLY SHORT PERIOD OF TIME AHEAD--
--TO THE UNEX-PECTED PHENOMENON OF A STRANGE AIRSHIP LANDING IN THE SHADOW OF THE CAPITAL BUILDING AND BEACON HILL.

I DON'T **SEE** ANYONE HERE TO **GREET** US.

YOU WOULD, IF **ANYBODY** WOULD-- WITH THOSE **NEW GLASSES** YOUR DOC PRESCRIBED!

SAYS THE KID WITH THE **DYED HAIR** AND **FRECKLE CREAM** ALL OVER HIS FACE!

WAIT! OVER THERE-- IN THE **SHADOWS**--!

TORCH! TORO! BUT-- WHO'S THAT **WITH** YOU?

HUH? DON'T YOU RECOG- **NIZE** ME, CAP? I'M THE **PATRIOT**-- THE GUY WHO'S MODELED HIS **WHOLE SPY-BUSTING CAREER** AFTER YOU-- **REMEMBER?**

ER, UH-- **SURE!** WHAT'S **UP?** WHO'S THAT YOU'RE **HOLDING?**

TELL HIM, TORCH!

"WHEN THE **BARE FACTS** WERE REVEALED...

..BUT YOU DON'T KNOW **WHICH** OF THE **TEN** DEMO- CRATIC CANDIDATES THIS "**ADAM-II**" PLANS TO PULL THE **SWITCH** ON?

NOT A **CLUE!**

THEN WE MUST CON- TACT THEM **ALL**-- BEFORE IT'S **TOO LATE!**

"MOMENTS LATER, WITH SCHEDULE-REVEALING **NEWSPAPERS** IN HAND, THE EIGHT SUPER-HEROES RUSHED OFF ON A MISSION PER- HAPS AS IMPORTANT AS ANY THEY EVER TACKLED DURING **WARTIME**...

"...YET WITHOUT UNDERSTANDING **WHY** THIS WAS SO.

OUR GUY SURE HAS A **BUSY SCHEDULE,** CAP!

WHAT **COUNTS,** LAD--

KENN ELEC

-- IS THAT WE'VE **FOUND** HIM!

...GLAD YOU FOLKS COULD **MAKE** IT HERE TONIGHT...!

JACK'S OUR BOY!

THE NEW GENERATION OFFERS A LEADER

KENNE VO

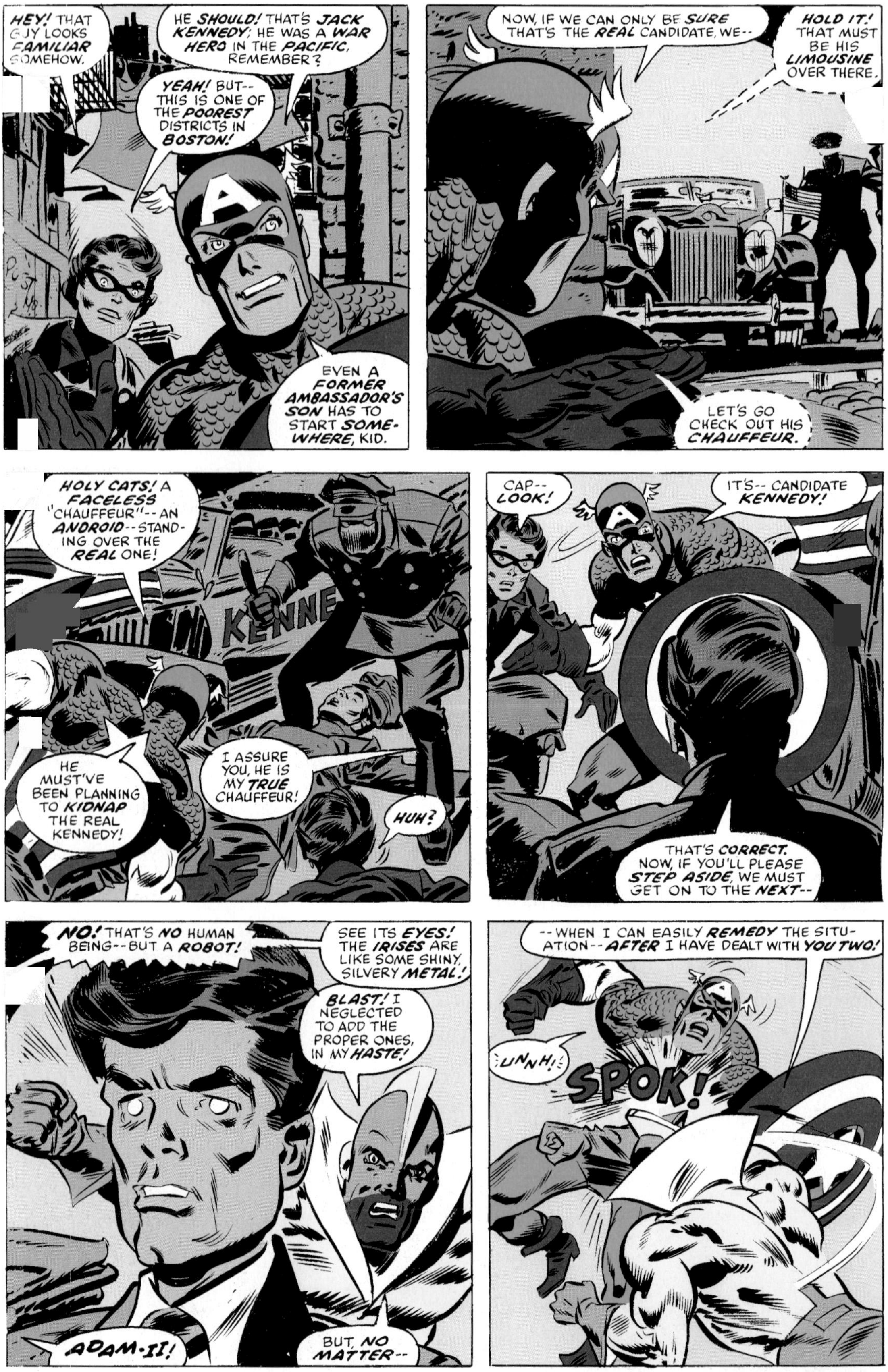
HEY! THAT GUY LOOKS FAMILIAR SOMEHOW.
HE SHOULD! THAT'S JACK KENNEDY; HE WAS A WAR HERO IN THE PACIFIC, REMEMBER?
YEAH! BUT-- THIS IS ONE OF THE POOREST DISTRICTS IN BOSTON!
EVEN A FORMER AMBASSADOR'S SON HAS TO START SOME-WHERE, KID.
NOW, IF WE CAN ONLY BE SURE THAT'S THE REAL CANDIDATE, WE--
HOLD IT! THAT MUST BE HIS LIMOUSINE OVER THERE.
LET'S GO CHECK OUT HIS CHAUFFEUR.
HOLY CATS! A FACELESS "CHAUFFEUR"-- AN ANDROID-- STANDING OVER THE REAL ONE!
KENNE
HE MUST'VE BEEN PLANNING TO KIDNAP THE REAL KENNEDY!
I ASSURE YOU, HE IS MY TRUE CHAUFFEUR!
HUH?
CAP-- LOOK!
IT'S-- CANDIDATE KENNEDY!
THAT'S CORRECT. NOW, IF YOU'LL PLEASE STEP ASIDE, WE MUST GET ON TO THE NEXT--
NO! THAT'S NO HUMAN BEING--BUT A ROBOT!
SEE ITS EYES! THE IRISES ARE LIKE SOME SHINY, SILVERY METAL!
BLAST! I NEGLECTED TO ADD THE PROPER ONES, IN MY HASTE!
ADAM-II!
BUT, NO MATTER--
--WHEN I CAN EASILY REMEDY THE SITUATION--AFTER I HAVE DEALT WITH YOU TWO!
UNNH!
SPOK!

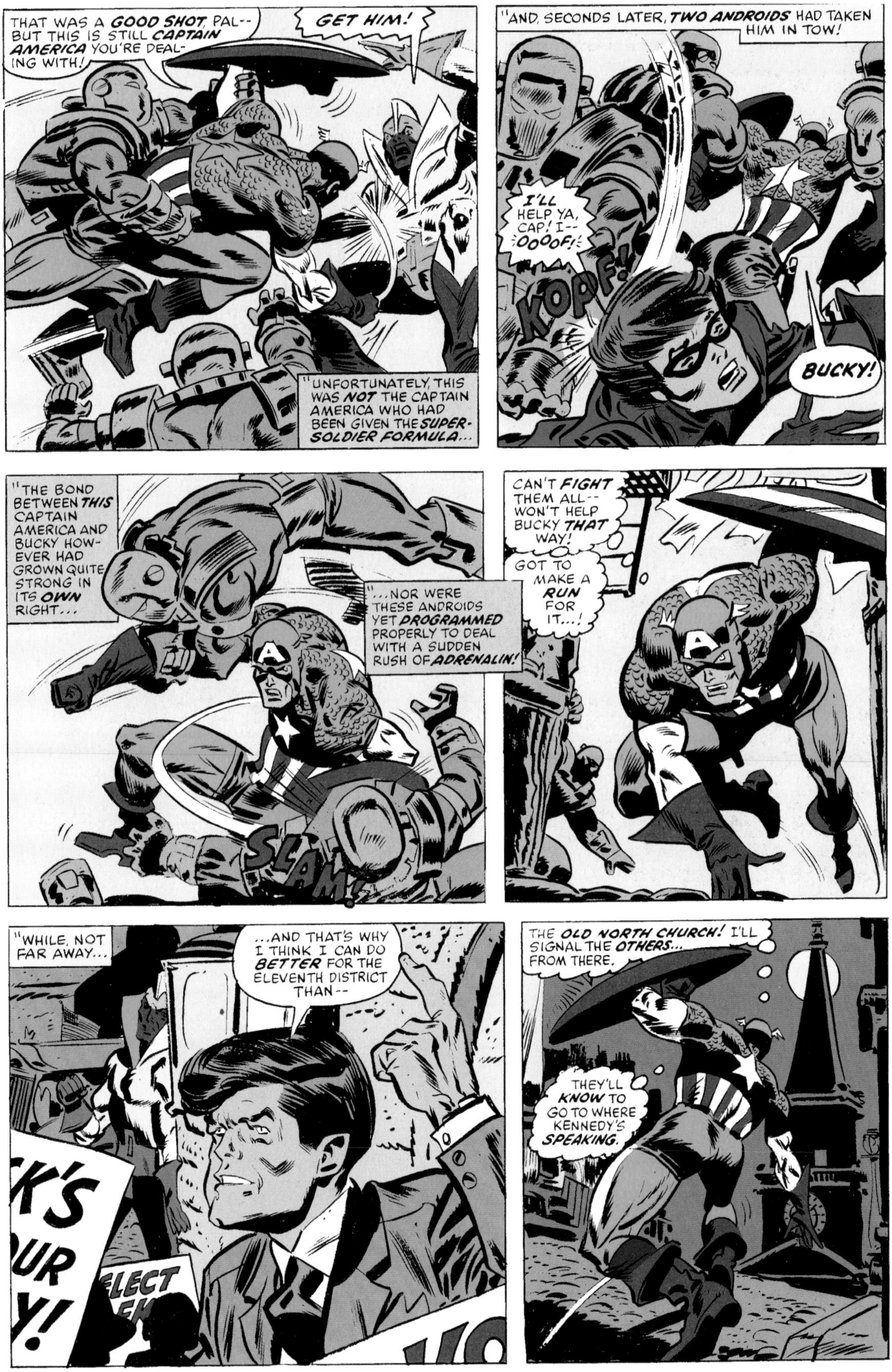
THAT WAS A GOOD SHOT, PAL-- BUT THIS IS STILL CAPTAIN AMERICA YOU'RE DEALING WITH!
GET HIM!
"UNFORTUNATELY, THIS WAS NOT THE CAPTAIN AMERICA WHO HAD BEEN GIVEN THE SUPER-SOLDIER FORMULA...
"AND, SECONDS LATER, TWO ANDROIDS HAD TAKEN HIM IN TOW!
I'LL HELP YA, CAP! I-- OOOOF!
KOPF!
BUCKY!
"THE BOND BETWEEN THIS CAPTAIN AMERICA AND BUCKY HOWEVER HAD GROWN QUITE STRONG IN ITS OWN RIGHT...
"...NOR WERE THESE ANDROIDS YET PROGRAMMED PROPERLY TO DEAL WITH A SUDDEN RUSH OF ADRENALIN!
SLAM!
CAN'T FIGHT THEM ALL-- WON'T HELP BUCKY THAT WAY!
GOT TO MAKE A RUN FOR IT...!
"WHILE, NOT FAR AWAY...
...AND THAT'S WHY I THINK I CAN DO BETTER FOR THE ELEVENTH DISTRICT THAN--
THE OLD NORTH CHURCH! I'LL SIGNAL THE OTHERS... FROM THERE.
THEY'LL KNOW TO GO TO WHERE KENNEDY'S SPEAKING.

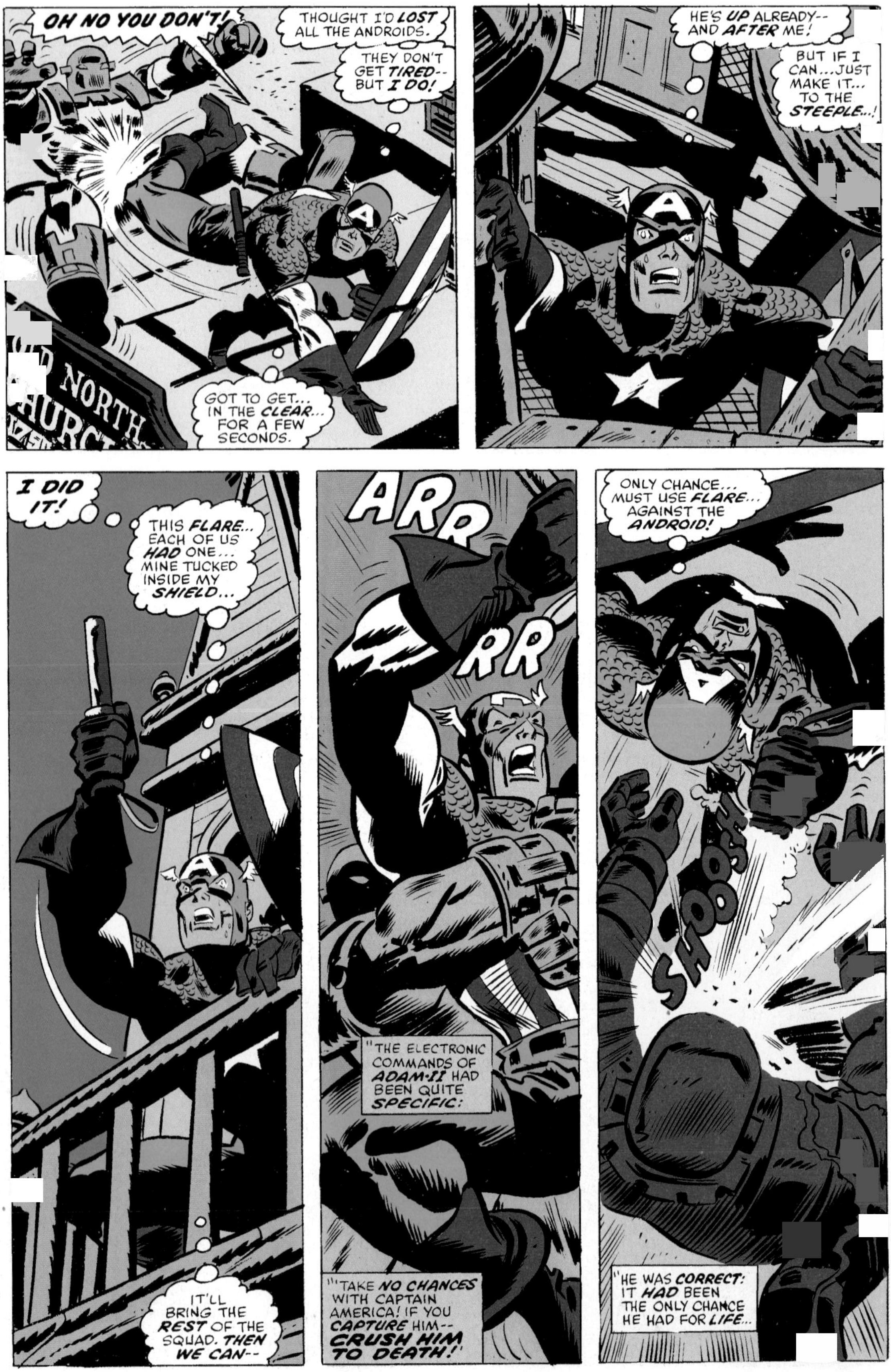
OH NO YOU DON'T!
THOUGHT I'D LOST ALL THE ANDROIDS.
THEY DON'T GET TIRED-- BUT I DO!
GOT TO GET... IN THE CLEAR... FOR A FEW SECONDS.
HE'S UP ALREADY-- AND AFTER ME!
BUT IF I CAN... JUST MAKE IT... TO THE STEEPLE...!
I DID IT!
THIS FLARE... EACH OF US HAD ONE... MINE TUCKED INSIDE MY SHIELD...
IT'LL BRING THE REST OF THE SQUAD. THEN WE CAN--
ARRRR
"THE ELECTRONIC COMMANDS OF ADAM-II HAD BEEN QUITE SPECIFIC:
"'TAKE NO CHANCES WITH CAPTAIN AMERICA! IF YOU CAPTURE HIM-- CRUSH HIM TO DEATH!'
ONLY CHANCE... MUST USE FLARE... AGAINST THE ANDROID!
SHOOSH
"HE WAS CORRECT: IT HAD BEEN THE ONLY CHANCE HE HAD FOR LIFE...

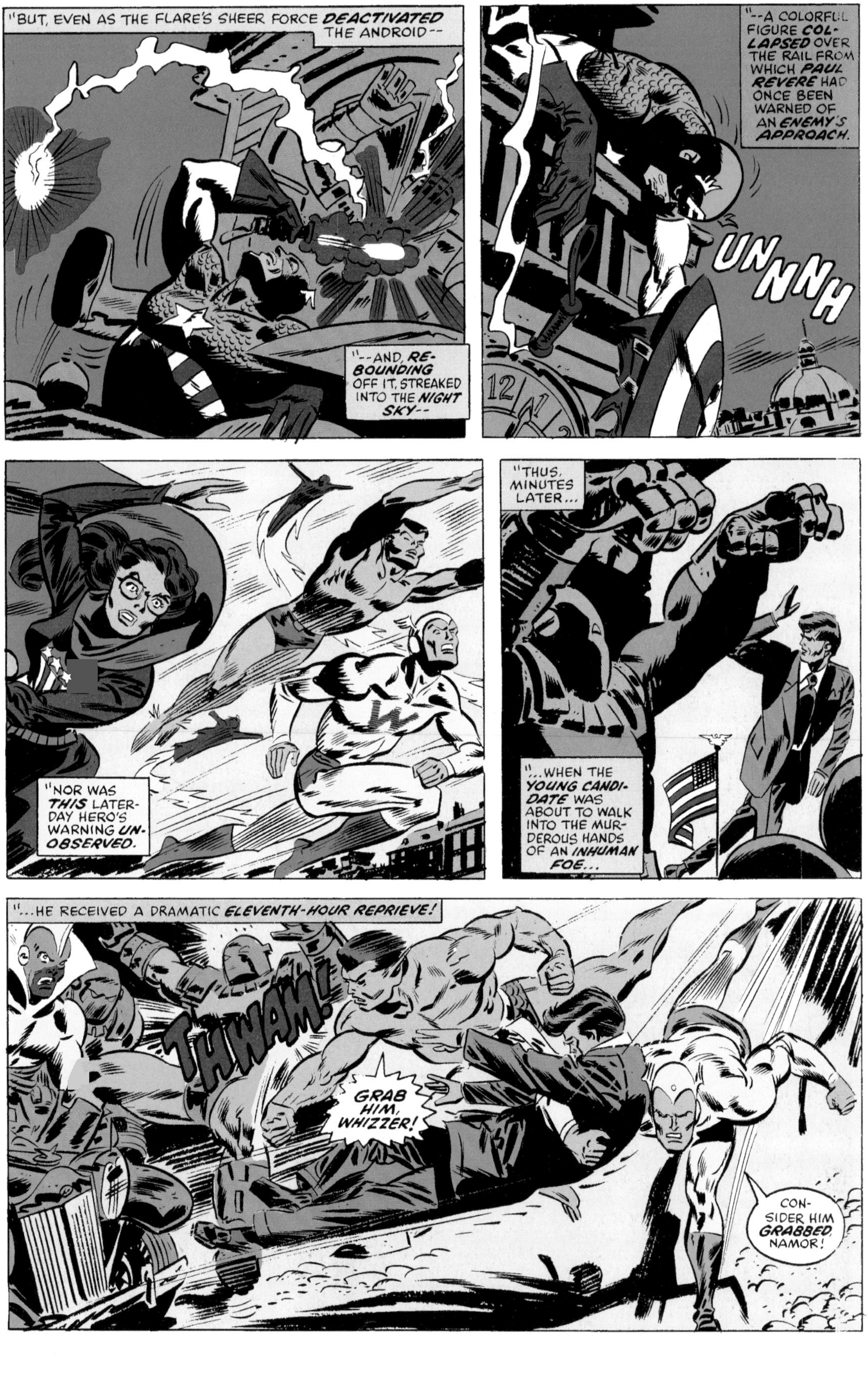
"BUT, EVEN AS THE FLARE'S SHEER FORCE DEACTIVATED THE ANDROID--
"--AND, REBOUNDING OFF IT, STREAKED INTO THE NIGHT SKY--
"--A COLORFUL FIGURE COLLAPSED OVER THE RAIL FROM WHICH PAUL REVERE HAD ONCE BEEN WARNED OF AN ENEMY'S APPROACH.
UNNNH
"NOR WAS THIS LATER-DAY HERO'S WARNING UNOBSERVED.
"THUS, MINUTES LATER...
"...WHEN THE YOUNG CANDIDATE WAS ABOUT TO WALK INTO THE MURDEROUS HANDS OF AN INHUMAN FOE...
"...HE RECEIVED A DRAMATIC ELEVENTH-HOUR REPRIEVE!
THWAM!
GRAB HIM, WHIZZER!
CONSIDER HIM GRABBED, NAMOR!

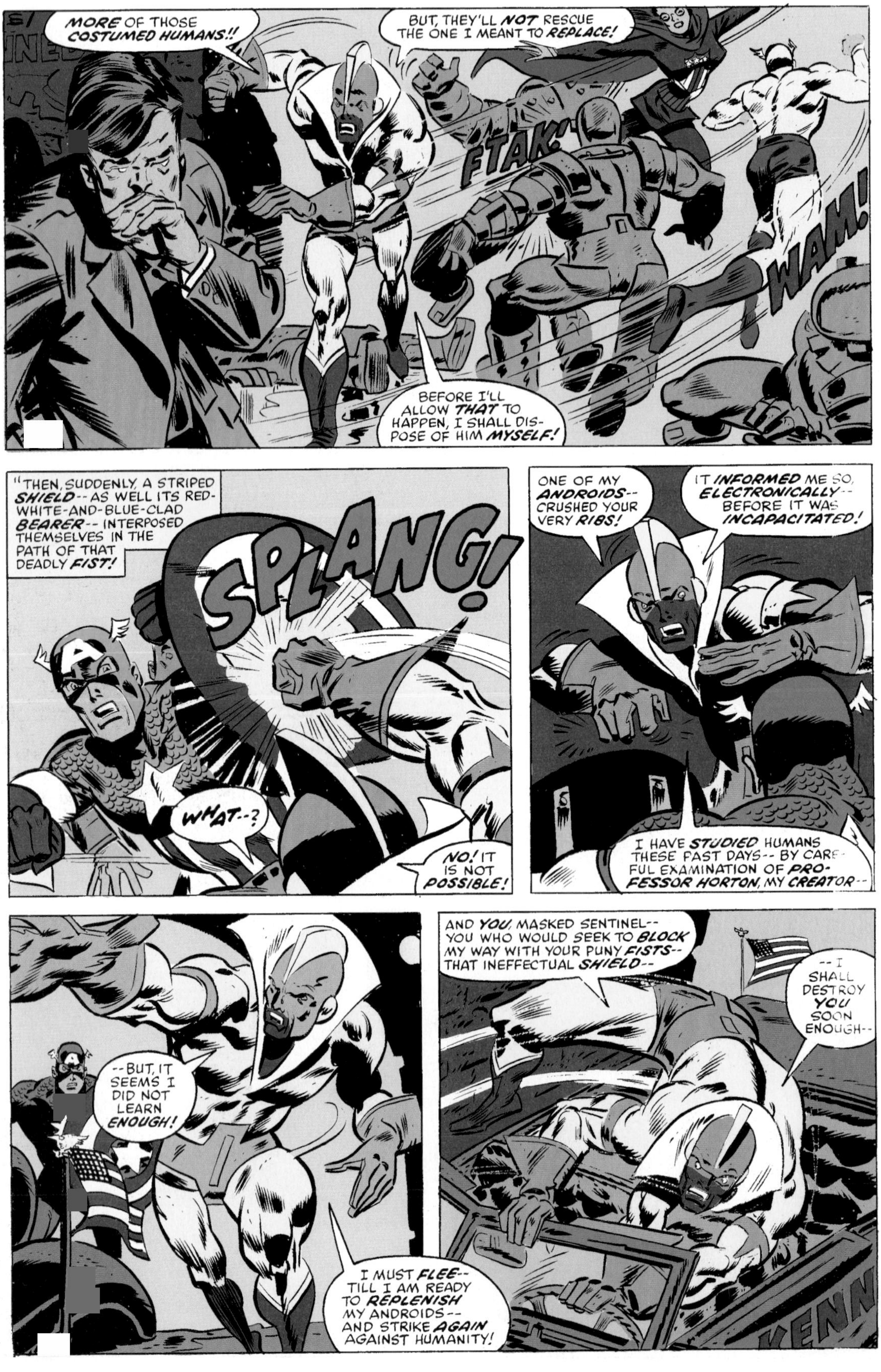
MORE OF THOSE COSTUMED HUMANS!!
BUT, THEY'LL NOT RESCUE THE ONE I MEANT TO REPLACE!
FTAK!
WAM!
BEFORE I'LL ALLOW THAT TO HAPPEN, I SHALL DISPOSE OF HIM MYSELF!
"THEN, SUDDENLY, A STRIPED SHIELD-- AS WELL ITS RED-WHITE-AND-BLUE-CLAD BEARER-- INTERPOSED THEMSELVES IN THE PATH OF THAT DEADLY FIST!
SPLANG!
WHAT--?
NO! IT IS NOT POSSIBLE!
ONE OF MY ANDROIDS-- CRUSHED YOUR VERY RIBS!
IT INFORMED ME SO, ELECTRONICALLY-- BEFORE IT WAS INCAPACITATED!
I HAVE STUDIED HUMANS THESE PAST DAYS-- BY CAREFUL EXAMINATION OF PROFESSOR HORTON, MY CREATOR--
--BUT, IT SEEMS I DID NOT LEARN ENOUGH!
I MUST FLEE-- TILL I AM READY TO REPLENISH MY ANDROIDS-- AND STRIKE AGAIN AGAINST HUMANITY!
AND YOU, MASKED SENTINEL-- YOU WHO WOULD SEEK TO BLOCK MY WAY WITH YOUR PUNY FISTS-- THAT INEFFECTUAL SHIELD--
--I SHALL DESTROY YOU SOON ENOUGH--
KENN

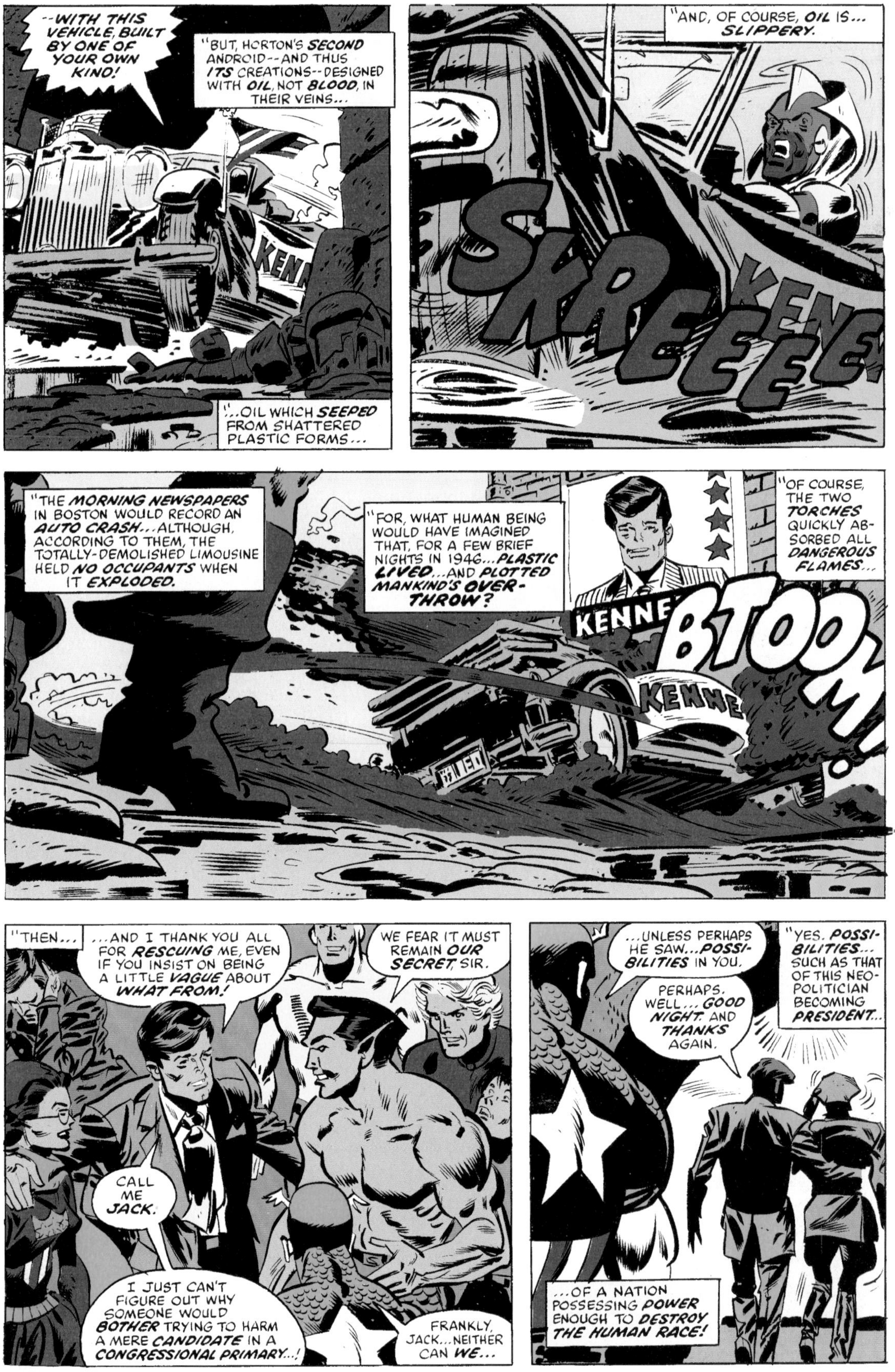
--WITH THIS VEHICLE, BUILT BY ONE OF YOUR OWN KIND!
"BUT, HORTON'S SECOND ANDROID--AND THUS ITS CREATIONS--DESIGNED WITH OIL, NOT BLOOD, IN THEIR VEINS...
"...OIL WHICH SEEPED FROM SHATTERED PLASTIC FORMS...
"AND, OF COURSE, OIL IS... SLIPPERY.
SKREEEE
"THE MORNING NEWSPAPERS IN BOSTON WOULD RECORD AN AUTO CRASH... ALTHOUGH, ACCORDING TO THEM, THE TOTALLY-DEMOLISHED LIMOUSINE HELD NO OCCUPANTS WHEN IT EXPLODED.
"FOR, WHAT HUMAN BEING WOULD HAVE IMAGINED THAT, FOR A FEW BRIEF NIGHTS IN 1946... PLASTIC LIVED... AND PLOTTED MANKIND'S OVER-THROW?
"OF COURSE, THE TWO TORCHES QUICKLY AB-SORBED ALL DANGEROUS FLAMES...
KENNE
BTOOM!!
KENNE
"THEN...
...AND I THANK YOU ALL FOR RESCUING ME, EVEN IF YOU INSIST ON BEING A LITTLE VAGUE ABOUT WHAT FROM!
WE FEAR IT MUST REMAIN OUR SECRET, SIR.
CALL ME JACK.
I JUST CAN'T FIGURE OUT WHY SOMEONE WOULD BOTHER TRYING TO HARM A MERE CANDIDATE IN A CONGRESSIONAL PRIMARY...!
FRANKLY, JACK... NEITHER CAN WE...
...UNLESS PERHAPS HE SAW... POSSI-BILITIES IN YOU.
PERHAPS. WELL... GOOD NIGHT. AND THANKS AGAIN.
"YES. POSSI-BILITIES... SUCH AS THAT OF THIS NEO-POLITICIAN BECOMING PRESIDENT...
...OF A NATION POSSESSING POWER ENOUGH TO DESTROY THE HUMAN RACE!

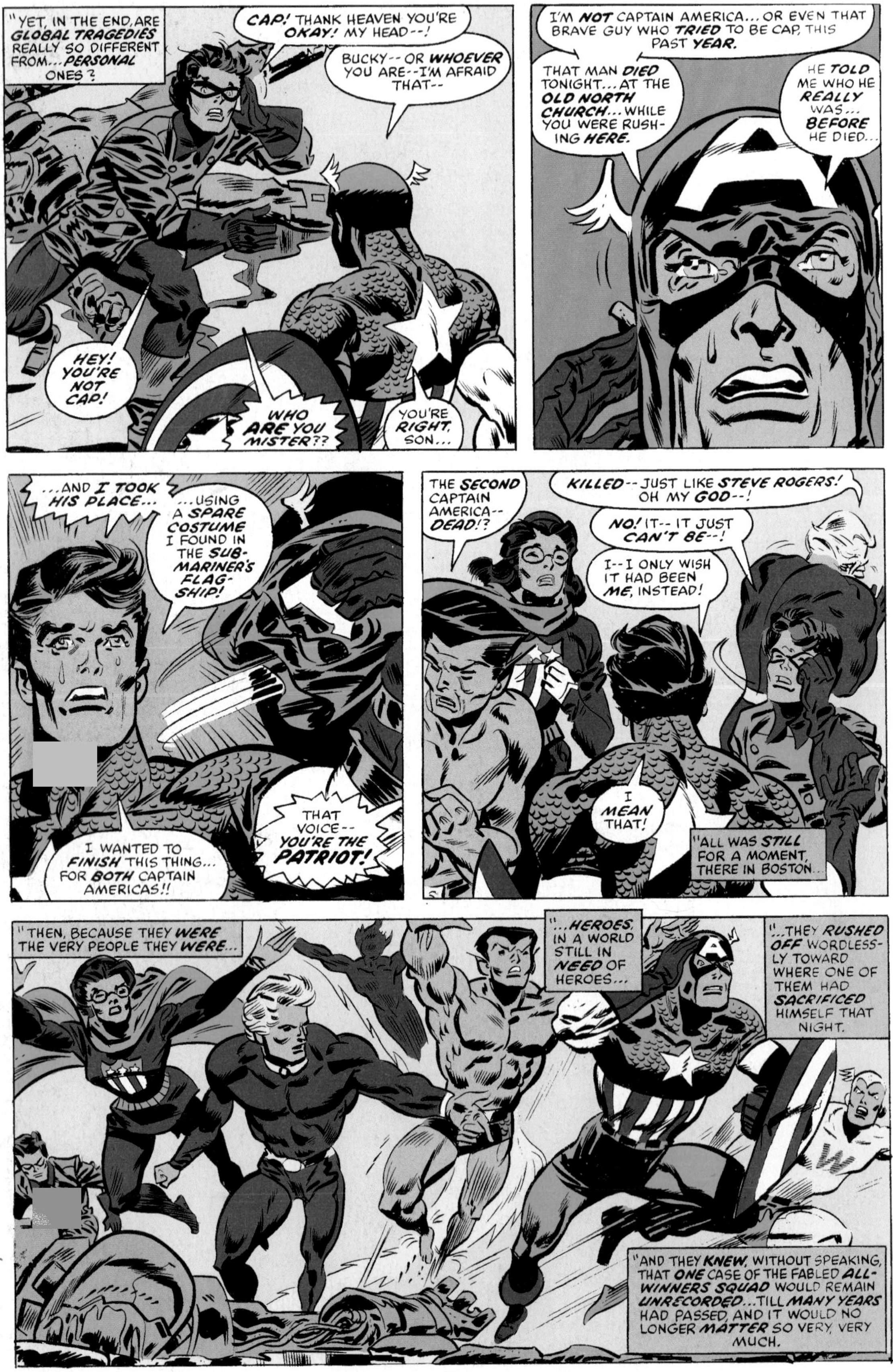
"YET, IN THE END, ARE GLOBAL TRAGEDIES REALLY SO DIFFERENT FROM... PERSONAL ONES?
CAP! THANK HEAVEN YOU'RE OKAY! MY HEAD--!
BUCKY--OR WHOEVER YOU ARE--I'M AFRAID THAT--
HEY! YOU'RE NOT CAP!
WHO ARE YOU MISTER??
YOU'RE RIGHT, SON...
I'M NOT CAPTAIN AMERICA... OR EVEN THAT BRAVE GUY WHO TRIED TO BE CAP, THIS PAST YEAR.
THAT MAN DIED TONIGHT... AT THE OLD NORTH CHURCH... WHILE YOU WERE RUSH-ING HERE.
HE TOLD ME WHO HE REALLY WAS... BEFORE HE DIED...
...AND I TOOK HIS PLACE...
...USING A SPARE COSTUME I FOUND IN THE SUB-MARINER'S FLAG-SHIP!
I WANTED TO FINISH THIS THING... FOR BOTH CAPTAIN AMERICAS!!
THAT VOICE--YOU'RE THE PATRIOT!
THE SECOND CAPTAIN AMERICA--DEAD!?
KILLED--JUST LIKE STEVE ROGERS! OH MY GOD--!
NO! IT--IT JUST CAN'T BE--!
I--I ONLY WISH IT HAD BEEN ME, INSTEAD!
I MEAN THAT!
"ALL WAS STILL FOR A MOMENT, THERE IN BOSTON...
"THEN, BECAUSE THEY WERE THE VERY PEOPLE THEY WERE...
"...HEROES, IN A WORLD STILL IN NEED OF HEROES...
"...THEY RUSHED OFF WORDLESS-LY TOWARD WHERE ONE OF THEM HAD SACRIFICED HIMSELF THAT NIGHT.
"AND THEY KNEW, WITHOUT SPEAKING, THAT ONE CASE OF THE FABLED ALL-WINNERS SQUAD WOULD REMAIN UNRECORDED... TILL MANY YEARS HAD PASSED, AND IT WOULD NO LONGER MATTER SO VERY, VERY MUCH.

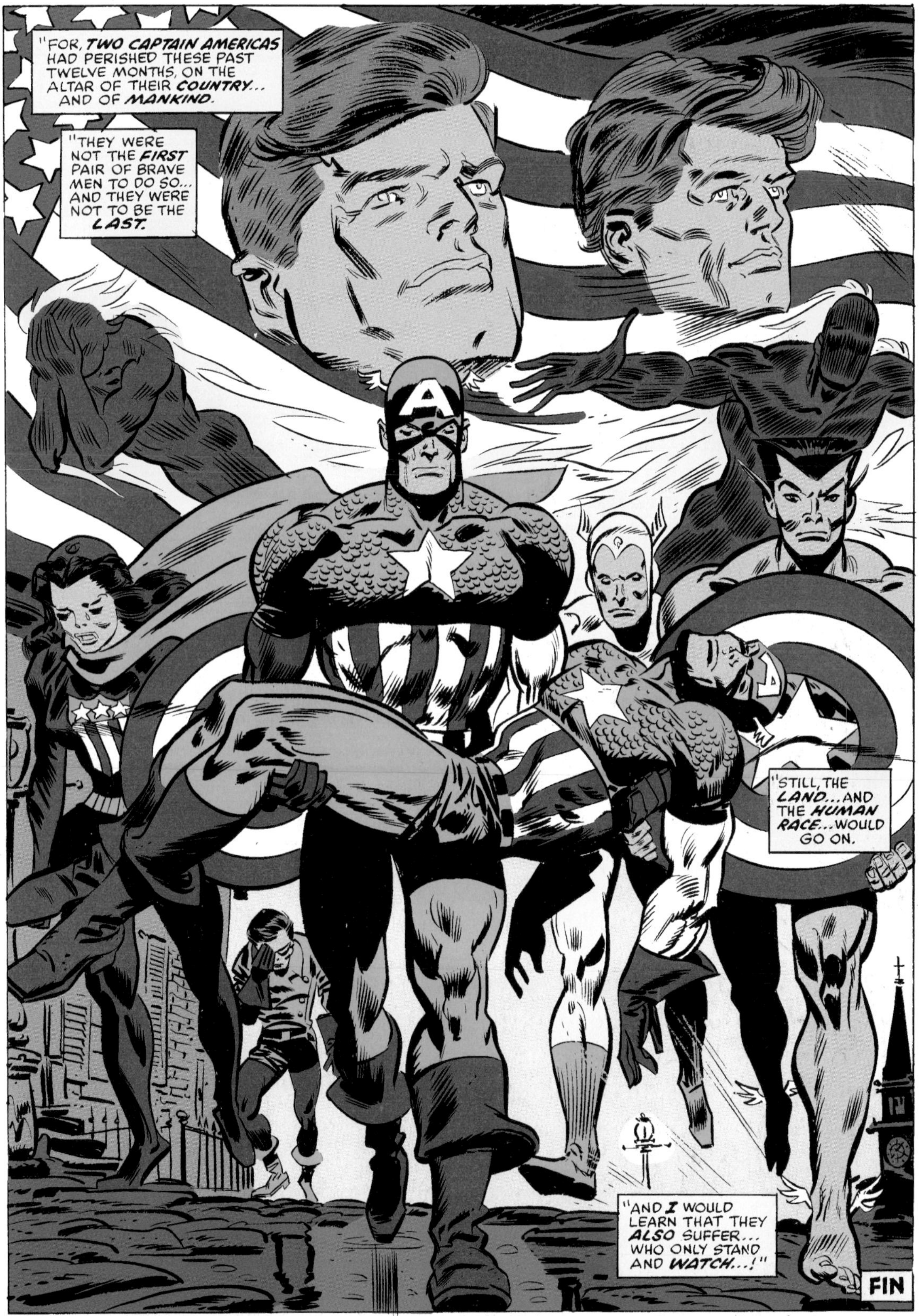
"FOR, TWO CAPTAIN AMERICAS HAD PERISHED THESE PAST TWELVE MONTHS, ON THE ALTAR OF THEIR COUNTRY... AND OF MANKIND.
"THEY WERE NOT THE FIRST PAIR OF BRAVE MEN TO DO SO... AND THEY WERE NOT TO BE THE LAST.
"STILL, THE LAND... AND THE HUMAN RACE... WOULD GO ON.
"AND I WOULD LEARN THAT THEY ALSO SUFFER... WHO ONLY STAND AND WATCH...!"
FIN

THE OTHER SIDE OF THE COIN! BY UNIVERSAL DEMAND!

NEXT ISSUE: WHAT IF CAPTAIN AMERICA *HADN'T VANISHED DURING WORLD WAR II?*

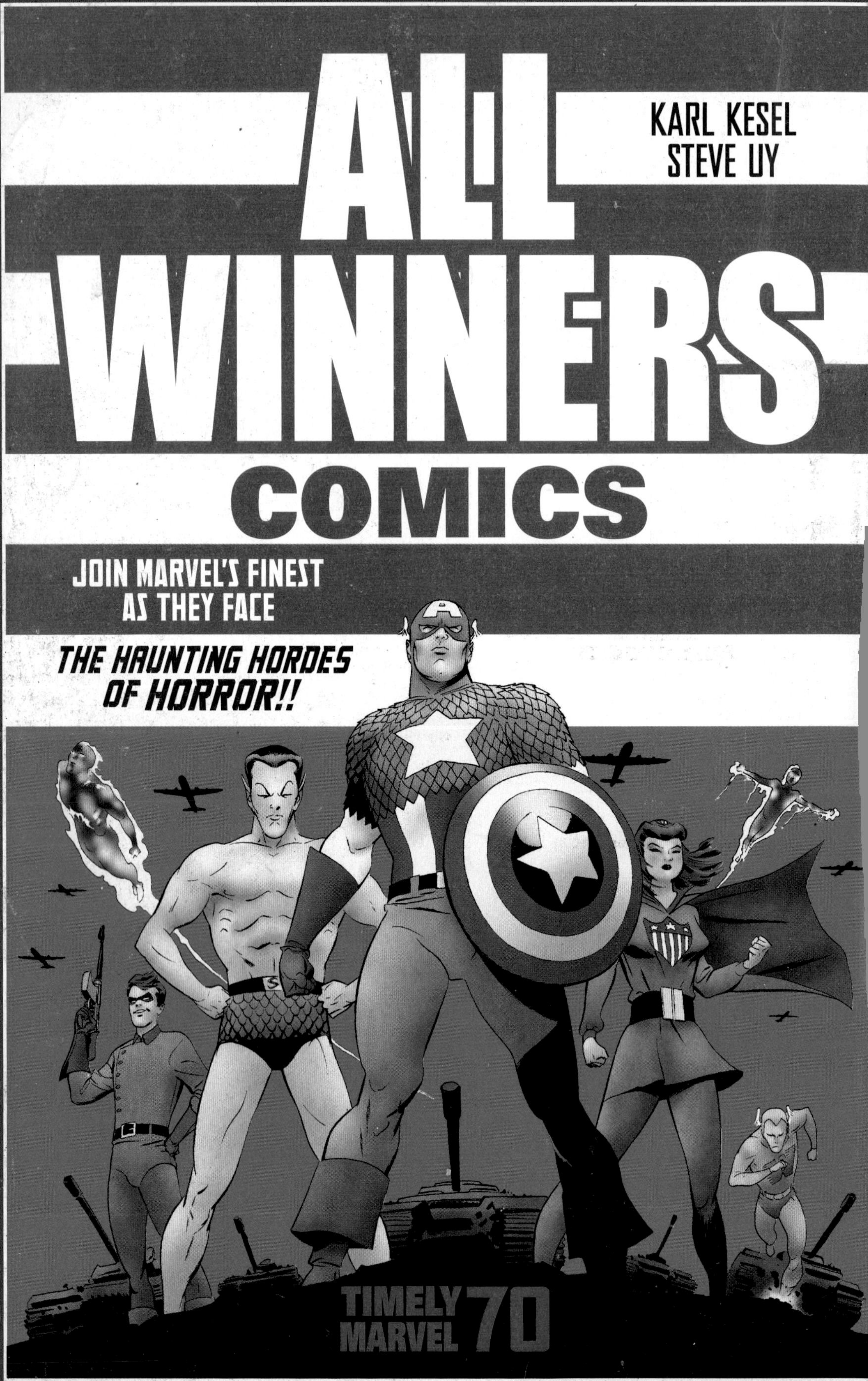
ALL WINNERS
COMICS
KARL KESEL
STEVE UY
JOIN MARVEL'S FINEST
AS THEY FACE
THE HAUNTING HORDES
OF HORROR!!
TIMELY
MARVEL
70

variant by Marcos Martin